Alternative Japanese Drama

Alternative

 UNIVERSITY OF

Japanese Drama

TEN PLAYS

Edited by Robert T. Rolf and
John K. Gillespie

HAWAII PRESS / HONOLULU

For Jim Araki
(1925–1991)

Publication of this book has been supported
by a grant from the Saison Foundation.

Library of Congress Cataloging-in-Publication Data
Alternative Japanese drama : ten plays / edited by Robert T. Rolf
  and John K. Gillespie.
          p.   cm.
    English translations with commentary.
    Contents: Alternative Japanese drama : a brief overview /
Takahashi Yasunari—The little match girl ; The legend of noon ;
The cherry in bloom / Betsuyaku Minoru—The sand of youth, how
quickly ; Those days : a lyrical hypothesis on time and forgetting ;
The dressing room : that which flows away ultimately becomes
nostalgia / Shimizu Kunio—Knock : street theater / Kishida Rio
and Terayama Shūji—The virgin's mask ; Two women / Kara Jūrō—
Ismene / Satoh Makoto.
    ISBN 0-8248-1347-2 (acid-free paper).—ISBN 0-8248-1379-0 (pbk.
: acid-free paper)
    1. Japanese drama—20th century—Translations into English.
I. Rolf, Robert.   II. Gillespie, John K. (John Kinsey).
PL782.E5A44   1992
895.6'2508—dc20   92–5185
                                                    CIP

Designed by Kenneth Miyamoto

CONTENTS

ACKNOWLEDGMENTS

THE EDITORS are grateful to the many people who generously assisted us in completing this book. The translations were checked with great care by Professors Sakata Shunsuke, Yokohama National University; Nakajima Kenji, Tsukuba University; Koike Misako and Matsumoto Emiko, Japan Women's University; and Nakamura Momoko, Kantō Gakuin University. Professor Kishi Tetsuo, Kyoto University, offered sound advice and encouragement. Tisa Chang, artistic/producing director, Pan Asian Repertory Theater, commissioned Chiori Miyagawa's stage adaptation of John Gillespie's original translation of Shimizu Kunio's play *The Dressing Room.* The Social Science Research Council (SSRC) funded John Gillespie's research in Tokyo during the summer of 1985. Publication was greatly aided by a grant from the Saison Foundation; Katayama Masao, program director, and Inaishi Natsuko, program officer, were extremely helpful. Professor James T. Araki, University of Hawaii, was instrumental in placing our manuscript in the hands of the University of Hawaii Press, whose editors Stuart Kiang, Iris M. Wiley, Sharon F. Yamamoto, and Cheri Dunn were supportive and expert throughout. Grace Yee and Laurie Mack, Clarke Consulting Group, with the assistance of Eric Wong, deftly keyed the final manuscript. Any errors, of course, emanate from our hands alone.

R.T.R.
J.K.G.

FOREWORD

J. Thomas Rimer

JAPANESE WRITERS and critics have come to regard the end of World War II as the beginning of a new era in the Japanese creative and literary arts. Nearly half a century has passed since then, yet a reasonably accurate cultural map of the period remains to be drawn, at least in the West. The amount of activity has been so extensive and the artistic approaches adopted to delineate the realities of society, the individual, and Japanese traditions so varied that the nature of any cogent synthesis, assuming it can even be created, still remains elusive. Nevertheless, it is clear, whatever one's vantage point, that the contemporary drama will be seen as a central contributor to the arts of the postwar period. No other form of literary expression—despite the excellence of postwar Japanese poetry, fiction, and criticism—has dealt to the same degree with the travails of this rapidly changing society. Similarly, just as Japanese attitudes and assumptions have come into closer consonance with contemporary life in Europe and the United States, so the concerns expressed in the kinds of remarkable dramas translated here have come to match in some uncanny way our own. In artistic skill and daring, these dramas, even read in translation, may appear sometimes to surpass what has been created in our own culture during that same span of years. These plays are at once familiar and mysterious, a set of shifting mirrors in which we occasionally see Japan but virtually always see ourselves.

As Takahashi Yasunari's brief overview makes clear, the strategies undertaken by these Japanese dramatists are by no means unfamiliar. Just as American audiences in the 1960s were forced to seek out the most trenchant social critiques off Broadway or off off Broadway rather than on the commercial stage, so Japanese dramatists during the same period found it necessary to begin a series of theatrical experiments that, in their choice of language, subject matter, and social concerns, led them far beyond the previous boundaries of the modern Japanese theater. The playwrights, performers, and other artists who joined these new avant-garde groups did so with a sense of commitment and passion that allowed the development, often at considerable individual self-sacrifice, of an authentic and powerful communal vision. What is more, the dramatists writing for these groups have remained a cultural force to be reckoned with in the larger society. In this regard, some of the reasons for the continued importance of these new theatrical movements are cultural as well as literary.

In the first place, by using tents and other unlikely environments as performance spaces, it was possible for these new groups to attract large and enthusiastic audiences, most often made up of young people, by charging very little for admission. Given the enormous size of Tokyo, theatrical productions of this kind were, and are, most often attended by those in their twenties, who can withstand the rigors of long commuting distances to their homes and who are on the whole not yet married and therefore not burdened with such responsibilities as child care. The enthusiasm of such an audience does not provide much revenue, however. Only simple and inexpensive productions, emphasizing lighting rather than scenery, made the early work of these playwrights possible. Contrast this situation with the difficulties encountered by the American director Peter Sellars, who in the mid-1980s valiantly attempted to run an avant-garde repertory company at the Kennedy Center in Washington, D.C. While he managed to build a certain core audience, the income generated could not support the high costs of professional, commercial productions. The project collapsed.

Second, the Japanese public happily was, and is, prepared to read printed versions of plays. Drama in published form has a long, honorable history in modern Japan. Even at the turn of the century, translated versions of Shakespeare, Ibsen, and Chekhov made the work of these great dramatists known long before fledgling producers and actors had developed skills sufficient to mount productions of such Western works. Later, during the prewar period, stage productions of modern drama were largely confined to Tokyo. Those living in other cities were reduced to reading dramas printed in books, magazines, and journals in order to learn about their own contemporary theater.

With this reading tradition strongly established, the dramatists included in this present collection, from Betsuyaku to Satoh, found publishers and a reading public almost from the beginning. In addition, in the last decade or so, other factors have made the work of the modern theater even more accessible. As various prefectures have developed economically, a number of halls and theaters have been built around the country. These institutions constantly seek works to mount for the growing regional public. Contemporary theater companies willing to tour have also benefited considerably from this continued interest. It is now possible for those who twenty years ago could only read new plays actually to see them performed in their own towns and cities. This change has benefited all concerned.

To say that the dramatic works of the gifted writers in this anthology provide a critique of their society, however, would suggest that there exists a certain negative focus in their work. Such is certainly not the case. It would in fact be more correct to say that these plays provide an alternative vision of contemporary life, a glimpse of reality at once more sobering, ironic, humorous, and lyrical than everyday consciousness can conjure up. These alternative probings can show such dramatic power because, in so many ways, these writers have reclaimed for themselves, either explicitly or implicitly, some of the great performance values of the traditional Japanese theater. Older Japanese drama, from the medieval *nō* that used masked actors to accomplish its metaphysical ends to the later seventeenth- and eighteenth-century puppet and *kabuki* plays, can roughly be categorized as presentational rather than representational. From the time of the great *nō* theorist Zeami, who lived and wrote early in the fifteenth century, the highest aim of the theater has been to capture the essence, not the surface reality, of the dramatic characters who inhabit the theatrical event being created. In breaking out of the kind of imported Western realism so important to modern Japanese theater until the 1960s, playwrights like Betsuyaku, Terayama, and Kara and directors like Suzuki Tadashi began to reclaim some of the deepest layers of traditional Japanese theatrical experience for their own work. This process was slow because for a long time traditional forms struck these playwrights as merely old fashioned; indeed, Suzuki himself has written with eloquence that his personal discovery of the power of the traditional *nō* theater occurred, remarkably, not in Japan but at an international theater festival in Paris sponsored by Jean-Louis Barrault.[1] On the whole, this fusion of old and new, politics and ritual, has been accomplished with great intellectual enthusiasm and an equally remarkable degree of literary and theatrical skill. The sense of commitment involved triumphs over any dangers of self-consciousness. These plays seem inevitable in performance, moving as they do through trajectories of physical movement and spiritual insight that draw on a thousand years of experience restructured through the tensions of modern consciousness. If Nietzsche and Foucault are in the mix, so are Chikamatsu, Zeami, and Tsuruya Namboku. In such a context, it is no wonder that the plays of the American writer Sam Shepard are, according to some reports, better appreciated by general audiences in Japan than in the United States. The shameful ghosts that inhabit *Buried Child* tend to make American audiences nervous; Japanese audiences have been accustomed to witness such spirits summoned forth for hundreds of years.

Finally, some comment is necessary concerning the incredible fecundity of these writers. The plays chosen for the anthology are certainly representative, but there are a dozen other titles by each author that might serve equally well to document their individual accomplishments. These writers are practical citizens of the theater who supply, from the amplitude of their responses to the world around and inside them, their own distinctive records of self-discovery. Reading their work, particularly in these felicitous translations, provides similar excitement for English-speaking readers. But remember, this collection represents merely an enthusiastic sampling. The availability of these translations marks, I hope, the beginning of our discovery of a body of work as difficult, exciting, and profound as any available in the world today.

1. See Suzuki Tadashi, *The Way of Acting: The Theatre Writings of Tadashi Suzuki,* trans. J. Thomas Rimer (New York: Theatre Communications Group, 1986), 69–76.

ALTERNATIVE
JAPANESE DRAMA:
A Brief Overview

Takahashi Yasunari

THE 1960s WAS, in many ways, a memorable period in modern Japanese history. In the performing arts, the decade will be remembered particularly as a privileged one that saw an upheaval of turbulent theatrical energy and eventually the birth of a new theater. It is easy to see now, from the vantage point of time, that signs of a profound change were already evident in the early 1960s, although few critics could have prophesied a flowering of movements that, continuing into the early 1970s, were to change the face of the theater almost beyond recognition. Insofar as this theatrical renaissance developed concomitantly with the counterculture at large, there is a sense now that it has outlived that culture. It remains true, however, that the new theater, precisely by being perhaps the most significant cultural achievement to come out of the period, has an enduring value that demands reappreciation and a power that, as this anthology is meant to prove, still disturbs and charms.

The plays included here were selected because they are by the most prominent playwrights to emerge from the Japanese counterculture of the 1960s. To be understood, they require at least some sense of the historical milieu in which they were conceived. The counterculture was of course part of the global phenomenon of the youth revolt. The students' strike in 1968 at the Medical Department of the University of Tokyo preceded the "May Revolution" in Paris by four months, without, in all probability, any consciousness of prophecy or synchronicity. By the end of the year, however, no fewer than 116 universities and colleges in Japan were experiencing campus turmoil, and the students were as fully conscious of global solidarity in their revolt against academic authority as in their denunciation of the Vietnam War and their admiration for the Beatles. At the intellectual level, fundamental modern Western or

1

Westernized values were being contested. Anthropology and antipsychiatry were fashionable topics (Lévi-Strauss' *Tristes Tropiques* was translated in 1967 and R. D. Laing in 1970), and students entrenched behind barricades were reading, among others, Bataille and Foucault. Perhaps the greatest cult name was Nietzsche, with his critique of Eurocentric rationalistic philosophizing and advocacy of "joyous" clownish wisdom. Among the younger generation in theater, it was avant-gardists like Artaud, Brecht, Beckett, Arrabal, Grotowski, and Julian Beck who were most avidly read and passionately discussed. Sartre was becoming passé despite his appeal around 1960; Arnold Wesker, although found congenial by some, was rejected by others as old fashioned. All this had a certain contemporaneity with what was happening in Western countries.

Nevertheless, it would be wrong to ignore specifically Japanese factors. No account of the new movement in Japanese theater in the 1960s would be complete without stressing the importance of one political event: the parliamentary ratification of renewal of the U.S.-Japan Mutual Security Treaty (Ampo) in 1960. Ampo was a symbolic site where the two great forces in postwar Japan, the conservative and the progressive, clashed head on. The progressive camp, comprising the Socialist and other opposition parties, the left-of-center intellectuals, students, workers, and artists, regarded the prevention of its ratification as a supreme task in the cause of Japan's true democratization and organized a huge campaign mobilizing nearly six million people on 30 June. The government won the battle, not, however, without the cancellation of President Eisenhower's scheduled visit to Japan before and the resignation of Prime Minister Kishi immediately after ratification. On the other hand, not only did the failure to prevent the renewal mean the demise of socialist power on the political scene, but it also forced intellectuals to rethink their very ideological standpoint.

For those young people in the theater, including most of the playwrights in this volume, who, barely twenty years of age, had participated actively in the anti-Ampo campaign, the effect was twofold: the traumatic experience irrevocably cured them of the Old Left dream and at the same time brought them into violent confrontation with *shingeki* (lit., new theater), the dominant force in modern Japanese theater. *Shingeki* had allied itself politically with socialism since prewar days and had adopted socialist realism as its artistic method, although a less political and more Chekhovian stance of psychological realism existed alongside it.[1] The defeat suffered in 1960 in a sense sparked the search by young Japanese theater figures for an alternative theater with a radically different ideology (or, more properly, without any ideology) and entirely new methods.

Ampo also heralded the start of the so-called era of high growth in the Japanese economy, which was to continue unhindered by the political turmoil of the next campaign against Ampo in 1970. This economic prosperity caused, as much as it was made possible by, a certain far-reaching "deideologization" of the nation's mind. The ideal of postwar democracy was thus considerably dampened, to the chagrin of the Socialists and Communists, and the political supremacy of the conservative Liberal Democratic party, which has remained in power to this day, was consolidated. Sociopsychologically, a weakening of the sense of national identity ensued, with a twofold effect: while people were just beginning to enjoy new affluence, they were at the same time searching the national conscience, ardently discussing what lay behind the material prosperity. Two events of the late 1960s, involving Mishima Yukio and Arnold Wesker, strike me as particularly symbolic of this ferment.

In May 1969, the year before his all-too-famous suicide, Mishima accepted a challenge by a group of radical students at Tokyo University (where I happened to be a young assistant professor) to hold an open debate with them on their campus. I managed to sneak into the packed auditorium and, in the tense yet strangely exhilarating atmosphere, watched and listened to the fascinating harangue in which the ultranationalist writer manifested his sympathies with and differences from the radically leftist students. Earlier in the year, the latter had achieved a spectacular *succès de scandale* when they were expelled by the police from the campus clock tower, the symbol of the university and intellectual authoritarianism, which they had been occupying for some weeks. (It was a truly spectacular event and received nationwide television coverage.) Mishima told the students that he was all for their attacks on the system of modern values authorized by universities and characterized by what he termed the "false affluence" of contemporary Japan and that he would have gladly joined them in their occupied citadel if only they had cried, "Long live the emperor!"—which brought forth raucous laughter from the students.

The other event that sticks in my mind occurred a few months prior to the fall of the citadel in September 1968. For an event called "Wesker '68," the British playwright was invited to a symposium in Tokyo with half a dozen Japanese theater directors and critics to discuss the situation of theater in contemporary society and what could be done to change it. I was on the platform as Wesker's simultaneous interpreter. There were mutual misunderstandings of both the Japanese and the British political and theatrical situation that prompted some futile although vehement exchanges, but there were also moments when the sheer force of the critique of the status quo, if not an outline of the possible strategies for "revolution," was movingly communicated. Inciden-

tally, quite a few of those in attendance were also among the audience at
the encounter with Mishima the next year.

The two episodes, I believe, help recall the political and social atmosphere in which the new theater movement, represented by the playwrights collected in this volume, was coming of age. The atmosphere of
moral and intellectual earnestness encouraged young theater people to
question everyday reality and to probe deeply into Japan's cultural
identity. The pervasive urge to talk of eschatology and utopia, of vision
and transcendence, of madness and carnival, nowhere bore more stim
ulating and substantial fruit than in the new theatrical movement of the
young.

A simple chronology of events in the late 1960s reveals the remarkable rapidity with which the major figures of Japan's new theater
appeared on the scene. Seemingly out of nowhere, the many little companies sprang up almost at the same time, led by charismatic talents
and producing play after play of menacing power:

> 1966: The Waseda Little Theater (Waseda Shōgekijō) makes its
> debut with Betsuyaku Minoru's *The Gate* (Mon), directed by Suzuki
> Tadashi. (Suzuki was one of the most important directors in the
> movement, producing influential plays such as *On the Dramatic Pas-
> sions* [Gekiteki naru mono o megutte] and *The Trojan Women* [Toroia
> no onna]. In 1983, Suzuki moved his headquarters to the small town
> of Toga in the hills near Toyama in northern Japan and renamed the
> troupe SCOT, the Suzuki Company of Toga.)
> 1966: The Free Theater (Jiyū Gekijō) opens with its leader Satoh
> Makoto's *Ismene* (Isumene). The company evolves into the Theater
> Center 68 (Engeki Sentā 68).
> 1967: Tenjō Sajiki (The Gallery) makes its debut with its leader
> Terayama Shūji's *The Hunchback of Aomori* (Aomori-ken no semushi-
> otoko).[2]
> 1967: The Situation Theater (Jōkyō Gekijō) introduces the phe-
> nomenon of tent theater with its production of one of the *Petticoat Osen*
> (Koshimaki Osen) series of plays, written and directed by the troupe's
> leader, Kara Jūrō. Founded in 1963, the Situation Theater had
> experimented with street theater in 1965 and an outdoor production
> in 1966.
> 1969: The Modern Man's Theater (Gendaijin Gekijō), founded by
> Shimizu Kunio and Ninagawa Yukio, produces Shimizu's *Such a Seri-
> ous Frivolity* (Shinjō afururu keihakusa), directed by Ninagawa
> (another important director of the period, later to become interna-
> tionally famous for his productions of *Macbeth, Medea,* and other adap-
> tations).

These companies did not rally around a common political slogan;
degrees of social commitment varied from Satoh's explicit New Left
"theater of revolution" to Terayama's agitation for "subversion

through theatrical imagination" to Suzuki's conscious refusal of any political reference. But they were unanimous in their passionate belief in a "revolution of theater" that would be total and far reaching, aiming at no less than a revolution of the consciousness of the audience. What they questioned first of all was naturally the relation of the stage to the audience. Some of the new companies chose for their performance spaces a small studio over a coffee shop or a room in the basement of an office building; others performed in movable tents, pitched in the courtyard of a shrine or in some other public area; others even used the open spaces of the streets. Sometimes they gave rise to scandals, affronting the civic code of peace and propriety. Admittedly, economics played a role in their choice of unconventional venues, but that did not nullify deeper convictions. The young Japanese avant-gardists believed, with some of their counterparts in the West, that the edifice of modern theater, with an invisible fourth wall neatly, almost hygienically separating the audience from the proscenium stage, symbolized the institutional structure of modern society that had appropriated the power of theater—theater as "pestilence" in Artaud's sense—and that this wall must be broken down.

Another object of attack was the hierarchical concept of the relations among playwright, director, and actor. The "myth" of authorial supremacy was undermined, and the role of director became important as it had never been before, especially because in a majority of cases the leader of a company was both director and playwright, with a few exceptions like Betsuyaku, who still limits himself to writing, or Shimizu, who turned to directing his own plays only in the mid-1970s. But what was emphasized to a supreme degree was the status of actor, or the physical presence of the actor's body on the stage. This was again part of a global trend, influenced by Artaud's ideas in *The Theatre and Its Double* and culminating in plays like Kenneth Brown's *The Brig* (1963) (which was in fact produced in translation in Tokyo in 1969). In Japan, however, it also had to do with a quest for an indigenous theatrical tradition. In *nō* and *kabuki,* which *shingeki* despised as premodern and irrational and from which it had completely severed itself, the actor is far more than simply the medium through which the author communicates his message. Instead, his body is accorded a privileged importance as the site where this social pariah called "actor," exposed to the humiliating regard of the audience, turns himself into a fascinating presence, where the audience watches an epiphanic manifestation of deepest desires, of the actor as well as of themselves. So the new apologists construed the aesthetics of the traditional theater, irrespective of their criticism of the existing institutional form of *nō* and *kabuki.*

It is no wonder that, during the late 1960s and the early 1970s, so many *kabuki* plays were revived in new forms at the hands of experimental directors of little theaters. Suzuki's *On the Dramatic Passions* incorporated some scenes from plays by Tsuruya Namboku, the *kabuki* playwright of the early nineteenth century, the great master of the grotesque. In 1970, Ninagawa produced Namboku's famous ghost play *The Macabre Story of Yotsuya* (Yotsuya kaidan) in a daring experimental style.

No wonder, too, that there existed among young theater people a deep admiration for the dancer Hijikata Tatsumi. A great charismatic figure of the time, Hijikata created a new performance art called *butō,* which he himself, however, considered a kind of "ur-*kabuki,*" a return to the roots of the indigenous sense of corporeality.[3] His haggard body, apparently at the nadir of ignoble impotence, moving with an extreme slowness reminiscent of *nō,* was the visible epitome of everything that was opposed to the comfortable intelligibility of modern culture. His art was at once a critique of modernity and a manifesto of a new aesthetics rooted in the "darkness" within the Japanese body and psyche. Not to mention his disciples in *butō* who were later to gain international fame, there are moments in Suzuki's or Ninagawa's works when one is reminded of Hijikata's lessons.

Finally, and most relevant for this volume, the structure and the texture of the dramatic text underwent great transformation. Insofar as an overt emphasis was put on performance at the expense of the literary independence of the text, it may be more difficult to reconstruct these productions from the printed text than realistic, dialogue-centered drama. But it would be unfair to regard the texts as we have them now as negligible drifts left by a once-mighty tide. Rather, they are enduring testimonies to the imaginative powers of playwrights who could draw rich sustenance from a collective and performative energy and create such incandescent artifices of dramatic language as the Japanese theater has rarely witnessed since the great ages of *nō* and *kabuki.*

It is difficult to pinpoint the varied characteristics of the plays written in the late 1960s, but one of the most salient features was certainly the playwrights' determination to reject a linear dramaturgy of realism and to devise a new technique to capture the full complexity of man and the world. In place of a causal, prosaic, and "syntagmatic" method, they fashioned a more aleatory, poetic, "paradigmatic" one. In most cases this involved a multiplication of time scheme. Virtually all the new dramatists were obsessed by the problematics of memory (including amnesia) and vied with each other for ever more effective ways of fusing time present with time past, of mixing desire with memory. Simple play-within-a-play structures like that of Tennessee Williams' *The Glass Menagerie* were left far behind in favor of incomparably more sophisticated ones. This dramaturgical innovation, however, must not be taken for technical cleverness for its own sake. Created by a powerful emotional and intellectual drive, the dizzyingly multidimensional and labyrinthine text was in fact inseparable from a rigorous act of critical examination of past and present, of personal memory and the nation's history. Against the grain of the notoriously oblivious mentality of the nation, these playwrights' plays are often shot through with traumatic memories of tragic events during the Shōwa era, from the invasion of Manchuria to the Rape of Nanking to the bombing of Hiroshima to the anti-Ampo demonstrations. The plays often feature images of the people or groups tied to those events, such as the Shōwa Emperor or Zengakuren (the union of radical students).

The principle of multidimensionality would seem valid at other levels as well. Characters are often intent on role-playing to an uncommon degree, thus intensifying the metatheatrical impression of the plays in which they appear. Again, this is not so much a sign of technical self-indulgence as an outcome of the struggle to find lost or multiple identities. It is no longer possible to retain firm outlines of individual selves when society as a whole seems to have lost its binding principle. The quest for an identity that is as it were lost in advance must necessarily take the form of multiple role-playing, and reality and fiction become indistinguishable.

Consider also the linguistic style of these plays. The text often eschews the linearity of realistic dialogue, lends itself to boldly poetic imagery, and loves to deal in ambiguities and non sequiturs. Another common stylistic trait that contributes to a polyphonic effect is frequent use of quotation, ranging from the classics to contemporary popular songs, both Western and Japanese. These textual devices, triumphantly different from the idea of realist drama and instead hearkening back to the premodern tradition of *nō* and *kabuki,* have broadened the expressive power of the contemporary Japanese language immensely.

The brilliant theatrical and dramatic upsurge in Japan in the late 1960s truly merits the appellation "renaissance."[4] It brought about a revolutionary change in the concept of theatrical representation, if not in the actual structure of society. This anthology includes four of the movement's five key playwrights, the choice of whom, I believe, cannot be contested by any standard. (While the other key playwright, Terayama Shūji, is discussed in the chapter on Tenjō Sajiki, he is unfortunately represented here only with a play that he conceived but that was in fact written by his closest associate, Kishida Rio. Terayama's mother, who has overseen his literary estate since his death in 1983, refuses to allow any translations of his works to be anthologized with those of other writers.) Each of the four playwrights included here is represented by one play from the 1960s and, with the exception of Satoh, also by at least one play from about a decade later. It is hoped that the reader will be convinced of how tenaciously these playwrights continued to deepen their visions and refine their techniques despite the vicissitudes of the social and theatrical milieu during the 1970s. The fact is that all of them are still no less productive now, at the beginning of the 1990s. That, however, is a matter for another volume.

Notes

1. Much of the story of *shingeki* and its development can be found in J. Thomas Rimer, *Toward a Modern Japanese Theatre: Kishida Kunio* (Princeton, N.J.: Princeton University Press, 1974). For translations and criticism of *shingeki* playwrights, see J. Thomas Rimer, "Four Plays by Tanaka Chikao," *Monumenta Nipponica* 31, no. 3 (1976): 275–298; David G. Goodman, ed., *Five Plays by Kishida Kunio,* Cornell University East Asia Papers, no. 51 (Ithaca, N.Y.: Cornell University East Asia Program, 1989); David G. Goodman, ed., *After Apocalypse: Four Japanese Plays of Hiroshima and Nagasaki* (New York: Columbia University Press, 1986), which includes plays by Tanaka Chikao and Hotta Kiyomi; Kubo Sakae, *Land of Volcanic Ash* (Kazanbaichi), trans. David G. Goodman, Cornell University East Asia Papers, no. 40 (Ithaca, N.Y.: Cornell University East Asia Program, 1986); Kinoshita Junji, *Between God and Man: A Judgment on War Crimes* (Kami to hito to no aida), trans. Eric J. Gangloff (Tokyo: University of Tokyo Press, 1979); and Yamazaki Masakazu, *Mask and Sword: Two Plays for the Contemporary Japanese Theater,* trans. J. Thomas Rimer (New York: Columbia University Press, 1980).

2. Given this troupe's great popularity under its Japanese name, we will continue to refer to it as Tenjō Sajiki.

3. For recent studies of *butō,* see Vicki Sanders, "Dancing and the Dark Soul of Japan: An Aesthetic Analysis of Butō," *Asian Theatre Journal* 5, no. 2 (Fall 1988): 148–163; and Susan Blakeley Klein, *Ankoku Butō: The Premodern and Postmodern Influences on the Dance of Utter Darkness,* Cornell University East Asia Papers, no. 49 (Ithaca, N.Y.: Cornell University East Asia Program, 1988). For photographic studies of *butō,* with extensive treatment of Hijikata, see Jean Viala and Nourit Masson-Sekine, *Butoh: Shades of Darkness* (Tokyo: Shufunotomo, 1988); and Ethan Hoffman et al., *Butoh: Dance of the Dark Soul* (New York: Aperture, 1987).

4. Indeed, this description has been used in the title of an excellent work in Japanese on the playwrights of this era. See Senda Akihiko, ed., *Gekiteki runessansu—gendai engeki wa kataru* (Theatrical renaissance: The modern theater speaks) (Tokyo: Riburopōto, 1983), which contains in-depth, annotated interviews with the playwrights included in this anthology. Translations exist of selected plays by Betsuyaku, Kara, and Satoh. See Betsuyaku Minoru, *The Move* (Idō) (1972), in *Modern Japanese Drama: An Anthology,* trans. Ted T. Takaya (New York: Columbia University Press, 1979), 203–272, and *The Elephant* (Zō) (1962), in *After Apocalypse,* 193–248; Kara Jūrō, *John Silver: The Beggar of Love*

(Jon Shirubā: Ai no kojiki) (1970), in *Japanese Drama and Culture in the 1960s: The Return of the Gods,* by David G. Goodman (Armonk, N.Y.: M. E. Sharpe, 1988), 237–288; Satoh Makoto, *Nezumi kozō: The Rat* (Nezumi kozō jirokichi) (1969), in *After Apocalypse,* 269–319, and *My Beatles* (Atashi no Bītoruzu) (1967) and (with Yamamoto Kiyokazu, Katō Takashi, and Saitō Ren) *The Dance of Angels Who Burn Their Own Wings* (Tsubasa o moyasu tenshitachi no buto) (1970), in *Japanese Drama and Culture,* 193–223, 301–311. For discussions of Shimizu Kunio's prizewinning play *Little Brother!—A Message to Sakamoto Ryōma from Otome, His Older Sister* (Otōto yo—ane, Otome kara Sakamoto Ryōma e no dengon) (1990) and Betsuyaku Minoru's recent critical success *Letters from the Wildcat—The Legend of Īhatōbo* (Yamaneko kara no tegami—Īhatōbo densetsu) (1990), see Robert T. Rolf, "Tokyo Theatre 1990," *Asian Theatre Journal* 9, no. 1 (Spring 1992): 85–111.

Betsuyaku Minoru

Betsuyaku Minoru (b. 1937) was the first major playwright to emerge from the new theater of the 1960s; three decades later, he remains a prolific author, a significant presence. To the degree that the dramatic text may be viewed as central to the theater's complex creative process, the new theater might almost be said to have begun with Betsuyaku. A student at Waseda University from 1958 until his intense involvement in the nationwide demonstrations against the renewal of the U.S.-Japan Mutual Security Treaty terminated his academic career in 1960, Betsuyaku participated in student theater with Waseda classmates, including Suzuki Tadashi and the actor Ono Seki. Their student troupe, the Free Stage (Jiyū butai), became a professional troupe of the same name after Suzuki and the others graduated in 1962; the following month, they staged the first masterpiece of the nascent movement, Betsuyaku's *Elephant* (Zō), directed by Suzuki. Betsuyaku, Suzuki, and Ono were again the principal figures in the foundation of the Waseda Little Theater in 1966, which received recognition through its productions of Betsuyaku's *The Gate* at the Art Theater Shinjuku Bunka in May 1966 and *The Little Match Girl* (Matchi-uri no shōjo) at the WLT Atelier in November 1966, both directed by Suzuki. For *The Little Match Girl* and *Landscape with Red Bird* (Akai tori no iru fūkei) (1967) Betsuyaku won the prestigious Kishida Prize for Playwriting. This was the first of many awards, including the Kinokuniya Drama Award (1970), Teatoro Theater Award (1982), and Yomiuri Literary Prize (1987).

Although artists such as Terayama and Suzuki were to work to reduce the primacy of the text, Betsuyaku, a pure playwright who neither directs nor acts, has been hesitant to endorse the diminution of the function of language and the authorial role in a play. In 1968, Betsuyaku thus found himself compelled to leave the WLT and part ways with Suzuki, who was thus free to lead the WLT into its well-known explorations of acting methodology and the nature of theatrical expression. Although Betsuyaku soon developed an enduring artistic affiliation with playwright/critic Yamazaki Masakazu and director Sueki Toshifumi, he has functioned basically as an independent playwright. He has succeeded in that role, a somewhat unusual one in the contemporary Japanese theater world. He captured the Aquarian spirit of the times in *I Am Alice* (Ai amu Arisu) (1970); explored the psychology supporting the imperial system in *The Legend of Noon* (Shōgo no densetsu) (1973), *Water-Bloated Corpse* (Umi yukaba mizuku kabane) (1978), and *The Snow Falls on Tarō's Roof* (Tarō no yane ni yuki furitsumu) (1982); treated the degeneration of leftist activism in *Red Elegy* (Sekishoku erejī) (1980); and portrayed the mindless anonymity of the Japanese "salary man" *(sararīman)*, the salaried worker in the contemporary Japanese company, in *A-Bubblin', A-Boilin'* (Abukutatta, nītatta) (1976) and *Thirty Days Hath September* (Ni shi mu ku samurai) (1977). Betsuyaku has also written several screenplays, produced a sizable opus of humorous juvenile fiction in addition to writing several plays for children, and frequently appeared on national television, discussing Western art, a lifelong interest.

INTRODUCTION

Robert T. Rolf

THE JAPANESE playwrights represented in this anthology were formed by a special time in their nation's history. They spent their childhood years during the intensely militaristic 1930s and early 1940s and the aftermath of Japan's defeat in 1945. To a great degree, Betsuyaku's artistic career has been an attempt to come to grips with that history, mirrored in his childhood.

Betsuyaku was born in Manchuria in 1937. His father, an administrative official in the Information Bureau of the General Affairs Agency of the Manchukuo puppet state, died in March 1945. From 1945 through 1948 Betsuyaku's mother struggled to support her five children. Crisis followed crisis: difficulties in obtaining food in Manchuria; nearly a year spent in Soviet-occupied territory; rampant illness aboard the repatriation ship. These were years during which Betsuyaku's mother took any available work, including itinerant peddling, before finally attaining some financial security operating a food cart (*yatai*) in Nagano, a city in the mountainous interior of Honshu, the main island of Japan. Betsuyaku's teenage years in the 1950s were increasingly stable, but he had acquired an intimate knowledge of the sad and anxious period that *The Little Match Girl,* one of his most important early plays, was meant to dredge up from the memories of audiences.[1]

Betsuyaku came to Tokyo in the late 1950s to study at Waseda University, but his time was totally consumed by theater and political activities. These two worlds—the artistic and the political—were closely interconnected for Betsuyaku in the 1960s. Today he is not the young activist who was passionately involved in the mammoth nationwide demonstrations against Japan's renewal of the U.S.-Japan Mutual Security Treaty in 1960 and in other campaigns in 1961, but his close scrutiny of contemporary Japanese society and its connections to earlier decades of Japan's modern history continues to be reflected in such works as *The Legend of Noon* and, somewhat more recently, *The Cherry in Bloom* (Ki ni hana saku) (1980).

The Little Match Girl

The title and basic plot of *The Little Match Girl,* Betsuyaku's most frequently performed play, are taken from Hans Christian Andersen's well-known tale "The Little Match-Seller," but the play evokes the Japanese historical experience. This Betsuyaku achieves through juxtaposing the Andersen story with a contemporary (1966) encounter between a middle-aged couple and a stranger, a young woman who appears at their home one evening claiming to be their daughter. She involves them in her painful childhood memories—of selling matches on the street at age seven, of performing a humiliating skirt-lifting routine for passersby—events described as taking place "about twenty years ago," the same time the couple lost their own seven-year-old daughter in a traffic accident. The audience realizes that these were the dark, impoverished days following the end of the war, about 1945–1947.

An off-stage narratress intrudes occasionally with quotations from Andersen's tale, lending a mythic dimension to the little girl's experiences. A connection between Andersen's and Betsuyaku's match girls is established through the similarities between their stories. Through the fairy-tale link Betsuyaku's story assumes an air of unreality that renders the stark immediate postwar years more approachable. And the fairy tale constitutes a structuring device, a means of freeing memory and linking the past with the present in a more suggestive way than with a conventional linear exposition. Betsuyaku's own thoughts are of great interest:

> What I like about fairy tales is, in a word, something that can be achieved through memory. Supposing you have read a fairy tale before, by juxtaposing the memory of reading that tale with the present day, one can discern rather clearly something like a time zone containing the vertical axis of the present day and perpendicular axis of the memory of when one read the fairy tale. If so, I think that when constructing an absurd space, it is useful to view the drama in terms of the relationship between the vertical axes of memory and the present day, rather than as a story which unfolds along a horizontal axis. So, it seems chiefly a matter of taking the memories that give form to the present day, the sediment from the past that forms the present, if you will, the vestiges of the past, and transposing them to the fairy tale so that they can be seen in another light. Not only are things simplified, there is also the rich texture of the fairy tale. The rich spatial texture of the *märchen* may well contribute to the spatial

enrichment of the absurd drama. In the main, I use the fairy tales we remember having read when children, to explore the temporal relationship between the vertical axes.[2]

Whereas Andersen's tale ends on a Christian note of deliverance, the humiliation of and responsibility for poverty are central for Betsuyaku. The skirt lifting represents an extreme debasement. The father's vehement denials of having had anything to do with it open the door for various psychological and historical interpretations, but one current among those who have staged the play implicates the emperor system.[3] The father or the couple can be taken as representing that system, the Japan that condones it, or the emperor himself.

In his opening Betsuyaku devotes considerable attention to the couple's ritualistic routine. Ritual patterns provide a sense of order, a manageable structure for experience. They constitute a defense against chaos. But when they become exclusive, such patterns become cold, empty, destructive; they shut out the helpless. There is an absence of life in the routine of the man and his wife. The real life in Betsuyaku's cosmos is on the street. Outside, where people are exposed, there is no hiding the truth. It seems fitting that the match girl brings the truth about the false family in from the street. As they fret over the details of their daily ritual in the opening, the middle-aged couple appear engaged in eminently civilized activity. But Betsuyaku's exaggeration of their routine shows that beneath the mannered facade is a pool of twenty-year-old memories—of deprivation, moral confusion, easy compromise. The affluent veneer that Japan had acquired by the 1960s could not erase the stark images of the 1940s lodged in the memories of the Japanese of all ages who had lived through the war years.

The Legend of Noon

The enigmatic title of this play would seem to refer to noon, 15 August 1945, the time of the emperor's nationwide broadcast announcing Japan's acceptance of surrender terms. At that moment what had been a living set of beliefs passed into the realm of history and legend. The play is about the dead-end absurdity of clinging to defunct, discredited beliefs and the anomie of living without the reassurance of acceptable ones.

Betsuyaku wrote *The Legend of Noon* at about the same time as he did the screenplay for Yoshida Yoshishige's film *Martial Law* (Kaigenrei) (1973), an important portrayal of the prewar ultranationalist theorizer Kita Ikki (1883–1937). As an autochthonous thinker (regardless of what stripe), Kita has long held a fascination for Betsuyaku and other artists of his generation.[4] Whereas *Martial Law* represents its subject in an almost oppressively serious manner, *The Legend of Noon* is characterized by vicious parody, irreverent and scatological humor, and unexpected pathos. It is almost as if Betsuyaku sought release from the deadly seriousness of the self-consciously avant-garde film in the irreverent but arguably more effective play. An awareness of the former, however, creates possible insights into the latter. Not only does "noon" seem to refer to 15 August 1945, but it also now suggests the mystical possibilities of the sun at its highest point, adds to the symbolic complexity of the Japanese flag (the *hinomaru*, lit., "sun circle"), prominent in both film and play, and perhaps even forms a connection with the sun goddess Amaterasu and her imperial "descendants."

The Legend of Noon is a one-act play with three scenes and four characters, Man, Woman, Wounded Veteran 1, and Wounded Veteran 2. The Man and Woman appear in the first scene, and the second is devoted to the two Wounded Veterans. In the final scene, the two pairs of characters encounter one another.

The Man and Woman meet on the street and struggle to form a relationship that both seem to need badly. Their uncertainty, however, leads to a relationship characterized by mistrust and misunderstanding. The scene parodies their emotional insecurity and narcissistic hypersensitivity, especially the Man's. The two Wounded Veterans, dressed in white clothing and military caps, are reminiscent of the legions of wounded soldiers who once begged on the streets of Japan, playing patriotic songs from the war era on simple instruments such as harmonicas. In contrast to the anomie of the Man and Woman, the relationship between Vet 1 and Vet 2 is symbiotic and obsessive. At the risk of oversimplifying the play's psychological and cultural complexity, we can see the first pair of characters as embodying the mentality of postwar Japan and the second pair that of prewar Japan.

Betsuyaku contrasts the relative freedom of the Man and Woman to the confinement of the Vets. The Woman demonstrates her freedom by walking. The Man reveals his through his fear of rootlessness—humorously overstated by the orange crate he carries everywhere so that there will always be a place for him. The Vets, on the other hand, are rooted to the ground and to their iconography—flags, uniforms, songs of allegiance. The Man and Woman are less tightly bound; they must still struggle with isolation and might even be friendless. Vet 1 has submerged his identity into that of Vet 2, who in turn has subordinated himself to some distant, mystical entity. The Man tries to establish a relationship with the Woman in terms of a financial contract. The Vets are bound to their way of life and to one another by ties of duty that are an extension of their military past.

In scene 3, the two pairs are thrown together. In the first scene the airy Woman had been pursued by the tedious Man, and she confessed her interest in him. But, in the face of the difficulties that his deep-rooted mistrust cause, the Woman is drawn in the end to the certainty and commitment of sorts represented by the veterans, especially Vet 2. She succumbs to their ethos despite its cruelty and irrationality, while the Man remains "rational" and loyal to his "values," such as they are, to the end, which finds him even more forlorn and repulsive than ever.

The two veterans make *The Legend of Noon* particularly memorable. Choice roles for actors with earthy comedic talents, they are intended to parody (and presumably condemn) mindless devotion to lost causes and irrational quests for pointless spirituality. They have been used by Betsuyaku in two other plays, and others of his generation have also employed such veterans in plays and films.[5] The two vets in *Legend* are in many ways grotesque, but their absurdity is extremely humorous, making them, if not likable, at least forgivable. After all, it is Vet 2 who strains mightily to maintain control of both his physiological functions and his singing of the de facto national anthem of Japan. Betsuyaku's irreverent regard for the Japanese imperial institution is relentless, but its followers at the grass-roots level are, however foolish, almost noble in the pathetic lengths of their quixotism. The pathos of the play's ending surely indicates a transformation from war maker to war victim, with the perhaps unforeseen result of putting a face on evil that, while foolish, is unnecessarily friendly. In that light, *The Legend of Noon* becomes all the more interesting as an example of a major postwar Japanese playwright grappling with ghosts from darker days of his nation's past.

The Cherry in Bloom

Whereas *The Little Match Girl* is an abstract work whose meaning must be inferred, *The Cherry in Bloom* is an undisguised statement of Betsuyaku's concern over the crises he perceives in contemporary education and child rearing. Specifically, he decries the rigidity, uniformity, and impersonality of Japanese education today. Beneath the current education system he discerns no adequate mechanism for nurturing the individuality of each child. This insufficiency is attributed to the absence of true local communities, which he views as having broken down by the early years of the Shōwa period (the mid-1920s through early 1930s). Only in communities that exist as a direct response to the demands of life can the humanity of each individual be recognized and nurtured, but the huge amorphous social institutions of modern Japan are unable to fulfill the instinctive need for such true community. The crisis thus created is best observed, he feels, in the details of certain crimes of passion. *The Cherry in Bloom* is a powerful portrayal of such an offense.[6]

In some ways *The Cherry in Bloom* is atypical of Betsuyaku's plays. Accompanying the uncharacteristic specificity of its social context is an attention to character delineation unusual for him. The characters are given the nondescript names that Betsuyaku is famous for—Old Woman, Man 1, Man 2, Man 3, Woman 1—but, yielding to the exigencies of realism to create a believable sense of family, the characters refer to one another by their given names or other appellations appropriate to Japanese family life. The Old Woman is Grandmother, Woman 1 her daughter Fumie, Man 1 Fumie's son Yoshio, Man 2 Fumie's husband Takaaki, Yoshio's father. Man 3 is the dead Grandfather, who appears on occasion and is visible only to the Old Woman. Their encounters allow her opportunity to express her disgust for the mild-mannered, unambitious natures of her father, her husband (Man 3), and her son-in-law Takaaki—three generations of men who are content with whatever cards life deals them. Her disdain fires her determination to "educate" her grandson Yoshio, to instill in him the resolve to strive, compete, and finish first at all costs. Specifically, Yoshio is to study intensively to enter a good university and then find good employment. He has no need for friends; his classmates are to be looked on merely as his competition. Yoshio's frustration grows and weighs him down. He comes to see that life can never be "won," but this realization is not accompanied by the feeling that life is to be lived. He often refuses to attend school; he becomes increasingly violent at home. Finally, he succumbs to despair.

In the contemporary social context of *The Cherry in Bloom,* Yoshio's violence against his parents and grandmother strikes an immediate chord of recognition among Japanese audiences. Such acts of violence are not everyday occurrences, but they are frequent enough to cause alarm in a nation that has traditionally placed a high value on filial piety, conformity, and the maintenance of innocence among its young. *The Cherry in Bloom* is topical but by no means "trendy." It represents the powerful response of an important artist to his times. Much of the play's power lies in the characterization of the Old Woman, one of the most formidable female characters in recent Japanese drama.

The set of *The Cherry in Bloom* also adds to its overall impact. The centerpiece is a cherry tree in full bloom, before which sits the Old Woman, a respectable representative of traditional authority. To her left rests, incongruously, a large wardrobe, an item found in most Japanese households and frequently acquired by newlyweds when setting up house. In *The Cherry in Bloom* the wardrobe represents the contemporary Japanese family. The living members of the play's family use it for entrances and exits. Sounds of violent family quarrels issue forth from within it, as if from the deepest unseen areas of the Japanese family. The stage directions state that the wardrobe has "no apparent relation to" the Old Woman and the tree. The cherry tree and the wardrobe may appear an odd pairing, but Betsuyaku's purpose is to illustrate the connection between them, that is, to illuminate the troublesome relation between the values the grandmother represents and the dilemma of the modern Japanese family faced with conflicting philosophies of child rearing and education.

The Look and Sound of Betsuyaku's Plays

Although in every sense the contemporary of the other playwrights in this anthology, Betsuyaku Minoru employs a dramaturgy different from theirs in significant ways. The most conspicuous difference is Betsuyaku's avoidance of the ebullient theatricality characteristic of Terayama, Kara, Satoh, and, at times, Shimizu. Betsuyaku might even be labeled a minimalist, but he has not sought the extreme simplification of the most celebrated theater minimalist, Samuel Beckett.

Betsuyaku prefers a mostly bare stage, frequently with a centerpiece such as a telephone pole, used so often it has become a trademark; a bus-stop sign; a dining table, as in *The Little Match Girl;* or the cherry tree in *The Cherry in Bloom.* Performances of his plays are often marked by a subdued atmosphere, a tense quiet untypical of the exuberant troupes of Terayama, Satoh, and, especially, Kara. *The Little Match Girl* and the first scene of *The Legend of Noon* lend themselves naturally to understated treatment; in *The Cherry in Bloom,* the impact of the violence is magnified by the pervasive quiet out of which it explodes.

Betsuyaku has absorbed a great deal from the dramaturgy of Beckett, whose *Waiting for Godot,* in particular, influenced Betsuyaku's works in various ways. The cherry tree of *The Cherry in Bloom* seems a curious Japanization of *Godot*'s forlorn, usually barren plant. The dynamic of the paired characters in *The Little Match Girl* (the Man and Wife, the Woman and her Brother) recalls Beckett's conception of characters in symbiotic pairs—Vladimir and Estragon, Lucky and Pozzo. As we have seen, the structure of *The Legend of Noon* involves throwing the play's two symbiotic pairs together. Each of the first two scenes is monopolized by one of the pairs, while the tension in the final scene results largely from the confrontation of the two pairs. Finally, *Match Girl, Legend,* and *Cherry* all move in a basically linear manner toward the most common Betsuyaku resolution, the death of the protagonist/victim. Still, Betsuyaku's slow-paced dramas do not seem far removed from the structural characteristics of *Godot,* with its absence of plot and movement and its static nature, where the same situation—waiting—is examined and reexamined from many puzzling angles.

The language of Betsuyaku's plays is distinctive and seems closely interrelated with their themes and structure. Many of Betsuyaku's plays explore the nature of human relationships through exaggeration, parody, and abstraction. Characters with no apparent relationship, familial or otherwise, encounter one another, thus beginning a relationship into which one party is drawn reluctantly. Simple everyday language is employed as the characters discuss the developing situation, the reluctant one trying mightily, but unsuccessfully, to explain his position. The Man and Wife of *Match Girl* are examples of characters in this predicament; another example can be found in the first and third scenes of *Legend.* The sympathy that the audience feels for the claims of the Woman and her Brother in the former is somewhat unusual for such plays; more often the character resisting the situation is clearly victimized. The language used is conversational, unexceptional, but generally inadequate for providing the characters with a simple clarification of the nature of their dilemma.

Betsuyaku is also capable of considerable humor. Humor is not employed in *Match Girl,* but it distinguishes *Legend.* The mindless bickering of the two Vets is a favorite technique of Betsuyaku's, the inspiration for which could possibly be traced to Vladimir and Estragon. Likewise, the bickering of the Old Woman and Man 3 in *Cherry* provides an example of the nonsensical play that Betsuyaku's characters often indulge in. The elderly couple's comic eating scene intrudes on *Cherry*'s thematic seriousness and fails to approach the great humor—reminiscent of the absurdists Beckett, Arrabal, and, especially, Ionesco—of Betsuyaku's many black comedies.[7] However, this comic relief has a thematic purpose—to provide insight into the relationship of the old couple, the character of the Old Woman, and her conception of the type of fun-loving man she works to prevent her grandson from becoming.

Although beginning his career enamored of the dramaturgy of such giants of the theater as Beckett and Ionesco, Betsuyaku is a Japanese original. The Japanese theater scene, dominated by troupes, pressures the independent playwright to write new plays steadily. A few of Betsuyaku's sixty some plays show signs of strain, but most are masterful works that probe the experience of Japan in the Shōwa era (1926–1989). These successes, such as *The Little Match Girl, The Legend of Noon,* and *The Cherry in Bloom,* exhibit what has kept Betsuyaku an important presence in Japanese theater for thirty years: avoiding the superfluous and ornamental in plot, staging, characterization, and dramatic language and evoking the intangible essence of psychological situations and sociopolitical phenomena.

Notes

1. For more information on Betsuyaku's life and work, see *Betsuyaku Minoru no sekai* (The world of Betsuyaku Minoru) (Tokyo: Shinchōsha, 1982); and Robert Rolf, "Out of the Sixties, Shimizu Kunio and Betsuyaku Minoru," *Journal of the Yokohama National University* 35, no. 2 (1988): 77–114.

2. Rolf, "Out of the Sixties," 102.

3. For example, Sueki Toshifumi, who has directed the greatest number of Betsuyaku's plays, in a transcribed interview by the editor, 14 July 1983.

4. Betsuyaku has written of his intentions for *Martial Law* that he conceived of Kita's relation to his emperor in the Kafkaesque terms of K's to the Castle (although he apologizes for adhering to his concept too schematically). See "Kita Ikki—eiga Kaigenrei" (Kita Ikki—the film *Martial Law*), in *Han-tennō-seiron* (Arguments against the emperor system), ed. Shin-Nihon bungakkai (New Japanese Literary Society) (Tokyo: Aki shobō, 1975), 34–57. The *Martial Law* screenplay, *The Legend of Noon,* and several relevant essays are contained in Betsuyaku's *Kaigenrei: densetsu Kita Ikki* (*Martial Law:* The Kita Ikki legend) (Tokyo: Kadokawa shoten, 1973). Kita Ikki is prominent in Betsuyaku's play *The Snow Falls on Tarō's Roof* and Shimizu Kunio's play *Dreams Departed, Orpheus* (Yume sarite, Orufe) (1986). For a useful description of *Martial Law* (which, however, makes no mention of Betsuyaku), see David Desser, *Eros Plus Massacre: An Introduction to the Japanese New Wave Cinema* (Bloomington: Indiana University Press, 1988), 72–75.

5. They appear, e.g., in Betsuyaku's *Water-Bloated Corpse* and *The Snow Falls on Tarō's Roof,* Kara Jūrō's *Kappa* (Kappa) (1978), and films such as Terayama Shūji's *Get Rid of the Books and Hit the Town* (Sho o suteyo machi e deyō) (1971) and, very briefly, Ōshima Nagisa's *A Treatise on Japanese Bawdy Songs* (Nihon shunkakō) (1967).

6. Betsuyaku's sociohistorical views contain similarities to those of noted "people's history" historian Irokawa Daikichi in his influential *The Culture of the Meiji Period* (Meiji no bunka) (1970), translation ed. Marius B. Jansen (Princeton, N.J.: Princeton University Press, 1985). Betsuyaku's views on education and community *(kyōdōtai)* are given in detail in the transcribed interview found in Rolf, "Out of the Sixties." As for Betsuyaku's interest in contemporary crimes, he attempts analyses of many such in his *Hanzai shindorōmu* (The criminal syndrome) (Tokyo: Sanseidō, 1981).

7. There are too many to enumerate them all, but Betsuyaku's most successful black comedies include *Kangaroo* (Kangarū) (1967), *Corpse with Feet* (Ashi no aru shitai) (1982), and three plays that could be termed his "medical trilogy," in each of which his protagonist/victim's destruction comes at the hands of the medical profession: *The Receptionist* (Uketsuke) (1979), *Corpse with Atmosphere* (Fun'iki no aru shitai) (1980), and *Sick* (Byōki) (1981).

Betsuyaku Minoru beside his well-known telephone pole, on the set of *Snow Falls on Tarō's Roof* at the Bungakuza Atelier, 1982. (Courtesy Robert N. Lawson.)

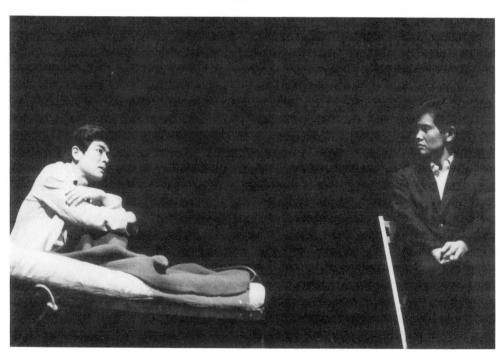

The Elephant was perhaps the opening shot in the theater revolution of the 1960s. The late Ono Seki *(left),* cofounder of the Waseda Little Theater, plays the *hibakusha* protagonist in a 1968 WLT revival. (Courtesy SCOT.)

Water-Bloated Corpse, which borrows from *The Legend of Noon,* began as an attempt to adapt Beckett's *Endgame.* Symbiotic characters and the familiar telephone pole are prominent. Bungakuza, 1978. (Courtesy Bungakuza.)

The Elephant depicts processes of victimization. The *hibakusha* protagonist, the Invalid, has his wife torture him until he can no longer stand it. Knack, 1978. (Courtesy Satō Jirō.)

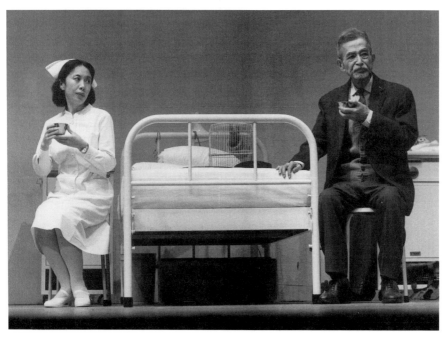

Corpse with Atmosphere shows Betsuyaku's reliance on *shingeki*'s best, such as Kishida Kyōko *(left)* and Nakamura Nobuo *(right)*. The play reflects his move toward the mainstream as leftist activism degenerated into internecine violence in the 1970s. En, 1980. (Courtesy En.)

The Little Match Girl

Betsuyaku Minoru

TRANSLATED BY ROBERT N. LAWSON

CAST OF CHARACTERS
WOMAN
HER YOUNGER BROTHER
MIDDLE-AGED MAN
HIS WIFE

(Center stage there is an old-fashioned table with three chairs, a little to stage left a small serving table with one chair.

This may be called an old-fashioned play, so it should open on an old-fashioned, slightly melancholy note.

The theater gradually goes dark, without it being noticed. From out of nowhere, a song from long ago, on a scratchy record, faintly comes to be heard. Then, unexpectedly, as if right in the next seat, a WOMAN'S VOICE, *hoarse and low, can be heard whispering.)*

WOMAN'S VOICE: It was the last night of the year, New Year's Eve, and it was very cold. It had already become dark, and snow was falling.

A poor little girl was trudging wearily along the dark, deserted street. She had no hat, nor even any shoes. Until a little while before she had been wearing her dead mother's wooden shoes, but they were too big for her, and, trying to dodge two carriages that came rushing by, she had lost both of them. Her little feet were purple and swollen, as she put one in front of the other on the stiffly frozen snow.

Her apron pocket was filled with matches, and she was holding one bunch in her hand. She had been trying to sell them, but no one had bought a single match from her that whole day. No one had given her so much as a single penny.

(From stage right a MIDDLE-AGED MAN *and* HIS WIFE *appear, carrying evening tea things. They begin to place them on the table, meticulously. In this*

household the way of doing such things is governed by strict rule, it seems. The
WIFE *sometimes makes a mistake, but her husband then carefully corrects it.*
Various things—taken from a tray, from the folds of their kimonos, from their
pockets—are carefully positioned. A teapot, cups, spoons, a sugar bowl, a milk
pitcher, jars of jam, butter, cookies, various spices, nuts, shriveled small fruits,
miniature plants and animal figurines, and other small things are all arranged
closely together. As this is going on, the two mumble to each other.)

MAN: Setting a table is an art, you know. If you arrange everything just
right, even a dried lemon will show to advantage.

WIFE: The people across the street place the powdered spinach next to
the deodorizer.

MAN: Hum, what kind of pretentiousness is that?

WIFE: Right . . . just what I said to them. "Isn't that pretentious?" But
listen to what they answered. "In this house we have our own way of
doing things."

MAN: Their own way, huh? Well, fine. But, even so, there should be
some principle . . . such procedures should be according to rule.

WIFE: That's right. Just what I told them. There should be some principle. . . .

MAN: Hey, what's that?

WIFE: Garlic.

MAN: Garlic is for morning. I never heard of garlic for evening tea.

WIFE: But we saw the sunset a little while ago. Don't you always say,
"Garlic for sunset"?

MAN: Garlic for sunrise. Onion for sunset.

WIFE: Was that it? Well, then, onions.

MAN: But let's not bother with them.

WIFE: Why?

MAN: They smell.

WIFE: Of course they smell. But is there anything that doesn't? You
can't name a thing that doesn't have some drawback. Ginseng may
not smell, but it has worms.

MAN: Yes, but those worms are good for neuralgia, you know.

WIFE: I like to eat onions. Then I don't feel the cold. One works for one
night. Two for two nights. So three will work for three nights.

MAN: Roasted crickets are good if you are sensitive to cold. I keep telling
you that. One cricket for one night.

WIFE: But there aren't any crickets now. What season do you think this
is? There's snow outside.

MAN: All right, then, do this. First, heat some sesame oil. Then, after
letting it cool, lick salt as you drink it. Lick and drink. Lick and
drink. Three times. It works immediately.

WIFE: Isn't that what you do when you haven't had a bowel movement?

MAN: No, then it's soybean oil. In that case you lick and drink four times. You don't remember anything at all, do you?

WIFE: Say . . . over there . . . isn't that cheese?

MAN: Hmm, it seems to be. It wasn't there last night. Well . . . where should we put it? In the old days, we used to put the cheese next to the dried dates, but. . . .

WIFE: *(Picking it up.)* I wonder when we got this. It's pretty stale, isn't it?

MAN: Yes, getting hard. Didn't there used to be something called hard cheese? Cheese that had become hard. . . . *(Thinking.)*

WIFE: Look, teeth marks. You took a bite and then left it, didn't you?

MAN: Ridiculous! Let me see. I'd never do an ill-mannered thing like that. Those are your teeth marks.

WIFE: My teeth aren't that sharp.

MAN: I don't know about that . . . but it could have been the cat.

WIFE: Well . . . maybe. In the old days we had a cat. Could it have been Pesu?

MAN: Pesu was the dog. Kuro was the parrot, Tobi was the goat, and the horse was Taro, so the cat . . . could it have been Pesu after all?

WIFE: The cat was Pesu. Kuro was the parrot, Tobi the goat, the horse was Taro, the dog . . . the dog . . . I wonder if the dog was Pesu. . . .

(A WOMAN *appears stage left.)*

WOMAN: *(Quietly.)* Good evening.

MAN: Huh?

WOMAN: Good evening.

WIFE: Good evening.

WOMAN: Are you having evening tea?

MAN: Well, after a fashion. . . .

WIFE: We never miss having tea in this house, from long ago.

WOMAN: It was that way in my family, too, long ago.

MAN: Ah, well, since you have taken the trouble to come, won't you please join us?

WOMAN: Yes, thank you.

WIFE: Please do. Not just for evening tea, but any time you have tea it's nice to have company. In the old days we frequently entertained.

MAN: Please sit down.

(The three of them sit down. The MAN *pours them tea.)*

MAN: Now then, before tea in your home, I mean before evening tea, do you say a prayer?

WOMAN: Ah . . . I don't really remember.

MAN: Well then, let's skip that. Actually, saying a prayer before evening

tea is not proper. You might even say it is a breach of etiquette. Do
you know why?

WOMAN: No.

MAN: Because it's not to God's liking. It says so in the Bible. (To HIS
WIFE.) Do you remember?

WIFE: No.

MAN: She forgets everything. Because of her age. Sugar? How many?

WOMAN: Yes . . . well, if it's all right, I'll serve myself.

MAN: Of course. Please do. That's the best way. People should be com
pletely free.

WIFE: In this house we always have guests who visit at night join us for
evening tea. Now, after so many years, you are the victim.

MAN: How many years has it been? But you are late in coming . . .
which way did you come from?

WOMAN: I came from City Hall.

WIFE: Ah, City Hall! That gloomy building? Don't you agree that it's
gloomy?

WOMAN: Yes, it's gloomy.

WIFE: Gloomy!

MAN: Would you like a sweet?

WOMAN: Thank you.

MAN: We have rich things, too, if you'd prefer. By the way, speaking of
City Hall, how is that fellow?

WIFE: What fellow?

MAN: That guy who sits there on the second floor and spits out the
window.

WIFE: Oh, he died. Quite a while ago.

MAN: Is he finally dead? He was a problem for everybody. As many as
thirteen times a day. People avoided passing that place.

WIFE: Well, no one avoids passing there these days. His son is sitting
there now, and that young man is very courteous. But did you come
directly from City Hall to our house?

WOMAN: Yes.

MAN: Directly here? That is to say, intending to come to our house?

WOMAN: That's right, directly here.

WIFE: Is that so? (A little perplexed.) Well then . . . ah . . . how nice of
you to come.

MAN: Yes. You are certainly welcome. We've had very few visitors lately.

WIFE: But what did they say about us at City Hall?

WOMAN: Nothing in particular.

MAN: That we are good citizens?

WOMAN: Yes.

WIFE: Exemplary?

WOMAN: Yes.

MAN: And *harmless?*

WOMAN: Yes.

WIFE: Well, that's certainly true. We are the best, most exemplary, citizens.

MAN: Last year the mayor went out on the balcony and gave a speech. Then, at the end, he said, "In our city we are pleased to have 362 citizens who are not only good, and exemplary, but also harmless." Those last two are us . . . really.

WIFE: The city tax isn't much, but we pay it right on time. And we don't put out much trash. And we don't drink much water.

MAN: Our ideas are moderate, too. We *are* both, relatively speaking, Progressive Conservatives. Those Reform party people are so vulgar. Neither of us can tolerate that. One of those guys, you know, will yawn without putting his hand to his mouth. Really! In the old days that would have been unthinkable.

WOMAN: *(With feeling.)* It is really . . . nice and warm here.

WIFE: Yes, isn't it? And refined, too. We aren't rich, but we try not to be unnecessarily frugal.

MAN: Now, to put it briefly, you've been sent here from City Hall.

WOMAN: No, I wouldn't say that exactly.

WIFE: Perhaps we should say, "dispatched."

WOMAN: No, that's not it. I heard about this place at City Hall. Something that made me want to visit you . . . so I came.

MAN: I see. I understand. You say that you heard something about us at City Hall. That made you want to visit us. And so, here you are— visiting us. That's certainly logical.

WIFE: *(In admiration.)* That makes sense. In short, since you wanted to visit us, you visited us. That's different from saying that you didn't want to visit us, but visited us anyway.

MAN: It's a goodwill visit, isn't it?

WOMAN: I just had to meet you.

WIFE: My, what a sweet thing to say. Another cup of tea? *(Offering tea.)*

WOMAN: Thank you.

MAN: In that case, whatever questions you have, or whatever requests, please just tell us. It is our established policy never to disappoint anyone who has come so far. Why are we so healthy in spite of growing old? Why are we so cheerful? So full of humor? Why, though we aren't rich, are we not unnecessarily frugal? How can we be both progressive and conservative at the same time? Why are we such good citizens? Why, to sum it all up, are we us?

WIFE: Go ahead and ask your questions. He will certainly answer them well, whatever they are about, I'm sure.

WOMAN: Thank you. But for right now it's enough just to be allowed to sit here this way.

MAN: Don't you have at least one of these "questions"? There are usually three questions for every person.

WIFE: And three for me, too.

MAN: And you know the answers already anyway, right?

WOMAN: Really, I   just to be sitting here   and you have even served me a warm cup of tea. . . .

WIFE: Ah, of course. This lady is interested in the domestic environment . . . our home's unique domestic environment.

MAN: I see. I understand. This so-called family atmosphere takes some doing. Now, the first thing you can't do without for that homey feel is a cat. Second, a fireplace, or something of the kind. Things like whiskey or home-brewed sake, like detective stories or fairy tales, knitting needles and wool yarn, or torn socks and gloves, and, to top it off, some reading glasses . . . right? We used to have a cat, too, but he seems to have disappeared recently. . . .

WIFE: If you'd given us a little notice that you were coming, we could have borrowed one from the neighbor. . . .

WOMAN: Please, never mind about that. I'm happy just to be here, in a warm place, with such kind people, quietly drinking tea. It's very cold outside. It's snowing. No one is out there.

MAN: I can well believe that. It's supposed to snow tonight. Did you walk all the way?

WOMAN: Yes, all the way. . . .

WIFE: Poor thing. You must be hungry. Please help yourself to whatever you'd like.

MAN: We always like to help those less fortunate as much as we can. That's our way. . . .

WOMAN'S VOICE: (From no particular direction.) The little girl was hungry now. She was shaking from the cold as she walked. The snow came drifting down on the back of her neck, to fall among the beautiful curls of her long golden hair. But from every window the light was shining, and there was the strong and savory smell of a goose roasting.

That was as it should be, the little girl was thinking. It was, after all, New Year's Eve. There was a small space between two houses. She drew her body into that corner and crouched down there, pulling her little feet under her. Even so, she could not escape the cold. . . .

WIFE: (In a small voice.) Dear, I think that this lady has something she'd like to say to us.

MAN: Is that so? Well then, please don't hesitate. For that matter . . . well . . . if you'd prefer, I could leave. I know that, as they say, women feel more comfortable talking to one another. . . . *(Beginning to stand.)*

WOMAN: No, please. Don't go. This is fine. Really. Just this, just sitting here quietly like this is fine. I'm perfectly happy this way.

WIFE: Well, if you say so. But you went to a lot of trouble to come here, and we'll feel bad if we don't do anything for you.

MAN: Right. We wouldn't want you to think we were so insensitive.

WOMAN: No, really, I wouldn't think anything like that.

WIFE: Ah, well, isn't there something you'd like to eat? If there is, I'd be happy to fix it for you.

WOMAN: Thank you, but not just now.

MAN: Well, just as she says . . . that's fine. She has just arrived, dear, and probably doesn't feel like asking questions or giving orders yet. That's what it is. It's better just to leave her alone. You know what they say about excessive kindness . . . now what is it they say? . . .

WIFE: Maybe you're right. *(To the* WOMAN.*)* Just make yourself comfortable. We're not in any hurry.

WOMAN: Thank you.

MAN: But, please don't hesitate. . . .

WOMAN: Yes . . . well. . . .

WIFE: As if it were your own home. . . .

WOMAN: Yes.

(MAN *starts to say something, and then stops. There is an awkward silence.)*

MAN: *(Suddenly thinking of something to say.)* Outside . . . was it snowing?

WOMAN: *(Nods.)*

WIFE: *(Eagerly pursuing the thought.)* Powdered . . . snow?

WOMAN: Yes. . . . *(Nods.)*

(Silence.)

MAN: *(Again thinking.)* You're tired . . . aren't you?

WOMAN: No.

MAN: *(To* HIS WIFE.*)* But she must be tired. Why don't you ask her to lie down for a little while? . . .

WIFE: That's a good idea. Why not do that?

WOMAN: No, this is just fine.

MAN: But. . . .

WOMAN: Really. . . .

WIFE: Well, whatever you think. . . .

(There is another awkward silence.)

MAN: Say, I've got an idea. Why don't you sing her a song?

WIFE: A song? I can't sing . . . not me!

MAN: "Not me?" Did you hear that? She's just being shy. Or too modest. I shouldn't brag about my own wife, but her singing is something to hear. Come on, sing something for her?

WIFE: I can't do that.

MAN: Of course you can. She'd like to hear it, too. Right? Wouldn't you like to hear her sing something?

WOMAN: Yes . . . but. . . .

MAN: See! Don't be so shy. Go ahead and sing. After all, she has taken the trouble to come. *(To the woman.)* She's not much good at anything else . . . just singing. But she's not bad at it. She's rather good.

WIFE: I don't have a good voice any more . . . at my age.

MAN: At your age? . . . Listen to that. Just yesterday she was saying that she could still sing pretty well in spite of her age, because she has always taken care of her voice. . . .

WIFE: But I just meant . . . for in the family. . . .

MAN: In the family, outside the family, what's the difference? Go ahead and sing. Try that song . . . "The snow is. . . . *(Trying to remember.)* The snow is. . . . *(Thinking.)* The snow is getting deeper . . . no *keeps* getting deeper. . . ."

WOMAN: *(Quietly.)* I was selling matches. . . .

WIFE: What?

WOMAN: I was selling matches.

WIFE: My, did you hear that, dear?

MAN: What's that?

WIFE: She's selling matches.

MAN: Matches? Ah, I see! Yes . . . I understand . . . finally. About buying matches. Well, it would have been better to have said so sooner, but . . . you went to City Hall to examine the city directory to find the household most in need of matches . . . and that was us. That's what it is! Fine. I can understand that. And we'll buy them. Buy them all. I don't know if you've got a truckload . . . maybe two . . . but we'll buy them all. Here and now. I promise.

WIFE: But we just bought matches. Far too many. Of course, since she took the trouble to come, we should buy some. Yes, let's buy some. But we can't use many.

WOMAN: No, that's not it. I was selling matches a long time ago.

MAN: Ah, a long time ago. . . .

WIFE: Then what are you selling now? If it's something useful around the house, we'll buy some. You've gone to so much trouble.

MAN: That's right. Even if it's a little expensive. . . .

WOMAN: Nothing in particular right now. . . .

MAN: Nothing? . . .

WOMAN: That's right.

WIFE: *(A little disappointed.)* Oh . . . well. . . .

MAN: Ah . . . I see. You were telling us a story about something you remember from when you were small. . . .

WOMAN: Yes, that's it.

WIFE: About selling matches? . . .

WOMAN: Yes.

MAN: How old were you?

WOMAN: I was seven. . . .

WIFE: It was terrible, wasn't it?

MAN: And you can't help remembering. . . .

WOMAN: Well, really, until just recently, I didn't understand it.

MAN: You didn't understand? . . .

WOMAN: It was twenty years ago.

WIFE: You don't say. . . .

MAN: And you had forgotten about it?

WOMAN: I didn't understand. Until just recently, I didn't understand at all. I was married and had two children. One, a boy, is four years old. The other, a girl, is barely two. So far as the girl is concerned, everything is fine, but a four-year-old boy requires a lot of attention.

WIFE: Isn't that the truth!

MAN: A boy of four can take care of himself.

WIFE: Nonsense!

WOMAN: People say that two children are too many at my age. But I don't feel that way.

MAN: You're right. Two is normal.

WIFE: They say you haven't really done your duty till you've had three.

MAN: Well, where are those children?

WOMAN: Don't worry about that.

MAN: Ah. . . .

WIFE: Are they healthy?

WOMAN: Yes, quite healthy. . . .

MAN: That's good.

WIFE: That's the important thing . . . for children to be healthy.

WOMAN: Then I read in a book. . . .

WIFE: In a book? . . . My. . . .

MAN: A child-care book?

WOMAN: No . . . fiction. . . .

MAN: Ah, that's good. When a woman gets married and has children, she usually quits reading books. Especially fiction.

WIFE: What was it about?

WOMAN: Various things.

MAN: Various things, indeed. Those writers of fiction write about all kinds of things, don't they?

WOMAN: Among other things, about a match girl. At first I didn't understand it. I read it again. Then I had a strange feeling.

MAN: Strange?

WOMAN: Yes. After that I read it many times, over and over. . . .

WIFE: About how many times?

WOMAN: Five . . . or more. . . .

MAN: Then? . . .

WOMAN: Then I saw it. I was amazed. It was about me.

WIFE: About you? . . .

WOMAN: Yes.

MAN: It was written about you?

WOMAN: That's right. I hadn't understood.

WIFE: About selling matches? . . .

MAN: . . . about the little match girl? . . .

WOMAN: Yes. It was about me. I was the little match girl.

WIFE: My goodness . . . that one? . . .

MAN: But. . . .

WOMAN: After that I remembered many things. Many things gradually became clear. . . .

MAN'S VOICE: *(Low, in a murmur.)* People were starving then. Every night was dark and gloomy. The town was built on swampland, sprawling and stinking. Here and there shops had been set up, like sores that had burst open. Small animals were killed in the shadows, and secretly eaten. People walked furtively, like forgotten criminals, and now and then, unexpectedly, something would scurry by in the darkness.

That child was selling matches at the street corner. When a match was struck, she would lift her shabby skirt for display until the match went out. People made anxious by the small crimes they had committed, people who could not even commit such crimes, night after night, in their trembling fingers, would strike those matches. Directed at the infinite darkness hidden by that skirt, how many times that small light had burned, until it had burned out. . . .

Those two thin legs held a darkness as profound as that of the depths of the sea, darker than all the darkness of that city floating on a swampland gathered together. As she stood there above that darkness, the little girl smiled aimlessly, or seemed empty and sad.

WIFE: Isn't there someone at the door?

MAN: Nonsense! In this cold? Aren't you cold?

WOMAN: No.

MAN: But then, how about that? Seeing yourself revealed in a story gives you a strange feeling, doesn't it?

WOMAN: Yes, very strange. After that I thought about it for a long time. I had suffered greatly. But there is still one thing I can't understand.

WIFE: One thing? . . .

MAN: What?

WOMAN: Why did I do a thing like that?

MAN: A thing like that?

WOMAN: Yes.

WIFE: Selling matches?

WOMAN: Yes.

WIFE: Well. . . .

MAN: Wasn't it because you were poor? I don't mean to be rude, but. . . .

WOMAN: Still, to do that kind of thing. . . .

WIFE: You shouldn't be ashamed of that. Everyone did such things then. Those who didn't, didn't survive. Children stole things. After I had worked so hard to make hotcakes for his birthday, they stole them. It was like that then.

MAN: You should forget the things from that time. Everyone has forgotten. I've forgotten, too.

WOMAN: But I want you to think back, to recall those memories.

WIFE: Well, even if you try, there are some things you can't forget. But what good does it do to remember?

MAN: I had to do such things, too. Just as you did, I tried to sell things as a peddler. It's not that important. It's nothing to be ashamed of. Really.

WOMAN: But how could I ever have thought of doing such a thing? I was only seven years old. Could a child of seven think of that kind of thing?

WIFE: That kind of thing? . . .

WOMAN: That kind of . . . of . . . terrible thing. . . .

MAN: . . . what kind of? . . .

WOMAN: I was selling matches.

MAN: Yes, selling matches . . . you were selling matches. . . .

WOMAN: . . . and while they were burning. . . .

MAN: . . . impossible. . . .

WOMAN: No, it's not.

MAN: I can't believe it. . . .

WOMAN: But that's the way it was. It was me. I was the little match girl. . . .

WIFE: Ah . . . you were the one. . . .

WOMAN: Yes, do you remember? That time? . . . that place? . . .

(A pause.)

MAN: But, well, all kinds of things happened then.

WIFE: That's true. All kinds of things. It was very different from now. No one knew what to do. It wasn't your fault.

MAN: It's nothing to worry about. That was all over long ago. An old story. My philosophy is to forget it. Forget everything. Without exception! Everything. If you don't   well, anyway   let life go on.

WOMAN: But I can't forget it.

WIFE: Why?

WOMAN: Because I have remembered.

MAN: I see. Yes, there is such a time in life. Just be patient a while. You'll soon forget. But, let's stop talking about it. Say . . . I'll make you forget in three minutes. Do you know the story of the kind weasel?

(WOMAN does not answer.)

MAN: How about fixing us another cup of tea, dear. . . .

WIFE: Fine, let me do that. It has gotten quite cold.

(Taking the pot, she leaves.)

WOMAN: Are mother's feet all right now?

MAN: Mother . . . ah, you mean my wife? No, they still aren't good, particularly when it gets cold. But I'm surprised that you know so much. Things like my wife's trouble with her feet.

WOMAN: I don't mind forgetting that story, either.

MAN: Please do. Just forget it. It happened twenty years ago.

WOMAN: But I would still like to know one thing.

MAN: What?

WOMAN: I'm sure that someone must have taught me to.

MAN: To what?

WOMAN: To do such a thing. . . .

MAN: Ah well, that's probably true. No doubt.

WOMAN: Was it you?

MAN: What?

WOMAN: Were you the one who taught me to?

MAN: Me?

WOMAN: Yes.

MAN: Me?

WOMAN: Yes.

MAN: Me? . . .

WOMAN: Yes.

MAN: . . . why would I have?

WOMAN: Don't you remember?

MAN: What?

WOMAN: Don't you remember me?

MAN: Remember you?

WOMAN: I'm your daughter.

MAN: You? . . .

WOMAN: Yes.

MAN: Impossible

WOMAN: There's no doubt about it. I've made inquiries. That's what they told me at City Hall, too. It's the truth.

MAN: It can't be. It's not possible. I don't have a daughter. We did have a daughter . . . but she died. She is dead.

WOMAN: I don't blame you for making me do that kind of thing. I don't bear a grudge. But I would just like to know. That's all. Why was I doing that? If someone taught me to, who was it? I . . . if I thought of something like that all by myself, when I was just seven years old . . . I can't believe that . . . that would be frightening. Absolutely frightening! I'd just like to know why. It bothers me so much that I can't sleep at night.

MAN: But it wasn't me. My daughter is dead. She was run over by a streetcar. I saw it . . . my daughter . . . right in front of my eyes . . . run over and killed. I'm not lying to you. My daughter is dead.

WOMAN: Father. . . .

MAN: Stop it. Please stop it. Your story is wrong. You have things confused somehow. That's it. A misunderstanding. Such things often happen. But a mistake is still a mistake.

(The WIFE *appears, carrying a pot of tea.)*

WIFE: What's going on, dear?

MAN: Well . . . a little surprise . . . she has just claimed that she is our daughter.

WIFE: Oh, my! Really?

WOMAN: It's true.

MAN: Don't be ridiculous! Our daughter is dead. Our daughter was run over by a streetcar and killed.

WIFE: That's true. But if she were living she would be just about this girl's age.

WOMAN: I *am* living. It is true!

MAN: But I saw it happen. I . . . with these eyes . . . right in front of me . . . very close.

WOMAN: I checked on that at City Hall, too.

WIFE: At City Hall?

MAN: Still. . . .

WIFE: But, dear, who can say for sure that she isn't our daughter?

MAN: I can!

WIFE: Why?

MAN: Because I saw it . . . I. . . .

WIFE: I saw it, too. But we need to remember the circumstances. Our daughter behaved a bit strangely. She often ran out in the middle of the night. The first time, she was just three years old. A fire alarm sounded in the middle of the night, and, when I looked, she wasn't there. We ran out after her, frantic. The bridge over the river outside the village was down. That child, drenched to the skin, was being held in the arms of a volunteer fireman. A bonfire was burning . . . I didn't know what to do. . . .

MAN: It happened a number of times. She died after we moved to town, so she was perhaps seven.

WIFE: She was seven.

MAN: I didn't know what happened. My wife shook me awake. It was in the middle of the night and it was raining. That child, still in her nightgown, went running out in the street where the streetcar line was, running in the deserted street. I ran after her. I called to her . . . again and again. Then, just as we turned the corner, there came the streetcar.

WIFE: That's right. It was raining that night . . . I remember.

WOMAN: Don't you remember me?

WIFE: *(Staring at her intently, then in a low voice.)* It's her.

MAN: You're wrong.

WIFE: But that kind of thing might be possible. . . .

WOMAN: It's me.

WIFE: Please, stand up for a minute.

(The WOMAN *stands, rather awkwardly. She walks a little.)*

MAN: Just who in the world are you?

WOMAN: The daughter of the two of you.

WIFE: *(To the* MAN.*)* She looks like her.

WOMAN: There's no mistake. The man in charge of family records examined many thick record books. That's how I found out. He said that my father and mother lived here.

WIFE: What do you think?

MAN: I don't believe it.

WIFE: But let's talk about it a little. Then we can see.

MAN: What?

WIFE: Oh, all sorts of things. But even if, let's say, she isn't actually our child, wouldn't that still be all right? She's had such a hard time.

MAN: I understand that . . . but. . . .

WOMAN: I . . . I don't blame you, Father . . . for that. . . .

MAN: Blame? . . . Me? . . .

WOMAN: I can forget even that, now.

MAN: You're wrong. It's all a mistake.

WIFE: That's all right. Let's just sit down. We'll sit and talk.

MAN: Yes, let's sit down. Standing won't get us anywhere. And since you went to the trouble to fix hot tea. . . .

WIFE: Right. Let's have our tea. After that, we'll have a long overdue parent-child conversation.

(The three of them sit down and begin to drink their tea, in a somewhat pleasant mood.)

MAN: Well, I don't deny that there's a resemblance. And, if she had lived, she'd have been just about your age. . . .

WIFE: She did live. I can't help feeling so.

MAN: Now, dear, don't say such things so lightly, even joking, because she is quite serious. . . .

WOMAN: What's best is to see that father and mother are well.

WIFE: My, how often have I thought I would like to hear that!

MAN: But, dear, I keep telling you, it is all a mistake.

WOMAN: Ah . . . I . . . it is difficult for me to say this, but . . . ah . . . my younger brother is still waiting outside.

WIFE: Younger brother?

WOMAN: Yes.

MAN: You have a brother?

WOMAN: Yes. We agreed that, if I found out that you really were our father and mother, I'd call him.

WIFE: But we had only the one daughter.

MAN: She was an only child. Of course, I always wanted a son, very much, but . . . we never had one.

WIFE: Your real brother? . . .

WOMAN: Yes, he is. So . . . your real son.

WIFE: That would seem to follow, but . . . but we really didn't . . . have a son. . . .

WOMAN: It's cold outside, and, if it's all right, I wonder if you could call him in? . . . *(Standing and moving off stage left.)*

MAN: But . . . just a minute. . . .

(The WOMAN reappears, bringing in HER BROTHER. She guides him to the small serving table.)

WOMAN: See, this is your mother.

BROTHER: Good evening, Mother.

WOMAN: And this is your father.

BROTHER: Good evening, Father.

WOMAN: Please sit down. *(Seats him beside the small table.)*

BROTHER: Yes. *(Sits.)*

WOMAN: You were probably cold, weren't you?

BROTHER: No, not at all. . . .

WOMAN: My brother has remarkable self-control. He has sometimes stood in the snow all night long. And he'd never even sneeze. Have some tea.

BROTHER: Yes. *(Taking a large cup, saucer, and spoon from a bag he is holding.)* *(The WIFE, holding the teapot, pours tea into his cup. While handing him the sugar, she observes him closely.)*

WOMAN: He likes tea very much. Two spoons of sugar. Always. Then he drinks slowly. I taught him that. They say it's best for the body, and for the heart, to drink slowly. *(The BROTHER drinks the tea.)*

WOMAN: Aren't you hungry?

BROTHER: No.

WOMAN: But take something. Since you haven't had anything since yesterday.

WIFE: My, since yesterday?

WOMAN: Yes, my brother's self-control is very strong. He has sometimes gone for over three days without eating. But he never says a word about it.

WIFE: Three days? . . . But that's not good for his health. Even Gandhi went only two days at the most. Well, there's not much, but please eat all you want.

WOMAN: *(Passing the plate of cookies.)* Please take one.

BROTHER: Thank you. *(Bows politely, takes one, and eats slowly.)*

WOMAN: Chew it well. The better we chew our food, the better it is for us.

BROTHER: Yes.

WIFE: You are a good sister. And your brother is very polite.

MAN: He's very sensible. That's an excellent quality.

WOMAN: When you are ready, tell father and mother your story.

BROTHER: All right. But it's not necessary.

WOMAN: Why?

BROTHER: I can tell them later.

WOMAN: My brother is very reserved. Shy. Bashful and uncommunicative besides.

WIFE: But that's good. Not to talk too much is excellent in a man.

MAN: Yes, that's true. Real gentlemen usually don't talk much. Still, to say that it is excellent not to talk misses the point. Speaking from my long experience, I would say that you should talk when it is time to talk. To be more precise, then, it is excellent in a man not to talk when it isn't time to talk.

WOMAN: Mother, won't you tell my brother something about when he was little?

WIFE: But, you know, you're confused about that. We never had a son.

MAN: We never had a son. We had a daughter. And she died. So there are no children. None. . . .

WOMAN: We can't get Father to believe us. . . .

WIFE: But . . . really. . . .

BROTHER: Mother. . . .

WIFE: Me?

BROTHER: A long time ago, you suffered from a bad case of asthma. I remember that very well. I used to rub your back. You'd be short of breath, and your face would get red. To see you bent over suffering like that was terrible. When I rubbed your back, that seemed to help, though, and you would go to sleep. . . .

WIFE: My, I wonder if that could be true. . . .

MAN: Did you ever have asthma?

WIFE: No.

MAN: Then this story doesn't fit, does it?

WIFE: But when a person catches a cold they cough a little.

WOMAN: That must be it . . . that mother had a cold, and that's what he's remembering. He has a very good memory. Would you like another one? *(Offering him the plate of cookies.)*

BROTHER: No, that's fine.

WOMAN: You needn't hold back. This is our home.

BROTHER: All right, then. Thank you. *(Takes one.)*

MAN: Now . . . please listen carefully. I want this quite clear.

WOMAN: He remembers everything . . . many things about Father and Mother in far greater detail than I can.

MAN: That's all very well, but . . . now listen! We did not have a son! I want to make that very clear. *Did not have!* That's the truth! We had a daughter. We had a cat. But no son. *There . . . never . . . was . . . one.* Do you understand? All right. Now, saying that doesn't mean that I want to put the two of you out. So please, just relax. Eat as much as you like. Drink as much as you like. I just want to make this one point. It may seem a mean thing to say, but I think it's important to be sure that it's clear. About this . . . this house. It is our home! You . . . are our guests.

WIFE: Dear, don't be so. . . .

MAN: I know. Yes, I know. Please don't misunderstand me. And if we agree on that one point, then we might welcome you as if you were a real daughter and a real son. Wouldn't you say that we have welcomed you almost as we might have a real son and daughter?

BROTHER: And Father suffered from neuralgia. Whenever it got cold, he had a pain in his hips. When that happened, he got irritable. Mother, and Sister, you both knew that. So, whenever he had an attack, you'd go out and leave me home alone with him. His sickness was the cause, of course, but he sometimes hit me and kicked me. At first I would yell, "It hurts! It hurts!"—and cry. But I soon stopped that. Because, no matter how much I cried, he still kept on. I just

learned to endure it. But, from that time on, my arm bends like this.
(Moves his left arm with a jerk.)

MAN: I never had anything like neuralgia. . . .

WOMAN: His endurance is remarkable. No matter what happens, he
never cries. Here, have another. *(Offering him the cookies.)*

BROTHER: Thank you. *(Taking one.)*

WOMAN: He's just naturally mistreated by everyone. He's hit and he's
kicked. But he bears it patiently. He keeps quiet; he crouches down;
he rolls up on the ground in a ball. But he doesn't cry.

MAN: I have never once used violence against another person. . . .

WOMAN: But, Father, he doesn't hold it against you. I have taught him
that that isn't good. It wasn't your fault. You were sick.

MAN: I had no son.

BROTHER: Father, I don't hold it against you. It was because you were
sick. That's what made you do it. Sometimes my arm hurts. When it
gets cold . . . just like with your neuralgia . . . there's a sharp pain,
right here. But I put up with it. I accept it. Sister said, "Please
endure it." So I do. I endure it.

WOMAN: His body is covered with bruises. It's terrible. But he doesn't
complain. He puts up with it. Show Father and Mother . . . so they
can see just how much you've endured.

BROTHER: Yes, Sister. *(Begins to unbutton his clothing.)*

WIFE: Stop! Please, stop. Don't do that! I understand. I believe you.
You probably are our son.

(The BROTHER, uncovering his upper body, stands up.)

MAN: *(Standing, solemnly.)* I see. You're the one. You were born. I wanted
it. I always wanted a son. So you were born. Evidently that's what it
is. They say that if you want something badly enough you'll get it,
don't they? That was you. And I never knew it at all . . . it's unbe-
lievable. I'm really surprised that you were born. *(Pause.)* This one
. . . kept quiet about it, and I never knew it. That's clear. And you
. . . you are my daughter. It's no mistake. I thought that you were
dead, but you were alive. The little girl I was chasing that evening
was someone else. You say that's so, so it must be. It was a dark evening. To me it was just a fluttering white thing dancing in the wind.
That wasn't you. You went flying the other way, running somewhere
else. And you never came back. That must be what happened. So
you are my daughter and son. My real daughter and son. I remember everything. So, then . . . what do you want? What now? . . .
Since I am your father, what do you want me to do for you? To look
at you with affection? To speak to you in a tender, caring voice? Or
do you want money? What is it? . . .

WOMAN: Father?

MAN: What?

WOMAN: *(Quietly.)* And Mother. We don't want you to misunderstand either. We didn't come here to trick you, or to beg for anything. We really are your son and daughter . . . that's all. . . .

MAN: Really? And I never knew. *(To HIS WIFE.)* Please ask these people to leave. We must go to bed now. We old people become sleepy earlier than you young people do.

WOMAN: Father.

MAN: Get out.

BROTHER: Not so loud. Please. The children have just fallen asleep.

MAN: Children?

WOMAN: My children. The two-year-old and four-year-old I told you about. I had them come in. It was presumptuous of me, I know. But I couldn't leave them out there in the cold. They were already almost frozen. They couldn't even cry. I felt so sorry for them. . . .

WIFE: Please leave.

WOMAN: Mother . . . don't be so cruel. . . .

WIFE: Please go. I beg you. Just go. I can't stand it. I'll give you money. It's so disagreeable. This is our house.

BROTHER: That's all right with me, Mother, but please think about the children. They're sleeping now, but they're very hungry. My sister has nothing to feed them. We kept telling them, as we came, "When we see Father and Mother, we'll ask them for something for you to eat." We barely got them to walk here. My sister is exhausted. Extremely exhausted. We walked for a long time.

WOMAN: But we are finally able to meet you, Mother. We walked a long way. It was very cold. Snow was falling. . . . *(Gradually laying down her head and seeming to fall asleep.)* Just for one look at Father and Mother . . . that's all we were thinking. . . .

WOMAN'S VOICE: To warm her freezing hands the little girl struck the match she was holding. The tiny stick flickered for a moment, enveloping the area in bright light. The ice and snow glittered a purple color. But, then, the match went out. The little girl remained there, crouching all alone on the cold stone pavement, with the wind blowing, freezing.

(The WOMAN's head is on her crossed arms on the table.)

WIFE: What happened to her? What's your sister doing?

MAN: She's sleeping.

BROTHER: Sleeping. Sometimes she sleeps. Then, sometimes, she wakes up.

WIFE: My, I wonder if she is crying . . . look. . . .

BROTHER: Yes, she's crying. She cries in her sleep. She's very unhappy.

MAN: Will you please wake her up, and leave? Look, I don't say that out of meanness. If you hadn't come with a strange trick like this, if you had come without saying anything, you would have received a warm welcome. Really. But now listen to me. Are you listening?

BROTHER: Yes.

MAN: Please leave.

BROTHER: But my sister is very tired.

MAN: Are you her real brother?

BROTHER: Yes, I really am. . . .

WIFE: Since when have you thought that?

BROTHER: What?

WIFE: How long ago did you become aware that she was your sister?

BROTHER: That was quite a while ago . . . quite a while. . . .

WIFE: Please try to remember clearly. It's very important.

BROTHER: But even when I first became aware of it, she was already my sister. . . .

MAN: Already at the time you became aware of it? . . . Well, that's not a very reasonable story.

WIFE: There had to be something before that.

BROTHER: There were many things. Many things. Then I suddenly realized . . . she was my sister.

MAN: It sounds like a miracle. . . .

(*Pause. The* BROTHER *gets up stealthily, takes a cookie from the table, goes back, sits down, and eats it.*)

MAN: (*Lost in thought. To* WIFE.) Can you remember back to that time? We were sitting somewhere on a sunny hill . . . the sky was blue, white clouds were floating lightly by, there was not a breath of wind . . . perhaps dandelions were blooming. . . .

WIFE: (*Prompted to reflection.*) There was that, too, wasn't there?

MAN: (*In the same mood.*) And then . . . some large thing was dead . . . alongside the road . . . what was it? . . .

WIFE: (*In the same mood.*) A cow . . . it was a large, gray-colored cow . . . just like a cloud. . . .

MAN: Ah, was it a cow? That thing . . . just like a cloud. . . .

WIFE: How about it, dear?

MAN: About what?

WIFE: These people . . . should we keep them overnight? . . .

MAN: Well, I was thinking that, too. We'll let them stay.

WIFE: I feel sorry for them.

MAN: Right, and people like that, no matter how they seem, they *are* unfortunate.

WIFE: Let's be kind to them.

MAN: Let's do that. Because there's nothing wrong in that.

WIFE: You two. It'll be all right for you to stay here tonight. We'll let you stay.

MAN: Make yourself at home. These other things . . . well, let's talk about them later. . . .

WIFE: Do you understand?

BROTHER: Yes, but that isn't necessary. Don't worry about us. Just leave us alone.

WIFE: Tell your sister, too, to put her mind at ease.

BROTHER: She already knows.

MAN: She already knows.

BROTHER: She told me that a while ago . . . that Mother had asked us to stay.

WIFE: Mother?

BROTHER: Yes.

WIFE: Meaning me?

BROTHER: That's right.

WIFE: So . . . then that's all right.

BROTHER: Is it all right if I take one more?

WIFE: Yes.

(He eats a cookie.)

MAN'S VOICE: Good evening.

MAN: Good evening.

MAN'S VOICE: I'm a city fire marshal. Is anything missing in your home. Is anything lost? Has anything disappeared?

MAN: Has anything?

WIFE: No.

MAN: It seems not.

MAN'S VOICE: So everything is in order?

MAN: I can't say that absolutely. You see, this is a very poor household.

MAN'S VOICE: How about your fire?

WIFE: It's all right. We haven't gone to bed yet.

MAN'S VOICE: Not yet? But you're not going to stay up all night, are you?

MAN: We'll check it before going to bed.

MAN'S VOICE: Did you notice?

MAN: What?

MAN'S VOICE: Can you hear the breathing of someone sleeping? Two small ones. . . .

WIFE: Children. There are children.

MAN'S VOICE: Be careful, please. Tonight is especially cold. Be careful that they don't freeze to death while they sleep. The city authorities are drawing special attention to that danger.

(There is the striking of wooden clappers, which gradually fades. Then, "Watch your fire," is heard from afar. The WOMAN *raises her head, as if still half asleep.)*

WOMAN: Father, while I was asleep, how many cookies did he eat?

MAN: Well, one, wasn't it?

WIFE: It was one, definitely. . . .

WOMAN: No, it was two. He ate two. I had counted them. I don't appreciate your letting him do that. Don't you remember, Father, how many times I asked you not to? He knows no limits. If you let him do it, he'll eat far too many. I have only eaten one so far. That's true, isn't it, Mother?

WIFE: Yes, but since there are plenty, don't feel that you have to restrain yourself. . . .

WOMAN: No, I don't mean it that way. I told him about it, but, no matter how often I tell him, he doesn't seem to understand. It's the same with Father. I've asked you so often!

MAN: But I didn't. . . .

WOMAN: No, I had spoken to you earlier. But it's not your fault. *(To* HER BROTHER.*)* You're the one. Mother, I hate to trouble you, but would you put these away?

WIFE: Yes, but there are plenty.

WOMAN: It will become a habit. Now apologize to Father and Mother.

MAN: Well, that's all right. Your brother was probably hungry.

WOMAN: Everyone is. Everyone is hungry. But people exercise self-control. You . . . you're the only one . . . doing such greedy things. . . . Well, apologize.

(She gives him a jab with her fingers.)

WIFE: Please, don't do that! Really, please stop. It's all right. In this house it doesn't matter at all.

WOMAN: Mother, don't interfere. This is our affair. I raised this child. Apologize. Why don't you apologize? Don't you feel ashamed? What did I always say to you?

MAN: Well, I understand your point very well. It's commendable. It's very commendable. However. . . .

WOMAN: Apologize!

MAN: Listen . . . will you? Here's another way of looking at it. What you say is sound, but don't tell me that if he gets hungry, it's his own fault? Really. Shouldn't you think again?

WOMAN: Please stay out of it. I'm the one who raised him. I taught him better.

MAN: Yes, I can understand how difficult that must have been.

WOMAN: No, you can't understand. You don't know how much I have done for him. From the age of seven. I have done things I'm ashamed to admit in front of other people in order to raise him. *(To* HER BROTHER.*)* Why can't you understand? Why don't you listen to me? Why don't you do what I tell you?

WIFE: He seems to obey you quite well.

MAN: That's certainly true. Your brother is very courteous.

WOMAN: *(Becoming more agitated.)* I'm a despised woman. It's because I became that kind of woman that you won't listen to me, isn't it?

(She twists HER BROTHER'S *arm. He stands up slowly, and then slowly crouches down on the floor.)*

WOMAN: What did I do that was so shameful? What do you say I did? And, if I did, who did I do it for? Just who did I have to do that kind of thing for? Tell me! Please tell me! Compared to what you have done, what does what I have done amount to? Which is worse? Tell me, which is worse? Tell us. Come on, out with it!

MAN: *(To the* BROTHER.*)* You'd better apologize. Please. Apologize. You shouldn't disobey your sister. You know that she's suffered many hardships to raise you. You understand that, don't you? And that she loves you. It's not good not to obey her instructions. That's bad.

WOMAN: Father! Please be quiet for a while! He doesn't understand yet. What I did . . . and who I did it for. And how miserable I have felt about doing it . . . to this very day. *(To* HER BROTHER.*)* Listen! What did I keep telling you? Did I say you could sink so low just because you're hungry? Did I teach you to be so rude in front of Father and Mother? Now apologize! Say "pardon me" to Father and Mother. I say apologize! Can't you see how ashamed I feel because of what you did? Then, apologize. Apologize! Apologize! Apologize!

(While saying this, she bangs his head, with a thumping sound, on the floor.)

WIFE: Please stop that! It's all right. Really, he doesn't have to. Don't be so harsh.

WOMAN: Please stay out of it! *(Increasingly violent.)* Whose cookie did you eat? Because of you, who won't have any?

WIFE: There are plenty. Plenty. We can't possibly eat them all.

WOMAN: Whose was it? Who won't get any? Please tell us!

MAN: Stop it. I'll go get them immediately. We have plenty. *(Grabbing her arm to stop her.)*

WOMAN: Let go of me, please!

MAN: *(Becoming angry.)* Stop! What in the world is this all about? What are you doing?

WOMAN: *(Startled, suddenly becoming humble, bowing her head to the* MAN*)* I beg you. I'll make him apologize. I'll make him apologize immediately. Please forgive him. He didn't mean anything. He'll apologize right now. He's usually more obedient. He's usually a well-behaved child.

MAN: *(A little bewildered.)* But that's all right. Because we're not really concerned about it.

WOMAN: I'll have him apologize, though, because I don't feel right about it. And, please, forgive him. He's already sorry about it, too,

in his heart. He *is* apologizing. He's crying. It's just that he can't say
anything.

WIFE: You. . . .

WOMAN: Please forgive me, Mother. I was wrong. I was a bad woman. I
did such a shameful thing. . . .

WIFE: That's not the point. It's all right.

WOMAN: No, it's not all right. But please don't say that my brother is
bad. He's feeling sorry. Forgive him. He's basically a gentle, courteous human being. He's usually very self-controlled. Please forgive
him. I'll make him apologize. Right now. He was hungry. That's all
it is. We can't blame him for that. Please don't blame him for that.
I'll make him apologize. I apologize, too.

MAN: *(Approaching her tenderly and trying to lift her to her feet.)* That's all right.
Let's stop all this. I understand.

WOMAN: *(Brushing him away.)* No, please forgive me. Don't touch me!
You must forgive me. I'm a bad woman. Please forgive me. *(Crawling
away from him as she says this.)*

MAN: What are you doing? *(Again extending his hand.)*

WOMAN: *(Retreating in the direction of the* WIFE.) Forgive me, Mother. I did
a bad thing. Please forgive me. At least give me your forgiveness.

WIFE: What's wrong?

MAN: What in the world is it? . . .

WOMAN: Forgive me, Father. *(Again retreating from the* MAN.) Forgive me,
Father. Forgive me, please. Matches. Please don't strike the
matches. . . .

(She bends down on the floor, covering her head, and remains motionless. The
MAN *and* HIS WIFE *stand dazed. The* BROTHER *rises slowly. They stand quietly for a moment. The* WIFE *is about to kneel down next to the* WOMAN.)

BROTHER: *(Quietly.)* Please don't touch her. She's a woman who can't
sink any further. That's why she doesn't want to be touched.

(He goes to her, hugging her and lifting her to his knee. The MAN *and* WIFE
stand bewildered.)

WOMAN: *(As from afar.)* Matches . . . don't strike the matches.

BROTHER: *(Murmuring.)* Father bought matches. Father bought matches.
Father bought matches. Every night . . . every night . . . for my
sister . . . night after night for my sister. . . .

MAN: No. . . . *(To* HIS WIFE.) I didn't do that. I never did that kind of
thing.

BROTHER: But I don't blame you. Whatever you did, I can't blame you.
Because my sister said, "Don't blame him. Don't blame him. . . ."

WOMAN'S VOICE: *(Low and hoarse.)* Then the little girl struck the rest of
the matches all at once, in a great hurry. In doing this, she hoped that
she would be able to hold firmly to her mother. The matches were

burning very brightly, lighting up the whole area, so that it became brighter than daylight. There was never a time when her mother looked larger, or more beautiful. She took the little girl in her arms, wrapped her in light and joy, and went climbing high, high up. There was no more cold, hunger, or fear. The two of them were called up to heaven.

MAN'S VOICE: *(Stealthily.)* Did you notice?

MAN: What?

MAN'S VOICE: You can't hear the children breathing in their sleep any more.

(There is the striking of wooden clappers, which gradually fades. Then, "Watch your fire," is heard from afar.

The MAN and HIS WIFE sit silently at the table, solemnly beginning "morning tea." . . .)

WOMAN'S VOICE: *(A little more clearly.)* It was a cold morning. The little girl, with red cheeks, and with even a smile playing on her lips, was dead.

The New Year's morning sun illuminated that little body. One hand held a bunch of matches, almost entirely burned up. People said, "She must have tried to warm herself. . . . " It was true. This child had been very cold.

In *The Little Match Girl,* the couple (Shiraishi Kayoko, *left,* and Ono Seki, *center*) welcome their "visitor" (Munakata Tomoko, *right*) until talk of responsibility begins. Waseda Little Theater, 1967. (Courtesy SCOT.)

The Little Match Girl dredges up memories of postwar deprivation. She attacks her brother for eating an extra cookie, saying someone will now go without. Waseda Little Theater, 1967. (Courtesy SCOT.)

The Little Match Girl is Betsuyaku's best-known play, performed by troupes of all ages for twenty years. Knack, 1978. (Courtesy Satō Jirō.)

The Legend of Noon

Betsuyaku Minoru

TRANSLATED BY ROBERT T. ROLF

CAST OF CHARACTERS

MAN

WOMAN

WOUNDED VETERAN 1

WOUNDED VETERAN 2

Scene 1

(A white stage. A young WOMAN *appears, her face hidden behind a red parasol. She stops center stage and lifts the parasol up high. She looks at the shadow on the ground for some time. A* MAN *carrying an orange crate appears and looks at her.)*

MAN: What're you doing?

WOMAN: *(Without looking up.)* Nothing in particular . . . just looking at the shadow.

MAN: *(Pointing at the shadow.)* It's moving. . . .

WOMAN: No, it isn't. . . .

MAN: Yes, it is. You can't tell just looking at it like this. Look at it through a microscope, closely, and it's moving just like a storm.

WOMAN: *(Relaxing her pose.)* What's that?

MAN: *(Looks at the crate in his hands, places it on the floor, and sits on it.)* A place; mine.

WOMAN: Do you always carry that around?

MAN: I sure do. You know how it is. Suppose I'm at a party. There's no place for me. I ask whoever's next to me very politely where my place is. But it's not his party; how should he know? The real host is never around. These days it's always some sort of a committee anyway. Everybody passing the buck—"I don't know, try asking him," that sort of thing. They look at me like, "Who invited him?" Every time. . . .

WOMAN: I'd never do that.

MAN: But I'm always prepared. Someone might offer me their place out
     of pity. I'd refuse. I'd tell them not to worry about it; I've got a place.
WOMAN: But I'd think perhaps they were being kind.
MAN: Maybe I do put everybody off. But there's nothing I can do about
     it. None of that bothers me. It's nothing compared to how bad I feel
     when I don't have a place.
WOMAN: I don't mind not having a place.
MAN: But what do you do?
WOMAN: I walk.
MAN: Walk? . . . At a party, a few steps, and that's it.
WOMAN: I just stroll around, slowly, taking it all in.
MAN: Slowly? . . . But how? . . .
WOMAN: Like this.
     (*The* WOMAN *walks slowly around the* MAN, *who sits knees drawn up in his
     arms on the orange crate.*)
MAN: Do you think of anything?
WOMAN: Nothing.
MAN: But don't people wonder what you're doing?
WOMAN: So what? Let them.
MAN: No, no. You can't have people wondering about you like that. The
     minute I thought people were thinking about me that way, I'd have
     to do something about it. And I would, too.
WOMAN: You're extremely inflexible.
MAN: I am. Awfully inflexible.
WOMAN: But don't people find your sitting on a box at a party strange?
MAN: They do. Everyone does. But only my sitting on the box. Nothing
     else.
WOMAN: I don't understand. . . .
MAN: You see, the worst thing is having everyone wonder about me.
     That hurts the most. I'd rather they just made up their minds that I
     am strange.
WOMAN: Rather complicated.
MAN: It is. I never thought life would be this complicated. But, as far as
     I can see, things seem rather easy for you, don't they?
WOMAN: Easy? . . . I don't know about that.
MAN: No, really. Say, what do you think of me?
WOMAN: Of you? . . . Nothing in particular.
MAN: But, haven't you been, you know, sort of taking an occasional
     peek at me? Like you were wondering what sort of person I am.
WOMAN: Could be . . . I may have been.
MAN: I was telling you all I could about myself; but you looked as
     though you didn't believe a word, and were just wondering what I'm
     really like.

WOMAN: You really are a nuisance.

MAN: I'm not trying to criticize you. I only wanted to be honest about myself, but you took it differently. I just want to ask you how I struck you differently. That sort of . . . You don't care to answer?

WOMAN: I would, but how?

MAN: Why not tell me what's on your mind? Don't hold back. . . .

WOMAN: I . . . *was* watching you. And . . . listening. And . . . that's all. Really . . . that's all. *(She walks slowly.)*

MAN: Going already? . . .

WOMAN: No. Either way's the same to me. I've no particular place to go, but no reason to stay here either.

MAN: Well, how about staying here? . . .

WOMAN: Well . . . all right.

MAN: Now . . . don't get me wrong, but what do you think? . . . Can I, you know . . . stay here, too?

WOMAN: I will go after all.

MAN: You got me wrong. Hey, wait. That's not what I meant. I don't know how you took it. Well, if . . . it sounded like I was giving you a bad time, I didn't mean it. I just thought I had to come out and ask, that's all.

WOMAN: This fussing is a bit annoying.

MAN: I understand. Please stay. Well, if . . . you don't mind, that is. Hope I can stay, too. If it doesn't bother you. . . . You stay over there and I'll stay here . . . I mean, what could be wrong with that? Act natural.

WOMAN: All right.

MAN: Then, uh . . . sometimes we might chat . . . without being annoying, of course. You don't have any place special to go and I don't . . . ah, maybe you were just being polite. Polite is a funny way to put it but people often act that way. They feel they mustn't look busy when they're with someone with nothing to do . . . and I thought that might be why you were being so considerate. Now, me, I. . . . Pick up something?

WOMAN: No.

MAN: Thought you did just now.

WOMAN: Just some glass.

MAN: What'd you think it was?

WOMAN: I didn't know. It was sparkling so I picked it up to see.

MAN: Oh, you did. . . . Myself, to continue what I was saying—don't mind this sort of talk, do you?

WOMAN: No . . . it's all right.

MAN: Looking for something?

WOMAN: Not in particular. . . .

MAN: Uh . . . me, I really don't have any place to go. I wasn't being polite; I just don't have anything to do. Really, I just wanted you to stay here so we could talk. But, you know . . . if I came out and said, "Stick around a while because I'm lonely and don't have anything to do or anyplace to go," you'd think I was pestering you, wouldn't you? And you wouldn't like that, would you?

WOMAN: No.

MAN: I guess not. I'm the same way about people pestering me. I really can't take that clinging. Just the same, you aren't looking for something?

WOMAN: I told you I wasn't, didn't I?

MAN: Sorry. Was I being a pest? But you sort of looked to me like you were. I think anyone would think so.

WOMAN: It's a habit.

MAN: A habit? . . . A childhood habit?

WOMAN: Yes.

MAN: Didn't your father or mother tell you not to?

WOMAN: Not especially. . . . Why?

MAN: No special reason. I'm not saying it looks bad. But don't fathers and mothers like to say things like that? Ridiculous, but they do.

WOMAN: They didn't say a word.

MAN: Uh . . . to continue what I was saying—you remember?

WOMAN: What? . . .

MAN: What? You know . . . I told you, didn't I? That awful feeling somebody's coming on to you. . . . You don't like it either, do you?

WOMAN: No.

MAN: Me, either. But . . . what I mean is not that but what I said before that. You know, before that when I . . . I said I've got nothing to do and no place to go—didn't you find that a little odd?

WOMAN: Odd? No.

MAN: But you must've. You did, didn't you? . . . Well, if you didn't, I'm sorry. I thought maybe you thought I wanted to follow you around. I mean, I thought that's what you thought. If not, I apologize. But I thought you might take it that way. Even though I didn't mean anything by it. I didn't mean what I said. I, you know, really, I said it before and say it again, I'm not the type to come on to somebody. They're pretty common though, aren't they? You've just met and don't know a thing about them, and they say something like, "Can I stay at your place tonight?"

(*The* WOMAN *squats down on her heels.*)

MAN: Sorry. I didn't notice. Sit on the box?

WOMAN: No, thanks.

MAN: But you must be tired. You should've told me. Of course I should've noticed, though.

WOMAN: I'm not especially tired. Just squatting like this.

MAN: Sit, please. It's far more comfortable. Don't worry about me. I've been sitting all this time, I don't want to sit anymore. Really! I'm not just being polite. That's the truth. If I wanted to sit, I would—this is my place. Besides, you know, when I want to sit, I'll tell you so honestly even if you're sitting there. I'll say, "I want to sit down, so make way." You'd like me to be honest about that sort of thing, wouldn't you? Don't worry, I'll come right out with it. So, in the meantime sit here, won't you? . . .

WOMAN: *(Rising and again strolling about.)* There's no wind here.

MAN: You'd like a wind?

WOMAN: Not especially . . . I merely remarked that there's no wind, that's all.

MAN: Do I smell? . . .

WOMAN: Smell? . . . No.

MAN: Yes, I do smell. I do. You know, I take a bath every day, but I still always stink a little.

WOMAN: No, no. I didn't mean anything like that.

MAN: Well, what then? . . .

WOMAN: Nothing. I simply said that there's no wind.

MAN: Maybe what's wrong is not the wind, but before that . . . the box. . . . That's it, of course. It was bothering me some, too. It's dirty. Well, not *dirty,* but I left it as it was after I'd sat on it. Now just maybe. . . . *(He turns over the cushion fastened to the orange crate.)* Right, this is what we need. . . . Now you can sit on it. That must have been it.

WOMAN: What? . . .

MAN: I mean, since you refuse to sit on it. It looks a little dirty but it's been washed. There are no germs on it. Hey, come on, have a seat.

WOMAN: That's not why I didn't sit on it.

MAN: I understand. I understand. But why not? No one's sitting there so why not sit on it? You know how it is. No one would want to sit on a warm cushion someone else's been sitting on. No matter whether you didn't like him, or you thought he was dirty, or what. It's all right. I don't let those things bother me. I mean, I don't take it to mean that people don't like me. Really! I might strike some people as awfully perverse, but I'm not.

WOMAN: I didn't say a thing.

MAN: You didn't. That's why I should've noticed the cushion myself.

WOMAN: That sort of thing never crossed my mind—not sitting on a warm cushion.

MAN: Maybe not. But even if it did, you would've thought it wrong to tell me. Say . . . well, hm, does all that matter? Have a seat. You must want to sit down.

WOMAN: No, I don't.

MAN: Why not? . . .

WOMAN: Why? . . . No special reason. I just don't. I'm always that way; no special reasons. I get hungry, I think, ah, I'm hungry. That's all.

MAN: You're hungry?

WOMAN: Just an example.

MAN: Well, I know that, but are you really?

WOMAN: I'm not hungry.

MAN: Really? . . . I mean, if you are, don't hesitate to tell me. I've got a little food. In the box. Actually, I thought you might be. But . . . a thing like that's hard to admit. A person's in fact hungry but puts it in terms of a for instance. . . . Of course I'm not saying that's what you did. But if you did, I would never hold it against you. I mean. . . .

WOMAN: I'm really not hungry.

MAN: Did you eat?

WOMAN: Yes.

MAN: When?

WOMAN: A little while ago. . . .

MAN: You did. . . . I hope so. Don't mean to harp on it, but, you know, if you suddenly get hungry, tell me so. Nothing unusual about saying you want to eat; I wouldn't consider you a liar for saying you ate just now. Of course, if you don't want anything, I certainly won't force you.

WOMAN: I would like to sit down. *(She sits down.)*

MAN: You do want something to eat?

WOMAN: I said I'd like to sit down.

MAN: But isn't that just the kind of thing I've been talking about? I mean, just a minute ago you were saying you didn't want to sit, weren't you?

WOMAN: True. But now I have suddenly gotten the urge to. So I am.

MAN: So like I said . . . say, come out and tell a guy these things. It's no big deal. You want something to eat? I've got it.

WOMAN: I only want to sit. I don't want to eat.

MAN: Sorry. Was I being a nuisance?

WOMAN: A bit. I don't mind, but if they saw, someone else might think you were.

MAN: This someone else is a friend of yours?

WOMAN: Yes.

MAN: You've got friends?

WOMAN: I do.

MAN: You must be very close.

WOMAN: Not too.

MAN: No . . . I'll bet you are, huh? . . . Am I wrong?

WOMAN: We're really not that close.

MAN: I don't have any friends. I know a few guys, but we're not friends. It's not important, though. I don't mean you should be that way. I mean, it's good you've got a lot of friends, and the fact that I don't is just one of those things and can't be helped. Besides . . . there's nothing in particular . . . between you and me. . . .

WOMAN: True. . . .

MAN: Sorry. I forgot. Doesn't it feel rough under your behind? Excuse me, could you stand up a second? *(He has her stand, and from a pocket attached to the cushion takes out a notebook and money.)* I was hiding this here. Always do. Now you can sit. My property and a record of my expenses. I keep track of them. I really have to keep at it. . . . I, uh . . . well, thought it might be uncomfortable for you to sit on. Of course . . . I wasn't worried that you might take them or anything.

WOMAN: I know.

MAN: But . . . you must be offended?

WOMAN: No.

MAN: Sorry. My fault. I didn't mean it. I never meant to mistrust you. Just, you know, I thought it must feel rough on your behind; I said as much, didn't I? I realized it suddenly, and so I took the things out. It did feel rough there, didn't it?

WOMAN: A bit, now that you mention it. . . .

MAN: You don't have to try to agree with me. I was just worried. You really didn't feel anything?

WOMAN: I didn't notice it much, but . . . well, as you said, it did seem a little rough.

MAN: Like I said, right? Well, anyhow, shall I put the things back? Will that make you feel better? . . .

WOMAN: I'm not particularly upset.

MAN: I'll put them back. When you think about it, it really was rude of me to do things like that. . . . Would you get out of the way?

WOMAN: *(Rising.)* I'd better be going.

MAN: Going? Where? I didn't mean for you to go. Like I've been saying, I'll tell you straight when I want you to give me the seat.

WOMAN: It's all right. I've been here long enough already; I'd better be going.

MAN: You don't like me?

WOMAN: I didn't say that.

MAN: Tell me, what don't you like about me?

WOMAN: Goodbye. It was fun. Maybe we'll meet again.

MAN: That's not true. You're just being polite. You don't ever want to

see me again. Tell me. What don't you like about me? I feel so bad I
won't be able to sleep tonight if you don't tell me.

WOMAN: I don't dislike you.

MAN: You do. I know you do. But I don't care. I just want to know what
it is about me you don't like. Come on, tell me. Am I being pushy?
Coming on a little too strong? Pursuing you too closely, perhaps? I
know, you thought just maybe . . . I might follow you home tonight,
didn't you?

WOMAN: No. Say, get out of my way!

MAN: I will. But, come on, this isn't the right way for us to part. We'll
both feel bad. We will. Just tell me what you don't like about me,
then we'll say a short and sweet goodbye. I mean it. I've no desire to
pursue you to the ends of the earth. I've got food, a place to sleep,
money . . . you saw it, look, look how much money I've got. *(Gathering up the money he has dropped when he took it from his pocket to show her.)*
I'm not going to bother you, not the slightest bit. Still, don't get me
wrong, but if you don't have a place to stay or need some money, I
can help you. . . .

*(He tries counting the money he has picked up. Something is wrong. He looks
about him. There is no more money on the floor. He tries counting his money
once more.)*

WOMAN: Something wrong?

MAN: Yeah.

*(He feels about in the pocket of the cushion once again. He tries searching his
own pockets. He tries looking about him and counting his money once more.)*

WOMAN: Short, aren't you?

MAN: Yeah.

WOMAN: I thought so. I just knew you would be. . . .

(They both stand without moving.)

(Blackout.)

Scene 2

*(In front of a white wall, on which is displayed the flag of Japan. In white clothing
and dark glasses* WOUNDED VETERANS 1 *and* 2 *sit side by side.* VETERAN 1 *is playing a small, metal-stringed harp and singing.)*

VET 1: *(While tuning the harp, sings deeply.)* Ki-mi-ga-yo-wa, Our em-per-or
up-on the throne! Ten thou-sand years live on. Till peb-bles. . . . [1]

(It is difficult to tell whether VETERAN 2 *is listening or not: he is motionless,
facing straight ahead.)*

VET 1: *(His song over, while tuning the harp.)* How was it? . . .

VET 2: Hmm. . . .

VET 1: You cold? . . .

VET 2: No. . . .

VET 1: You want to try it this time? . . .

VET 2: No, it's all right.

VET 1: What's wrong? . . .

VET 2: Nothing. I don't want to sing. . . .

VET 1: *(Playing again.)* Our em-per-or up-on the throne. . . .

VET 2: Hey, stop it.

VET 1: What? . . .

VET 2: Quiet for a while.

VET 1: Something wrong? . . .

VET 2: I'm all right. I'm OK, just a little. . . .

VET 1: You're sweating.

VET 2: Yeah. . . .

VET 1: Feel sick?

VET 2: No. I'm OK, just leave me alone a while.

VET 1: But, listen . . . if you're sick. . . .

VET 2: I said forget it. I'm not sick. I just have to take a crap. . . .

VET 1: A crap? . . .

VET 2: Right, so give me a minute. . . . I'll get over it in a minute.

VET 1: But, in that case, shouldn't you just go ahead and do it?

VET 2: No problem. Have it under control soon.

VET 1: Control? . . . But that's no good. The best thing's to just *do* it.
  No paper?

VET 2: I got some. Paper's not the problem. Forget it.

VET 1: Forget it, you say. . . .

VET 2: Leave me alone. Please, turn the other way a minute. I can't tell
  what might happen with you fooling around there.

VET 1: Is it that bad?

VET 2: It's terrible, and why shouldn't it be? It's been since last night.

VET 1: Since last night? . . .

VET 2: No, maybe longer. Anyway . . . I forget really. . . .

VET 1: I think you ought to get it over with. . . . If paper's the problem,
  I've got some.

VET 2: Shut up. Move a little farther off. Don't touch me.

VET 1: I'm not touching you, am I? *(Moving slightly away.)* This better?

VET 2: Ah. . . .

VET 1: Hurt? . . .

VET 2: Yeah. . . .

VET 1: Drink some water? . . .

VET 2: No.

VET 1: If there's anything I can do, just tell me.

VET 2: Ah. I will. . . .

VET 1: But . . . tell me, why?

VET 2: Why what?

VET 1: Why won't you do it? . . .

VET 2: Hm . . . I just don't feel like it. . . .

VET 1: You don't. . . . Then that's that.

VET 2: You . . . never felt that way? . . .

VET 1: What way?

VET 2: I mean, you have to go, but just don't want to.

VET 1: Me? . . . Hm. Don't think so.

VET 2: Probably because you're insensitive, wouldn't you say?

VET 1: Insensitive? Me?

VET 2: Don't talk so loud, idiot. See, just like I said—insensitive.

VET 1: Maybe I am insensitive after all. . . .

VET 2: Sometimes just the sight of you irritates me.

VET 1: It does? (Taking something from inside his shirt, he begins munching.) Wonder why? . . .

VET 2: Now I've got to go again.

VET 1: Rub your back for you?

VET 2: It's OK, you idiot. How many times do I have to tell you—leave me alone.

VET 1: All right. But I can't relax with you like that. None of it's my fault. . . .

VET 2: What're you eating?

VET 1: Beans.

VET 2: Give me some.

VET 1: But . . . is it OK?

VET 2: Of course it's OK.

VET 1: You know, beans aren't that good for your stomach.

VET 2: I don't have diarrhea or anything. Put some over there.

VET 1: Chew them up good. They're no good for your digestion even if you don't have diarrhea.

VET 2: Hey, look, you spilled them off the paper. You can't do anything right. Snap out of it.

VET 1: I'll give you this many. I've more; eat these, I'll give you some. But maybe this is enough for today.

VET 2: (Picks up a bean and puts it in his mouth.) What kind of beans are these?

VET 1: They're leftovers from winter.[2] Some old lady brought them.

VET 2: Winter leftovers? Hey, no more for me. Stick them over there.

VET 1: What's wrong?

VET 2: I don't want to eat any more. Put them away. Out of my reach. Out of my sight.

VET 1: I told you not to eat any.

VET 2: Over there, so we don't spill them.

VET 1: I'll set aside your share.

VET 2: I'm in awful pain; not that I care, though. . . .

VET 1: Of course you are. What you're doing is not natural. No wonder it hurts.

VET 2: It comes in cycles. Lasts just a minute. . . . If I can just get through this one. . . . Are you? . . .

VET 1: What?

VET 2: Still eating?

VET 1: Still? I just started, didn't I?

VET 2: Stop.

VET 1: Why should I? I've got plenty. I'm saving you your share.

VET 2: The noise irritates me. Just the sound of you munching away.

VET 1: OK. I'll stop. *(He puts another handful into his mouth.)*
    (Since VET 2 *can hear the sound, he glares at* VET 1 *as if to say, "Haven't you stopped?")*
    *(*VET 1 *mumbles and indicates he has put the bag away.)*

VET 2: Hey. . . .

VET 1: What? . . .

VET 2: Play your harp.

VET 1: My harp? . . .

VET 2: I feel like singing.

VET 1: Now?

VET 2: Now.

VET 1: You all right? . . .

VET 2: I'm OK, so play.

VET 1: In that case. . . . *(Pulls the harp to him.)* Here goes. . . . *(Plays.)*

VET 2: Our em-per-or up-on the throne! Ten thou-sand years live on. . . .

VET 1: What's wrong? . . .

VET 2: It's no use. Hey, this is awful. Do something.

VET 1: Do something? What can I possibly do? Say, how about it, go ahead and do it. What else can you do?

VET 2: I don't want to. I don't want to do it. Come on, help me. Just for a minute.

VET 1: *(Moving to hold him in his arms.)* Like this? . . .

VET 2: Stop, fool, what're you doing? . . . *(Sings.)* Till peb-bles shall. . . . It doesn't help.

VET 1: Great rocks be-come. . . .

VET 2: Cut it out, idiot. Give me a hand.

VET 1: What are you going to do?

VET 2: Try to stand up.

VET 1: You going to do it?

VET 2: No, I'm not. I just . . . want to stand up . . . and try to walk. *(He stands.)* Hmm. Don't rush me. Take it easy.

VET 1: Watch your step.

VET 2: Hmm. Don't drag me, I tell you. I want to take it slow.

VET 1: All right. . . . How's that? . . .

VET 2: Hmm. . . .

VET 1: Has it passed? . . .

VET 2: Mostly. Hmm, walking's wonderful.

VET 1: It is? . . .

VET 2: I . . . feel like I'm walking for the first time. Hey. . . .

VET 1: What happened? . . .

VET 2: *(Squatting down.)* Wait a minute. Just a second.

VET 1: Did it come again? . . .

VET 2: Pretty soon. It'll pass soon. Hmm. . . . Better already. *(He stands up.)*

VET 1: Going to walk? . . .

VET 2: Yeah. Easy, now. Good. . . . Like this a while.

VET 1: You mean walking?

VET 2: Yeah. . . . Why? . . .

VET 1: No reason. . . .

(The two of them walk about slowly.)

VET 2: Did the beans taste good?

VET 1: Bad. Lousy.

VET 2: Then why'd you eat them?

VET 1: I wonder, why did I eat them? . . .

VET 2: You're addicted.

VET 1: Addicted?

VET 2: Addicted to beans. And so you gobble down those lousy-tasting beans. They're good for absolutely nothing.

VET 1: No, they're not. Beans have nutritional value.

VET 2: Fat chance. Beans?

VET 1: Yes, beans. Even horses eat them, don't they?

VET 2: Horses do eat beans. But that's a pretty crude kind of nutrition. You have to eat a ton of them, like a horse. Real nutrition, you just eat a little and—it hits you. Like lemons. Lemons have vitamin C.

VET 1: Lemons? . . . Yeah, I think I heard they're nutritious. . . .

VET 2: They are, they're nutritious. Starting tomorrow I'm eating lemons.

VET 1: But you can't eat nothing but lemons.

VET 2: Why not. They've got vitamin C. A man can get by as long as he's got vitamin C.

VET 1: He can? Just vitamin C? . . .

VET 2: *(Comes to a halt.)* I'm tired.

VET 1: Going to rest?

VET 2: Yeah. . . . But after I walk a little more. Do you want to rest?

VET 1: No, I'm OK. I just thought maybe you wanted to.

VET 2: I'll make my own decisions. . . .

VET 1: I guess so. I can keep going until you say when

VET 2: Can't you say when for yourself?

VET 1: What? . . .

VET 2: Listen, you make your own decisions. This is my business. If I don't want to take a crap, it's my business. So you don't have to worry about it. It's got nothing to do with you. I'm the one fighting off taking a crap.

VET 1: I understand.

VET 2: No, I really don't think you do.

VET 1: What are you saying anyway? That I'm only doing things because I have to?

VET 2: No, no. Not at all. How can I put it? . . . Don't you think what I'm doing is weird?

VET 1: I do. I do. I just told you I did. Didn't I ask you why you were doing it? . . .

VET 2: You should think it's even weirder than you do. But not you. You act like you get it right away, but you're just trying to humor me. And I can't stand that. I can't stand that insensitivity of yours.

VET 1: But what can I do? I'm just trying to be kind to you. . . .

VET 2: That's not kindness. That's not real kindness.

VET 1: Well, what the hell am I supposed to do?

VET 2: Thought I told you: Make your own decisions. *(He sits.)*

VET 1: Going to rest?

VET 2: I'm going to rest. But that doesn't mean you are.

VET 1: I know.

VET 2: Say.

VET 1: What?

VET 2: Have you ever committed hara-kiri?

VET 1: Hara-kiri? . . . No.

VET 2: I mean, have you ever seen hara-kiri?

VET 1: No.

VET 2: No? . . . Well, it stinks.

VET 1: Stinks?

VET 2: Uh-huh, it's a real nose-bender. That day, a man did it right before my very eyes. It stunk. It's awful. I hadn't realized it'd be like that.

VET 1: Then? . . .

VET 2: Huh? . . .

VET 1: What happened after that? . . .

VET 2: Nothing. Isn't that enough? I learned this much: hara-kiri stinks.

VET 1: Why tell me?

VET 2: No special reason. I just suddenly remembered it.

VET 1: *(Playing his harp and singing low.)* Our em-per-or up-on the throne. . . .

VET 2: Hey, I'm in trouble now. . . .

VET 1: Going to stand up? . . .

VET 2: No, far from it. . . .

VET 1: What should I do? . . .

VET 2: You don't have to do anything. It'll pass in a minute.

VET 1: A little while ago you felt better when you stood up, didn't you?

VET 2: Yeah. . . . Say, think maybe I ought to drink some water?

VET 1: Water, yeah. . . . Want me to pour you some?

VET 2: No, wait a bit. I'm not sure. It might make me worse. Let me think about it.

VET 1: Might be good just to moisten your lips.

VET 2: I said it's all right. Give me a minute. I'm thinking.

VET 1: Anyway, I'll set the water here.

VET 2: Not there. I might knock it over when I move. It's OK. I don't want any. I'd better not drink it after all.

VET 1: It might refresh you. It all depends on how you feel. *(He tidies things up.)* You want some, tell me.

VET 2: I don't need any. Water's no good.

VET 1: Best I don't sing? . . .

(VET 2 is silent.)

VET 1: I won't for a while. . . .

VET 2: What did we eat last night? . . .

VET 1: Last night? . . . Potatoes, beans, and meat; with miso soup and rice . . . and pickled radishes. . . . That's about it. That's all we had.

VET 2: Potatoes? . . . That's definitely it.

VET 1: They gave you a stomachache?

VET 2: That's not what I mean. And how about this morning? . . .

VET 1: This morning, miso soup, rice, raw eggs, and pickled vegetables.

VET 2: We really ate a lot of different stuff.

VET 1: We did. And you ate an awful lot.

VET 2: What about lunch yesterday? . . .

VET 1: I can't remember all that.

VET 2: Try.

VET 1: Why do you have to know that stuff?

VET 2: Don't worry about it; just think.

VET 1: Let's see. Yesterday for lunch . . . I think we ate noodles. . . . Noodles. It was noodles.

VET 2: I wonder, why does man eat?

VET 1: I wonder. . . . Now that you mention it, I wonder, why does he? . . .

VET 2: Idiot. What're you talking about? People eat because they're hungry. Anybody knows that. That's not what I mean. That's not what I *mean*. I mean, why does *man eat* . . . that's what. . . .

VET 1: And I said, why does he eat; it's the same thing.

VET 2: No, it's not. That's not what I meant. Why must you be such a fool. Forget it. Just keep quiet.

(VET 1 *quietly plucks his harp; he does not sing.*)

VET 2: Don't sing.

VET 1: OK. . . .

VET 2: You have to play that?

VET 1: No, not really. . . .

VET 2: Then stop.

VET 1: All right. . . .

VET 2: Doesn't . . . doesn't it bother you?

VET 1: Me? . . . No, not at all. I went this morning.

VET 2: Not that. I'm not talking about that. Idiot. I mean . . . from that day right down to today, it hasn't bothered you at all? . . .

VET 1: Well . . . I guess not. . . . At least I don't think so. . . .

VET 2: Idiot. *(With deep feeling.)* You are really an idiot. . . .

VET 1: Has . . . something bothered you?

VET 2: It has. Isn't that why I'm doing this? But I just realized last night.

VET 1: Last night? . . .

VET 2: Yeah, last night after we ate, I realized. Why didn't I realize it before we ate, I wonder. . . .

VET 1: What did you realize?

VET 2: That! Hey, water.

VET 1: Sure. Wait. . . . Here. . . .

VET 2: Yeah. . . . *(He drinks.)* Good. . . . I should've had a drink earlier.

VET 1: Say, what was it you realized?

VET 2: That, idiot. How many times do I have to tell you. That since that day we just haven't given it everything, haven't thrown ourselves into things.

VET 1: But haven't we suffered a lot?

VET 2: We have suffered. But we lacked total effort; we haven't thrown ourselves into things. Do you see, we've been wrong. We thought we were forgiven that day. . . .

VET 1: But we weren't forgiven?

VET 2: We were forgiven. There was forgiveness. . . . But that wasn't the end of things. Hey, water. . . .

VET 1: You've got some. Over there.

VET 2: That wasn't the end. We were forgiven that day, but it didn't last down to today. All this time we've had to go on being forgiven, over and over again, day after day, hour after hour. You see, hey, it's the truth. You're dead wrong if you think you're forgiven once and that's the end of it. It goes on and on forever. Every day you have to be forgiven all over again. See, you didn't know that, did you? We didn't know. That's why I say we just haven't thrown ourselves into things.

VET 1: Hmm. . . .

VET 2: Do you understand? . . .

VET 1: And so . . . what should we do then?

VET 2: Idiot. That's why I said you're an idiot. You have to think it out for yourself. What else, it's your business.

VET 1: Ah, I get it: that's why you don't want to take a shit.

VET 2: That's not what I mean. That's not it. . . . But . . . I've got no other choice, do I? Because I don't know what he thinks. . . .

VET 1: I get it; so that's it. . . . Well, what if I don't take a crap anymore, either? . . .

VET 2: That's no good, you idiot. Don't do what other people do. You see, hey, what use is it to copy somebody else? Discover it for yourself, for yourself. . . .

VET 1: I don't know . . . I could never do it. . . . I could never think of something like that. I've never been able to.

VET 2: You will think. And if you throw yourself into it—body and soul —even you can think of something. . . . Hey, I think I want to lie down. . . .

VET 1: Has it started? . . .

VET 2: Yeah . . . but it's not that bad. It's nothing that bad. . . .

VET 1: Shall I wipe the sweat off you?

VET 2: No, don't. Just think.

VET 1: OK. . . .

VET 2: I'm in pain, it hurts . . . but somehow it makes me feel alive. . . . As if, little by little, the forgiving keeps going on. . . . We weren't living; we thought we were forgiven and that was it. But that's not the way it was. That's not the way it . . . was. Hey, you thinking? . . . Really think; hurl yourself at it. . . .

(Blackout.)

Scene 3

(A white stage. The young WOMAN *is sitting motionless on the orange crate, hold-ing her red parasol above her head; the* MAN *is standing by her side.* VET 1 *soon appears ministering attentively to* VET 2. *He spreads their straw mat, sets down their paraphernalia, has* VET 2 *lie down alongside, and stretches the Japanese flag up on the wall.)*

MAN. Shall we go? . . .

(WOMAN *does not answer.)*

MAN: Come on, let's go.

(VET 2 *moans.)*

VET 1: You all right? . . .

VET 2: Yeah. . . . Sing.

MAN: Let's go. Really, that's not what I meant. That's not what I meant at all. It's a coincidence. Of course I didn't think for a second that you took it. How could I have? So I shouldn't have said anything . . . but I thought that would've seemed odd, too, since I really was short.

WOMAN: I understand. Of course. I realized. But look how things turned out. . . . I blame myself for that.

VET 1: *(Sings.)* Our em-per-or up-on the throne! Ten thou-sand years live on. Till peb-bles. . . .

MAN: Don't talk like that.

VET 1: *(Singing.)* Shall great rocks be-come.

MAN: What a racket!

(A brief pause.)

VET 2: What'd he say? . . .

VET 1: He said, "What a racket."

VET 2: What is? . . .

VET 1: The song.

VET 2: Why? . . .

VET 1: I don't know.

VET 2: Ask him.

VET 1: Why's it a racket?

MAN: Hey, let's go. Come on, let's go somewhere else and talk. Here is so . . . you know.

WOMAN: Why don't you search me to see if I took it?

MAN: I've been trying to tell you. . . . I don't suspect you.

WOMAN: Then what did happen to your money?

MAN: I don't know.

WOMAN: That's not good enough. I was suspected.

MAN: I said I didn't.

WOMAN: Not by you.

MAN: Then by who?

WOMAN: I don't know by who. Anyway, by somebody.

VET 2: Hey! . . .

MAN: Somebody? . . .

VET 2: *(To VET 1.)* Why doesn't that guy answer?

VET 1: *(To the MAN.)* Hey, why don't you answer?

MAN: Sorry. I didn't mean anything.

VET 1: Says he didn't mean anything.

VET 2: Then why'd he say we were making a racket?

VET 1: Why'd you say we were making a racket?

MAN: You weren't. You weren't bothering me.

VET 1: He says we weren't bothering him.

VET 2: He did say, "What a racket."

VET 1: He did. *(To the MAN.)* Hey, you did say, "What a racket."

MAN: So I'm apologizing, aren't I?

VET 2: I don't want apologies.

VET 1: He doesn't want apologies.

MAN: Then what in the world do you want?

VET 2: Tell him to kill me.

VET 1: He says to kill him.

MAN: Hey, let's go. Let's go somewhere else and talk.

WOMAN: How much were you missing?

MAN: Forget it. Let's change the subject. It might be my mistake, and besides. . . .

WOMAN: How much?

MAN: A thousand yen. . . .

WOMAN: *(Taking it from her pocket.)* Here's a thousand. Here. . . . I mean, this seems to be where this talk is leading. Of course this is my money. But how can I prove it to you?

VET 2: What are they talking about?

VET 1: Money.

VET 2: Hm, thought they probably were. Water.

VET 1: Sure. In pain? . . .

MAN: Prove it? . . . But isn't that your money? . . .

WOMAN: It is.

MAN: Then . . . what's the problem? Just leave it at that. . . .

WOMAN: How can I prove it to you? . . .

MAN: It's not my money.

WOMAN: No use *you* saying that.

MAN: Then who should? Only the two of us know about this, you know.

WOMAN: That's what I mean. Both of us can say this money is ours.

MAN: Would I say something like that?

WOMAN: But you could think it. And I want it so that you can't do that.

MAN: How will you manage that?

WOMAN: Any way I can.

VET 2: You know, I might die.

VET 1: Don't be so downhearted. We've toughed it out this far. . . .

VET 2: We certainly have. We've toughed it out. . . .

MAN: Let's go. Someplace better.

WOMAN: I don't want to.

VET 2: Say, ask that guy if he's got a knife.

VET 1: Hey, you got a knife?

MAN: What? . . .

VET 1: I said, you got a knife?

MAN: Knife? . . . No.

VET 1: He said no.

VET 2: Well, lend him one.

VET 1: *(Pulling it out.)* Hey, I'll lend you one.

MAN: What? . . .

VET 1: I'll lend you one. Here. . . .

MAN: No, thanks. . . .

VET 2: Tell him to take it and stab me in the throat.

VET 1: He said to take this and stab him in the throat.

MAN: Let's go. Come on, enough is enough. This is ridiculous. We can't
   stay here. I don't care—you can keep the money.

WOMAN: I can keep it?

MAN: Well, no. . . . I didn't mean that. I didn't mean it that way.
   I. . . .

   (WOMAN *waits for him to continue.*)

MAN: Well . . . you're right. It might've been like you said after all. I
   mean . . . I did suspect you. I thought you stole it.

WOMAN: I did not steal it.

MAN: Of course not. Of course you didn't.

WOMAN: How do you know? . . .

MAN: How? . . . Well, I suspected you until now. I must confess I did.
   It was wrong of me. But, now. . . .

WOMAN: Why was it wrong of you? . . .

MAN: I just told you. I suspected you. Until now.

WOMAN: But you lost a thousand yen, and I had a thousand yen, so isn't
   it natural to suspect me?

MAN: Well, it's natural. Still. . . .

WOMAN: What?

MAN: Nothing. I'm not sure I understand anymore. . . .

WOMAN: That's right. You don't understand. No one understands
   whose money this is. We both know; but, all the same, we don't

understand. You see, we're finally at the starting point. *(She stands and walks.)*

VET 2: Give that guy the knife and tell him how to use it.

VET I: Hey, take this.

MAN: Leave me alone. *(He brushes it aside.)*

WOMAN: Io ho oiok?

VET 2: No, Miss, I'm not sick. I'm just living life seriously—throwing myself into it.

WOMAN: You're not sick, but then how do you go about "throwing" yourself into life?

VET 2: Certainly it requires a bit of ingenuity. In my case, I'm swearing off taking a shit.

WOMAN: My, I'd like to try throwing myself into life like that, too.

VET 2: Why not do the same as I'm doing?

WOMAN: I couldn't. I haven't had a thing to eat for some time.

MAN: You haven't? . . . Then you lied to me, didn't you? Didn't you tell me you just ate?

WOMAN: I did. I lied. What of it? But that money's mine. That isn't a lie.

VET I: Hey, I told you I'd show you how to use the knife.

MAN: And I told you to leave me alone. Come on, let's go.

WOMAN: No.

MAN: Say, in that case, how about this? I just got an idea. We'll each take five hundred yen. . . .

WOMAN: No. Why? Why're you like that? You haven't understood a thing.

MAN: Now . . . come on, just what do you think I should do?

WOMAN: There's nothing you can do. Nothing at all, but, just the same, why can't you be more serious about all this?

MAN: Me, not serious?

WOMAN: You are not serious.

VET 2: He doesn't throw himself into things.

WOMAN: This man's perspiring. . . . He might be in pain.

VET I: He is. But that's fine. Because whatever else you might say, he's putting everything into it—body and soul.

WOMAN: Shouldn't we wipe off the perspiration?

VET I: No, no. He wouldn't like you to do that. Doesn't he seem to feel good all covered with sweat?

MAN: He seems to be saying something?

VET I: He says to stab him in the throat. With this knife. He wants you to.

MAN: That's not funny.

WOMAN: Why don't you? . . .

MAN: Why don't I? . . . What're you saying?

WOMAN: You probably believe this money's yours, don't you?

MAN: But I told you, didn't I? . . .

WOMAN: All right. Do you believe the money's mine?

MAN. Yes, I do.

WOMAN: Then stab him.

MAN: But why? . . .

WOMAN: Do, and I'll be satisfied, too. I'll be convinced. I'll believe you really believe the money's mine.

MAN: What are you talking about?

VET I: It's OK. He wants you to, too. Look, he told you to, didn't he? He told you to stab him.

WOMAN: You don't want to?

MAN: I have no idea what you're talking about. I mean, it makes no sense whatsoever.

WOMAN: Then I'll do it. In return you just believe that the money's mine.

MAN: Cut it out, I said. How many times have I told you already that I believe you?

WOMAN: Talk's cheap. You have to really believe me.

MAN: I really do.

WOMAN: You don't believe me. Give me the knife.

VET I: Know how to use it?

MAN: Stop it. Don't do something foolish. Isn't this ridiculous over just a thousand yen?

WOMAN: Hold him back.

VET I: Right.

MAN: Stop it, you fool. Hey, don't. I've got plenty of money. Hey. Stop. Hey. . . .

(*The* WOMAN *readies the knife and squats down near* VET 2*'s head. She looks down intently at* VET 2*'s face. Then she realizes.*)

WOMAN: He's dead. . . .

(VET I *releases the* MAN, *and they slowly approach* VET 2*'s corpse.* VET I *puts his hand to* VET 2*'s nostrils to verify that he is dead.*)

WOMAN: (*Putting the knife down and standing.*) This is the end. I don't understand anything now. (*The thousand-yen note falls from her hand and flutters to the stage.*)

VET I: But you tried to stab him. I saw it.

WOMAN: I didn't stab him. . . .

(VET I *gathers up his things and, slinging* VET 2 *over his shoulder, stands up.*)

VET I: I've got to come up with something ingenious, like he did, so that I can throw myself into life, too. Goodbye. (*He leaves.*)

(*The* WOMAN *opens her parasol and sits on the orange crate.*)

MAN: Let's go. There's nothing we can do. It's too late to do anything now. And let's leave that other thing as is. I know: I'll give you a thousand yen. Rather, I'll lend it to you. Say, how's that? Pay it back whenever it's convenient for you. Don't take it so much to heart; it's only a thousand yen. . . . If you like, you know, I can lend you a little more. I say lend, but . . . you know what I mean. I only put it that way because it'd be rude to say give.

Notes

1. This represents a slight adaptation of a venerable rendering of *Kimigayo* by "Dr. Gordon of Dōshisha, Kyoto." The Gordon version reads, "O Prince upon the throne! / Ten thousand years live on. / Till pebbles shall great rocks become / With moss all over grown!" (see Wada Shin'ichirō, *Kimigayo to banzai* [*Kimigayo* and *banzai*] [Tokyo: Kōfūkan shoten, 1932], 224). The "harp" is a *Taishō-goto* (Taishō koto), an inexpensive instrument about two feet in length. Dating from the Taishō period, it has nostalgic associations.

2. The Japanese original refers to beans used in observances to mark the traditional last day of winter and first day of spring.

The Legend of Noon juxtaposes today's mentality (the young couple) with that of the past (the veterans). *Front:* Era Jun *(left)* and Satō Jirō *(right). Back:* Akiyama Toshiko *(left)* and Funabashi Saburō *(right).* Knack, 1978. (Courtesy Satō Jirō.)

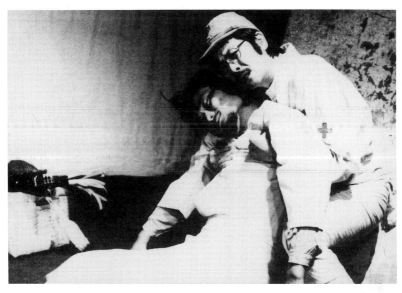

In *The Legend of Noon,* Veteran 2 throws himself at life, to atone for his halfhearted attitude. His companion holds him at the close. Knack, 1978. (Courtesy Satō Jirō.)

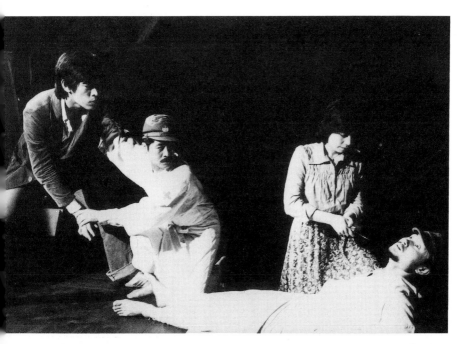

In *The Legend of Noon,* Veteran 2 *(right)* finally wants to be killed for his indifference. Revolted at the self-centered Man *(left),* the Woman moves to oblige. Knack, 1978. (Courtesy Satō Jirō.)

The Cherry in Bloom

Betsuyaku Minoru

TRANSLATED BY ROBERT T. ROLF

CAST OF CHARACTERS
OLD WOMAN
MAN 1
MAN 2
MAN 3
WOMAN 1

(A cherry tree in full bloom. Beneath it is a straw mat on which a gray-haired OLD WOMAN *is drinking sake, a vermilion lacquered serving table in front of her. Situated off to the left a bit and with no apparent relation to this is a large wardrobe. "Sakura, Sakura" gently plays; cherry petals are floating down constantly.)*

OLD WOMAN: A beautiful day . . . peaceful as if the whole world's gone mad. . . . It's true, Yoshio. . . . You're ill. . . . I've known a long time. . . . Your brain is white and soft; it trembled in fear at even the tiniest breeze. . . .

(Looking about a little.) Spring weighs me down. . . . It's always heavy, like damp bedding. . . . Say, Yoshio. . . . You remember. . . . Once you and I were singing under this tree, and you told me, "Grandma, my brain feels heavy." . . . "Is it, is it heavy?" I said and rested your head on my lap. . . . Your head *was* heavy, Yoshio. . . . Heavy, warm, throbbing. . . . "Now, now, Yoshio, you can stand it," I kept telling you, but . . . now I see . . . you didn't know what to stand or how. . . .

(Sings faintly, almost in a murmur.) Sa-ku-ra, sa-ku-ra, ya-yo-i no so-ra wa. . . . Another spring, Yoshio. . . . Spring again, with its cherry blossoms as usual. . . . That must be it. . . . That must be why you didn't know what to stand. . . . Summer is hot and winter is cold, but what can you say about spring? . . . There's nothing but the cherry in bloom. . . .

(The gathering dusk changes to a sunset that seems adrip with blood. The door of the wardrobe opens, and MAN 1 *appears, his large head wrapped in a white bandage, a grammar school knapsack on his back.)*

MAN 1: Grandma, I'm home. . . . *(He sits on her mat, his head drooping.)*

OLD WOMAN: Hello. . . . What happened to your head? . . .

MAN 1: I fell down the stairs. . . .

OLD WOMAN: Don't lie to me.

MAN 1: I got pushed.

OLD WOMAN: *(Gently.)* Who did it? . . .

MAN 1: I don't know. . . . I was on my way to the crafts room after second period and someone pushed me down the stairs. . . .

OLD WOMAN: Who was there?

MAN 1: I don't know. There were a lot of kids and I got pushed from behind. . . .

OLD WOMAN: You told Mr. Uemura, didn't you? . . .

MAN 1: Yeah . . . but he thinks I tripped on something. . . .

OLD WOMAN: You were shoved? Pushed down the stairs? You do remember clearly?

MAN 1: Yes, I felt someone's hand touch my back, then he pushed me. . . .

OLD WOMAN: . . . What did Fumie say? . . . Your mother. . . . And what about your father? . . .

MAN 1: They told me not to say bad things about my friends. . . .

(A brief interval.)

OLD WOMAN: It's all right, Yoshio. . . . Take off your knapsack and come here to Grandma. Put your head on my lap like you always do and rest. . . . *(Has him rest on her lap.)* . . . Don't be afraid; Grandma knows all about it. . . . Even who pushed you down the stairs. . . . *(Rather enjoying herself.)* Ah, I know who it was. That boy. . . . You know who. That boy. It has to be him. He's no good in his studies, so he's jealous of you because you are. Remember, Yoshio: he may smile, but in his heart he hates you. . . . All the more reason for him to push you down the stairs. . . . Now you see, don't you? . . . You've nothing to be afraid of. . . . Stick to it. You'll show him someday. . . . Graduate from a good university and be somebody; he'll learn his lesson then. . . . Go to sleep. . . . For now just be quiet and sleep. . . . Grandma knows all about you. . . .

(It is night; the moon is out. The OLD WOMAN, *still with* MAN 1 *on her lap, listlessly sings him a lullaby. Soon* MAN 2 *and* WOMAN 1 *appear from inside the wardrobe.)*

WOMAN 1: Is Yoshio with you Grandma?

OLD WOMAN: Yes. . . .

MAN 2: Looking at the blossoms in the moonlight? . . .

OLD WOMAN: Shh. He just fell asleep. . . .

WOMAN I: Let me take him.

OLD WOMAN: You two didn't even ask about Yoshio's injury? . . .

MAN 2: We did. I had Fumie call the school a while ago. . . .

WOMAN I: I've heard from Mr. Uemura; Yoshio may well have tripped and fell. . . .

OLD WOMAN: Yoshio says someone pushed him. . . .

WOMAN I: That part's not clear. . . .

OLD WOMAN: If it's not, don't you think you ought to make it clear?

WOMAN I: True. . . . But Grandma, Yoshio is always telling on his friends.

OLD WOMAN: So what? If he really was pushed, shouldn't we find out just what happened? He was hurt.

MAN 2: Now, now, Grandma. Even if he was, it's the children's business. Besides, I don't think it's good for him to tell. . . .

OLD WOMAN: Why? What's wrong with finding out exactly what happened?

WOMAN I: Grandma . . . Mr. Uemura has told me any number of times; nobody likes Yoshio. He doesn't have a single close friend. Even you must be aware of that, Grandma. . . .

OLD WOMAN: He doesn't need friends. . . . If he does what's right but they won't make friends with him, he's better off without friends like that. . . .

MAN 2: That's true, Grandma, but in Yoshio's case. . . .

OLD WOMAN: When Grandpa was alive he always told you—remember? —"Never want friends!" . . . And you didn't, did you: you never had any friends. . . .

WOMAN I: But now I regret that. . . .

(MAN I *rises abruptly and, his big head swaying unsteadily from side to side, slowly disappears into the wardrobe.*)

OLD WOMAN: Yoshio. . . .

(MAN 2 *and* WOMAN I *look at one another.*)

MAN 2: Was he awake?

OLD WOMAN: Don't make Yoshio ashamed of not having any friends. . . . It'll make the boy weak. . . .

(*The three of them are silent. Blackout.*

When the lights come up, it is spring once more. The cherry in full bloom. The OLD WOMAN *is drinking sake.*)

OLD WOMAN: Spring again. . . . Time after time, spring. . . . The blossoms practically sneering. . . . Fumie, Fumie, I'm out of sake. Heat some and bring it here, Fumie. . . . I'm gradually falling, like something slowly rotting. . . . I feel heavy. . . . And when I'm under these blossoms, that much heavier. . . . (*Sings wearily.*)

(WOMAN I *appears from the wardrobe, bringing some sake and a small dish of food.*)

WOMAN I: More sake, Grandma. . . .

OLD WOMAN: Ah, thank you. . . .

WOMAN I: *(Putting down the little dish.)* Just some things I boiled. . . .

OLD WOMAN: Good. Have a look at the blossoms, too.

WOMAN I: All right. . . .

OLD WOMAN: They've bloomed nicely. . . .

WOMAN I: But too much, don't you think? I don't particularly care for the Somei Yoshino blossoms.[1] . . .

OLD WOMAN: Well, what do you like? . . .

WOMAN I: Something like the wild cherry. . . . Wouldn't you say that even these have more charm when the leaves have come out and there are only a few blossoms left here and there? . . .

OLD WOMAN: You don't know how to appreciate cherry blossoms. . . .

WOMAN I: I don't? . . .

OLD WOMAN: No. Because the flowers have life, too. . . .

WOMAN I: What do you mean? . . .

OLD WOMAN: They're mad. Mad and they can't help but bloom. . . .

(WOMAN I *pauses.*)

OLD WOMAN: Life goes mad when spring comes. . . . You can't understand cherry blossoms if you don't understand that. . . . *(Offers her sake.)* Have some. . . .

WOMAN I: No. . . .

OLD WOMAN: Just look . . . the tree's gone mad; it's a miracle how quietly. . . . Why don't you drink? . . .

WOMAN I: It's daytime. . . .

OLD WOMAN: Somei Yoshino are the flowers. . . . What else is there? . . . This is all. It's only when they're just full of flowers that you realize that they bloom because they can't help it. . . . It's true, Fumie. . . .

WOMAN I: What? . . .

OLD WOMAN: Do you even know why people drink when the cherries bloom? . . .

WOMAN I: No. . . .

OLD WOMAN: Of course you don't. . . .

WOMAN I: Why do they? . . .

OLD WOMAN: Because it's unbearable. . . . People can't stand to see the cherry trees go mad like this. . . . And . . . and so you should drink, too. . . .

WOMAN I: Then I'll have just a little, Grandma. . . . *(While the* OLD WOMAN *is pouring for her.)* I hope it won't show because I've got to go shopping soon. . . .

OLD WOMAN: Don't worry. . . . I'm not telling you to get carried away.
. . . Am I? . . . Do I look like I'm getting carried away? . . .

WOMAN I: No.

OLD WOMAN: No one is. . . . Everyone's holding it in; the flowers, I
mean. . . . They're unbearable. . . . *(Sings softly.)* You and Takaaki
were quarreling last night, weren't you?

WOMAN I: Yes. . . .

OLD WOMAN: What about? . . .

WOMAN I: Nothing. . . .

OLD WOMAN: Isn't that unlikely? . . .

WOMAN I: Grandma, please leave us be. It's just between him and
me. . . .

OLD WOMAN: About Yoshio? . . .

(WOMAN I does not answer.)

OLD WOMAN: It was about Yoshio, wasn't it? . . . Tell me. . . .

WOMAN I: Takaaki's opposed to Yoshio's going to a cram school.[2] . . .

OLD WOMAN: Why? . . . Yoshio wants to. . . .

WOMAN I: I know that, but. . . .

OLD WOMAN: You don't know, you two. Yoshio is desperate to get ahead
of those kids.

WOMAN I: What kids?

OLD WOMAN: You don't know them. . . .

WOMAN I: Who? Who are "those kids"?

OLD WOMAN: Why, Uchida, Tanimura, and that bunch, of course.

WOMAN I: Why Uchida and Tanimura? . . .

OLD WOMAN: You don't know? They're the ones who scribble in Yoshio's
arithmetic book and tear up his notebooks. They don't show up for
cleaning when he's in charge.

WOMAN I: Don't say that, Grandma. They've been Yoshio's closest
friends since elementary school.

OLD WOMAN: What are you talking about? You don't know, you two.
You don't know a single thing about Yoshio. . . . Yoshio and I can
handle our own affairs; we're the only ones who understand
them. . . .

WOMAN I: Please stop it, Grandma. Don't be like that. I've met Uchida
and Tanimura myself; they're nice boys.

OLD WOMAN: Listen, Fumie. . . . Leave Yoshio's problems to me. . . .
Don't worry. He's my grandson. . . . I mean, even you can't want
Yoshio to turn out like Takaaki? . . .

(WOMAN I is speechless.)

OLD WOMAN: Naturally I won't say a thing about the two of you. That's
your business. . . .

(WOMAN I remains silent.)

(As petals softly fall, it gradually becomes dusk. From out of the wardrobe appears MAN I, *reading a book.)*

OLD WOMAN: Yoshio. . . .

MAN I: Yeah. . . .

OLD WOMAN: What are you reading? . . .

MAN I: A book. . . .

OLD WOMAN: What book? . . .

MAN I: You wouldn't understand it Grandma

OLD WOMAN: Don't be ridiculous. . . . Read it to me. . . .

MAN I: *(Reads.)* There was a traveler who lost his way in the wilderness. At dusk he finally found a deserted house, where he decided to spend the night. . . .

OLD WOMAN: See, even Grandma understands that. . . .

MAN I: *(Reads.)* In the middle of the night a red demon came along carrying a corpse.

OLD WOMAN: My, my, it's a fairy tale. . . .

MAN I: *(Reads.)* Then along came a blue demon, who began to fight over the corpse with the red demon.

OLD WOMAN: A common story. . . .

MAN I: *(Reads.)* They fought and fought, to no decision. The blue demon paused and asked the traveler, "Whose corpse is this?" The traveler was frightened but answered, "The red demon brought it here, so I think it's his."

OLD WOMAN: That's the correct answer. . . .

MAN I: *(Reads.)* At this the blue demon became angry, tore off the traveler's right arm, and threw it outside. But the red demon took pity on him, tore off the right arm of the corpse, and attached it to the traveler. The blue demon tore off the traveler's left arm and threw it outside. The red demon tore off the left arm of the corpse and attached it to the traveler. The blue demon tore off the traveler's right leg and threw it outside. The red demon tore off the corpse's right leg and attached it to the traveler. . . .

OLD WOMAN: Enough!

MAN I: *(Reads.)* When the corpse and the traveler had become completely interchanged, even the red demon and blue demon were both exhausted. They divided the corpse they had thrown outside evenly between them, ate it, and left. . . . In the abandoned house someone remained alone. . . .

(A slight interval. Blossoms fall. The three are silent. At length MAN I *slowly begins to leave.)*

OLD WOMAN: Wait. . . .

MAN I: What? . . .

OLD WOMAN: What does the story mean? . . .

MAN 1: I don't know. . . .

OLD WOMAN: Then why did you read it to Grandma?

MAN 1: But you asked me to yourself. . . .

OLD WOMAN: It's all right. Come here. Come to Grandma and sit down.

(MAN 1 slowly approaches the OLD WOMAN *and sits.)*

OLD WOMAN: Somebody told you to read that to Grandma, didn't they? . . .

MAN 1: No. . . .

OLD WOMAN: Your father? . . .

WOMAN 1: Grandma. . . .

OLD WOMAN: Your father told you to, didn't he? . . .

MAN 1: No.

OLD WOMAN: Then who?

MAN 1: Nobody.

OLD WOMAN: Don't lie, you.

MAN 1: I'm not lying. I just brought it here and read it, that's all.

OLD WOMAN: Yoshio, tell the truth.

WOMAN 1: Grandma, let's forget it.

OLD WOMAN: No. Yoshio, Grandma'll never forgive you if you don't tell the truth.

MAN 1: That is the truth.

OLD WOMAN: It's a lie. Come on, Yoshio, tell me. That can't be the truth; you'd never read something like that to your Grandma.

WOMAN 1: Grandma. Stop it.

OLD WOMAN: Yoshio. Tell me. Who? Who told you to read that kind of thing? Yoshio, Yoshio. . . . Tell me, Yoshio. . . .

(The sun is down. Blackout. After a brief interval, fade in. Light, perhaps of the moon. The OLD WOMAN *is lying on the mat. A little off from her stands* MAN 1, *facing away and listlessly playing "Luxuriant Greenery"[3] on the harmonica. At length* MAN 2 *appears from inside the wardrobe carrying a blanket.)*

MAN 2: *(Covering the* OLD WOMAN *with the blanket.)* Grandma, Grandma. . . . Shouldn't you get up and go in the house? . . . You'll catch a cold. . . . Grandma. . . .

(Since the OLD WOMAN *does not move,* MAN 2 *gives up, walks over to* MAN 1, *and stands there.*

MAN 2: Yoshio . . . I've been wanting to have a long talk with you. . . .

MAN 1: *(He goes on playing the harmonica.)*

MAN 2: How about tonight? . . . I'm free. . . . Do you have anything to do? . . .

MAN 1: *(He continues playing the harmonica.)*

MAN 2: Well . . . if you do, it doesn't have to be tonight. . . . C'mon, Yoshio. . . . I've got a lot of things I want to ask you. . . . Like what you want to be when you grow up . . . what kind of life you want to lead. . . .

MAN 1: *(He continues playing the harmonica.)*

MAN 2: How about it, huh, Yoshio? . . . Man to man. . . .

(MAN 1 suddenly stops playing the harmonica and disappears inside the wardrobe. A brief interval. MAN 2 *hums "Luxuriant Greenery" softly. The* OLD WOMAN *sits up slowly.)*

OLD WOMAN: Takaaki. , , ,

MAN 2: *(Turning around.)* Ah, Grandma. . . . Were you awake? . . .

OLD WOMAN: Did you hear about this afternoon? . . .

MAN 2: This afternoon? . . . Yes, I heard a while ago from Fumie. . . .

OLD WOMAN: That was your book? . . .

MAN 2: Yes. . . . That kid, he must've dug it up somewhere. . . .

OLD WOMAN: What kind of story was that? . . .

MAN 2: Indian. . . . A kind of ancient Indian fable. . . .

OLD WOMAN: You must understand it, Takaaki. Please explain it to me. After the demons leave, someone is left alone in the abandoned house. Who is that? . . .

MAN 2: I don't know, Grandma. No one does. It's an enigma. . . .

(Blackout. It soon brightens somewhat; the OLD WOMAN *is sitting motionless, alone on the mat.)*

MAN 1: *(Voice only.)* The red demon and the blue demon divided the corpse they had thrown outside evenly between them, ate it, and left. . . . In the abandoned house someone remained alone. . . .

(Suddenly, from inside the wardrobe, the sounds of MAN 1 *shouting and furniture being overturned; soon it is still.* WOMAN 1 *comes staggering out.)*

OLD WOMAN: What's wrong? . . .

WOMAN 1: It's Yoshio. . . .

(MAN 2 comes out of the wardrobe.)

MAN 2: What happened, Fumie? . . .

WOMAN 1: I don't know. All of a sudden Yoshio just got angry. . . .

(MAN 1 comes forth slowly from inside the wardrobe, carrying a notebook and a bamboo yardstick.)

OLD WOMAN: What's wrong, Yoshio? . . .

MAN 1: *(Glaring at* WOMAN 1.) Somebody read my diary. . . .

MAN 2: Your diary? . . . *(To* WOMAN 1.) Did you read it? . . .

WOMAN 1: Of course not. What're you talking about, Yoshio. I'd never do a thing like that.

MAN 1: Then who did?

OLD WOMAN: I did. . . .

MAN 1: *(Caught unawares.)* Grandma? . . .

OLD WOMAN: I read it. . . .

MAN 1: Why?

OLD WOMAN: Why? . . . Grandma just wanted to know what you're thinking. . . .

(*A brief interval.* . . . MAN 1 *slowly squats down and begins to tear up the notebook.*)

MAN 2: (*Stopping him.*) That's foolish, Yoshio. . . . (*Holds him from behind.*)

MAN 1: (*Breaking away.*) Stay away. Let me go. Damn it. I said let go. . . .

WOMAN 1: But it's your diary. Why do that?

MAN 1: (*Squirming to get free of MAN 2.*) Stop it. This thing's not a diary or anything anymore. (*Kicks the notebook.*)

OLD WOMAN: (*Standing up.*) Yoshio.

MAN 1: (*To MAN 2.*) I told you to let me go, damn you. . . .

WOMAN 1: Stop it, Yoshio.

MAN 1: (*To WOMAN 1.*) Shut up. Keep out of this, you.

OLD WOMAN: (*Picking up the yardstick.*) What do you mean talking like that. (*To MAN 2.*) It's all right. Let him go.

MAN 2: But, Grandma. . . .

OLD WOMAN: It's OK, so let him go. . . .

(MAN 2 *releases* MAN 1. MAN 1 *loses heart on the spot and slumps to the ground.*)

OLD WOMAN: What's this commotion? Just for looking at your diary. . . .

(MAN 1 *is silent.*)

WOMAN 1: But, Grandma, it's not nice to read someone's diary. . . .

OLD WOMAN: Did you hear that, Yoshio? . . . It seems your father and mother don't have the nerve to read their own child's diary. . . . But Grandma is different. . . . Not only your diary, but how much money you've got in your wallet, and what you've got hidden in the back of the third drawer of your desk. . . .

WOMAN 1: Grandma. . . .

OLD WOMAN: I know everything. . . . What time you got up last night and went to the kitchen for a drink of water, how long it took you to get back to sleep after you went back to bed . . . everything! . . . That's my . . . that's Grandma's way of doing things. . . . So you don't have to worry about a thing. . . . (*She jerks his head up.*) Look, there's still a clear scar . . . from when you were in elementary school and got pushed down the stairs. All you have to remember is who did that. Who tore up your notebooks, who skipped their turn at sweeping up, who scribbled in your arithmetic book. . . . Understand? That's all you have to remember. . . .

(MAN 1 *is still silent.*)

OLD WOMAN: (*Poking him.*) OK, tell your father and mother. Neither of them has read your diary, so they don't have the slightest idea what you're thinking. Tell them, Yoshio. Who was it that pushed you down the stairs?

MAN 2: Grandma, let's forget about that. . . .

OLD WOMAN: Well, Yoshio, tell us. Who was it?

MAN 1: Nobody. . . .

OLD WOMAN: How could it be nobody? . . .

MAN 1: Nobody. I tripped and fell.

OLD WOMAN: Yoshio, what're you saying?

MAN 1: I lied. The truth is I tripped and fell, but I said somebody pushed me down. . . .

OLD WOMAN: Nonsense, Yoshio, tell the truth.

MAN 1: It's true. I was alone when I fell. I tripped and fell by myself. And I tore up the notebooks and scribbled in my arithmetic book. I did it all myself.

OLD WOMAN: Don't lie.

MAN 1: I'm not. I did it all myself and blamed it on the others.

WOMAN 1: Why? Why would you do something like that, Yoshio?

OLD WOMAN: Stop it. Don't ask why; it's obvious. You see, Yoshio, Grandma understands everything. I know—you let those kids beat you, didn't you? . . .

MAN 1: I did not. . . .

OLD WOMAN: Then why're you telling us all this *now?*

MAN 1: Because it's true.

OLD WOMAN: It is not.

MAN 2: Grandma, please stop. Yoshio's telling the truth. He was wrong to lie all this time, but it's good that he's honestly admitting it. *(To MAN 1.)* That's what I think, Yoshio. You're doing the right thing.

OLD WOMAN: What's so good about this liar? *(Kicks him with her foot.)*

WOMAN 1: *(Restraining her.)* Grandma. Yoshio's telling the truth now. . . .

OLD WOMAN: You mean you two still don't understand? The boy's lying. He wasn't before, but he is now. Isn't that so, Yoshio? Aren't you ashamed of yourself?

MAN 2: Grandma. . . .

OLD WOMAN: Shut up. I'm right, aren't I, Yoshio. They beat you, so you say these things to get in good with them. You want them to make up with you and be your friends, don't you? Say it! *(She strikes him soundly with the yardstick.)*

WOMAN 1: Grandma, stop it.

OLD WOMAN: You know they're sneaks, liars, cowards, cruel, lazy; and you're still going to wag your tail for them? Hey, say something. Are you that afraid of being alone? *(Hits him.)*

MAN 1: No.

OLD WOMAN: Then why don't you tell the truth? Yoshio. Speak. (*Hits him.*) The truth. (*Hits him.*)

MAN 2: Grandma, quit it.

OLD WOMAN: (*Continues to hit him.*) Well, talk. If you're not afraid, out with it. Yoshio. (*Half crazed, she continues to beat him.*) Yoshio. Talk. Talk. Talk.

MAN 1: I will, Grandma. . . .

(OLD WOMAN *pauses.*)

MAN 1: You're right. . . . The truth is I really was pushed down the stairs. . . .

OLD WOMAN: Who did it? . . .

MAN 1: Uchida. . . .

OLD WOMAN: Who tore up your notebooks? . . .

MAN 1: Tanimura. . . .

OLD WOMAN: And who scribbled in your textbook? . . .

MAN 1: Higaki. . . .

OLD WOMAN: Don't forget it. When you start wanting to forget it, it means you're growing weak. . . .

MAN 1: Right. . . .

OLD WOMAN: Pick up your diary and go to your room. . . . You must have some homework? . . .

(MAN 1 *picks up the diary he dropped and slowly disappears into the wardrobe.* WOMAN 1 *hurries into the wardrobe. The stage darkens;* MAN 2 *is standing and the* OLD WOMAN *sitting, with no apparent relationship to one another.*)

MAN 2: Grandma. . . .

OLD WOMAN: Stop calling me Grandma when Yoshio's not present.

MAN 2: Mother. . . . Do you really think Yoshio was pushed down the stairs? . . .

OLD WOMAN: What do you think? . . .

MAN 2: I . . . don't know. . . .

OLD WOMAN: Me, either . . . I don't know. . . .

(MAN 2 *pauses.*)

OLD WOMAN: But I know Yoshio. . . .

MAN 2: Was that Yoshio? . . .

OLD WOMAN: That was Yoshio. . . .

(*A brief interval.*)

OLD WOMAN: Are you and Fumie going to separate? . . .

MAN 2: No, why? . . .

OLD WOMAN: Fumie said you were. . . .

MAN 2: I've no intention of separating. No matter what Fumie, Yoshio, or you say. . . . I want to get along with all of you. . . . And I'm confident that I can. . . .

OLD WOMAN: Get inside. . . .

MAN 2: All right. I'm going. . . .

(He does not move. Blackout. Soon it brightens. As before, the OLD WOMAN *is sitting on the straw mat, drinking sake alone beneath the cherry blossoms in full bloom. A gay melody begins, a number of women in kimonos do a slow, gentle dance, holding small cherry branches.)*

OLD WOMAN: Spring goes by. . . . the blossoms scatter. . . . Spring is always slowly moving. . . . From here to there. . . . Like it's falling forward. . . . Moaning . . . Like people who died full of resentment. . . . Like people unable to bear their own passing. . . . Spring goes by. . . . the blossoms scatter. . . . Go then. I'm not moving. I'm staying here. . . . However often spring comes and the cherries bloom . . . I'm staying here; here, motionless, breathing low; here. . . .

(A middle-aged man in a dark suit staggers in, blindfolded, his arms extended in front of him casting about for someone. The women dancing about nimbly evade him; he gradually nears the OLD WOMAN. *Watching this apprehensively, the* OLD WOMAN *stands up. As* MAN 3 *draws nearer to the* OLD WOMAN, *the women cease dancing, break formation, and cling to a corner as if in fear.)*

MAN 3: *(Finally grabbing the* OLD WOMAN.*)* I found you. Got you. *(Laughs.)* Who're you?

(The OLD WOMAN *gives* MAN 3 *a resounding slap on the cheek. The women quickly disappear.* MAN 3 *is startled and removes his blindfold.)*

MAN 3: Oh, it's you. . . .

OLD WOMAN: What do you mean "you"! Stop acting like a fool. . . .

MAN 3: Guess I was, but. . . . *(Looks around him.)*

OLD WOMAN: Something wrong? . . .

MAN 3: No . . . I was wondering what happened to everybody. . . .

OLD WOMAN: Who's everybody? . . .

MAN 3: Everybody. . . . I was playing blindman's buff just now with the kids down at the government office. . . .

OLD WOMAN: Grandpa, you quit the government office last year. . . .

(MAN 3 becomes dimly aware of that.)

MAN 3: How many times have I told you to stop calling me Grandpa when Yoshio's not around. . . .

(MAN 3 steps onto the mat and sits down hugging his knees.)

OLD WOMAN: Would you like some sake? . . .

MAN 3: Don't need any. . . . You'd better ease up on it, too; it's daytime. . . .

OLD WOMAN: I'm viewing the flowers. . . .

MAN 3: Alone? . . .

OLD WOMAN: Yes, alone. . . . I'm always alone. . . .

MAN 3: What happened to Yoshio and the others? . . .

OLD WOMAN: Yoshio and Fumie went out. . . . They're going shopping and then walk along the Yotsuya[4] embankment on their way home, or so I heard. . . . Even though we've got cherry blossoms right here, too. . . . Would you like something to snack on? . . .

MAN 3: No, thanks. . . .

OLD WOMAN: Did you hear what happened to Yoshio at kindergarten yesterday? . . .

MAN 3: Forget it. I don't want to hear about Yoshio now. . . .

OLD WOMAN: Why not? . . . You brought up the subject yourself. . . .

MAN 3: I get scared every time I look at him how is a boy like that ever going to survive? . . .

OLD WOMAN: He'll make it. . . . That child is the heir of this family. . . .

MAN 3: Looks like Takaaki won't make section chief after all. . . . I called Sekine and asked last night; he says it'll be a fellow who joined the company the same time as Takaaki. . . . Ogōri was his name, I think. . . .

OLD WOMAN: His name is Ogōri; he came to the house once. . . .

MAN 3: Seems he'll be the one. . . .

OLD WOMAN: I knew it. . . .

MAN 3: You knew? . . .

OLD WOMAN: From the first time Fumie brought Takaaki here. He's the same type of person as you. . . .

MAN 3: But becoming section chief doesn't mean anything. . . .

OLD WOMAN: But someone with the same seniority getting ahead of him does. The same thing happened to you. . . .

MAN 3: Blaming me, huh. . . .

OLD WOMAN: No, I'm talking about myself. . . . Because my father was the same: had someone with the same seniority become section chief before he did and said it didn't matter. . . .

MAN 3: Then why'd you pick me? . . .

OLD WOMAN: Because I didn't know. . . . I realized for the first time when Fumie brought Takaaki home that something made us choose the same type of man. . . . My mother must've done the same thing. And her father must've been the same type, too. . . .

MAN 3: *(Stands up absently.)*

OLD WOMAN: But Yoshio's all right. . . .

MAN 3: What makes you think so? . . .

OLD WOMAN: Because, no matter what, I'll never say anything like that to Yoshio, that becoming section chief doesn't matter. And I won't let Fumie or Takaaki, either. . . .

MAN 3: What happened after that? . . . To your father? . . . You know . . . after he couldn't become section chief? . . .

OLD WOMAN: He wrote haiku, that sort of thing. . . .

MAN 3: Haiku? . . .

OLD WOMAN: There was one poem by Katō Shūson that moved father very much: "A mackerel sky / not a thing to be told to others."[5] The way he explained it to me—and he did so a great many times—there is a sky filled with fleecy little clouds, in rows like the streaks on a mackerel, and he feels something, but it's not anything you can make people understand. . . .

MAN 3: A mackerel sky, not a thing to tell others. . . .

OLD WOMAN: Yes. . . . But I thought that if it's something you can't tell people, then you shouldn't put it in a haiku or let yourself get excited by it either. You certainly shouldn't read it to people and try to explain it to them. . . .

(MAN 3 stands more or less transfixed, then begins to walk absently.)

OLD WOMAN: Where are you going? . . .

MAN 3: Just for a walk. . . .

OLD WOMAN: *(Standing up.)* But it's already getting dark. . . .

(MAN 3 absentmindedly disappears stage right.)

OLD WOMAN: Shouldn't you put something on? . . . Grandpa . . . Grandpa. . . .

(MAN 2 appears from inside the wardrobe.)

OLD WOMAN: Grandpa. . . .

MAN 2: What's wrong? . . .

OLD WOMAN: *(Turning around.)* What? . . .

MAN 2: Did you just say Grandpa? . . .

OLD WOMAN: Yes, there, just now. . . .

MAN 2: Grandpa? Our dead Grandpa? . . .

OLD WOMAN: No. . . . *(Gazing at MAN 2's face, she comes to her senses vacantly.)* Yes, I found myself thinking of him. . . . *(Sitting down slowly.)* Grandpa died without saying a thing. . . . It was a cold night. . . . I left the room for a second, ate some noodles in the kitchen, and when I got back, he was dead. . . .

MAN 2: What made you think of him now? . . .

OLD WOMAN: I wonder. . . .

MAN 2: Do you know where Fumie is?

OLD WOMAN: No. Probably went shopping, don't you think? . . .

MAN 2: Shopping. . . .

OLD WOMAN: Why're you two bickering the way you do every night? . . .

MAN 2: Is Yoshio at the cram school? . . .

OLD WOMAN: Apparently. . . . He wasn't in his room. . . .

MAN 2: Actually, Grandma, I'd like a word with you. . . .

OLD WOMAN: What about? . . .

MAN 2: I . . . listen carefully, Grandma . . . the truth is . . . we have to move out. I talked it over with Fumie again last night. . . . Please understand, Grandma, we're not abandoning you or anything like that. . . . It's just that we need to make a new start now, just the three of us. . . . If we don't, it'll be too late. . . .

OLD WOMAN: Too late for what?

MAN 2: For Yoshio. . . . You haven't noticed? Yoshio's been strange lately. . . .

OLD WOMAN: Strange?

MAN 2: Yes. . . . During the ceremony for the first day of classes, he suddenly collapsed. We thought it might be anemia because he felt better after they had him lie down in the infirmary. . . . But afterward it happened again in class. . . . I found out that it happened a couple of times in the third term, too. . . .

OLD WOMAN: Have you had a doctor look at him?

MAN 2: A doctor of internal medicine. He said nothing's wrong with him.

OLD WOMAN: Nothing's wrong with him?

MAN 2: Right. . . .

OLD WOMAN: Yoshio did it on purpose? He did, didn't he?

MAN 2: No, the doctor said it's psychogenic, caused by extreme tension, and that he should see a psychiatrist if it gets much worse. . . .

(OLD WOMAN pauses.)

MAN 2: Yoshio is damaging his nerves. . . .

OLD WOMAN: Why? . . .

MAN 2: What? . . .

OLD WOMAN: Why? Why didn't someone tell me sooner?

MAN 2: I wouldn't let anyone. . . . I thought it was better not to. . . .

(OLD WOMAN is silent.)

MAN 2: Fumie thought so, too, you know. . . .

OLD WOMAN: And Yoshio? . . . What did Yoshio say? . . .

MAN 2: Yoshio didn't say anything. . . . He doesn't even know he's sick. . . .

(Twilight gradually thickens until finally the area is entirely hidden.

When after a while it brightens to the level of moonlight, on the straw mat the OLD WOMAN *and* MAN 3 *sit close together, quietly drinking sake and picking at the things in their tiered lunchboxes. They murmur to one another off and on.)*

OLD WOMAN: Say. . . .

MAN 3: What? . . .

OLD WOMAN: Aren't you cold?

MAN 3: No. . . . What's this?

OLD WOMAN: A potato. Taro.

MAN 3: Hm. . . .

OLD WOMAN: Not going to eat it? . . .

MAN 3: Well . . . I was just wondering if there wasn't something else. . . .

OLD WOMAN: What do you mean "something else"? . . .

MAN 3: I mean, something besides.

OLD WOMAN: Fish? . . .

MAN 3: No, no. . . .

OLD WOMAN: Boiled butterbur, perhaps? . . .

MAN 3: Not that

OLD WOMAN: Then what? Anyway, this is all there is.

MAN 3: Oh, this is fine; I was just wondering. . . .

OLD WOMAN: Well, please don't. Shall I pour you some sake?

MAN 3: Yeah. . . . *(He holds out his sake cup, but his back itches, and he moves.)*

OLD WOMAN: Hold it still, Dear. . . .

MAN 3: All right. . . . *(He moves again anyway.)*

OLD WOMAN: What's wrong?

MAN 3: It itches.

OLD WOMAN: Itches? . . .

MAN 3: Yes. . . .

OLD WOMAN: Where? . . .

MAN 3: Where? . . . My back. . . .

OLD WOMAN: Think maybe an ant got under your shirt? There're lots of ants around here. . . .

MAN 3: Come on. . . . *(Puts down sake cup.)* It's no ant. . . . *(He cannot reach the itch.)* Isn't there anything around here? . . .

OLD WOMAN: Like what? . . .

MAN 3: Anything. . . . A stick or something. . . .

OLD WOMAN: I don't have anything like that. . . .

MAN 3: It doesn't have to be a stick. . . . Don't you have anything? . . . *(Stands up.)*

OLD WOMAN: Is it that itchy? . . .

MAN 3: Are you kidding? . . . What could it be? . . .

OLD WOMAN: Shall I scratch it for you?

MAN 3: Yeah. . . . There's no stick?

OLD WOMAN: No. Now please watch your step. You don't want to step on something.

MAN 3: Then try scratching it for me.

OLD WOMAN: Fine. Where? . . .

MAN 3: *(Sits with back to the* OLD WOMAN.*)* My back, it. . . . *(The* OLD WOMAN *tries to put her hand down under his collar.)* Hey, quit it, wait a minute. What is that?

OLD WOMAN: What? My hand.

MAN 3: Hand? . . . Well, that's OK then.

OLD WOMAN: What're you talking about. I'm hardly going to use my foot.

MAN 3: I didn't think it was your foot. . . . No, not there, not there, lower, lower. . . .

OLD WOMAN: Here? . . .

MAN 3: No, not there, more to the side.

OLD WOMAN: Side? . . . Which side?

MAN 3: Which side? . . . The side, idiot. . . .

OLD WOMAN: Here? . . .

MAN 3: Not there. . . .

OLD WOMAN: Ah, here. . . .

MAN 3: Yes, yes, a little higher. . . .

OLD WOMAN: Here? . . .

MAN 3: There, there, there, there. . . . Ah, yes, yes. . . . Ouch. Don't claw me, you.

OLD WOMAN: Sorry. . . .

MAN 3: Ah, there. . . . Oh, that feels good. . . . Finally under control. . . . Ouch, ouch, ouch, ouch. . . .

OLD WOMAN: *(Removing her hand.)* What's wrong? . . .

MAN 3: What do you mean what's wrong? . . . Scratched me, didn't you? . . .

OLD WOMAN: I didn't scratch you.

MAN 3: Might've raised a welt. . . .

OLD WOMAN: What're you talking about? After I went to the trouble of scratching it for you. Is that enough? . . .

MAN 3: Yes, enough. . . . It's stopped itching. Burns a little though. . . .

OLD WOMAN: It's an ant. An ant bit you.

MAN 3: *(Returning to his seat.)* Well, now, what was I doing? . . .

OLD WOMAN: What? . . .

MAN 3: Nothing, but wasn't I about to do something before I got itchy? . . .

OLD WOMAN: You were going to eat some potatoes but decided not to. . . .

MAN 3: Yes, I decided not to. . . .

OLD WOMAN: And then . . . ah yes, I was about to pour you some sake. . . .

MAN 3: That's right, some sake. . . . *(Holding the sake cup, he has her pour.)* And then? . . .

OLD WOMAN: And then *what?* . . .

MAN 3: And then what was I going to do, I wonder. . . .

OLD WOMAN: I don't know. . . .

MAN 3: Shall we do something? . . .

OLD WOMAN: What? . . .

MAN 3: Anything. . . .

OLD WOMAN: How about eating? . . .

MAN 3: Well . . . I'm tired of eating. . . .

OLD WOMAN: Tired of eating? . . .

MAN 3: Tired of it. . . .

OLD WOMAN: Well, want to drink something? . . .

MAN 3: No . . . I'm tired of drinking, too.

   (A brief interval.)

MAN 3: Hey. . . .

OLD WOMAN: *(Eating by herself.)* What? . . .

MAN 3: Want to *janken?*[26] . . .

OLD WOMAN: *Janken?* . . .

MAN 3: Yes. . . .

OLD WOMAN: All right, but why? . . .

MAN 3: Why not? Anyway, let's try it. . . . Ready? . . .

OLD WOMAN: Yes. . . .

MAN 3: Here we go: *Jan, ken, pon!* . . .

   (The OLD WOMAN *shows "paper";* MAN 3 *shows "stone.")*

MAN 3: You win. . . .

OLD WOMAN: That's right. . . .

MAN 3: Happy? . . .

OLD WOMAN: Not especially. . . .

MAN 3: You're not? . . . Guess not. . . . Doesn't mean anything special
   to me, either. . . .

OLD WOMAN: *(Suddenly looking up.)* Say. . . .

MAN 3: What? . . .

OLD WOMAN: Were you really itchy? . . .

MAN 3: What're you talking about. . . .

OLD WOMAN: You were lying, weren't you? You weren't itchy; you were
   just playing.

   *(*MAN 3 *says nothing.)*

OLD WOMAN: Why? . . . Tell me. I don't mean to criticize you. I simply
   want to know. Why are you always like that? . . . Am I wrong? You
   always have to be doing something: just can't sit still. And so . . .
   you do stupid things like that. . . . Why? Well, dear? Dear. . . .

   *(*MAN 3 *is as motionless as a rock. . . . Soon it darkens.*

    When it brightens, the cherry is in full bloom. White paper in one hand,
   chopsticks in the other, the OLD WOMAN *is squatting near the straw mat killing*
   ants. She puts the ants she has killed in the white paper. Listening carefully, one
   can hear her singing faintly, almost a murmur, "Sakura, Sakura." From out of
   the wardrobe MAN 1, *dressed for school, ambles in absently.)*

MAN 1: Hi, Grandma. . . .

OLD WOMAN: *(While at her work.)* Oh, hello. . . .

MAN I: What're you doing? . . .

OLD WOMAN: *(Looking up, only now realizing.)* Yoshio . . . what're you doing here? . . .

MAN I: Just dropped by to see how you're doing. . . .

OLD WOMAN: But what about school? . . .

MAN I: It's already over for today. . . . What's that? . . .

OLD WOMAN: Ants. . . . When the cherry blooms, it never fails. . . . They come out to suck the nectar. . . .

MAN I: *(Squatting down.)* You kill them? . . .

OLD WOMAN: Yes. . . . *(Sets to work.)*

MAN I: These? All of them? . . . *(Tramples them.)*

OLD WOMAN: Stepping on them's no good. Have to squash them carefully one by one. . . .

MAN I: But that's hard. . . .

OLD WOMAN: It's hard, but what can you do? . . . The ants won't die unless you do it that way. . . .

MAN I: *(Squashing them with his fingers, he begins placing the dead ants in his left hand.)* I tore them apart, but they're still moving. . . .

OLD WOMAN: Don't tear them apart; squash them. Grab it, press the head, and squash it. . . . It'll die then. . . .

MAN I: But I did and it's still moving. . . .

OLD WOMAN: Don't worry. . . . In a minute. It'll stop moving in a minute. . . . It's just suffering a little. . . .

MAN I: I wonder if ants're insects?

OLD WOMAN: They are; they've got six legs. . . .

MAN I: Wings, too, I guess. . . .

OLD WOMAN: Wings, too, four wings. . . . Because they're insects. . . .

MAN I: *(Looking up.)* Got any . . . paper? . . .

OLD WOMAN: Paper? . . . Should be some rice paper there. . . .

MAN I: *(Transferring the dead ants in his left hand to the paper.)* What do you do with the dead ones? . . .

OLD WOMAN: Burn them. . . .

MAN I: Why? . . .

OLD WOMAN: Because then they won't come back to life. . . .

MAN I: Then there won't be any more next year?

OLD WOMAN: Next year new ones'll come out again.

MAN I: You'll kill them again? . . .

OLD WOMAN: Kill them again. . . .

MAN I: You don't think you can fix it so that there absolutely won't be any more. . . .

OLD WOMAN: No. There are new ants every year. You have to go on killing them year after year. . . .

MAN 1: Forever? . . .

OLD WOMAN: Forever. . . .

MAN 1: *(Stopping his work.)* Grandma. . . .

OLD WOMAN: What? . . .

(MAN 1 *pauses.*)

OLD WOMAN: What is it, Yoshio?

MAN 1: Nothing. . . . *(Setting to work.)* There's a nest here. Shall we dig it up and squash the eggs? . . .

OLD WOMAN: Forget it. Leave it alone. I'll pour kerosene on it later and burn it. Or else the ones inside won't die. . . .

MAN 1: Grandma, will there be new ants next year all the same?

OLD WOMAN: Yes. They'll come out again next year all the same. . . .

MAN 1: Why?

OLD WOMAN: Ants spring up from the ground. As long as there's ground, come spring, out come the ants. . . . You see, Yoshio, there's nothing you can do about it. . . .

MAN 1: *(Rising absently.)* Then how can we win?

OLD WOMAN: We are winning, aren't we? . . . We're killing the ants this way. . . .

MAN 1: But won't there be new ones next year? . . .

OLD WOMAN: Yes. And so next year we'll kill them again. . . . Understand, Yoshio? That's what winning is. . . . There's no victory where you win it all at once and that's it. . . . No one can do that. All we can ever do is to stay a little ahead. . . .

(MAN 1 *drops the paper he is holding, picks up his schoolbag, and slowly disappears into the wardrobe.*)

OLD WOMAN: Yoshio. . . . *(She returns to her work, and the rest is said as if muttering to herself.)* No need to hurry, take it slow. . . . Just keep killing them one by one. . . .

(*A telephone rings inside the wardrobe.*)

OLD WOMAN: Little by little, just keep at it. . . .

(*The telephone continues to ring. The* OLD WOMAN *slowly gets up and enters the wardrobe. . . . The area gradually darkens. . . . There is only the voice of the* OLD WOMAN *talking on the telephone.*

MAN 2 *appears, dressed as if just back from the government office; he stands abstractedly beneath the cherry tree, listening to the* OLD WOMAN *talking.*)

OLD WOMAN: Hello. . . . Fumie? . . . Yes, I'm fine. . . . Getting along somehow. . . . What? I don't mind. Don't worry about me. . . . I see . . . Yoshio isn't? . . . He's not going to school? Why not? What for? . . . I don't know. How would I? Who's the one who snatched Yoshio away from me? . . . I don't know. . . . Yes . . . he came here just once. . . . No . . . he didn't say anything. . . . He helped me kill ants. . . . He went home without saying a thing. . . . Yes, that's about when it was. . . . Then he stopped going to school the next day. . . . Fumie, bring Yoshio back here. No matter what happens. All right, Fumie? . . . Fumie . . . if you don't, he'll turn out no good. Now this is not the time to say things like that, Fumie, Fumie. . . .

(She hangs up and, after a brief pause, emerges slowly from the wardrobe. Her eyes meet those of MAN 2.*)*

MAN 2: *(Darkly.)* There's a reason why Yoshio stopped going to school. . . .

OLD WOMAN: What sort of reason?

MAN 2: The father of one of his classmates was transferred overseas, and Yoshio was the only one not invited to the going-away party. . . .

OLD WOMAN: Who was it? . . .

MAN 2: That doesn't matter. . . .

OLD WOMAN: It does. Who?

MAN 2: Kataoka's the boy's name. . . . But you don't know him, Grandma. . . .

OLD WOMAN: Then it has nothing to do with me. . . . Yoshio wouldn't let a thing like that get him down; he's never been one to. . . .

MAN 2: True . . . but this time I happened to know the boy's father a little, so I called him and asked him to invite Yoshio, too. . . .

*(*OLD WOMAN *is silent.)*

MAN 2: The boy told the whole class about it. . . .

(A slight interval.)

MAN 2: I intend to go to the school tomorrow and talk to everyone in the class. . . . I'll tell them I did it entirely on my own, that Yoshio didn't know a thing about it. . . .

OLD WOMAN: *(Rather quietly.)* Don't do that, it's ridiculous. . . .

MAN 2: *(Indignantly.)* It is not. What else can I do to make them understand the truth? You see that, don't you? Don't worry. I'm sure they'll understand if I have a heart-to-heart talk with them. I'm even willing to go down on my knees to get them to. . . . I mean . . . listen, Grandma, that's why I came here, that's why Yoshio must be made to think seriously about himself. Not about this one incident, but the root cause, the fact that nobody likes him. Of course, Yoshio is probably not entirely to blame. But that's beside the point. Yoshio's been at fault, too. If Yoshio apologizes, the others'll think things over, too. And even if they don't, at least it'll be the key to breaking the ice. Someone'll understand Yoshio. They'll make friends with him. Don't you see, Grandma? . . . That's why I'm going to school tomorrow. . . . If Yoshio doesn't come around, it won't do any good no matter how I grovel to them. . . .

OLD WOMAN: So? . . . What do you want me to do about it? . . .

MAN 2: I want you to talk to Yoshio and try to bring him around. . . .

OLD WOMAN: Why don't you talk to him yourself? . . .

MAN 2: I did. . . . He refused. . . .

OLD WOMAN: So you're here to get on your knees and beg me? . . .

MAN 2: Yes, Grandma. . . . I'll get down on my knees and beg. *(He does.)* Please. Please talk to him. . . . I understand the way you've taught him. But Yoshio's not as strong as you think, Grandma. He's not a boy who can go on competing with everyone. He needs friends. . . . I beg you, Grandma. . . .

OLD WOMAN: I refuse. Stop this nonsense. . . .

MAN 2: Grandma. . . .

OLD WOMAN: *(Moving.)* How unspeakably impudent you look down on your knees like that. And, as strange as it sounds, obscene. . . . You're probably enjoying yourself. . . . I won't do it; don't play me for a fool. I know your type down to the dirt on your heels. I've had people work on me like that so many times I'm sick of it.

MAN 2: Grandma. . . . *(The* OLD WOMAN*'s anger is completely unexpected to* MAN 2.*)*

OLD WOMAN: Get out of here. You make me puke.

*(*MAN 2 *rises slowly and leaves in dejection. Soon it darkens.*

A slow fade in; the OLD WOMAN *is sitting on the straw mat while* MAN 1 *sleeps, his head resting on her lap. She listlessly sings "Sakura, Sakura.")*

OLD WOMAN: *(In the middle of her song, blankly.)* It's so dark . . . Yoshio . . . don't you look up now. . . . There'll be blossoms in full bloom, blooming just like they're holding their breath. . . . Quietly now. . . . We have to hold our breath, too, pretend not to notice them and walk on by—that's the trick. . . . Mustn't look. . . . Or we'll go crazy, too. . . . Once long ago there was a boy who struck a match in the dark to look at the flowers that seemed to cover everything . . . he never got home. . . .

(Suddenly there is the sound of WOMAN 1 *screaming; the stage quickly darkens. In the dark the sound of things crashing.* WOMAN 1 *is heard screaming, "Yoshio, Yoshio, stop it. Yoshio, Yoshio. . . . " Fade in; the* OLD WOMAN *is sitting alone on the straw mat, and* WOMAN 1 *comes out of the wardrobe screaming.)*

OLD WOMAN: What happened? . . .

WOMAN 1: Yoshio's run wild again. . . .

OLD WOMAN: You said something to him, didn't you? . . .

WOMAN 1: No . . . I just told him that if he wasn't going to school, he should at least stop sleeping all day. . . .

(From deep within the wardrobe are heard MAN 1*'s shouts, the clatter of things breaking, the sound of glass shattering.)*

OLD WOMAN: Hasn't Takaaki been able to do anything? . . .

WOMAN I: He's no help. . . . He hasn't said a thing to Yoshio since the day we moved back in here. . . .

(OLD WOMAN *pauses.*)

WOMAN I: What'll we do, Grandma? . . . His teacher told me to try going to the Educational Counseling Office; he gave me a letter of introduction.

OLD WOMAN: Don't do anything ridiculous. . . . What possible good would that do? . . .

WOMAN I: But Grandma, his teacher said that the number of students suddenly refusing to go to school is increasing. And they are all violent toward their parents, just like Yoshio. . . .

OLD WOMAN: Yoshio's different. . . .

WOMAN I: But isn't he doing the same thing? . . .

OLD WOMAN: No. I know Yoshio better than anyone. . . .

WOMAN I: Then what should we do? . . .

OLD WOMAN: Let him alone. . . .

WOMAN I: He'll destroy the house. . . .

OLD WOMAN: What if he does? You two always said you wanted to be nice to Yoshio. Well, be nice. Let Yoshio do what he wants—that's being nice, isn't it? . . .

(WOMAN I *disappears into the wardrobe, dejectedly but somehow harboring determination.*

The stage darkens, and, at almost the same time, the sound of things crashing, MAN I*'s moans, and* WOMAN I*'s screams, "Stop it, Yoshio. Stop. Stop," are heard once again. The* OLD WOMAN *sits on the mat, motionless as if frozen stiff. . . . The noises and screams gradually grow more terrible and are finally joined by* MAN 2*'s voice, too, "Yoshio. That's enough, Yoshio. . . ."*

A police siren is heard in the distance; it gradually grows closer and stops in front of the house. The noises inside the wardrobe cease abruptly.

Soon from inside the wardrobe MAN I *emerges, in a daze, a kitchen knife in his hand. He stands facing away. . . .*)

OLD WOMAN: Yoshio. . . . Come here. . . .

(MAN I *does not move.*)

OLD WOMAN: *(Sharply.)* Get over here! . . .

(MAN I *slowly approaches the* OLD WOMAN *and sits near her.*)

OLD WOMAN: Give it to me. . . .

(MAN I *hands the* OLD WOMAN *the kitchen knife.*)

OLD WOMAN: Put your head on Grandma's lap and rest. . . .

(MAN I *lies down and lays his head in her lap.*)

OLD WOMAN: When we're like this . . . I know your brain is right here. . . . Your white, soft brain crammed full of all kinds of things. . . .

(*There is a faint clatter from within the wardrobe; finally the patrol car is heard gradually receding in the distance.*)

OLD WOMAN: This brain wants so bad to do something, but doesn't know what it should do. . . . Don't forget though. . . . Grandma knows. . . . You remember, one spring . . . Grandma had you on her lap like now. . . . Your brain was still quite small, but you knew more clearly then who you hated. . . . That's right. . . . You were always hating someone.   Mustn't forget that. . . . It's your only strength. . . .

(MAN 2 *absently emerges from the wardrobe; he stands staring at the two of them.*)

OLD WOMAN: You, huh . . . you called the police? . . .

MAN 2: Yes . . . Yoshio tried to stab Fumie with a kitchen knife. . . .

(MAN 1 *raises his head from the* OLD WOMAN*'s lap and sits up straight, eyes cast downward.*)

OLD WOMAN: And? Did he stab her? . . .

MAN 2: No. . . .

OLD WOMAN: How's Fumie? . . .

MAN 2: I gave her a sedative and put her to bed. . . .

OLD WOMAN: *(To* MAN 1.*)* You still want to stab Fumie? . . .

(MAN 1 *does not answer.*)

OLD WOMAN: If you do, tell Grandma. I'll stab her for you. *(She stands up.)*

MAN 2: Grandma. . . .

OLD WOMAN: Stay out of this. I don't have anything more to say to you.

MAN 2: I realize that. . . .

OLD WOMAN: I'm talking to Yoshio. . . . What about it, Yoshio? . . .

MAN 2: Now let's drop it. Grandma. . . .

OLD WOMAN: You're going to tell me, Yoshio. Want to stab your mother? I said I'd do it for you. Well, Yoshio, what about it?. . . .

(MAN 1 *still gives no answer.*)

OLD WOMAN: Where should I stab her? The chest? The heart? Grandma won't fail like you. Hey! *(Pokes him.)* Yoshio, speak. . . .

(MAN 1 *remains silent.*)

OLD WOMAN: I get it. . . . It's Kataoka you want to stab, isn't it. . . . Because he didn't invite you to his going-away party. . . . Right? . . . Then let's go to Kataoka's. Grandma'll kill him for you. Well . . . *(She grabs him by the scruff of the neck and pulls him along.)* Come along, c'mon. We're going to Kataoka's place. . . .

MAN 1: *(Resisting being dragged along.)* It doesn't matter. . . .

OLD WOMAN: What do you mean it doesn't matter? You hate him, don't you? Want him dead, don't you? Grandma'll stab him for you. Come on, now. . . .

MAN 1: I mean it. . . . Kataoka's not here anymore. He went to a foreign country. . . .

OLD WOMAN: His old grandparents are here. His house is here, right? Why don't we kill them and burn down their house? Grandma'll do it for you. Now, you're coming. . . . Or do you want to get Uchida instead? . . .

MAN 1: *(Being dragged along.)* No. . . .

OLD WOMAN: What do you mean no? You think Grandma can't do it? You don't know me. So come. I'll show you. I'll have Uchida covered with blood and writhing in agony. Well, c'mon. Yoshio. . . . You're coming, Yoshio. . . .

MAN 1: *(Falls prostrate on the ground and, resisting being dragged along by the* OLD WOMAN, *almost in a moan.)* It doesn't matter. It doesn't matter. Grandma. . . . It's really all right; you don't have to do anything like that. . . .

(The OLD WOMAN *finally releases him.)*

OLD WOMAN: Then it's really all right. . . .

MAN 1: *(Faintly.)* Yeah. . . .

OLD WOMAN: You haven't let those guys beat you, have you? . . .

MAN 1: . . . No. . . .

OLD WOMAN: Starting tomorrow you go back to school. . . . And you won't care how that bunch looks at you, what they say behind your back, or whether anybody talks to you or not. . . . Not if you really hate them. . . . Right? . . .

*(*MAN 1 *nods slightly.)*

OLD WOMAN: Get some rest. . . . Get ready for tomorrow. . . .

*(*MAN 1 *gets to his feet and slowly disappears into the wardrobe.)*

MAN 2: Grandma. . . .

OLD WOMAN: You still here? . . .

MAN 2: Yes. . . .

OLD WOMAN: Didn't I tell you I didn't want to talk to you? . . .

MAN 2: Yes, but I don't care about myself. . . . I don't care how much you despise me. . . . It's just that. . . .

OLD WOMAN: I'm talking about that repulsive way of talking of yours. . . .

MAN 2: What do you mean? . . .

OLD WOMAN: Why don't you care about yourself? Why doesn't it matter how much you're despised? . . .

MAN 2: It's only Yoshio that I'm. . . .

OLD WOMAN: I'm talking about Yoshio, too. . . .

MAN 2: But Grandma. . . .

OLD WOMAN: How can Yoshio hate a person who says, "I don't care about myself" or "I don't care if I'm despised"? . . .

*(*MAN 2 *says nothing.)*

OLD WOMAN: The fact that Yoshio hasn't stabbed you doesn't mean that he doesn't hate you. . . . He just didn't know how to go about hating you. . . .

(MAN 2 *pauses.*)

OLD WOMAN: Of course you're not the only one. . . . The world's full of people who say they don't care about themselves, that they don't care if they're despised. . . . They gang up on Yoshio, dodge his hatred, and instead get him in a choke hold, as if they were strangling him with silk floss. . . . It's true, you . . . now you're trying to choke him to death the same way. . . .

(A brief *interval.*)

MAN 2: Is that a fact, Grandma? . . . Then I'm the one you hate, aren't I? . . .

OLD WOMAN: That's right. . . . I'm teaching Yoshio just how to hate you. . . .

MAN 2: But why? . . .

OLD WOMAN: Be on your guard. . . . Someday he's sure to figure things out. . . . Then he'll stab you. . . .

MAN 2: Why? . . . I just don't understand. . . . Why must I be hated so? . . .

OLD WOMAN: You wouldn't understand. . . . Even after he stabs you, you still won't understand. . . .

(*Blackout. After a while it brightens again. The* OLD WOMAN *is sitting on the straw mat under the same cherry in full bloom. There is the gentle melody of* "Sakura, Sakura.")

OLD WOMAN: It was one spring. . . . Wasn't it, Yoshio. . . . Blue sky. . . . White clouds. . . . The sun shining. . . . Your face was pale, your temples strained and twitching. . . . You went off to school like you were going off to be murdered. . . . It was the same the next morning and the morning after that. . . . Your hatred was transparent and extremely fragile . . . so you trembled at the tiniest breeze like it was a storm. . . . But, it's true, Yoshio. . . . You'll soon find out. . . . Hate is something you can just keep inside. . . . You don't have to tell anybody. . . . You don't have to exchange it for anything. . . . But if you do . . . don't let anyone know why . . . be like the trees when they change to flowers in the spring. . . . Aren't I right, Yoshio. . . . To look at the blossoms, who would know they're caused by the tree's hating. . . .

(WOMAN 1 *appears from inside the wardrobe and, somewhat confused, stands transfixed. She has come to speak to the* OLD WOMAN, *but her resolution is dulled the moment she sees her.*)

OLD WOMAN: What's wrong with you? . . .

WOMAN 1: I. . . .

OLD WOMAN: Tell me. . . .

WOMAN I: I just had a call from school. They want to know if Yoshio's come home. . . .

(OLD WOMAN *listens quietly.*)

WOMAN I: One of his classmates, Kanayama, lost his money; he noticed it after lunch. . . . Yoshio was the only one who stayed in the class-room during lunch period. . . .

(OLD WOMAN *still says nothing.*)

WOMAN I: The classroom was in an uproar, so the teacher in charge came in. No one said a thing about Yoshio, but he suddenly jumped up and said he took it . . . then ran off somewhere without a word. . . .

OLD WOMAN: *(Holding her stomach, apparently in some pain.)* I know. . . .

WOMAN I: You know? . . .

OLD WOMAN: Yoshio was just here. He told me everything. . . . But there's no cause for alarm. Yoshio didn't do it because he wanted the money. . . . That's not why he stole it. . . . I understand Yoshio perfectly. . . . He only did it so that he and his classmates would hate each other. . . .

WOMAN I: That's not true, Grandma. . . .

OLD WOMAN: Yes, it is. I understand everything. Don't go branding Yoshio a thief. That's not why the child did it. . . .

WOMAN I: No, Grandma, the money wasn't stolen. It was in the boy's locker. He had the key, too. He'd forgotten. . . .

(OLD WOMAN *is speechless.*)

WOMAN I: Yoshio doesn't know. He left without finding out. He's the only one who doesn't know. . . .

(*A brief interval.*)

OLD WOMAN: But he said he took it. . . . He said, "Grandma, I've wound up as a thief. . . . Now I'm a criminal. . . ."

WOMAN I: Grandma. . . .

OLD WOMAN: Fumie, go look for him. Hurry.

WOMAN I: But where? . . .

OLD WOMAN: Somewhere. Quickly. *(Groaning in apparent pain.)* He's made a mistake. . . .

WOMAN I: *(Noticing the* OLD WOMAN's *pain for the first time.)* Grandma, is something wrong? . . .

OLD WOMAN: Don't worry about me; find Yoshio quickly. . . . If you don't hurry, it'll be too late. . . .

WOMAN I: I will. . . .

(WOMAN I *hastily disappears into the wardrobe.*)

OLD WOMAN: *(At times holding her stomach in pain.)* Yoshio, what a terrible mistake. . . . I thought I'd made a mistake when you told me you were a thief but . . . this is much worse. . . . You didn't do any-thing. . . . You may've tried to trade your hatred for something more solid, but in the end you didn't get anything for it. . . . You weren't a thief, were you? . . . Yoshio . . . don't go there. . . . There's nothing there, Yoshio. . . .

(A patrol car approaches in the distance, then slowly speeds by outside. Listening to it, the OLD WOMAN *slowly raises her head, having realized something.)*

OLD WOMAN: Fumie, Fumie   The government office, Takaaki's place. . . . Fumie, call Takaaki's place. Yoshio's there, Fumie. . . . Call Takaaki and tell him to get away quick. . . . Fumie . . . I didn't tell you: Yoshio's got a knife. . . . Fumie, the office. . . . Tell Takaaki . . . Fumie. . . .

(The telephone rings several times, then suddenly stops. The patrol car can be heard faintly in the distance; it, too, stops.

MAN 3, *cane in hand, wanders in from right and stands lingering beneath the cherry blossoms.)*

MAN 3: They've bloomed. . . .

OLD WOMAN: Yes. . . .

MAN 3: Do you know the story about corpses being buried under cherry trees in full bloom?[7] . . .

OLD WOMAN: No, what does it mean? . . .

MAN 3: Nothing. . . . That's all there is to the story. . . .

OLD WOMAN: Why're you always saying things that don't mean anything? . . .

MAN 3: Hm . . . I don't know why myself. . . . I just heard once somewhere about a corpse being buried beneath a cherry tree in full bloom. . . . *(Moves slowly to right.)*

OLD WOMAN: Grandpa, where are you going? . . .

MAN 3: I thought I told you never to call me Grandpa when Yoshio's not around. . . .

OLD WOMAN: But where are you going? . . .

MAN 3: Nowhere. . . .

OLD WOMAN: Grandpa. . . .

*(*MAN 3 *slowly walks off at right. At about the same time,* MAN 2 *appears from inside the wardrobe. His clothes show that he has just returned from the government office.)*

MAN 2: Grandma, has something happened to Yoshio? . . .

OLD WOMAN: Oh, you've come home from work? . . .

MAN 2: Yes, I just had a call from Fumie. What's happened to Yoshio?

OLD WOMAN: He left, running. . . .

MAN 2: Where to? . . .

OLD WOMAN: You didn't see him? . . .

MAN 2: No . . . not me. . . .

OLD WOMAN: Your place. . . . I thought he probably went straight to you. . . .

MAN 2: Me? . . .

OLD WOMAN: *(Evidently in increasing pain.)* To stab you. . . .

MAN 2: *(Noticing the* OLD WOMAN*'s state.)* Grandma, what's the matter? . . .

OLD WOMAN: I'm all right. . . . Leave me be. . . . It's Yoshio who needs help . . . save him, Takaaki. . . . The boy's gotten into awful trouble this time. . . .

MAN 2: Something's happened, hasn't it? Hasn't it, Grandma. . . . *(He spies the first-aid kit by her side.)* What's the first-aid kit doing here? . . .

OLD WOMAN: Leave me alone. . . .

MAN 2: Are you hurt? . . . Did Yoshio do something? . . . Grandma, please tell me. Grandma. . . .

(The OLD WOMAN *tries to say something, but suddenly falls forward on the straw mat from the excessive pain.)*

MAN 2: Grandma. . . .

(From stage right WOMAN 1 *slowly appears, followed by two men in white coats bearing a stretcher.* MAN 1 *lies on the stretcher. His face is covered with a white cloth.* MAN 2 *staggers to his feet.)*

WOMAN 1: *(Darkly.)* Grandma, Yoshio's come home. . . .

(The OLD WOMAN *twists herself in an attempt to move, but is unable to raise herself.)*

WOMAN 1: *(Leaning over the* OLD WOMAN *and shaking her.)* Grandma, it's Yoshio. Do you hear? . . . Yoshio's killed himself. He's dead, Grandma. . . .

(The two men in white coats put the stretcher down in front of the OLD WOMAN *and leave slowly.)*

WOMAN 1: *(Shaking her more.)* Grandma, listen to me, Yoshio's killed himself. . . . He jumped off the roof of the housing development down the street. . . . Grandma, do you hear me, Grandma. . . .

OLD WOMAN: *(Virtually groaning.)* I hear you. . . . *(Briefly raising herself partially.)* Is that Yoshio? . . .

WOMAN 1: Yes, it is, Grandma; it's Yoshio. . . .

OLD WOMAN: It breaks my heart. . . . Breaks my heart, Yoshio. . . . Now I see. . . . You took your own life so that you could never hurt anyone again. . . . So that you could never hate anyone else again. . . . *(Loses her strength once more and collapses.)*

WOMAN 1: *(Supporting her.)* Grandma. . . .

MAN 2: *(Darkly, quietly.)* Grandma, too; she's been stabbed. . . .

WOMAN 1: Grandma, too? . . .

OLD WOMAN: It was Yoshio. . . . He was just here; he stabbed me. . . . If only I'd realized it then. . . . See? . . . He did it so I'd never have to hate anyone again. . . . *(To* WOMAN 1.) Stop it, don't touch me. . . .

*(*WOMAN 1 *rises and moves away from the* OLD WOMAN.)*

OLD WOMAN: Now Yoshio and I can never hate anyone again. . . .
(The sunlight fades, the blossoms continue to flutter down, and "Sakura, Sakura" plays softly.)
OLD WOMAN: Fumie . . . it's so peaceful. . . . Like I'm slipping far away. . . .
(WOMAN 1 and MAN 2 both stand rooted, "Sakura, Sakura" gradually grows louder.)

Notes

1. A variety of cherry tree prized for its numerous and gorgeous blossoms.

2. Refers to *juku,* the private schools designed to supplement the regular schooling of Japanese children, preschool through high school, to give them a competitive edge in their many school entrance examinations.

3. "Luxuriant Greenery" (Aoba shigereru) is a song of feudal devotion—to one's father and to the emperor. By the militaristic years of the 1930s and early 1940s, it was an indispensable item in the education of Japanese schoolchildren (see Ivan Morris, *The Nobility of Failure* [New York: New American Library, 1976], 106–142; an English translation of "Aoba shigereru" is found on pages 131–132).

4. Yotsuya is an area of Tokyo.

5. Katō Shūson (b. 1905). This haiku is from the late 1930s.

6. The "scissors-paper-stone" game played endlessly in Japan to decide things (e.g., who goes first) or for amusement.

7. The notion of the cherry in full bloom as oppressive and menacing, with corpses buried beneath and inducing madness in those who stop to gaze at the blossoms, has been exploited in such well-known modern short stories as "Under the Cherry Tree" (Sakura no ki no shita ni wa) (1928) by Kajii Motojirō and "Beneath the Cherry Grove in Full Bloom" (Sakura no mori no mankai no shita) (1947) by Sakaguchi Ango. The latter has inspired contemporary dramas, most recently, *A Fake "Beneath the Cherry Grove in Full Bloom"* (Gansaku: sakura no mori no mankai no shita) (1989) by Noda Hideki (b. 1955).

The Cherry in Bloom treats education and socialization. Yoshio's grandmother—a representative of Japanese tradition—offers to kill anyone he wants. Seinenza, 1980. (Courtesy Seinenza.)

The tree in *The Cherry in Bloom* dominates both stage and imagery. Cherry blossoms, the song "Sakura," and the flower-viewing custom are given sinister associations. Seinenza, 1980. (Courtesy Seinenza.)

Shimizu Kunio

SHIMIZU KUNIO (b. 1936) is an accomplished playwright whose best works are marked by thematic complexity and lyric intensity. He was a vital figure on the youthful new theater scene of the 1960s, but today his plays appeal to mature audiences. He began writing plays while a student at Waseda University. On graduation in 1960 he worked for Iwanami Films for five years, where, among other activities, he wrote scenarios for noted director Hani Susumu: *A Full Life* (Mitasareta seikatsu) (1962); *She and He* (Kanojo to kare) (1963); and *The Song of Bwana Toshi* (Buana Toshi no uta) (1965), which involved a lengthy stay in Tanzania in 1964 that Shimizu feels affected his outlook greatly. Shimizu did television documentaries on the tragic 1963 coal mine accident that inspired his play *Those Days* (Ano hitachi) (1966).

He carved his own niche in the new theater by establishing the Gendaijin Gekijō (Modern Man's Theater) with Ninagawa Yukio in 1969. Their first production was Shimizu's *Such a Serious Frivolity* (Shinjō afururu keihakusa), published in 1968 and performed at the Art Theater Shinjuku Bunka under Ninagawa's direction, the first of five annual plays that Shimizu wrote and Ninagawa directed there from 1969 to 1973. Located in the teeming hub of Tokyo's Shinjuku Ward, the Art Theater was a significant cultural center from 1962 to 1974, showing art films and staging plays. Shimizu was the most active playwright there, but the theater also saw productions of works by Betsuyaku, Terayama, and Kara. In 1976 Shimizu began his current company Mokutōsha (Winter Tree Troupe) with his wife, the actress Matsumoto Noriko. Their first production, *Night: Night of Youth That Raises My Hackles with Screams and Anger* (Yoru yo ore o sakebi to sakage de mitasu seishun no yoru yo), in November 1976, won Shimizu the Kinokuniya Drama Award. His *When We Go Down the Great Unfeeling River* (Bokura ga hijō no taiga o kudaru toki) had already earned him the Kishida Prize for Playwriting in 1974. For *Little Brother!—A Message to Sakamoto Ryōma from Otome, His Older Sister* (Otōto yo—ane, Otome kara Sakamoto Ryōma e no dengon), Shimizu received the Teatoro Theater Award for best play of 1990.

Many of Shimizu's plays, like the notable *An Older Sister, Burning Like a Flame* (Hi no yō ni samishii ane ga ite) (1978) and *Dreams Departed, Orpheus* (Yume sarite, Orufe) (1986), are set in a mythic small town near the Sea of Japan, which is modeled on Shimizu's home in Niigata Prefecture and is, he feels, ideal for developing such themes as memory, insanity, change, decay, and the nexus between illusion and reality. In other works he places such themes within the context of Japanese history, in particular the thirteenth-century *Tales of the Heike* (Heike monogatari): *By Illusion His Heart*

Pushed to Madness—Our Masakado (Maboroshi ni kokoro mo sozoro kuruoshi no warera Masakado) (1975); *My Spirit Is the Sparkling Water* (Waga tamashii wa kagayaku mizu nari) (1980), which won the Izumi Kyōka Literary Prize that year. Among Shimizu's prose works, *Off to Buy a Tsukigata Sickle* (Tsukigata kama o kai ni iku tabi) was nominated for the Akutagawa Prize in 1988.

INTRODUCTION

John K. Gillespie

WHATEVER THE BALANCE between reality and illusion in his plays, even those that verge on the absurd, Shimizu Kunio creates dialogue that is resolutely realistic. This is perhaps the most distinctive aspect in his style of playwriting, setting him immediately apart from Betsuyaku's Beckettian absurd, Terayama's relentless stylization, Kara's vaudevillian slapstick, and Satoh's recourse to Japanese mythology. Shimizu is, in short, the most literary of these five playwrights.

Shimizu did not set out, however, to become a playwright. The son of a policeman in Niigata near the coast of the Sea of Japan, Shimizu entered Waseda University in 1956 planning to major in design and drawing. But after working in a small student theater group formed by his older brother, he switched his concentration to literature and theater. His graduation thesis was on Tennessee Williams, whom he cites as an important influence on the way he conceives dialogue. He earned his initial recognition as a playwright in 1958, when his first play, *The Signatory* (Shomeinin), won a Waseda University playwriting competition. On graduating in the spring of 1960, Shimizu was commissioned by the Seihai Theater Company to write the play that became his first to reach the stage, *Tomorrow I'll Put Flowers There* (Ashita soko ni hana o sasō yo).[1]

The date of this commission is significant, coming as it did during the summer of nationwide student and leftist protests over the renewal of the U.S.-Japan Mutual Security Treaty. Shimizu took part in the demonstrations along with thousands of other Japanese youths (including the other playwrights in this anthology). Yet *Tomorrow I'll Put Flowers There* is barely colored by political proclivities. He was, he maintains, simply one who went out and demonstrated like everybody else. His work is affected far less by the specific political nature of the protests than by the passion that characterized the time.

A look at the major themes of Shimizu's plays indeed proves him to be a child of his age, nurtured as a youth by the often wrenching changes of the Occupation years, brought to adulthood in the increasingly affluent yet tumultuous and tentative culture of the late 1950s and early 1960s. Shimizu's plays largely reflect this experience: nudged by the West (mainly the United States) along a systematic path toward postwar economic recovery, Japan achieved many and stunning successes, quite abruptly, before inwardly taking stock and attempting to come to terms with itself. Shimizu's concerns spin off from there. Chief among them is the problem of identity as exemplified through probing the nature of memory, through the fervent quest in postwar Japan for home or a homeland by turning to the past, or through stark portrayals of the ephemerality of youth and of youth disoriented in the advance of time.

In fact, the plays of Betsuyaku, Shimizu, Terayama, and Kara all "begin and end," according to the critic Satō Tadao, with the question, "Who am I?"[2] Shimizu deals with this question principally through characters who, like Pirandello's (also an important influence on his work), have trouble remembering the past. They may even have amnesia. As they confront one another, they encounter the inevitable problem of existence—distinguishing reality from illusion. Who were they really? Is their present idea of self merely an illusion? These characters often sense the unceasing advance of time keenly; they can hardly return to the situation of the past, even if they knew exactly what it was. Their situation is ambiguous, but Shimizu's larger implication is not. Cut off from a past full of verities, contemporary Japan is caught up in such frenzied, pervasive economic activity that it is often oblivious to the long-range human implications of what it is doing. In Shimizu's view, contemporary Japanese recall the past only vaguely, if at all, and grasp the present tentatively at best. For them the question of identity is elusive, inextricably tied to the shifting complexities of Japan's modern history.

Elusive Identity: **Those Days** *and* **The Sand of Youth, How Quickly**

Shimizu makes the elusive nature of modern Japanese history the focus of two works, *Those Days* and *The Sand of Youth, How Quickly* (Seishun no suna no nan to hayaku) (1980), which are dramaturgically quite different from each other. *The Sand of Youth, How Quickly* is a short, tightly wrought, sometimes lyrical portrayal of human passion and psychology. *Those Days,* on the other hand, is an ambitious, somewhat sprawling, generally realistic play that, nevertheless, possesses considerable significance as a link between the earlier *shingeki* social problem play and the alternative drama of the 1960s. While still concerned with social issues, Shimizu and his contemporaries in the burgeoning new drama of the 1960s displayed a fundamental mistrust of what they saw as Japan's orthodox, superficial view of its history and national psyche; they sought to probe that view on a deeper psychological level. Both the older concern with social issues and the new sensibility are at work in *Those Days*.

In that play, to discuss the earlier of these two fascinating works first, Shimizu treats the question of identity vividly. Staged in 1966 by the Seihai Theater Company and published in 1967, *Those Days* is based on a real event, the 1963 explosion at the Miike Coal Mine at Ōmuta in Kyushu, in which the carbon monoxide was so overwhelming that a large number of the survivors suffered a kind of brain damage diagnosed as retrograde amnesia. They were still able to recall certain motor skills, such as how to strike a match, but they did not know who they were.

Shimizu's play suggests two possible approaches to the dilemma. One, espoused by the character Ikki (who has survived the explosion, memory intact), is to re-create as exactly as possible what happened in the past, who the amnesiacs were, and what were their relationships. The other, advanced by the character Yamamoto Kaneko, is to forget trying to reestablish the past and start anew with the present. Neither approach is free of difficulty. On the one hand, delving into the past is less enlightening than confusing for the characters in this play. Whose account of the past is one to believe? As in the play, witnesses to the same situation or the same event can have radically different reactions. When the character Tokugawa, for example, finds himself sexually attracted to the beautiful young woman Hanako, who, he is told, is his daughter, his conflicting emotions render him hopelessly perplexed. On the other hand, to ignore the past entirely is the epitome of rootlessness.

Shimizu's intention with this dialectic is to raise the specter of identity. What have our human relationships been, he asks, and what have been the obstacles to realizing them? An advantage of amnesia, Shimizu suggests, is that, in releasing one from relationships, those obstacles too disappear. Before the explosion the characters Uragami and Ikeno were at each others' throats, in part because of implied marital infidelity involving Ikeno and Uragami's wife or perhaps Uragami and Ikeno's wife. They now find themselves, survivors with no memory, close friends. Matters are made all the more complex by Shimizu's notion, particularly as expressed through the characters Yamada (who has total amnesia) and Kaneko (his estranged wife who tries to recast their relationship), that one must certainly lose the past to be free but, having lost it, will just as certainly encounter the desire to return to it. Thus, the question posed at the beginning of the play remains. On whose account of the past can one safely depend? In short, according to Shimizu, the search for identity, anchored in our social relationships and shaped by our faulty remembrance, is fraught with problems.

The characters in *The Sand of Youth, How Quickly,* Shimizu's first play included here, are no less bedeviled by confusion over the search for self. Although published in *Teatoro* in 1980, this was originally a radio play entitled *Passing Strangers* (Yukizuri no hitotachi yo), written in 1974. The only change from the radio version, however, is the addition at the beginning and end of a poem by Louis Aragon. This play too concerns the problem of identity—wrapped in a veneer of generational conflict and inevitably passing youth—rendered here in a far more stylized fashion than in *Those Days.* Four characters, Older Man, Doctor, Woman Who Claims to Be the Wife, and Woman Who Claims to Be the Mother (the two women also appear as schoolgirls), haggle over the identity of the fifth character, Man. The Man allegedly suffers from a psychologically induced loss of memory, but it is hardly clear from the assertions of the others who the Man is—or even who they are. The Older Man and the two Women are perhaps as out of touch with the reality of the past as the Man who has no memory. Is he the companion of the Older Man or the husband of the one Woman and the son-in-law of the other? Or are all of them patients in an asylum? (Even the Doctor has at least one irrational outburst.)

Shimizu's concerns here are twofold. First, he is underscoring his view that, in the change-infested contemporary age, family relationships are so deeply infected as virtually to preclude coming to terms with one's identity through them. With the exception of the Doctor, the play's other four characters are perhaps related in various configurations, but their relationships are shrouded in suspicion. The Older Man, for example, even wants to verify whether the two Women are in fact related to each other. But his relationship to the Man is so tentative he can conclude only that "it's possible" he is a relative. Later, the Older Man appears to voice Shimizu's sense of "how fragile and thin the ties are between one person and another."

Second, as the critic Ōzasa Yoshio observes, Shimizu is expressing his conviction that a consciousness of self must be based on intuition. Shimizu possesses no intuition into the past, Ōzasa goes on; he can intuit only the present.[3] The very form of a play, then, to Shimizu's mind, can be a point of departure for approaching this problem; by focusing on the present, he attempts to fuse past and present into a single instant. The immediacy and visual nature of the theater allow past and present to crystallize on stage simultaneously. This, for Shimizu, is the essence of theater and serves to explain why so many of his plays deal with questions of memory and insanity, of consciousness of self and identity.

A clue to the answers of the questions posed by *The Sand of Youth, How Quickly* emerges, therefore, in the form of the play itself. Consider the fluctuating relationship of the Man with the Older Man. When the Man says, "I wanted to believe anyone who came along," he confesses his dependence on the Older Man. But with time the relationship has reversed itself: the Older Man has become dependent on the younger, just as a youth, although once dependent on parents, eventually must take care of them. The time between being young and older streams so rapidly through one's consciousness—as imperceptibly as the shifting sand of Shimizu's title—that it hardly registers; the complex relationship between the Man and the Older Man, rendered on stage in the single present instant of the play, may well be one of time. Is the Older Man really the Man at a different point on life's continuum? Is the one claiming to be the mother really the Man's wife in a different temporal phase of her existence? Perhaps the changes wrought by time's advance are so wrenching that we are all, in the Older Man's words, merely "passing strangers" with ourselves. Identity, Shimizu might be saying, whether personal or national, is neither static nor discernible in static sources but continually evolving. Attempts, therefore, to establish one's identity as unchanging are, in the parlance of this play, "fake." Shimizu's characters here will continue to seek theirs out. Lacking a set of clearly defined relationships—in a larger sense, a home or homeland—to return to, their quest is at best inauspicious, at worst futile.

The Dressing Room

That is also the fate of the characters in Shimizu's other play here, *The Dressing Room* (Gakuya), first performed at the renowned Jean-Jean Theater in Shibuya in July 1977 as the second production by Shimizu's troupe, Mokutōsha, and published the following month in *Shingeki* magazine. Undergirded by a series of ironies, this intriguing play embodies Shimizu's notions of the effect on the quest for identity of the advance of time, remembering the past, and the difficulty of returning to one's homeland or even of recognizing it.

The four characters, Actresses A, B, C, and D, generally behave in the dressing room as one might expect. They apply makeup, rehearse lines, and talk about their lives in the theater, about roles desired but never attained. An existential overlay is quickly apparent as it becomes clear that Actresses A and B are ghosts observing Actresses C and D, who are alive. Moreover, Actress C is rehearsing the role of Nina in

Chekhov's *The Sea Gull,* a character who aspires to the stage with scant chance of success. Actress D, who had been C's prompter until she took ill, comes on stage clutching a pillow from her sickbed and demands to exchange it with Actress C for the role of Nina. The paltry, soiled pillow is emblematic of her painfully ineffectual attempt to obtain her desired role, underscored as Shimizu juxtaposes Actress D's situation with Nina's, whose own hapless aspirations are emblematized in the slain sea gull. Enraged by Actress D's insistence, C brings a bottle down on her head, effectively moving her into the realm of Actresses A and B.

Shimizu's approach is, in certain ways, reminiscent of the classical Japanese *nō* theater. The main character in a *nō* play, the *shite* (doer), is always a ghost who renders a moment of intense agony, passion, or pathos from a famous event. Most *nō* plays open with the subordinate character, the *waki* (onlooker), in the role of a priest traveling to a historic temple or battle site. The *waki* encounters the *shite,* a nondescript ghost, who hints at his or her identity and promptly disappears. Then, while offering a prayer for the repose of this departed being's soul, the *waki* dozes off and dreams. The second of the play's two parts concretizes the dream and is in effect a play within a play: the *shite* returns magnificently clothed to reenact the fateful moment from the past.

Shimizu's characters in *The Dressing Room* call immediately to mind the roles of *shite* and *waki,* and he employs the play-within-a-play structure. Moreover, he seeks to render palpable, as in *nō,* a deep-seated passion that informs the play throughout. By no means, however, does Shimizu adhere in every particular to a traditional *nō* structure; the differences forge the telling impact of his play. For example, he does not conclude with the play within a play but uses it from the beginning until toward the end, when Actress C makes her final exit. Actresses A and B, the *waki* figures, are not alive but ghosts, and Actress C, the *shite* figure, is not a ghost but alive. Actress D, while she is alive, is a kind of shadow *waki,* manifesting the eternal aspirations of all four actresses for substantial, *shite*-like roles—they would be great doers rather than mere onlookers, leading players rather than lowly prompters. Indeed, after she dies, Actress D joins A and B, *waki* figures all, in a thoroughly inauspicious effort to become *shite* as the female leads Masha, Olga, and Irina in Chekhov's *The Three Sisters.*

Although *nō* plays often end in a similarly bleak atmosphere, the context and consummate artistry of what is happening on stage can subsume the bleakness in a sense of spiritual fullness. The *waki*'s crystallized dream entices the spectator into a self-enclosed, eternally present moment that gains vitality as it probes the multiple synapses of an intensely felt passion culled from the memory of days gone by. The effect is kairotic and transporting. It is a moment ostensibly from a simpler time in Japanese history, replete with the familiar, comforting verities of one's true homeland.

That is not the case with Shimizu's plays. His characters reflect his fundamental notion that their erstwhile homeland, where they yearn to shut out life's clutter and know who they really are, has, with the passage of time, been irretrievably altered. What they find is a place that only vaguely resembles the homeland they remember so fondly. The people they encounter there only vaguely resemble the people they once knew so intimately. Ōzasa penetrates this aspect of Shimizu's worldview: "Then where is the hometown one should return to? Nowhere. It has become frighteningly ambiguous."[4] Shimizu's plays often end with his characters perplexed by this ambiguity, overwhelmed by frustration; he allows hardly a glimpse of spiritual fullness as in some mythical homeland.

The dressing room is an ambiguous, symbolic homeland for Shimizu's actresses. Actress C's attitude toward her mirror-laden dressing room yields, ironically, a clear reflection of the ambiguity. She rails against her surroundings, in part because of her inability to recognize the past, represented by the ghosts, Actresses A and B. Glaring at the space they occupy, Actress C sums up her frustration: "Rotten, foul air always hovers around here." Actress D, when she was alive, had perceived the past, but only vaguely, in the dressing room. "It was never clear," she explains to Actresses A and B after becoming a ghost, "but I always felt your existence. . . . I always heard voices . . . silent voices." Shimizu thus sees the dressing room as a place where the past is itself a kind of prompter, moving the actresses to some sort of action that is calculated, in their minds, to enhance their stage careers. But Actress C's action is a frenetic attempt merely to swap one inadequate dressing room for another. "That's it!" she cries in frustration. "I will demand a different dressing room tomorrow." And Actresses A, B, and D, themselves stage prompters, seem resigned to using the dressing-room only for random rehearsals, leading nowhere. This dressing-room homeland, Shimizu suggests, yields an aura at once insecure and unfamiliar.

Here is the crux of Shimizu's play. No matter how hard these actresses try to realize the dressing room's alluring promise—an eternal moment of stardom on the stage—it remains elusive. The frustration created by this dilemma constitutes a leitmotiv shaping the play. For example, Actress C reflects her own unsettled mind in reciting over and over Nina's unconvincing lines: "I am a sea gull. . . . No, that's not right. I'm an actress. Ah, well. . . ." No longer young, Actress C manifests her frustration further as she struggles to explain herself to the youthful Actress D by referring willy-nilly to the ephemerality of youth, which is the antithesis of the eternal moment of stardom; confused by her own reasoning, she hurriedly suggests that what is more important than youth is the "accumulation" of various experiences necessary to realize the rarefied glitter of success. A metaphor for her past, the "rotten, foul air" that Actress C perceives as hovering in the dressing room is one kind of accumulation. Actress D alludes to another after she has become a ghost when she approaches Actresses A and B about their activities in the dressing room: "You just sit here doing your makeup night after night for nothing. You wait here for your turn forever . . . for the opportunity that will never come. Am I right?" Late in the play, when Actresses A, B, and D compulsively decide to take on the central roles of Chekhov's *The Three Sisters*, Actress B poignantly limns their common frustration by raising a toast "to our eternal rehearsal."

The contrast with *nō* is stark. Instead of crystallizing on the stage an eternal moment, whole and unchanging, Shimizu's actresses can only string out a chronology of moments, fragmented and finite, drawn from their stockpile of "accumulations." As Actress B says, initiating Actress D to the dressing room's netherworldly dimension: "You know, we are not just wasting our time waiting. We keep trying, really. We recollect our past accumulations." But instead of rendering a past that indeed has happened, as in *nō*, Shimizu's actresses rehearse a future that will not. Instead of experiencing the infinite, comforting sense of fullness engendered by a re-created, timeless homeland, they are rooted only in their amorphous accumulations, at odds with their past, bereft of a secure, familiar homeland.

Actress C sharply punctuates their shared predicament in two ways. First, just before her final exit, she cites another of Nina's lines, a passage from Turgenev: "Happy the man who on such a night has a roof over his head, who has a warm corner of his own." This utterance harks ironically back to Actress C's dissatisfaction with her dressing room and her impulsive desire to give it up for another one; happiness will elude her in the measure that warm-cornered, sweet-smelling homelands are in extremely short supply.

Second, when Actress C, the *shite* figure, leaves the stage, nearly a quarter of the play remains. In *nō*, just as the role of *waki* needs the larger one of *shite* to realize the full force of the drama, so the play within a play cannot stand alone but requires the main play's larger context in order to work its intended effect. Indeed, when the *shite* leaves the stage, the *nō* play is over. But instead of ending Shimizu's play, Actress C's departure leaves a vacuum that Actresses A, B, and D, mere *waki* figures, seek to fill in the desperate belief that they can assume *shite*-like proportions with the roles of Masha, Olga, and Irina. This plot twist creates a stirring irony in that, while Shimizu's three actresses are already dead, Chekhov's three sisters, alive but steeped in the ennui of an ossified aristocratic life, might as well be. Yet, although the *shite* in *nō* is a ghost who re-creates an elevated moment of great pathos, the actresses, also ghosts, seem capable in their re-creations only of moments characterized by unremitting bathos. We are no more confident of Shimizu's three actresses seizing success in major roles than we are of Chekhov's three sisters sustaining happiness by working for their livelihood.

The dressing room, the actresses' homeland, can be seen, therefore, as a place of betrayal. Obsessed with their makeup, the actresses prepare for the roles that have always eluded them; recollecting their accumulations, they perceive the past only vaguely. Thus prompted, they attempt in vain to realize the dressing room's hoary promise of stardom. The irony comes full circle in that Actresses A, B, and D do not become stars in major roles but remain merely prompters. They are themselves the past that they recollect. They are themselves one more accumulation. They embody precisely the kind of insecure, unfamiliar, vaguely articulated homeland to which they belong.

This is Shimizu's view of the quest for identity. His actresses stand hardly a better chance of success than the amnesiac coal miners in *Those Days* or the contentious, confused family members in *The Sand of Youth*. Their respective plights fuel the conclusion, in Shimizu's idiom, that at best they are all caught up in an "eternal rehearsal," not of the certain past, but of a vague future that will never come.

Notes

1. For more information on Shimizu's life and work, see *Shimizu Kunio no sekai* (The world of Shimizu Kunio) (Tokyo: Hakusuisha, 1982); and Robert Rolf, "Out of the Sixties, Shimizu Kunio and Betsuyaku Minoru," *Journal of the Yokohama National University* 35, no. 2 (1988): 77–114.

2. Satō Tadao, "Watashi wa dare deshō?" (Who am I?), *Shingeki* (July 1970): 18.

3. Ōzasa Yoshio, *Dōjidai engeki to gekisakkatachi* (Contemporary plays and playwrights) (Tokyo: Geki shobō, 1980), 197.

4. Ibid., 199.

Shimizu Kunio's language, humor, and theater sense make him one of Japan's most accomplished playwrights. (Courtesy Shimizu Kunio.)

Little Brother!—A Message to Sakamoto Ryōma from Otome, His Older Sister (1990). To deny the death of imperialist samurai Ryōma (1835–1867), characters create a surrogate, who also dies. Mokutōsha, 1990 (Courtesy Shimizu Kunio.

Dreams Departed, Orpheus explores myth making. To his older sister's *(right)* dismay, a teacher *(left)* claims to meet prewar nationalist Kita Ikki (1883–1937), two years after his death. Mokutōsha, 1988. (Courtesy Shimizu Kunio.)

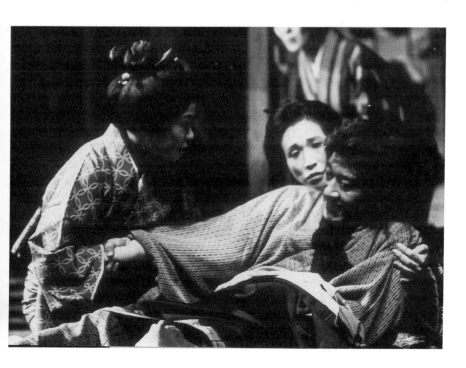

Tango at the End of Winter (Tango, fuyu no owari-ni), set in a small town on the Sea of Japan, explores loss and decay. A 1986 production by Ninagawa Yukio, who directed an English-language version in London in 1991. (Courtesy Shimizu Kunio.)

For Some Reason Youth (Nazeka seishun jidai; 1987) conjures up the 1960s. Shimizu's plays under Ninagawa's direction often feature stages crowded with actors. (Courtesy Shimizu Kunio.)

The Sand of Youth, How Quickly

Shimizu Kunio

TRANSLATED BY ROBERT T. ROLF

CAST OF CHARACTERS

MAN

OLDER MAN

DOCTOR

WOMAN WHO CLAIMS TO BE THE WIFE

WOMAN WHO CLAIMS TO BE THE MOTHER

(Both women also play schoolgirls)

(Piano music suddenly flows into the darkness. Two women in high school uni-forms float into view like a wind rising. It has the feel of the corner of a schoolyard in the memory of a day somewhere faraway.

One of them picks flowers; her face is already that of an old woman. The other holds a book of poetry [by Aragon]; she, too, is a woman past her prime. The high school girl with the poetry begins to read.)

> How quickly it has slipped through my fingers
>> The sand of youth
> I am like a person who has only danced,
>> Startled by the dawn
> I've squandered, I don't know how,
>> The season of my strength
> Life is here that finds another lover
>> And divorces me.[1]

(The two women fade out; the piano music continues.

The piano music is abruptly rent by shouts, sounds of two men grappling, screams, resounding and overwhelming everything before receding.

The stage brightens.

[Several characters will appear, and the stage is set up so that each is receiving "interrogation" in his respective separate room. The WOMAN WHO CLAIMS TO BE THE WIFE *and the* WOMAN WHO CLAIMS TO BE THE MOTHER *are in the*

127

*same room. If at all possible, the feeling of separate rooms should be produced
without partitioning the stage space.*]

 The MAN *is on a chair.*)

MAN: What do you want me to say? I don't want to talk. Give me a cigarette, will you?

(*The* OLDER MAN *is on a chair.*)

OLDER MAN: Yes, sir . . . I'm really sorry to cause so much trouble.
Actually, the injury's not serious; can't you just forget it?

MAN: (*Laughs.*) He said that? Well, that should do it, shouldn't it? He's
the one who's hurt, so let's forget it, like he says.

OLDER MAN: You must be joking. Why should I protect him? Our relationship's not that intimate. We're more or less passing strangers.
. . . (*Anxiously.*) Has he said something? . . .

MAN: Hey, look, like I said, would he cover for me? He just wants to get
rid of me fast; it's that simple. Hey, tell that guy something: I don't
even want to see his face!

OLDER MAN: Water, a glass of water. . . . Thanks. . . . Who does he
think he is, doesn't want to see my face. He's the one who hurt me
like this. Tell him something for me. Let me think a minute. All
right, tell him, tell him to get lost! Drop dead! I hope he gets run over
by a car!

MAN: Cut it out! I'm fed up with this. . . . You people know I'm sick.
What can I tell you? . . . Ask him. He practically forced me to run
away from the hospital, so ask him.

OLDER MAN: Now let me make myself clear. I didn't make him leave the
hospital; he begged me to get him out. Why should I? . . . As I told
you before, I'm a passing stranger. . . .

MAN: I've got nothing to say. . . . Give me a cigarette.

OLDER MAN: I will not. There is no reason I should be the one to talk.
Uh, I wonder if I could have another glass of water? Yes, sir. . . .

(*The* DOCTOR *enters.*)

DOCTOR: Sorry to be late. I've heard most of the story. You have my
sympathy; our hospital's already been put to it, too, by that pair.
Say, can I borrow your phone later? It's urgent. Here's the gist of
what happened. It was about two months ago, yes, late December.
The older man came to our hospital. He said he was an agricultural
equipment salesman; he had a younger man with him, the rude one.
He said they'd become acquainted on a train and the young man was
behaving strangely. He said he didn't appear insane, but didn't seem
to know his own name, his age, where he'd come from, or where he
was headed. He thought the young man might have amnesia. . . .

 I took charge of examining him because I just happened to be the
one free in the psychiatrics department. I'll spare you the technical

medical detail, but after various tests my diagnosis was retrograde amnesia, in short, loss of memory. There were no external injuries to the head or elsewhere. It can be considered psychogenically induced, that is, a loss of memory due to some psychological shock. At any rate, I contacted the local police. His story most probably reached the newspaper through the police. It was a small article, but he did get in the news. A few days later we were contacted by a woman who said he appeared to be her husband.

(*The* WOMAN WHO CLAIMS TO BE THE WIFE *and the* WOMAN WHO CLAIMS TO BE THE MOTHER *enter. They are the two schoolgirls of the opening. Of course they are not wearing the schoolgirl middy blouses.*)

WIFE: Yes, that's right, I'm his wife, Nagasaki Harue. He's Nagasaki Shūichi. But at this point who cares? Calling me down to a place like this after all this time—just a nuisance, right? I mean, you people'll make up some excuse and take him away from me in the end anyway, won't you? If you *are* going to give him back to me, why not hurry up and do it? . . . I'm sorry. My attitude is unforgivable. . . . Do you have an ashtray? Ah, there's one. Thank you. . . . You asked me about the newspaper, didn't you? I don't read the papers much, because of my job, you know. If I were the accountant at the average company, I'd work from nine to five and be done. But not at our place; the S. P. Chain's got five cabarets alone. I total up all the receipts, the whole thing by myself. They close at 11:30 at night . . . then we gather the sales slips from the various locations and. . . . Well, none of that matters. Anyway, I read two or three days' news-papers at one sitting. So I happened to see his picture in the paper. He'd been gone three months, and the picture wasn't too clear. But we'd been living together for five years; I recognized him right away. "Estimated age, twenty-six or twenty-seven," that fit him perfectly, too. So I talked it over with my mother here, and we caught the train up at once.

DOCTOR: To tell the truth, I was relieved to hear his family had turned up because it was my first amnesia case. And the director had been grumbling about my keeping an uninsured patient in the hospital; I let her see the young man immediately.

She took one look at him and, well, uh, she clung to him and screamed, "Darling!" They struck me as really husband and wife, but not because of the way she held on to him . . . I just knew. Her mother stood there speechless, half in a daze. . . . But he . . . it's natural when you think about it, he broke loose from the woman and fled to a corner of the room, as if he were afraid suddenly. It's embarrassing, but for a minute I didn't know how to deal with it.

WIFE: I've got nothing against that doctor. He did seem a trifle unreliable, and it was unpleasant that he rather disapproved of my being the older. But I thought that couldn't be helped, either. I'm five years older than my husband; I've gotten those looks enough before, haven't I, Mother? . . .

(*The* WOMAN WHO CLAIMS TO BE THE MOTHER *is slowly and meticulously eating her cold box lunch.*)

WIFE: I'm sorry. You've probably been thinking her odd. My mother can hear, but she can't speak. Otherwise, she's perfectly healthy— just look at her appetite. . . .

(*The* WOMAN WHO CLAIMS TO BE THE MOTHER *gives her a ferocious kick; hereafter, she will let fly these kicks from time to time.*)

WIFE: Sorry, Mother. . . . What made me furious was not the doctor but the man who brought my husband in, that "salesman." He jumped in between us and started screaming that it was absurd not to check whether we were really relatives. What need would I have to come down here claiming to be the wife of a man I didn't know and even bring my mother along? If he were rich it'd be different. But he's a sick man without a cent.

OLDER MAN: So she's finally turned up? She's a slicker talker than she looks; don't let her fool you. No, I'm not saying that she's definitely a fake, but . . . well, I don't have to keep quiet just because she's here. . . .

I became acquainted with the man roughly as you heard, but not exactly. For one thing, take that business that has her furious with me. I wasn't that outspoken. To begin with, I was practically relieved when she showed up. I'm a salesman. I travel all over getting orders. I couldn't afford to get stuck in a place like this; I thought at least now I'll get out of this. Really! . . . But he began to get frightened the moment he saw her. You say she says he ran to a corner of the room, but he hid behind me. He held on to my arms from behind. He was shaking. Pathetic, isn't it? He'd only known me a few days, and he was depending on me. . . . I stood there like a wall between her and the guy. She was all excited and trying to hold on to him. All I did was stand there quietly like this. Don't you see? This is the important thing. I had no desire whatsoever to meddle in their affairs. Please remember that point clearly.

MAN: Looks like they finally believe I'm sick. It took them long enough. But then how can I answer your questions? I still can't believe any of this; that's right, none of it. . . . And the same goes for that woman. Even if you brought her here right now, the result'd probably be the same. It wouldn't change a thing. No matter how much I want to believe it, I can't. . . . You people don't know what it's like. . . . Everything's a blank . . . nothing fits. Who wouldn't get scared and run away when people suddenly show up claiming they're your family? Am I wrong? . . . I don't remember exactly what happened that time, just that the woman was real excited and kept pleading with me about something. . . . But I couldn't understand her. What got to me more was that woman who claims to be her mother, standing next to her, not saying a thing, her big eyes wide open. For some reason the old hag just stared at me without a word . . . In the meantime, I didn't react at all to the younger woman, which really burned her up. She started talking wild. She said I was lying and tricking her; that I didn't have amnesia, I was faking to try to get away from her. She got me mad, too. . . . What do you think? The woman's crazy, isn't she? . . .

WIFE: Yes, I said those things; I was so upset. What's wrong with that? Put yourself in my place. Just three months. A mere three-month blank—does that wipe out five years of living together? How could I suddenly accept that? I believed the doctor at first. That's why I was crying and begging. I was frantic. I wanted my husband to recall something of our life, absolutely anything. . . . But he didn't look at me; he just watched my mother. I could take his showing no reaction whatsoever, but why keep looking at her? What for? Why would he stare at my mother like he was afraid of her?

(The MOTHER kicks, to calm the WIFE down. But for some reason she also assumes a triumphant air.)

OLDER MAN: (Laughing.) I see. So she's brought up that sort of thing. Well, as a third party who was there, I can state clearly that when she began to scream, I found it odd. The doctor diagnosed amnesia, but she suddenly starts shouting that it was fake and she was being tricked. And that's not all. She ran on about their family affairs: how he'd left them because he couldn't get along with her mother; that he should've told her because she'd've left her mother if he wanted. She said she could earn enough to support her mother, and he could go on writing his songs like he wanted. . . . I must admit it was a rather believable story. But him a songwriter? Look for yourself: the fellow's sunburned and has rough hands like a laborer. . . . And I'll tell you, that's not all that made me suspicious. I mean, it was the way she talked. All the while she was calling his amnesia a fake she was skillfully telling him about herself and selling him on what a good position he'd be in living with her. And why was she so impatient to settle the matter? For a reasonable person, this sort of thing should take time. Wouldn't she realize he needs time? That's when the wild idea began to hit me. . . . The woman might be a fake. Even her "mother"—it was suspicious that she couldn't speak. She might've hired her and made her a mute so that she wouldn't say something she shouldn't. So I suggested to the doctor that things should be handled more cautiously. . . .

WIFE: Hey, see, now he's changed his story. All that about not saying a word and standing between us like a wall is a big lie. That should be enough to tell you what he is. And all that stuff about getting suspicious after a while is nonsense. He had his mind made up from the start that I was an impostor. Then, of all things, he even suspects my mother. Hey, Mother, be angry! Get mad! Oh, she burns me up just sitting there eating. . . . *(She quickly dodges a kick.)* Anyway, I'm the one who wanted time, who said to give things time. Please understand, I'm the one who said that first.

DOCTOR: Hm, wait a minute. It's hard to say who said it first now. . . . *(He is worried about the time and looks alternately at his wristwatch and his pocket watch.)* No, she didn't. I remember: *I* did. I couldn't just stand there. I said give me time. . . . You see, they'd placed me in a curious position, like a judge. With a day or two's time, we could get some objective evidence. For example . . . if she were his wife, we could even have her go get a photograph of them together or a certified copy of their family register. . . . That's why I explained to them that I wanted time. Yes, that's exactly what happened.

MAN: *(With a forced laugh.)* Who cares what happened? . . . I don't. . . . Dig up all that stuff you want, it's got nothing to do with me. Leave me alone! Leave me alone!

(His voice echoes. Signs of night steal onto the stage. The DOCTOR *is on the telephone.)*

DOCTOR: . . . Hello, Sensei.[2] Thanks for your help the other day; I thought you might be home already. . . . No, it's about my daughter again. . . . That's right, she still wants to use her left hand first on the piano. . . . I know, lots of children tend to break up the chords and play them arpeggio to some extent. But . . . but *Sensei*, no matter how many times I tell her, it doesn't help; she still hits the keys with her left hand a little ahead of her right. I almost want to jab that left hand of hers with an awl. What? An awl. A-W-L. . . . Of course I'd never do anything like that but, but, if we don't correct it soon, it'll be beyond fixing. . . . No, I'm not at home now. I'm, well, kind of working now. . . . What? Well, later at my house? I'll be waiting. Thank you. *(Hangs up.)*

(The WOMAN WHO CLAIMS TO BE THE WIFE *drinks tea from the pot of the* WOMAN WHO CLAIMS TO BE THE MOTHER.)

WIFE: It's pretty cold for this time of year. . . . Or maybe it's cold even in the summer in a place like this.

(The WOMAN WHO CLAIMS TO BE THE MOTHER *starts a new meal.)*

WIFE: *(Matter-of-factly.)* But, you know, if you stop and think a minute, it might all be a trap laid by that salesman. Really. And our having to stay in the hospital that night—he arranged that neatly, too. There's no other way to look at it. Because everything's gone his way.

OLDER MAN: Has she started again? I'm amazed. How've things gone my way? I mean, believe me, that night the woman completely changed her strategy. When she saw that words wouldn't work, she resorted to direct action—she turned physical. Making the most of her feminine weapons. . . . *(Laughs.)* I couldn't bear to watch her. Is that the attitude a wife'd take? She acted like she was sex crazy. . . .

WIFE: Let me see him. Let me see that man this minute. How dare he talk like that. I work in a cabaret, but I'm the accountant. He takes things that way because he's been against me from the beginning. Mother, say something. You saw—was I acting sex crazy? . . . How awful. And I tried so hard. All that talk about proof. . . . I can see now that I should've at least brought along a photo, but who would think of such a thing at a time like that? What woman would think she needed proof to see her own husband? I was too preoccupied. All I could think of that night was whether he'd remember. That if he didn't, everything would be ruined forever, so . . . I knew it was brazen of me. But I was beside myself! . . . Then that man, pretending to be so honest, put poison in my husband's head. That's right, awful poison. . . .

OLDER MAN: She's gotten even more dramatic. Poison? Was that "poison," I wonder? And I didn't put any ideas into his head. She's lying. Her making up to him was simply awful, and I told her so. I told her no matter how much she acted as if she wanted me out of the room . . . it just wouldn't work. She and I were like stones to him; he takes his first few faltering steps, and we're the first things he stumbles on. In that sense, we were the same to him. He doesn't know who's telling the truth and who's lying. . . . I mean, from his point of view, even I might be a relative of his. . . . Well, if that's too extreme, maybe at least a friend or a man who knows his past. Something, some compelling circumstance, might be making me act like a passing stranger. It's a possibility, you must admit.

(A steam whistle. The sound of a train. The light closes in on just the MAN.)

MAN: That's right. It was on a train. I met him on a train. . . . But I don't remember clearly. . . . He was sitting cater-corner in front of me. . . . I remember, he was eating an apple. . . . He seemed to be enjoying it. . . . Then I realized I was eating an apple, too. . . . I don't know why. It's funny. I got embarrassed. . . . Then he might've gotten embarrassed, too. He sort of smiled. . . . For a while after that we munched our apples without saying anything. . . . Then suddenly I . . . realized I didn't know him. . . . We were both eating apples, so I'd been completely assuming we were together, but we weren't. . . . I was confused all of a sudden, and real quick threw away my apple. . . . When he saw that, the guy spoke for the first time . . . to ask what was wrong. . . . I kept quiet. . . . Pretty soon he asked me another question. . . . Where I was headed. . . . That's when. That's when I knew for sure the guy was a complete stranger. . . .

(The sound of a train dying away in the distance. The lights go up.)

OLDER MAN: Oh, no, even you people're taking it that way. . . . I was being sarcastic. I lost my temper, so I was being sarcastic. Put yourself in his place, and everyone's suspect; it's possible even I am a relative or acquaintance. . . . That's all I meant.

WIFE: That's the poison I'm talking about. See? He says that anyone's suspect, which makes sense, but what he's really doing is denying me and cleverly selling himself. It's not what he says but the nuance. He didn't look at me while he said these things; he kept his eyes riveted meaningfully on my husband's. . . . I used to have a girlfriend who attracted men the same way. He's exactly like her—in essence the man's a woman.

OLDER MAN: Idiotic delusions. Beneath comment. As I stood there an uneasy feeling came over me when I realized how fragile and thin the ties are between one person and another. I merely put that another way. I spoke only out of total sympathy for the man.

WIFE: Oh, really? That's sympathy? If he really does sympathize with him, why turn around and say things to agitate him? I mean, you people must find it odd, too. In fact, I couldn't bear to watch him he was so agitated. He shouted at us, like some beast shrieking, Get out you two! *Please* leave me alone!

DOCTOR: Yes, of course I was there. I told them both to leave the room because any further stimulation would have an adverse effect on the patient. But when I did, the patient underwent a sudden transformation and began to plead: "Wait! No one leave! Don't leave me alone!" Well, I'd guess you'd call it total confusion. Unlike before, the patient began to exhibit an extremely manic condition. *(Looking at his watch.)* What's the time now?

MAN: *(In apparent irritation.)* Manic condition? Where does he get that stuff? Just what did that doctor do for me? Gave me a shot or two of some vitamins everyday, that's all. . . . And that other guy, coming out with that wierd stuff all of a sudden. . . . "If you put yourself in his place, everyone's suspect." . . . I see what he means, but he's got it all wrong. He doesn't understand anything. . . . I wanted to believe. I wanted to believe anyone who came along. Otherwise, I wouldn't know what to do. I'm not changing my story. I really did want to believe, but I couldn't seem to, not entirely. But. . . . But I still wanted to believe someone. That's why . . . I called to those two to stop. . . .

WIFE: *(Turns around with a start.)* Could that be true? Did he really say that? . . . If he did, it's ridiculous.

OLDER MAN: Yes, it certainly is ridiculous. Because that woman has misunderstood everything.

WIFE: That's right. I misunderstood. I misunderstood everything. But all because I was taken in by that slick-talking salesman!

OLDER MAN: That's accusing me falsely. You people must realize that from what you've heard so far. She simply took it into her head that he was agitated. Specifically, she was convinced that he'd begun to doubt her. . . .

WIFE: No, that's not true. That's not true. He's the one my husband began to doubt—him, not me. And that was very convenient for him, too. Look, it's common psychology. Rather than believe the person who says he's the real one, people start believing the person who claims not to be. . . . My husband fell very neatly into that psychology. I'm insisting I'm his wife; the salesman's doing his best to convince him he's a passing stranger. If it were you, which would you choose? He wants to believe someone, but both seem suspicious. Who would you believe at a time like that? The answer's clear. That's right, just as you thought, he chose him over me.

OLDER MAN: *(A little perturbed.)* To say he chose me is exaggerating things but . . . it's like the woman says . . . a surprising change did occur in the man. . . . That is, uh. . . . Truthfully, I was completely confused. His doubts caught me totally by surprise. . . . Wasn't I lying? . . . I was too nice to him to be a passing stranger he happened to meet on a train. . . . Wasn't *I* the one deceiving him? Mightn't I be a person who has a deep relationship with him? . . .

WIFE: How shameless. Saying he was caught by surprise when everything went according to the scenario he devised. The poison's started to work. The poison he implanted has clearly started to work. . . . "Put yourself in his place, and everyone's suspect." "Which means there's a possibility even I'm his relative or friend." That's exactly what he said. You heard him. That's what he said exactly.

OLDER MAN: I definitely did say that. But as I might be repeating endlessly, I had not the slightest intention of putting ideas like that into his head. Please believe at least that. And I can't imagine even him being carried away merely by what I said. I don't know how or why such a change occurred, but he suddenly said my face looked familiar. Somehow my face looked familiar. . . . Would he talk that way just carried away by what I said? Or was it all a big lie of his? . . .

DOCTOR: A word about that. . . . As I explained to everyone at the time, on no account was the young man lying. But then neither did any change occur partially restoring his memory. He was indeed influenced by what the salesman said. It acted as a stimulus, and the young man's desire to believe someone manifested itself as the fictitious recollection that the older man seemed familiar. It's a common phenomenon.

MAN: He doesn't understand. Doesn't understand anything. That doctor must think he got a look at my feelings with his gastroscope. . . . The fellow's face really did start to look familiar. No, to be exact, not just his face but the way he talked, his stooped shoulders, that messed-up hair full of dandruff, his chewing his fingernails like a kid though he must be over thirty. . . . I know that man from somewhere. Maybe the train, but I think not. It was before that. Somewhere before that. . . . We're not just passing strangers. Before, somewhere, we . . . lived together. . . .

WIFE: *(Sneering.)* He's mistaken. He's got things confused with some old movie he saw. How could they've been living together? He was living with me all the time. With me all the time. . . .

OLDER MAN: Of course I denied it. I've no reason to deceive him. Think about it calmly, and it's obvious. For instance, suppose I was his acquaintance. Or even that we did live together. For what possible reason would I bring him to a hospital, claiming we were passing strangers? Well, for what?

MAN: To get rid of me. That's for what.

OLDER MAN: That's crazy!

WIFE: *(Excited.)* Yes, it really is crazy! Who got rid of who? Listen, everybody! The one that was gotten rid of was me!

MAN: . . . That's what she was shouting then all right. But it's not true. I was positive. The one they were trying to get rid of was me. . . . That's why I was begging him. . . . Please don't leave me. . . . Please. . . .

(An ambulance siren drawing near, then receding. The WOMAN WHO CLAIMS TO BE THE MOTHER *has fallen asleep. The* WOMAN WHO CLAIMS TO BE THE WIFE *kicks her lightly. The* WOMAN WHO CLAIMS TO BE THE MOTHER *opens her eyes and indignantly returns the kick.)*

WIFE: . . . The salesman's finally got what he wanted. . . . He's got my husband completely in his clutches. He's snatched my husband away from me. . . .

OLDER MAN: Snatched him away? What for? She said as much herself. He's a penniless amnesiac. What would I gain? What reason would I have to steal him?

WIFE: How would I know? . . . But I can imagine. . . . I think all of you can, too. Look at that salesman. . . . Messed-up hair, worn-out suit, beat-up briefcase full of catalogs for farm equipment or something. . . . He can't have a wife and kids looking like that. . . . He wanted a buddy. It's like some famous man said—"Solitude is a wonderful thing, but having someone to tell that to is the far greater joy." That was it. He had too much solitude. He wanted a buddy. He wanted a buddy to talk about his wonderful solitude with. . . . And a man who'd loot his memory would be perfect. . . .

OLDER MAN: I appreciate your sympathy. . . . Tell her that, and thank her, too. And tell her one more thing, that everything she said applies to her, too. I imagine she's about my age. The accountant at a cabaret. . . . I don't mean to say anything about her job, but assuming she's single . . . it must be a lonely life. Sleeping in the daytime and starting on the receipts at 11:30 at night. . . . Living like that, no wonder she hit on a bold plan. A man who's lost his memory is, in a sense, like a clean slate. . . . She's not pressed for money. And for a woman beyond the marriageable age the guy was a bit of a catch. But she's a bad actress. She didn't think her plan through. That mute mother was a laugh. . . . That's why he turned to me. He wanted to trust one of the two people he saw before him; either would do. . . . He couldn't help but choose me. . . .

DOCTOR: I am not a judge! How are you saying I should've handled it at a time like that? What do you think a mere psychiatrist can do? . . . I told the patient, Don't trust people so easily. I know you want to believe, but it's merely a wish on your part. . . . I told him over and over.

MAN: It's no wish. . . . I wanted to believe someone. I couldn't stand it otherwise. . . . I was afraid.

DOCTOR: Shut up! Pig! So what if he was afraid! What does he mean afraid! Does he think I'll stand for that talk! Die! *(He smashes a chair to pieces.)*

OLDER MAN: That man is really a doctor? It's beyond me. He's too arbitrary, far too naive. He says don't believe people, doubt, and all the while he himself completely forgets to doubt. . . . Me. I'm talking about me. Why doesn't he consider doubting me? All of you seem puzzled, too. . . . Listen, I've denied being his acquaintance all along. But where's the proof that I'm not lying? The man's intuition may have been right. He and I were acquainted. But he got in the way, and I got rid of him. . . . That might be the real truth.

MAN: Stop it! Let me sleep!

(Later that night. The DOCTOR makes a telephone call.)

DOCTOR: Hello, it's me. Sorry to bother you again. . . . *(Turning around.)* I know. I'll be done in a minute. *(Returning to the phone.)* Sen-

sei, uh, what I said before, that I wanted to stab the child's left hand with an awl; it's about that. . . . Actually, actually I already stabbed her. Yes, three, four, five, six times. . . . *(Moans.)* I'll call you again later. *(Hangs up; turns around.)* Let's see. We were talking about what the two did after that. That night, about dawn I believe, the two men made a brilliant escape and went into hiding. Of course I don't know anything of what happened after that; I've been busy. I guess I should've treated him properly and thoroughly when I had the chance. . . .

WIFE: The same goes for me, too. I've no idea what happened to them after that. I'm a woman who was thrown away like a rag. From that day on I've tried desperately to forget. I've had enough of men. . . . I'll live my life in quiet with this mute mother of mine. . . .

(The sound of a train . . . street noises . . . then the sound of a train again.)

OLDER MAN: We caught a train. I wish you'd stop exaggerating and saying we escaped. I just went back again to my job as a salesman traveling around the provinces. Of course I didn't resist his coming along. . . . We traveled mainly in the warmer areas in the west. . . .

MAN: Everything was fresh and new. . . . It's natural, but wherever I went was unfamiliar territory. . . . We often drank milk at stands in stations, lining up five or six bottles and emptying them one after another. At times like that he was like a kid playing and shouting. . . .

OLDER MAN: He was the one acting like a kid. Always shadowboxing and, well, that sort of thing doesn't matter. . . . Hm, it wasn't a bad trip. . . .

MAN: True. . . . All in all, it wasn't a bad trip. . . .

OLDER MAN: Of course we didn't run into anything especially worth talking about. Things you usually see when you travel. . . . Yes. A festival. A big sale in a shopping center. Schoolgirls on an outing. The sea in winter. A fire on a ship in the harbor. . . .

MAN: And . . . the opening ceremony for a new bridge. . . .

OLDER MAN: Ah, yes . . . the opening ceremony for a new bridge. . . .

(Lively music . . . loudspeaker announcements . . . a storm of applause . . . balloons dancing in the sky. Soon these fade out.)

OLDER MAN: Then we came to this town. My sales bring me here two or three times a year. . . . Traveling together over two months a kind of rule had quite naturally developed, that while I was working he would take a room and wait there. That became the custom. One day I finished work and returned to the inn, where he was supposed to be waiting. But he wasn't there. I was beside myself. You know he can't go about on his own. I looked all over town. I focused my search particularly on the vicinity of the station. But he wasn't there. . . . An hour later . . . I finally discovered him in the school-yard of a girls' school on the outskirts of town. In the dusky school-yard. He seemed to be listening to piano playing. It was coming from a music classroom, I guess.

(Intense piano music. The MAN *listens. The* DOCTOR, *too, gives a start and turns toward it.)*

OLDER MAN: I don't know how to describe my feelings when I found him. . . . I was relieved and, at the same time, determined never to lose my buddy again. Whatever happened I could not be without the guy. Then I blurted out things that even surprised me. "Listen. Don't ever leave me. If you do, I'll never forgive you. Now I can tell you, you and I were old friends after all. That's why we can travel together so smoothly like this. You must've known. You must've felt it. . . . I'll never lie to you again, so you have to trust me. . . ." But the moment he heard my confession, a sort of cold smile I'd never seen before played across his face. That's right. Such a cold smile that for a minute I seemed frozen. . . .

(During these lines, the DOCTOR *staggers off stroking his left hand.)*

MAN: Cut out the stupid questions. How would I know what kind of expression I had on my face? But . . . but I can tell you what I felt. . . . As soon as I heard his confession, I thought, this guy's a fake. He's no friend of mine. He really is just a passing stranger. . . . It was intuition. There's no better way to describe it. I felt it intui-tively. . . . He would've done better not to do any confessing. . . .

OLDER MAN: He can take it that way if he wants. But when I saw that cold smile of his, something else hit me. This isn't the smile of some-one who's lost his memory. He's a fake. It's like the woman said, he's pretending to have amnesia. He's the one who shouldn't've lowered his guard and smiled like that. . . .

MAN: *(Laughs.)* Really. In that case, I'm some actor. . . . But it's weird. After that the guy was suddenly timid and got tame as a kitten. Why was that? . . . Well? Why get so servile all of a sudden?

OLDER MAN: *(Perturbed.)* I didn't particularly become servile. . . . Things simply got a bit eerie. . . . *(Irritated.)* You people know how it is . . . with a person who is thinking and scheming no one knows what. . . . It's unnerving. . . . *(Looking around at his surroundings.)* This room's suffocating; why's the window so small? . . . I mean it. I really got a little scared. . . .

MAN: *(Triumphantly.)* Not me. After I found out the guy was a fake, I felt relieved. You see, he'd been really leading me on, dragging me around, but he wasn't the man he appeared to be. . . . He was the one who needed me. He couldn't stand being alone. . . . It was sud-denly absurd to me. Why do I have to slink along behind him doing

what he says. He ought to tag along behind me! He has got to play
up to me! He's *my* slave!
(The noise of the harbor resumes. During the following lines of the MAN, *the*
OLDER MAN *becomes bothered by the small space he is in, touching the walls and
pacing along them. A curious interplay between his actions and the content of the*
MAN*'s lines is desirable.)*

MAN: After that I started to walk around town everyday. Just as I
pleased. The harbor, the amusement park, the boulevard, back to
the harbor. . . . I destroyed that rule that I'd wait at the inn while he
worked. He gave up his selling and started following along behind
me just like a pet dog. . . . He was something to see. I want some ice
cream. I want a can of beer. . . . I had only to say it, and he was off
dashing around the port buying things. . . . *(Laughs.)* . . . Before
long I wanted to tease him more. . . . So one day I went to where all
those barges are in the harbor. . . . Dozens of barges are tied
together there, as you know. . . . I started hopping from barge to
barge. . . . It's kind of fun . . . skillful balance, limber jumping
ability, strong legs. . . . As I figured he would, he followed me. . . .
For a guy five or six years older than me it was rough work, waddling
along, chasing me like an overweight duck. . . . I picked up my
speed. He was sure to get his feet tangled any second. . . . But no,
the spoilsport, he followed desperately, teeth clenched, face con-
torted. . . . I suddenly got mad. What an ass. Worn-out, middle-
aged, but shit, what horsepower. . . . I stopped and faced him; he
was frantically trying to cross over to me. . . . Then he seemed to
misjudge something. His face was pale. He began to smile. And
. . . he stretched his hand out to me like he wanted me to baby him.
. . . I tenderly reached out my hand. Just when he was suspended in
mid-air about to take hold of it . . . I pulled my hand back. . . .
(Laughs.) . . . Splash, right into the ocean. . . . As I had figured, the
guy fell right into the water. . . . *(Laughs. The sound of raging waves
overlaps his laughter.)* . . . What followed was hilarious, too. He
thrashed around in the water a while; then, of all things, he stretched
his hand out as far as he could in my direction. . . . Can you believe
it? I had just tricked him beautifully, but he's holding his hand out to
me for all he's worth. . . . What a clown. . . . I laughed so hard I
almost cried. . . .
(Silence.)

OLDER MAN: . . . *(A low laugh.)* Is he the better actor or am I? . . . If he
really believes what he just said, he is an extremely naive man, too.
. . . Because I fell into the ocean on purpose. . . . I knew all along.
He wanted to drop me into the ocean. . . . I was waiting for the right

chance to fall in just like he wanted me to. . . . No, I'm not lying. I worked hard to make it appear natural. . . . And after I fell into the ocean, I even held my hand out to him because I knew he wanted me to. You see, I put on that little performance because I knew he expected it. . . .

MAN: That's a lie! Stop talking nonsense! And tell him I said so! . . . Why? . . . Why would he have any need to do that? . . .

OLDER MAN: Need? I had no need. . . . He simply wanted me to. . . . And I wanted to myself. . . .

MAN: That's stupid! How can he say that? Why would I want him to do something like that. . . .

(Harbor noises fade out; poignant piano music fades in.)

OLDER MAN: . . . On our way home from the harbor we again passed that girls' high school. . . . He stopped in his tracks and wouldn't move. We stood at least thirty minutes without a word. I got impatient and suggested we get back. To which he said, Back where? So I told him . . . "Where? . . . To our room, of course." . . . To our room? he said. He suddenly smiled a cold smile. That same smile of his. And the smile wasn't all. This time he spat it out clearly. . . . You're a fake! I've known you're no friend for a long time! You dirty, lousy hypocrite! Get lost!

MAN: So what. All of a sudden he got worked up and started screaming himself. You're the fake! You fraud! That spoiled face of yours makes me want to puke! I'll kill you! I'll strangle you like a pig! Die! You bum! Die! Die! Die!

(The stage is swiftly enclosed in darkness. From out of the darkness come the same noises as in the opening . . . scuffling . . . shouts . . . which shortly fade out. Slowly the lights come up.)

WIFE: *(Laughs.)* It serves them right. I wish they'd fought until they killed each other. Why stop just because one got hurt? Why didn't they go all the way? . . . What's the use now of saying "it's like the woman said." The dusky schoolyard . . . the piano music. . . . That should show you he's a songwriter. What's so strange about a songwriter who's tanned and has rough hands like a manual laborer. I'm not saying that because I want to get him back. What I'm telling you is the truth. I want everyone to understand that. The way I feel now, I'd like to tell everybody off. My husband, that "salesman," you people . . . I'd like to tell you all off and laugh you away. Right, Mother, you must feel the same. Laugh them away. Even a mute ought to be able to laugh. Well, Mother, laugh. Why not laugh? Why stare at me with such eyes? Come on, laugh. Mother, for me, laugh. . . . *(Changes to sobbing.)*

(*For acting thus, the* WOMAN WHO CLAIMS TO BE THE MOTHER *kicks the* WOMAN WHO CLAIMS TO BE THE WIFE *and leads her off with an air of resolution.*)

OLDER MAN: . . . They did? The woman went home? She outdid herself in her parting lines. But she still doesn't understand. That no matter how many words are wasted, the truth remains rather obscure Enough is enough. I think I told you in the beginning. Just forget it, please. . . . Please. . . .

(*The piano piece resumes. Off in the darkness the two schoolgirls of the opening fade in. Each has a white bandage on her left hand. . . . One picks flowers. One reads from the book of poetry.*)

> (That monotonous spring)
> One can tell nothing interesting
>   In spite of its baroque airs
> I was just a passing stranger
>   Mired in that time
> Far in the past now all of that appears
>   filled with
> Adventure, intoxication, blasphemy

(*The piano piece continues.*)

OLDER MAN: I told you, you can take my confession however you want. I don't care anymore what people think about me. . . . Just one thing . . . I know now how stupid it was to fight. . . . I don't want to lose him this way. . . .

MAN: I think the fight was dumb, too. The guy's really weak. I finished him so quickly I should've been the one screaming. . . . Who cares who's a fake? What's done is done. It's got nothing to do with me now. I couldn't go on if I worried about that stuff. . . .

OLDER MAN: I feel the same way. Stop digging up this stuff from the past. The man and I met by chance and got along great traveling together. Why not leave it at that? What's he doing now? Aren't we finished yet? Hurry, let me see the man, please.

MAN: He must've stopped bleeding by now. You're wasting time. Hurry up and let me see the guy.

OLDER MAN: Hurry, let me see him, please!

MAN: Hurry up and let me see him!

OLDER MAN: Please!

MAN: Come on!

OLDER MAN: Shit! Hurry, I want to see him!

MAN: Hurry, let me see him!

(*Everything is plunged into darkness. The piano music increases in intensity.*)

Notes

1. The Aragon poetry in *The Sand of Youth, How Quickly* was rendered by M. Cristina Frontini from the French original, "Comme il a vite . . ." in Aragon's *Le Roman inachevé* (1956).

2. *Sensei* (llt., born before) is a term of respect with such meanings as teacher, instructor, and professor.

The Sand of Youth, How Quickly requires a feeling of separate rooms without partitioning. Characters address unseen interrogators, but often seem to be talking to one another. Haiyūza, 1983. (Courtesy Shimizu Kunio.)

In *The Sand of Youth, How Quickly,* the plausibility of the woman's claim to the young man is pitted against his emotional tie to the salesman. Haiyūza, 1983. (Courtesy Shimizu Kunio.)

The premiere of *The Sand of Youth, How Quickly* tackled the problem of Shimizu's stage directions by frequent use of a large revolving platform, on which everything was situated. Seinenza, 1980. (Courtesy Seinenza.)

The Sand of Youth, How Quickly exploits the problematics of memory. One version of events seems as believable as the next; "truth" seems almost not to matter. Seinenza, 1980. (Courtesy Seinenza.)

Those Days: A Lyrical Hypothesis on Time and Forgetting

Shimizu Kunio

TRANSLATED BY JOHN K. GILLESPIE

CAST OF CHARACTERS

NAGAOKA, *the associate director*
SARUSHIMA, *head trainer*
KURAMOCHI, *trainer*
YAMAMOTO KANEKO, *trainer*
YAMAGISHI, *doctor*
TAKEMOTO, *nurse*
SAKINO, *nurse*
IKKI, *the only miner whose memory
    was unaffected by the accident*
OLD HANDYMAN
YAMADA
URAGAMI, *patient*
IKENO, *patient*
TOKUGAWA, *patient*
KITADA, *patient*

KATŌ, *patient*
NISHI, *patient*
KANAYAMA, *patient*
PIT-FACE MAN I
PIT-FACE MAN II
KATŌ'S UNCLE, *a village headman*
NISHI'S FATHER, *a coal miner*
URAGAMI RYŌKO, URAGAMI'*s wife*
IKENO YŪKO, IKENO'*s wife*
TOKUGAWA HANAKO, TOKUGAWA'*s
    daughter*
KATŌ'S WIFE
WOMAN, YAMADA'*s wife?*
NEWSPAPER REPORTER

(Place: A mental rehabilitation center for laborers, located on the outskirts of a coal mining town in Kyushu.)

ACT ONE

Scene 1

(A dimly lit pit face. Jarring echo, like a large excavating machine. Shadows of men squirming. Suddenly, a deafening roar of profound strength. The men are blown down. A strange hissing sound flows in. The men shout back and forth.)
The gas! It's exploded!
Lie down! Don't stand up!
Soak the towels! Hurry!

Run! Feel your way along the tracks!

Some light, we can't see a thing!

(A light is suddenly turned on. [The stage lights simultaneously illuminate the pit face.] Then it becomes evident that, contrary to expectation, the "pit face" is in fact a model constructed in the garden of the rehabilitation center. What sounded like a large excavating machine was IKKI *[thirty-two years old], at stage right, using an electric chainsaw. On the wall at stage left, the* OLD HANDYMAN *is pasting up old newspapers one after another. He is the one who turned on the light switch.)*

IKKI: Who said you could turn on the lights?

HANDYMAN: You're the one who wanted some light.

IKKI: At any rate, you really acted well. You've gotten so good it's too bad you're a handyman.

HANDYMAN: I may be old, but I can still manage. See, I used to act in farces.

*(*IKKI *turns toward the spectators.)*

IKKI: What's this look like? Does it look like the pit face of a coal mine? This is a museum model, which I hope looks like a real pit face. The black rocks, the coal, are to remind us of a time when the earth was still in its infancy. In addition, the model of a coal mine pit face invites us to dream of the golden age of the Japanese coal mining industry.

(The HANDYMAN*'s attention is drawn to one of the newspapers.)*

HANDYMAN: Terrible, that's terrible! Look, there was a big explosion!

IKKI: *(Approaching to look at the article.)* That paper's three years old!

HANDYMAN: It's terrible, even if it did happen three years ago. Isn't this the accident you were in? . . . *(Reads the newspaper.)* "10 November, 11:00 A.M., at the Misawa Miyama Coal Mine in Kyushu, an outbreak of explosions, the number of dead has climbed to 450.[1] The accident was triggered by an explosion of coal dust, and it appears that almost all the two hundred who were rescued were overcome by carbon monoxide poisoning."

IKKI: You might remember this incident. But you don't know what happened afterward. The fact is the two hundred or so who were rescued lost their memory because of the carbon monoxide. And this huge group of amnesia victims has still not recovered. They're living at a convalescent center in Kyushu.

(The HANDYMAN *continues reading here and there in the newspaper. Lights up gradually on an exercise room. Patients doing calisthenics.)*

IKKI: I was rescued. Miraculously, I was without a scratch, and even without amnesia. . . . In pit face number five, I was the only one who was safe. This was the start of my bad luck. I guess I shouldn't say anything, but look, you'd have to be really stupid not to wonder why when a miracle happens to you. People now, you know, they say this, they say that, but don't in the least try to believe in miracles. No matter how much I try to explain why I was the only one who got rescued, they don't understand. Well, I can understand the grief of the bereaved families. But they're nuts if they think that I did something wrong to get rescued when hundreds of others got killed. That's crazy. It's an accident that occurred in the bowels of the earth—there's no logic to that. *(Shakes his head.)* They don't believe me. The bereaved families weigh in against me with hatred and reproach in their eyes. I've been subjected to a kangaroo court no less than fifty-eight times in one year. I have only one last hope—it's for those two hundred victims of amnesia. If they could only recover their memories, they would vindicate me. I don't have much money saved up, but it's all going to go for that. *(Caressing the pit face wall.)* Well built, isn't it? You can't trust medical science these days. Isn't that right? Two years already, and they haven't recovered a bit. . . . I'll go about it my own way—there's the story of Columbus' egg, miracles can happen. . . .

(The lights focus on one of the spectators' seats. A woman stands up and heads toward the stage.)

Scene 2

(A medical office with white walls. Associate Director NAGAOKA *[forty-seven years old] and the woman from the spectators' seats,* YAMAMOTO KANEKO *[twenty-six years old], are there.* KANEKO *is wearing glasses.* NAGAOKA *is intently studying her resumé.)*

KANEKO: Is there anything that you would like to ask me about?

NAGAOKA: I make it a point to read things like medical charts and resumés very carefully.

KANEKO: As you think best.

NAGAOKA: But the charts are by far the more interesting. When you look into the history of a person's illnesses, you can understand him quite well.

KANEKO: I'm sorry, the office said it was all right to keep my personal history simple.

NAGAOKA: Did you ever have any serious illnesses?

KANEKO: Yes . . . pneumonia, when I was a student.

NAGAOKA: I see. If I had to say anything, a person whose respiratory system is bad suits my taste better than a person whose digestive system is bad. Why did you quit the nursery school and come here?

KANEKO: I saw in the paper that you had a shortage of workers. . . .

NAGAOKA: In general I think you know about the Mental Rehabilitation

Center. It is a sanitarium that aims at recovery for those with memory disorders. You won't be a nurse or a schoolteacher. That's what's difficult about being a trainer in the Mental Rehabilitation Center.

KANEKO: Yes.

NAGAOKA: Do you have a driver's license?

KANEKO: No.

NAGAOKA: Of course, you've never gone to a driver training school.

KANEKO: Will that be necessary?

NAGAOKA: No. I'm just wondering if you know about the instructors at such places. Your job here would be somewhat similar to what they do.

KANEKO: Yes.

NAGAOKA: To some extent, just do whatever you think's best. No need for theory. Just determination to keep the training moving right along. As to the medical effectiveness, we doctors will consider that.

KANEKO: Do you think a woman can do the job?

NAGAOKA: If anything, a woman suits my taste better than a man. Just joking. No need to worry. What we're doing here amounts to a new departure; the Japanese medical community is watching us closely. (*The head trainer,* SARUSHIMA [*thirty-seven years old*], *enters.*)

SARUSHIMA: Dr. Nagaoka, things are really out of hand, to put it mildly.

NAGAOKA: Hey, slow down! Here is the very person. . . .

SARUSHIMA: Oh! Is she the one who is to be connected with the model in the courtyard? Well, I'll say it clearly—if that sort of bizarre surrogate gets their memory back, then I, Sarushima, will resign.

NAGAOKA: Pull yourself together! You misunderstand. She has just been taken on as a trainer. . . .

KANEKO: My name is Yamamoto Kaneko.

SARUSHIMA: I see. I'm Sarushima, the head trainer. But Dr. Nagaoka, aren't you too against it? Didn't you say that it spoils the view of the hospital? . . . That guy, he's been stirred up by Dr. Yamagishi. . . .

NAGAOKA: I expected he'd give up halfway through, that guy Ikki. When you are in constant contact with those in the sanitarium, you completely forget that there are still people out there who won't give up.

SARUSHIMA: Dr. Nagaoka, that's why. . . .

NAGAOKA: Look, no need to be so irritable. You've never been sick, have you?

SARUSHIMA: When I was twenty, I had my appendix out. . . .

NAGAOKA: And?

SARUSHIMA: That's it.

NAGAOKA: So you see, am I not right? If you've only had your appendix out, that proves you're a simple man.

SARUSHIMA: I always catch colds when the seasons change. . . .

NAGAOKA: Since you're the one in charge of the training, if you can just do that properly. . . .

SARUSHIMA: *(Sullen.)* I understand.

NAGAOKA: Good, then I'll leave her to you

(NAGAOKA exits.)

SARUSHIMA: *(Irritated.)* It's got nothing to do with my appendix. These characters who pass for doctors just don't like healthy people.

(Picks up KANEKO's resumé from the desk. A chorus is audible from outside the window.)

KANEKO: What's? . . .

SARUSHIMA: Oh, that's the patients.

(KANEKO listens attentively.)

KANEKO: Doesn't this mean they've remembered something? A song they knew in the past? . . .

SARUSHIMA: If that's the case, we trainers are out of jobs. It stimulates their brain cells, you see, teaching them songs they all apparently used to know.

KANEKO: You mean by educating them over again? . . . *(Sighs deeply.)*

SARUSHIMA: From your resumé here, it's not clear whether you are married or unmarried.

KANEKO: I separated from my husband, three years ago.

SARUSHIMA: Oh, husband unfaithful? Or maybe. . . .

KANEKO: Personality conflict. Nothing of any great interest.

SARUSHIMA: *(Clearing throat.)* Let me give you a general explanation of what goes into our training. The patients are divided into twenty classes. The general categories of training consist of classroom study and physical exercise. For classroom study, we have them do arithmetic and voice dictation. For physical exercise, we have them play badminton, softball, volleyball, work out on the horizontal bar, weed the garden, ring toss. . . .

KANEKO: Ring toss?

Scene 3

(The training room. In the center is a large swing. The patients are wearing white uniforms and playing ring toss. The patients are URAGAMI [thirty-five or thirty-six years old], IKENO [twenty-eight or twenty-nine], TOKUGAWA [forty-one or forty-two], KATŌ [twenty-three or twenty-four], NISHI [twenty-two or twenty-three], KITADA [about forty], KANAYAMA [twenty-five or twenty-six], YAMADA [indeterminate age]. The trainer KURAMOCHI [twenty-five] is working out with weights. Only KANAYAMA, on crutches, is not playing ring toss but just watching KURAMOCHI's workout.)

IKENO: Toku, your timing is off.

TOKUGAWA: I'm getting old.

URAGAMI: Aren't you still just thirty-five?

TOKUGAWA: Forty-five. You're the one who's for sure thirty-five.

URAGAMI: I thought I was thirty-six.

IKENO: Since I'm six years younger than Ura, I'm thirty

TOKUGAWA: Well, who's thirty-five?

KITADA: Someone was thirty-five

NISHI: I'm twenty-three.

URAGAMI: I'd like to be twenty-three too.

IKENO: You look like it, you look like you're twenty-three! If that's the case, I'm six years younger than you, which makes me seventeen. *(Becomes uneasy.)*

TOKUGAWA: Isn't it Kita who's thirty-five?

KATŌ: I'm tired. I mean, that's eighty-one.

NISHI: Eighty-one what?

KATŌ: Eighty-one times I've thrown.

(Continuing his weight lifting workout, KURAMOCHI speaks.)

KURAMOCHI: Hey, cut the nonsense. You've got thirty more to go.

(KANAYAMA looks with admiration at KURAMOCHI's workout.)

KANAYAMA: That's really difficult, isn't it?

KURAMOCHI: I'm definitely looking to enter the national trials this fall.

KANAYAMA: . . . I must have worked out that way everyday too.

KURAMOCHI: Mr. Kanayama, you were a sprinter, weren't you? The marathon starts like this. *(Shows him.)*

KANAYAMA: They say I placed sixth at the Kumamoto Labor Games.

KATŌ: I entered that meet as a swimmer.

TOKUGAWA: Wasn't it Ura's wife who played volleyball?

URAGAMI: Yep, she did.

NISHI: Really?

IKENO: Are you saying that's not right?

NISHI: Maybe it was my wife.

KITADA: Certainly, it's Nishi's wife. Make up your minds.

IKENO: I thinks it's Ura's wife.

KATŌ: That's because, Ike, you take Ura's side, whatever it is.

IKENO: It's bad when friends can't get along, right, Ura?

URAGAMI: Right. We were pretty close friends before the accident. Everyone told us we had been, so there's no doubt about it.

(KURAMOCHI is engrossed in his workout.)

KURAMOCHI: *(To KANAYAMA.)* What do you think? Change of grip was good, wasn't it?

KANAYAMA: *(As if coaching.)* No, no, your old grip was better.

(KURAMOCHI sets to work seriously.)

TOKUGAWA: Anyway, we shouldn't make mistakes. Whatever relates to yourself, you really have to get it straight in your mind.

KITADA: Right. You've got to take care of your own matters yourself. . . .

KATŌ. I know about myself! I was born in Kagoshima, graduated from junior high school there, then went to work at a lumberyard in Miyazaki. Three years ago I came here to this town. I met my wife in Kumamoto, we got married. . . .

IKENO: It was Beppu. I got tired of hearing the same stuff.

KATŌ: If I don't repeat it from time to time, I get nervous.

URAGAMI: You're still pretty well off. There's one here who's got a lot more to worry about. He can't delve into his past at all. . . .

(YAMADA abruptly stops playing ring toss and goes to the swing. The rest of the patients, seeing this, exchange meaningfully animated signs. KURAMOCHI notices YAMADA.)

KURAMOCHI: What's wrong, Mr. Yamada. Keep on with your training.

(Ignoring him, YAMADA begins to swing. Enter SARUSHIMA and KANEKO.)

SARUSHIMA: Who's the one? Please be honest and raise your hand. Who teased Mr. Yamada?

KANEKO: Mr. Yamada. . . .

(KANEKO stares fixedly at YAMADA. With lighting changes, YAMADA at times look like a small boy, at times like an old man.)

KURAMOCHI: He's a patient who's difficult to deal with. He'll immediately sulk like a child.

(KANEKO has been standing straight as a stick but in the next instant approaches the swing.)

KANEKO: Wow! What a nice, big swing! *(Turning to YAMADA.)* You like to swing? Me, too, I've got really pleasant memories of swinging. . . .

YAMADA: I hate it. . . . It scares me.

SARUSHIMA: Ms. Yamamoto, this is Mr. Kuramochi, your coworker.

(KANEKO greets KURAMOCHI. The patients laugh loudly.)

KURAMOCHI: *(Amiably.)* Pleased to meet you.

SARUSHIMA: I'd like to set up her schedule right away.

KURAMOCHI: But what about here?

SARUSHIMA: *(To KURAMOCHI.)* Why don't we have her supervise for a while. *(To patients.)* Let me present you with your new teacher. Ms. Yamamoto.

KURAMOCHI: Well, get started everybody. . . . Mr. Katō, your navel is showing. *(To KANEKO.)* Now, then, all you have to do is watch them till the hour's up.

SARUSHIMA: *(To KANEKO.)* Please remember that the swings are for the patients' use.

(SARUSHIMA and KURAMOCHI exit. The patients begin to play ring toss again,

but everybody's attention is focused on KANEKO. KANEKO *approaches the swing.)*

KANEKO: *(To* YAMADA.*)* Shall I give you a push?

(Frightened, YAMADA *shakes his head.)*

KATŌ: Miss, you mustn't indulge him.

KITADA: That's right,

KANEKO: I'm sorry. *(Currying favor.)* I'll never be a strict trainer.

IKENO: What did you do before you came here?

KANEKO: I was a teacher in a nursery school.

IKENO: A nursery school? That's why you came here. Most of the trainers here are people like that, aren't they?

KITADA: Mr. Sarushima used to be a junior high school teacher. Mr. Nakano was at a school for the blind and dumb.

KANAYAMA: Not Mr. Kuramochi.

NISHI: He was formerly in the Self-Defense Forces. He's good at drilling the troops.

IKENO: How long were you at the nursery school? Is it here in this town?

URAGAMI: *(Reproaching him.)* Ike.

IKENO: Would you like to play with us? *(Holding out to* KANEKO *rings for ring toss.)*

TOKUGAWA: Don't be rude. She's not a patient. What did you do before you were a nursery school teacher?

KANEKO: I worked in a small factory.

URAGAMI: A glass factory?

KANEKO: No. Why do you ask?

URAGAMI: Because I like glass factories . . . or was it porcelain?

IKENO: *(Reproaching him.)* Ura.

*(*TOKUGAWA *and* KITADA *suddenly begin exercising.)*

TOKUGAWA: *(Casually.)* Married . . . are you married?

KITADA: Yes . . . are you married?

KANEKO: Now, I'm single.

(Everyone falls into deep thought over this.)

URAGAMI: You mean, you are separated by death?

IKENO: One can also be separated by life, you know.

*(*KANEKO *answers, her eyes fixed in* YAMADA*'s direction.)*

KANEKO: No.

URAGAMI: *(To* IKENO.*)* What's the story then?

KANEKO: He's on a trip.

IKENO: Far away, right?

KANEKO: Yes, very far away. . . .

URAGAMI: Went by train, right?

IKENO: I've got it. By . . . what's that thing . . . flying? *(Spreads hands out.)*

URAGAMI: A crow?

IKENO: Faster than that.

URAGAMI: Airplane?

IKENO: I wonder if he went off by plane?

URAGAMI: It's surely across the ocean.

IKENO: Across the ocean? What's there?

URAGAMI: You mean you don't know?

IKENO: You think you know?

URAGAMI: On a clear day you can see, can't you, from the hill in back of us?

IKENO: The island!

URAGAMI: You can see the island.

IKENO: You can see the island, just bobbing up there.

URAGAMI: A long time ago, I went out to it, just jumped right out to it.

IKENO: What about me?

URAGAMI: Let's go together some time.

IKENO: *(To* KANEKO.*)* Why did he go away and leave you all alone?

KANEKO: *(To* YAMADA.*)* You don't ask any questions at all, do you?

YAMADA: You . . . might be prettier if you'd take off your glasses.

KANEKO: What?

URAGAMI: Please don't get offended. He tends to offend people.

KANEKO: And you don't? For the last few minutes you all seem to want to put me through an interview.

(All, as one, are reproached into silence.)

KANEKO: But this doesn't mean I'm offended. Why are you so concerned about my past, I wonder?

TOKUGAWA: Because you're the newest person here.

IKENO: Because we've mostly heard all about the nurses and the doctors.

KANAYAMA: Awful. Digging up the past has gotten to be a habit.

KITADA: You see, we can't remember a thing about our own pasts.

URAGAMI: What we do is ask our families and the people around us things, and then we finally get some idea what kind of people we were.

(YAMADA gets off the swing and begins to play ring toss alone in a corner.)

KATŌ: We've been pretty inquisitive, haven't we?

NISHI: Even still, at times we forget everything.

KITADA: It's gotten to be a bad habit. The nurses don't like us for it.

TOKUGAWA: We know we shouldn't . . . but somehow we can't stop.

(Enter Nurse TAKEMOTO *[twenty-seven years old].)*

TAKEMOTO: Mr. Uragami, you didn't take the brain-wave test yesterday, did you?

URAGAMI: I was feeling nauseous right then.

TAKEMOTO: Mr. Ikeno, how about you?

IKENO: Me too . . . I had a headache and was feeling nauseous. . . .

TAKEMOTO: Strange, you two. When one of you is bad, without fail the other one is too.

IKENO: *(Seriously.)* That is true.

TAKEMOTO: It appears to be, so it's up to me to point it out to you. Even Dr. Yamagishi can't figure it out. Please take the test next week for sure. *(Looks at* KANEKO.*)* My name is Takemoto, from the second ward. *(Exits.)*

TOKUGAWA: That girl. She must've changed men five times.

KITADA: I know. Now it's Dr. Yamagishi, right? What a chump to let himself get sucked into that.

*(*NISHI *tries to say something but is cut off by the rest of the group.)*

IKENO: The first man was what's-his-name, the intern who went to Osaka, wasn't it?

KANAYAMA: Number two was the kangaroo.

KANEKO: Kangaroo?

TOKUGAWA: The intern with the long neck.

URAGAMI: The third one is . . . hold it a sec, third was. . . .

KANEKO: That's enough of this.

KATŌ: Before coming here, he worked at a mental asylum in Kumamoto. His family was in the hosiery business.

IKENO: Not the one in hosiery. It was someone else. . . .

KATŌ: Absolutely, it was the one in hosiery.

KANEKO: All right, everybody, please continue with ring toss.

(All return to the game.)

TOKUGAWA: Since we got here, how many times you think we've done this?

KITADA: Maybe two thousand times? Shall we count them up?

URAGAMI: No, it's five thousand times.

IKENO: I think it's about five thousand times, too.

KANAYAMA: *(Clumsily searching his pockets for his cigarettes.)* All right if I smoke?

KANEKO: Please.

(With his crutches under his arms, KANAYAMA *clumsily tries to take out a cigarette. He almost topples over.* KANEKO *holds him up.)*

KANAYAMA: My kneecap was shattered in the accident.

*(*KANEKO *gives him a light.)*

KANAYAMA: That's very kind of you. Were you at the nursery school a long time?

KANEKO: *(Not wanting to go through it again.)* Two years.

(Dr. YAMAGISHI [*thirty-four years old*] *of the medical staff enters. He stands silently behind the patients.)*

KANAYAMA: And, uh, before that? . . .

TOKUGAWA: She worked in a small factory.

KATŌ: Not a glass factory.

URAGAMI: Is that when you met your husband?

IKENO: Married just that one time, right?

KANEKO. *(Angry.)* Please stop.

(YAMAGISHI breaks into the discussion.)

YAMAGISHI: Doesn't that satisfy you enough?

(Like children, they all become quiet.)

YAMAGISHI: Worthy of research. You have a nasty way of amusing yourselves. . . . I'm Yamagishi of the medical department. Are you the
one who just joined the training staff?

KANEKO: My name is Yamamoto.

YAMAGISHI: I expected someone older. *(Looks hard at the patients.)* At any
rate, you've probably heard talk about how I'm overflowing with
humanity.

KANEKO: Yes.

YAMAGISHI: We're long since used to it. For enjoyment that's all this
crowd has, you see. I want them to dig into their past, but only
among their own close friends.

(The group gradually begins playing ring toss. YAMAGISHI *approaches*
KANEKO.*)*

YAMAGISHI: Those gas patients are medically interesting, but socially
they can even inspire hate.

KANEKO: The way you talk . . . will hurt their feelings.

YAMAGISHI: Soon you might come to hate them too.

KANEKO: *(Decisively.)* No. I won't hate them. *(Like a young girl.)* I came
here to love.

YAMAGISHI: *(Dumbfounded.)* Oh, my! I think I'm capable of some human
interest, at least in you.

KANEKO: *(Snickering laugh.)* I'll tell you the truth. The reason I came here
is because the pay is two thousand yen higher than at the nursery
school where I was before.

YAMAGISHI: *(Laughing.)* You appear to be a good person.

KANEKO: You appear to be a bad person.

YAMAGISHI: I know, I know.

KANEKO: Please be gentler with them.

YAMAGISHI: Because I said I hate them? If I did, I might carry out some
drastic treatment on them, you know.

KANEKO: I thought doctors were all calm and collected.

YAMAGISHI: The calmness sharpens our judgment, and that's good, but
doctors need more. They need determination, and the thing that
spurs determination is emotion, even if it's dark feelings of hatred.

KANEKO: *(Distantly.)* What an awful thing it must be, to have lost sight of the past. . . .

YAMAGISHI: For someone like me, it's in a sense enviable. How great to be able to erase the past completely . . . there is nothing so disagreeable as a trip back into one's memory.

TOKUGAWA: *(Reprovingly.)* But, Doctor, my past was not so bad.

KITADA: I was an ordinary human being. My honeymoon was at Mt. Aso. . . .

IKENO: Mt. Aso, what's it like?

KITADA: I hear it spouts flames up into the sky.

URAGAMI: How so?

(Making various sounds, they each try to imagine what the volcano is like.)

KITADA: I don't remember it at all.

NISHI: Mine isn't the sort of past that people can tell me this and that about. I was the vice-chairman of the regional labor union committee.

KATŌ: Considering that, you're not much good at speaking, are you?

NISHI: Even here, didn't I organize a strike and make it so there were enough uniforms for everybody?

YAMAGISHI: The only thing you didn't forget was your strike know-how. *(Sarcastically.)* You were all such wonderful people. Well, that's what you want to say, isn't it?

KITADA: I'm saying I'm just an ordinary human being.

YAMAGISHI: You may have been a more wonderful person.

TOKUGAWA: I don't like this. Being spoken to like that gets on my nerves.

KATŌ: *(Pointing to* YAMADA.*)* For him the world's a different place, but our minds are at peace. Our families and relatives wouldn't lie to us.

IKENO: No, why would they?

KANAYAMA: Dr. Yamagishi, are you saying we shouldn't believe what the people around us tell us?

KANEKO: No, you misunderstand. It's okay for you to believe what everyone says.

URAGAMI: We haven't been told anything but to believe.

KANEKO: *(To* YAMADA.*)* Why don't you ever say anything? Mr. Yamada . . . wasn't it?

YAMADA: I'm not Yamada.

KANEKO: But your name tag. . . .

YAMADA: It's a temporary name. The easiest to come up with, see. As for my name . . . if you know it, let me know.

YAMAGISHI: The fact is he's caused some consternation for both the hospital and our office. He was certainly there in the pit face when the accident occurred, but his name isn't in the office register. Nor has his family as yet made themselves known.

KATŌ: There were as many as four unidentified bodies.

KANEKO: No clues at all?

YAMAGISHI. He was probably a member of a subcontract group. It's really careless, isn't it, to know neither his identity nor even the number of people in a subcontract group?

TOKUGAWA: A member of a subcontract group? They say a lot of them have criminal records, don't they?

YAMADA: I may even have murdered someone.

KITADA: You don't have to be so obsessed.

NISHI: What he means is that that possibility's strong.

YAMADA: It's okay to call me a murderer. If I do have a criminal record, my fingerprints will let me know my past. Who did I kill anyway?

(Sounds of chimes in the distance.)

URAGAMI: Ah, well, that's finally over.

KITADA: It's over. We can relax.

KANAYAMA: What next?

IKENO: Arithmetic. I can do multiplication and division, but I wonder why I can't do subtraction.

URAGAMI: Subtraction's cruel, isn't it? What you subtract completely disappears.

(Nurse SAKINO [nineteen years old] enters.)

SAKINO: *(Looks meaningfully in the direction of YAMAGISHI and KANEKO.)* Oh! Dr. Yamagishi, weren't you looking for Ms. Takemoto?

YAMAGISHI: Not at the moment. Wouldn't she be over in the second ward?

SAKINO: Mr. Katō, how about it? Did you learn the steps?

(KATŌ shrinks back but is caught. SAKINO, snapping her fingers, runs through the steps of a popular dance.)

SAKINO: This will never do. Look sharp, you've got to get into it more. . . . Mr. Ikeno, how about you?

IKENO: *(Escaping.)* Ura, let's go prepare our lessons.

URAGAMI: Right. Let's cool off in the shade.

(URAGAMI and IKENO exit as if sneaking away.)

YAMAGISHI: Ms. Sakino, you're the only one who's getting into it.

(SAKINO stops.)

SAKINO: The bare minimum, aren't they? These people. I've been here a year and still haven't been pinched on the backside—not even one time.

(Swinging her hips, SAKINO moves toward KANAYAMA.)

SAKINO: Well, Mr. Kanayama (KANAYAMA *timidly takes hold of her*), what do you say? I don't bite.

(In SAKINO's *grip,* KANAYAMA *begins to move about.)*

KANAYAMA: A bit slower. My bones will break!

SAKINO: Your bones aren't broken. Have a little faith in your X-rays.

KANAYAMA: No, they're breaking apart.

SAKINO: Bothersome illness, this numbness of the brain. . . .

   *(*KANAYAMA *and* SAKINO *exit.)*

TOKUGAWA: Silly girl, isn't she.

KANEKO: What? I'd say terrific. A sprightly Miss Voluptuous.

KITADA: What's so interesting about her? There's nothing to her past. It's totally boring.

   *(*TOKUGAWA, KITADA, NISHI, *and* KATŌ *exit. The* OLD HANDYMAN *enters and begins to straighten up the training room.* YAMADA *gives him a hand.)*

HANDYMAN: Three times—morning, noon, and night—three times they eat and can't clean up a thing afterward.

KANEKO: Who's that old fellow?

YAMAGISHI: Seems to take a philosophic view of life, doesn't he? But life is not so simple and clear. The fact is he, too, has some misfortune that can't be undone. On the day of the accident, he went to see a comic animal farce in Hakata. He let a decisive moment slip away. It's a great loss. He missed the chance of a lifetime. Look at him. Picking up the old newspapers and magazines, acting like he's all made up for his journey to the next world. . . .

HANDYMAN: *(Reads from an old newspaper.)* The company president spoke on 13 November, huh. "Some say the recent accident was due to increased production that ignored operational safety, but the truth is that production that ignores operational safety is impossible. A coal dust explosion could easily blow up the whole mine. The reason I think that isn't what happened in Misawa is that we were scrupulous about operational safety."

   *(*KANEKO *gets on the swing.)*

KANEKO: *(Swinging to her feet, addresses* YAMADA.*)* Hey, how about a push?

   *(*YAMADA *looks disoriented, but finally goes to the swing and slowly pushes it.)*

KANEKO: A long time ago, my husband and I used to do this a lot together. There was a tiny, tiny park, just a narrow little bit of ground, really. There used to be a broken bike beside the horizontal bars . . . a small pair of red-thonged clogs abandoned in the sand box. . . .

YAMAGISHI: Husband? You're married?

KANEKO: Divorced. Three years ago. . . .

   *(*YAMADA *looks around with a puzzled expression.)*

KANEKO: What is it, that sound?

YAMAGISHI: Tenaciousness personified is working on his model of the coal mine pit face.

KANEKO: A while ago the head trainer Mr. Sarushima was angry with him.

YAMAGISHI: The reason is he's attempting an occupational therapy based on a faithful re-creation of the scene of the accident. The idea smacks of amateurism. . . . Of course we can't dismiss it out of hand. There are even questions about the rehabilitation carried out here, how much basis there is for it, its effectiveness. . . .

(YAMADA *unobtrusively exits.*)

KANEKO: You must be exhausted. Your speaking like that, it's upsetting.

YAMAGISHI: But the hard fact is . . . that's the way it is. As for the assistant directors, with mass media showing us some interest, they are probably proud enough . . . but not me.

KANEKO: A long time ago, I saw it in a movie. About a man whose memory by some chance returned.

YAMAGISHI: Such a thing might possibly happen in case of memory loss in war or in a traffic accident. But, in the case of carbon monoxide poisoning, the brain cells may well suffer complete deterioration.

KANEKO: That's . . . not clearly established, is it?

YAMAGISHI: No, not in today's medicine. There were 450 dead bodies, but not even one autopsy was done.

KANEKO: Why not? (*Gets off swing.*)

YAMAGISHI: Because their families were against it, and what's more, the doctors too were confused. During the first month what sort of treatment do you think they gave? They only had them drink an over-the-counter nutritional supplement. . . . But the human body is incomprehensible. Even that fellow's approach may not be altogether lacking basis. In the medical world, too, some are of the opinion that recovery may be enhanced by returning them as quickly as possible to work. I tried it once, even going so far as to oppose the director. I was really into it then.

KANEKO: You were tireless. . . .

YAMAGISHI: But it wound up a failure. On top of that, they forgot where they had set up the dynamite and so caused yet another accident. Everyone was criticizing me. They said I used patients like guinea pigs in an experiment. After that I couldn't even return to my university.

KANEKO: Did you recommend the model of the pit face?

YAMAGISHI: No . . . only if. . . .

KANEKO: There's no assurance at all that those people will recover their memories, is there?

YAMAGISHI: You too are looking for assurance?

KANEKO: For such an uncertain objective, they are going to keep on with their ring toss, their chorus, their arithmetic, and all the rest of it until they die?

Scene 4

(The pit face. IKKI *is working on the construction.)*

IKKI: Who's there?

*(*YAMADA *enters timidly.)*

IKKI: Uh, so it's you. What do you think? Looks pretty good, doesn't it? I've gotten the stuff together and busted my rear end over this.

*(*YAMADA *stares goggle eyed.)*

YAMADA: There's no water spilling out. . . .

IKKI: Water?

YAMADA: Water.

IKKI: I guess I forgot the water. Let's see, water spilling out, that's the way it really was. . . . But it's not possible. We don't have the budget for it. I had all I could do just to make this.

YAMADA: It's somehow nostalgic . . . the smell of the river . . . the thistles . . . when was all that, anyway?

*(*YAMADA *starts to go into the construction. Startled by this,* IKKI *pulls him back.)*

IKKI: So, you said water, huh? Maybe you remembered that. Well, that's right, isn't it?

*(*YAMADA *shakes his head slowly.)*

YAMADA: When I was rescued, my shirt and pants were soaked.

IKKI: Hey, you remember! When the man-powered tramway ran amok, weren't you right there beside it? Don't you remember my face?

YAMADA: . . . everybody slept lying all around. Only our cap lights were on. Hundreds of them crossed beams, like searchlights, and shone against the ceiling. I didn't know what had happened. I didn't understand that where we were was more or less the bowels of the earth. Why am I in the bowels of the earth? It was a sea of mud. There was a sound. A dreadful sound. A sound like snakes slithering. No, it's a sound I've heard somewhere before. I kicked them away and ran out. The sound came after me. That sound. I can't stand it. Stop that sound. . . .

*(*YAMADA *runs out.)*

Scene 5

*(*KANEKO *and* YAMAGISHI *in the training room.)*

KANEKO: What's that voice?

YAMAGISHI: It's coming from the courtyard.

*(*YAMADA *comes running in as if frightened.* IKKI *follows helter-skelter.)*

YAMAGISHI: What's wrong?

IKKI: Nothing, just this guy coming into the construction model. . . .

KANEKO: Did he do something?

IKKI: No, but . . . he seems to have remembered something about when he was rescued. Dr. Yamagishi, it looks like you can see results already with this thing. Yamada is the first to recover his memory.

YAMAGISHI: But things aren't always what they seem—that is, not for a real researcher.

(IKKI *draws near* YAMADA.)

YAMADA: Thanks, I'm okay now. You know, you're a kindhearted person.

KANEKO: That's cruel. Scaring him like this.

IKKI: No, no. He is to be trained in the very place where they were working.

KANEKO: Do you enjoy tormenting people?

IKKI: The harder the work, the keener they'll return to their senses.

KANEKO: I don't know. I don't know. Why must we go to such lengths just to push these people back into the same types they were before?

YAMAGISHI: Recovery is going back to the source, isn't it? These people are patients.

KANEKO: I'll never be able to think of them as patients.

IKKI: Doctor, who is she anyway?

YAMAGISHI: She's a trainer who just joined us.

IKKI: *(Referring to* KANEKO.) That's reckless talk. If the trainers start getting soft and lax, we'll never get results.

YAMAGISHI: *(To* KANEKO.) Why get so excited about it? I know what you wanted to say. That we should recognize them as people with completely new personalities and use that as a starting point for communication with them. . . .

KANEKO: I'm sorry . . . it's just that I don't really understand why everybody is concerned only about their past. If it doesn't look like their memory will come back, shouldn't we be thinking about their future?

IKKI: You can't just bring up the future like that. You can't construct the future by omitting the foundation of the past.

KANEKO: I'll give these people new lives, new jobs, new loves. . . .

YAMAGISHI: You came here to love . . . you said that a while ago too. But, you see, this place is a rehabilitation center for recovering the past. You and I are retained solely for that function.

(KURAMOCHI *enters playing a guitar.* YAMADA *stands up and abruptly bursts forth in song. With* YAMAGISHI, KANEKO, *and* IKKI *watching him, he walks around slowly, on key with the guitar.*)

YAMADA: *(Sings.)*

>Those days
>Like the shepherd and the maiden.
>Always full of joy

No strange events
No new regrets. . . .²

(YAMADA *stops by the entrance and turns around.*)

YAMADA: *(To* KURAMOCHI.*)* Why did you stop playing?

KURAMOCHI: But. . . .

(KURAMOCHI *begins to play his guitar again.* YAMADA *continues singing.*)

KANEKO: *(To* YAMADA.*)* Why do you know that song?

YAMADA: *(Sings.)*

Those days
Like a puzzle never solved
Smiles swearing love unchanging
Flowering thistles in among day lilies
A nice, childlike dream
When was it that it was. . . .

ACT TWO

Scene 6

(Sickroom. Four beds. URAGAMI *and* IKENO. URAGAMI *is lying in a bed.* IKENO *is devotedly transporting a tray with medicine and a glass of water.*)

IKENO: Ura, here, take your medicine. *(Cheerfully.)* Shall I go to the garden and bring some flowers? No vase here, is there?

URAGAMI: Stop treating me like an invalid.

IKENO: When your stomach hurts, better lie down. When the others aren't here, it's quiet and cool, isn't it?

URAGAMI: It's just about time for the bus to arrive. Ike, don't you want to hurry down and meet your wife?

IKENO: I don't hear it yet.

URAGAMI: Hey, just listen.

IKENO: It's your stomach growling.

URAGAMI: I'm all right. You go ahead.

IKENO: If I go, you come with me.

URAGAMI: I'm ill.

IKENO: And I'm right beside you. Isn't there anything else I can do? Rub your stomach?

URAGAMI: Going together won't help a thing. We are, after all, not related. And our wives, too, are different.

IKENO: Your stomach is soft. Feels good. Now, what are you teed off about?

URAGAMI: I'm sure to die sooner than you. I'm at least six years older.

IKENO: I wonder if I really was a man before the accident. If I were a woman then. . . .

URAGAMI: What a creepy idea.

IKENO: Listen, Ura, hadn't you better take your medicine?

URAGAMI: Don't worry about me.

IKENO: Did I do something wrong? If there's something bothering you, out with it.

URAGAMI: You're betraying me.

IKENO: That's unfair! When I've been doing everything I can for you.

URAGAMI: How come my stomach hurts, but yours doesn't.

(IKENO *looks nonplussed.*)

URAGAMI: Up to now, whenever you've had diarrhea, I've had it too, without fail. . . .

IKENO: Yes, it's strange.

URAGAMI: Sure it's strange.

IKENO: Funny . . . I don't hurt anywhere.

URAGAMI: Are you sure? Didn't you say just this morning that you felt some pain around your appendix? This afternoon, I was thinking about that and I began to hurt something fierce.

IKENO. (*Lies down on a bed and anxiously feels his body here and there.*) I must have got over it.

(*With* IKENO *worrying about himself,* URAGAMI, *apparently relieved, takes his medicine.*)

IKENO: I'm worried. I think I'll have Dr. Yamagishi take a look right away.

(URAGAMI *looks out the window.*)

URAGAMI: Someone's heading this way on a bike.

(IKENO *also looks out.*)

URAGAMI: Looks like a white butterfly.

IKENO: A white butterfly? I'd say sort of dazzling.

URAGAMI: I'll say.

(*Below the window, a young girl goes by humming.*)

URAGAMI: Whose family does that girl belong to, I wonder?

IKENO: What's certain is that she is not your wife or mine.

URAGAMI: Of course not. Our wives are not that young.

IKENO: Right, they got after us when we asked about their age.

URAGAMI: Women aren't supposed to be honest. Maybe they're not telling their real age.

IKENO: They always come together, but I wonder if the wives too are really good friends, like us.

URAGAMI: They live right next door to each other. Their friendship is everyday going and crying on each others' shoulders. Or so they say.

(IKENO *moves away from the window.*)

IKENO: Strange, isn't it. How we've come to be such good friends.

URAGAMI: Maybe we were childhood friends. Who knows, maybe we went to the same kindergarten.

IKENO: Weren't they saying I grew up in Miyazaki?

URAGAMI: And me in Kobe.

(The two look each other in the face with puzzled expressions. Sounds of a bus in the distance.)

URAGAMI: The bus, isn't it?

IKENO: Right, the bus.

URAGAMI: Wish our wives'd come separately. . . .

(IKENO looks at URAGAMI inquiringly.)

URAGAMI: At the first meeting, remember? We didn't know whose wife was whose, and didn't they get after us for it?

IKENO: It's not that way anymore.

URAGAMI: You get to the point where you mistake your own wife, and you're no longer human.

IKENO: Women, they all seem the same, don't they? Like with pigeons, it's hard to tell one from another.

URAGAMI: But it's a lot easier remembering your wife's face than your own hospital room.

IKENO: Well, shall we head on down?

URAGAMI: Yeah, let's go.

(The two get up to go. First, one loses his footing and falls over, then the other.)

IKENO: How did that happen?

URAGAMI: You fell down.

IKENO: Guess so.

URAGAMI: That's right.

Scene 7

(Training room. KURAMOCHI picking at a guitar and singing.)

KURAMOCHI: Please come back again
        Day with blue clouds streaming
        Day with the afternoon star
        Flickering. . . .

(Enter YAMADA.)

KURAMOCHI: Visiting day is gloomy, isn't it? Want me to be with you?

YAMADA: It's all right, I'm always alone.

KURAMOCHI: How about singing?

YAMADA: What?

KURAMOCHI: What you sang recently?

YAMADA: What I sang?

KURAMOCHI: Didn't you sing it just like this? . . .

KURAMOCHI: *(Sings.)*

> Those days, those days,
> Please come back
> I've grown up
> Till I'm full
> To overflowing
> I tremble in sadness. . . .

YAMADA: It's a wonderful song. But I don't know it at all. I've never heard it.

KURAMOCHI: Aren't you worried, being so forgetful?

YAMADA: Worried? I think I'd rather worry. Look, it's worry that makes people go on, isn't it? Without time and without worry in my life, I become passive.

KURAMOCHI: Who did you hear that from? Why are you giving such a difficult speech to me? I'm no doctor!

Scene 8

(The pit face. It is dark. YAMAGISHI enters. From the shadow of a mining cart, Nurse TAKEMOTO suddenly appears and embraces YAMAGISHI.)

YAMAGISHI: What is it, calling me out to such a place. . . .

TAKEMOTO: Just a while ago, that woman left.

YAMAGISHI: Do you mean the new one, Ms. Yamamoto?

TAKEMOTO: I just assumed she was seeing you.

YAMAGISHI: It's just your lack of imagination.

TAKEMOTO: It's not a question of imagination, it's a persistent rumor.

YAMAGISHI: Look, rumors are 80 percent imagination.

TAKEMOTO: Maybe if it's a rumor in the general public. But not here. The patients here trace their facts thoroughly.

YAMAGISHI: What we have here is two hundred detectives?

TAKEMOTO: *(With an ill-tempered smile.)* This place, it's hell!

YAMAGISHI: Well, it's supposed to be the bowels of the earth. But . . . I wonder why Ms. Yamamoto came to such a place as this?

TAKEMOTO: Does it bother you?

YAMAGISHI: What if I said it does?

> *(YAMAGISHI reaches out trying to embrace TAKEMOTO. Playing hard to get, she flees.)*

TAKEMOTO: She, she really looked scared.

YAMAGISHI: Did she see you?

TAKEMOTO: I hid. And then. . . .

YAMAGISHI: And then?

TAKEMOTO: The mining cart just happened to come running out and almost crash into her.

YAMAGISHI: . . . You're pretty scary.

TAKEMOTO: Since no one saw it, I don't have any explaining to do.

YAMAGISHI: I don't understand. Why would you want to kill her so badly?

TAKEMOTO: *(Laughs.)* Want to kill her—that's going too far. . . . But even a falling leaf can make a woman angry enough to kill.

YAMAGISHI: Indeed . . . is all I can say here.

TAKEMOTO: . . . The woman's in love with somebody.

YAMAGISHI: Oh . . . the two hundred detectives've investigated that, too?

TAKEMOTO: This is woman's intuition. . . .

YAMAGISHI: Woman's intuition, huh? And if she is in love with me, a desire to kill on your part would fall within the realm of reason.

TAKEMOTO: One thing for sure. You're uncommonly concerned about her.

YAMAGISHI: Is that too intuition?

TAKEMOTO: *(Leeringly.)* Last night Mr. Kuramochi and Ms. Sakino sort of borrowed this model.

YAMAGISHI: *(Taking a cigarette from his pocket.)* No smoking in the mine pit?

TAKEMOTO: Very funny! It's just a model.

YAMAGISHI: *(Sardonic smile.)* It is well made, don't you think? It's funny how Ikki enjoys working on this thing. The whole notion of realism, see. To create the very illusion of reality by making things closely resemble reality. It's the work of a maniac, you know, this whole thing. Besides, as long as he is confined to this place, he's able to avoid being grilled by the relatives of the victims.

(With a meaningful glance, TAKEMOTO *begins to undo the buttons of her blouse.* YAMAGISHI *backs away.)*

YAMAGISHI: This afternoon was the neurological test, wasn't it?

TAKEMOTO: It's visiting hours now. . . . It's all right, isn't it?

YAMAGISHI: *(Darting his eyes about, as if suddenly frightened.)* I feel surrounded by piles of corpses here.

TAKEMOTO: Don't look at me like that. . . .

YAMAGISHI: I was the first doctor into the mine pit after the accident. I'd never had such an experience before. Since becoming a doctor, it was the first, I mean, dealing with so many dead bodies. I wonder if you've ever seen bodies done in by carbon monoxide poisoning? They're rose colored. A strangely transparent rose color. Because the carbon monoxide destroys the oxygen in the blood. It was pretty. Their skin was transparent and faintly reddish. It was oddly peaceful. . . .

TAKEMOTO: I'm afraid of getting old, really afraid.

YAMAGISHI: *(Wearying of the discussion.)* Your strong point is that you are interested only in the present progressive tense.

TAKEMOTO: What about her?

YAMAGISHI: She said, "New lives, new loves." She sometimes acts like a coed.

TAKEMOTO: Stop talking about her.

YAMAGISHI: You started it.

TAKEMOTO: I'll tell you what. The present progressive tense means, you see, time going by is precious.

(The two embrace.)

TAKEMOTO: Lately I can't sleep, I'm afraid of the hands of my watch. Before I know it I'm counting the seconds out loud: two seconds, three seconds, four seconds.

(Their embrace gradually becomes fervent. A noise from the rear, the two look up.)

YAMAGISHI: Are you sure there's nobody there?

(TAKEMOTO bursts out in laughter.)

YAMAGISHI: What is it?

TAKEMOTO: I thought of something really strange. *(Giggles.)*

YAMAGISHI: Something strange?

TAKEMOTO: Right. It's just occurred to me. If you have your bust enlarged, it'd be really wierd when you get old.

YAMAGISHI: That would be wierd.

TAKEMOTO: Ugh . . . not me. *(Continues laughing.)*

YAMAGISHI: *(Fumbling around.)* I forgot to smoke my cigarette.

(TAKEMOTO becomes angry.)

YAMAGISHI: Because you're so concerned about the present progressive tense.

(YAMAGISHI lights a cigarette. On second thought holds the lighted match to the wall of the pit face.)

YAMAGISHI: Surprisingly rough, isn't it? Strange. Looks like it was broken on purpose.

TAKEMOTO: He really tried to outdo himself.

(IKKI suddenly appears from the rear.)

IKKI: Where is it? The part that's broken.

(YAMAGISHI and TAKEMOTO are surprised and part in a flurry.)

YAMAGISHI: You startled us.

IKKI: *(Does not so much as glance in their direction. Turns on light switch.)* Terrible, this is terrible. Who would do such a thing?

TAKEMOTO: It must be her.

IKKI: Who? Ah, I know. Her. Has to be her. Dammit! What she won't do! Dr. Yamagishi, that woman, who in hell is she?

YAMAGISHI: Well, I'm not interested in anyone beyond the patients.

IKKI: She might be a spy, hired by the bereaved families.

TAKEMOTO: That prim expression, you don't know what she's thinking. The bread truck driver said he'd seen her on a "strange" street in Hakata.

YAMAGISIII: A "strange" street?

TAKEMOTO: Right, a street where men go looking for women.

Scene 9

(The training room. The afternoon sun casts deep shadows. URAGAMI*'s wife* RYŌKO *[twenty-six years old] and* IKENO*'s wife* YŪKO *[twenty-six years old].* KITADA *enters as if looking for someone.)*

RYŌKO: There is not as much breeze here as I expected.

YŪKO: I wonder where they went, those two.

RYŌKO: I heard from the nurses some malicious gossip about their being gay, that they go everywhere together, even the toilet.

YŪKO: *(Fingering flower petals in the flower pot she has brought.)* I shouldn't forget to water it in the evening.

*(*NISHI *and* NISHI'S FATHER *[forty-six years old] enter from the courtyard.)*

NISHI'S FATHER: What a ridiculous thing he's making. You could say your brother was killed by that man three years ago.

*(*NISHI *is munching on a banana, probably brought by his father.)*

NISHI'S FATHER: Medical science is making no progress at all, is it? Building such a thing right in the middle of the hospital, he's dead wrong if he thinks this kind of hocus-pocus can make the four hundred bereaved families trust what he says and does. Do you see what I'm saying to you? . . .

NISHI: *(Eating.)* What you're saying? I understand already!

NISHI'S FATHER: *(To* RYŌKO *and* YŪKO*.)* Sometimes, I'm absentminded and can't get down to work. Don't you know the young man Nishi, who was a leader in the Great Strike?[3] He used to be vice-chairman of the regional labor committee. . . .

NISHI: Everyone already knows all about me.

KITADA: Hey, no need to be so shy. . . .

NISHI'S FATHER: I'm talking about your older brother who died. And here you are, in this shape, the younger brother who has survived. . . . I wonder if my son will ever be normal again? It's amazing how you wives are able to put up with them.

*(*KITADA *exits, grinning broadly.* KANEKO *enters. She is without her glasses, and her clothes have undergone a gorgeous transformation. The others stop talking and watch her.)*

KANEKO: *(Greets everyone lightly, then to* NISHI*.)* I wonder if you've seen Mr. Yamada?

NISHI: Um, are you getting married?

KANEKO: Yes, but just temporarily. He's all alone, right? And so today I thought I would become a surrogate family for Yamada.

NISHI'S FATHER: He's the one, Yamada. Was standing on his head in the garden! He'll say he can see the world differently.

KANEKO: My, those flowers look like they're about to burst into flames.

YŪKO: They'll last only three days.

(KANEKO *exits.*)

RYŌKO: It was silver pink, her lipstick.

YŪKO: That sort of person is a lot older than one might think.

(IKENO *and* URAGAMI *enter.*)

RYŌKO: Where did you go?

(IKENO *and* URAGAMI *are hesitant.*)

URAGAMI: We went to the bus to meet you.

RYŌKO: Oh, that's odd. I wonder why we didn't see you there?

YŪKO: Mr. Uragami . . . your complexion has gotten a lot better.

IKENO: On the way, we saw some strange bugs, didn't we?

URAGAMI: Small black bugs in a procession.

YŪKO: Small black bugs?

IKENO: They weren't mice.

URAGAMI: They might've been camels—they had humps, right?

RYŌKO: In that case, it must be ants.

IKENO: They had wings.

RYŌKO: You've been looking at bugs. What a waste of time. Um, say, dear, would you take off your shirt for a minute?

(URAGAMI *is stupefied.* RYŌKO *takes a new colored sports shirt from a package.*)

RYŌKO: Hurry up and take it off.

URAGAMI: I'm embarrassed.

(URAGAMI *nervously begins to take his shirt off.*)

IKENO: I am really embarrassed.

(IKENO, *too, begins to take his shirt off.*)

YŪKO: Not you. (*Produces the potted plant.*) Here, this is for you.

(IKENO *holds the plant in his arms.*)

RYŌKO: (*Looking at* URAGAMI*'s naked upper body.*) Oh, your body seems to have gotten somehow firmer . . . hasn't it, Yūko?

IKENO: But he's got some pimples.

(YŪKO *turns her eyes away from* URAGAMI*'s body.*)

YŪKO: Don't forget to water it.

IKENO: Pretty, isn't it? (*To* URAGAMI.) We can put it right between our two beds. What do you think?

(URAGAMI *is struggling to put on his new shirt over his head.*)

URAGAMI: I can't see a thing.

(KATŌ'S UNCLE [*fifty-two years old*], KATŌ'S WIFE, *and* KATŌ *enter.*)

KATŌ'S UNCLE: (*In a fairly loud, arrogant voice.*) Quite a nice place, wouldn't you say? Even the air is good. The sea is close by. And the greenery is not bad. The building's even better than our community center.

KATŌ: Who is he? Tell me again.

KATŌ'S WIFE: (*Hits* KATŌ *lightly. She has a habit of indiscriminately hitting people in this way.*) That's not good. It's your uncle talking to you.

KATŌ'S UNCLE: Hello, you're all families visiting? I am the uncle of Katō, who is in group number seven. I'm working as village headman down the coast in Ariake.

NISHI'S FATHER: The part famous for being reclaimed by drainage?

KATŌ'S UNCLE: It's scary during typhoons. We're all in the same boat, as they say; still, please forgive my nephew.

(*With a resigned air, everyone acknowledges him.*)

KATŌ'S UNCLE: But say, you girls are pretty enough to be on TV. Do you always come on visiting day?

RYŌKO: Yes. We work, so on visiting day, we just take a little time off.

KATŌ'S UNCLE: I'll bet you work in a cabaret or something. Whereabouts?

YŪKO: With the help of the union, we are at a sewing factory, making work clothes. . . .

RYŌKO: Don't we look like the wives of laborers?

NISHI'S FATHER: Aren't 80 percent of the patients' wives working? The worker's accident insurance alone is just not enough.

KATŌ'S UNCLE: It must be difficult. No matter how strange he becomes, you should never turn your back on your own husband. But how about it—hasn't the old urge bugged you, you know, to play around?

KATŌ'S WIFE: Uncle!

KATŌ'S UNCLE: Right, I'm out of line. The one who's been bugged by the urge is, I should say, yours truly.

(YŪKO, RYŌKO, *and* KATŌ'S WIFE *practically burst into laughter.*)

URAGAMI: "Bugged?"

IKENO: He said "bugged."

(SARUSHIMA *enters in uniform and carrying a notebook.*)

SARUSHIMA: Everyone, thanks for your trouble. My name is Sarushima. I'm the one in charge. (*He has a fit of coughing.*) Please, just make yourselves at home.

(*Each of the families greets him.*)

SARUSHIMA: If you have any questions about the subsequent progress or how they're doing in their studies, please do not hesitate. . . . Mr. Uragami, where is your uniform?

RYŌKO: I'm sorry. We're just seeing whether his new shirt fits.

SARUSHIMA: It would be good to put a large identification tag on the shirt. The patients often put on the wrong shirts. In any event, the trouble is both the one who makes the mistake and even the guy whose shirt is taken are totally unaware of it and act as if nothing has happened.

NISHI'S FATHER: My son says he's having trouble with *kanji* dictation.

SARUSHIMA: Mr. Nishi? Let's see, Mr. Nishi. . . . *(Leafs through his notes.)*

*(*TOKUGAWA *and* TOKUGAWA*'s daughter,* HANAKO *[sixteen years old] enter. She is humming a tune to herself.)*

HANAKO: Daddy, do you know when your birthday is?

TOKUGAWA: Surely not today, is it?

HANAKO: It's the day after tomorrow.

(Looking shy, TOKUGAWA *is pulled along by* HANAKO. URAGAMI *and* IKENO *exchange glances.)*

HANAKO: *(To* KATŌ'S UNCLE.*)* Doctor, I wonder if it's all right to give Daddy a ride on the bike?

KATŌ'S UNCLE: The doctor's over there.

HANAKO: Oh, I'm sorry. I thought he was a patient.

SARUSHIMA: *(Grim faced.)* It's not advised, as a rule.

HANAKO: *(Waving her camera.)* I want to get one shot with the ocean as background. That's OK, isn't it?

SARUSHIMA: *(Face beaming.)* A picture? Just let me see that. *(Takes camera in hand and examines it like a maniacal expert.)* Probably good enough for an amateur. The range finder is a bit dark. Go out of the courtyard, and there's a gate on the left. Go straight out there, and you'll find a splendid hill with the sea as background.

HANAKO: Let's hurry, Daddy.

TOKUGAWA: Calm down, calm down, the sea will still be there. . . .

*(*KATŌ'S UNCLE *looks here and there out the window.)*

KATŌ'S UNCLE: Wonderful place. Wouldn't be a bad hotel. If only there were no wire fence around it.

NISHI'S FATHER: The building doesn't really matter.

KATŌ'S UNCLE: People, somehow or other, grow into whatever contains them. . . .

KATŌ: *(To his* WIFE.*)* You didn't tell me about the uncle before, you know.

KATŌ'S WIFE: He suddenly came in yesterday from the country. He said when you were small you always spent summer vacations at his house.

*(*SARUSHIMA, *who has been talking to* RYŌKO, *suddenly speaks.)*

SARUSHIMA: It's really strange, you know. During physical training, Mr. Uragami is totally unable to balance on one foot. According to the doctors, that part of his brain with the sense of balance was more seriously affected than in the other patients.

RYŌKO: How can that be?

SARUSHIMA: Mr. Uragami, would you first try to do it?

(URAGAMI *stands on one foot. He perfectly maintains his balance.*)

SARUSHIMA: More and more strange. Try it one more time.

(*Copying* URAGAMI, IKENO, NISHI, *and* KATŌ *also try.* URAGAMI *maintains his balance perfectly. Sound of someone falling over with a bang.* SARUSHIMA *and the others turn around to see that* NISHI *has fallen over.*)

SARUSHIMA: My mistake. It was Mr. Nishi who couldn't. . . .

KATŌ'S UNCLE: (*To* KATŌ.) Don't remember at all. You used to pester your father, "Let's go to the country and see that dance, the *menfuryū*, let's go to the country and see the dance. . . ."

KATŌ'S WIFE: But, Uncle, it's not possible. . . .

KATŌ'S UNCLE: I know. He's ill and all that, but you see, we can't have him forget the *kagura* dance too. It's quite famous, you know. It's been officially declared by the government an Intangible Cultural Property. You've often danced it together with my son, haven't you. Look! Allow me! The *menfuryū*, a wonder drug for memory recovery.

(KATŌ'S UNCLE *abruptly launches into a dance. The others all stop talking and stare at him.* KITADA *enters.*)

KITADA: I wonder if you've seen my wife.

HANDYMAN: It's a festival! Take it in quietly.

(KANAYAMA *and* SAKINO *enter.*)

SAKINO: Hurry up, we won't make it in time!

KANAYAMA: At the Miyama Mines festival, even I could do the Coal Miner's Dance[4]—or so I hear.

SARUSHIMA: (*To* KATŌ'S UNCLE.) Oh my! Are you from Saga too? Do you know the Ureshino area?

KATŌ'S UNCLE: (*Dancing.*) You mean the area west of Hizen?

SARUSHIMA: Right, to the west. I was there for about three years. Wow, what a strange coincidence!

(SARUSHIMA *too joins with* KATŌ'S UNCLE *and begins to dance. When at times he forgets his steps, he watches* KATŌ'S UNCLE, *who is an accomplished dancer, and follows along.* YAMAGISHI *and* TAKEMOTO *enter.*)

YAMAGISHI: The *menfuryū* dance?! Does this mean that the days of yore have finally taken the stage?

(NAGAOKA *enters.*)

KURAMOCHI: Join us, Dr. Nagaoka, please.

NAGAOKA: For a long time, I've waited and hoped for this kind of warm, heart-to-heart contact.

(*The tempo of the* menfuryū *dance picks up a bit, then vigorously. Suddenly,* KATŌ *lets out a scream and runs off.*)

KATŌ'S WIFE: Hey, where are you going?

(KATŌ'S WIFE *chases after him.* KATŌ'S UNCLE *stops his dance.*)

KATŌ'S UNCLE: It's not working, is it? Without some sacred wine and revelry, after all. . . .

(KATŌ'S UNCLE *too runs off stage.*)

NISHI'S FATHER: *(To* SARUSHIMA.*)* I want to speak with that doctor. You don't know what's going on.

(SARUSHIMA *chases after* NISHI'S FATHER, *trying to explain.*)

SARUSHIMA: If I can just tell you about the detailed data we have

(*Opens his notebook.*)

(NISHI'S FATHER *and* NISHI *exit.* SARUSHIMA *closes his notes in confusion and exits as if chasing them.* HANAKO *takes* TOKUGAWA *by the hand.*)

HANAKO: To the sea!

(HANAKO *and* TOKUGAWA *exit.*)

URAGAMI: I'm a little sleepy.

IKENO: I'm sleepy too.

SAKINO: I wonder where they went, Takemoto and the doctor? Mr. Uragami, Mr. Ikeno, you haven't had the brain wave test yet, have you? They just now came from the university, you know. *(To* RYŌKO *and* YŪKO.*)* Is it all right?

RYŌKO: Please, go right ahead.

SAKINO: *(To* IKENO *and* URAGAMI.*)* Better to get it done quickly.

(SAKINO *goes out in the direction of the courtyard.*)

URAGAMI: I wonder if it's okay to have the brain wave test when you're sleepy.

IKENO: *(Still carrying the potted plant.)* Why not have the brain wave test done on this too?

(IKENO *tries to go.* YŪKO *gently takes the plant from him.* URAGAMI *and* IKENO *exit. Thunder.*)

RYŌKO: It's summer for sure now.

YŪKO: The third summer. . . .

(*The lights focus on the stairway landing.* KANEKO *and* YAMADA *are playing hopscotch.*)

YAMADA: Thunderstorm might be coming.

KANEKO: I don't mind a thunderstorm.

YAMADA: You sound like somebody who'd have a strong appetite, too.

(SAKINO *returns with* IKKI *from the direction of the garden.*)

IKKI: I wonder where she is? The lowest estimate is twenty thousand yen damage, you know. Anyway, I won't be satisfied unless we make her pay.

(IKKI *exits the training room in the direction of the entrance to the main building. Lights again on the stairway landing.*)

YAMADA: . . . somebody's looking for somebody.

KANEKO: It's all right. We're playing hide-and-seek. . . .

(*The two continue to play hopscotch. The lights on the stairway landing fade out.*)

SAKINO: If you'll just allow me to smoke a cigarette? . . . It's a real bummer, you know, not being allowed to smoke on duty. (*Looks at* RYŌKO *and* YŪKO.) You always come together, don't you?

RYŌKO: Yes.

YŪKO: Yes.

(SAKINO *puffs on the cigarette and lightly does a few dance steps.* RYŌKO *and* YŪKO *look at each other.*)

RYŌKO: Listen, my husband and Mrs. Ikeno's husband, there's someone spreading a rumor they're gay. Do you know about it?

SAKINO: (*Flatly.*) They couldn't be gay. Not those two. Their sex drive is still defunct. Homosexuals lacking a sex drive, it's like a highball without alcohol.

YŪKO: That's why we're not worried.

RYŌKO: They can't help it if they're good companions. They've been close friends since a long time ago.

SAKINO: (*Giggles.*) I've got sharp ears.

YŪKO: What do you mean?

(YAMADA *and* KANEKO *enter the training room, still playing hopscotch.*)

YAMADA: I was with someone—who was it, I wonder?—walking by the river. Those long legs . . . maybe it was stilts . . . were reflected in the water . . . a weed-grown embankment ran all along the. . . .

KANEKO: How about a swing?

YAMADA: A swing I don't remember.

KANEKO: That's enough. You're completely worn out, aren't you. Come on, let's go.

YAMADA: Flowering thistles . . . that's it, flowering thistles in among day lilies.

(SAKINO *stops her dance steps.*)

SAKINO: But, it's strange. . . .

YŪKO: What's strange?

RYOKO: Yes, what?

SAKINO: Oh, you are good at pretending. Mr. Uragami gets along so well with him now, but before, they hated each other so much they could've killed one another.

(KANEKO *and* YAMADA *stop their hopscotch and listen.*)

YŪKO: What are you saying?

RYŌKO: Something must be wrong with her.

SAKINO: (*Turning toward* YŪKO.) You must be the cause.

YŪKO: That's a lie.

SAKINO: One's husband and lover both lose their memories . . . a little tragic, eh?

(KANEKO steps in between them.)

KANEKO: *(To SAKINO.)* Whatever the situation, it probably doesn't matter to you. Children shouldn't interfere.

RYŌKO: Let's have the whole story.

YŪKO: It's totally cock and bull.

RYŌKO: If so, you've got nothing to fear.

YŪKO: I'm not afraid of anything.

SAKINO: Well, I've got to go. I'm sorry.

(SAKINO exits. RYŌKO and YŪKO, as though testing each other's feelings, stand speechlessly. YAMADA seems almost to fall over with silent laughter.)

KANEKO: Mr. Yamada. . . .

YAMADA: She said those two, those two who are always together, hated each other so much they could've killed one another. . . .

KANEKO: What's so funny about that?

Scene 10

(A small hill from which the sea is visible. Light. TOKUGAWA's daughter HANAKO.)

HANAKO: *(Facing the sea.)* Hey! Hey, there!

(TOKUGAWA enters.)

TOKUGAWA: Who are you calling?

HANAKO: You, Daddy.

TOKUGAWA: Daddy? Isn't that me? I'm right here.

HANAKO: *(Still facing the sea.)* Hey!

TOKUGAWA: I'd just like to ask you something. What was it I used to call you when you were little?

HANAKO: Hanako, Hanachan, Hanabo, Ohana, Hanabei.

TOKUGAWA: And which name do you like the best?

HANAKO: Let's see, now, I guess Hanabo. Oh, look! A rainbow!

TOKUGAWA: So it's Hanabo, is it?

(TOKUGAWA looks at HANAKO from behind as if dazzled by her youth and beauty.)

TOKUGAWA: It's really all right to believe, is it, that you're really my daughter?

HANAKO: Daddy, don't talk like that. Then whose child would I be anyway?

TOKUGAWA: Probably . . . my child. It's just, if you were a child of two or three, I could think of you as my daughter, but such a grown one as you, well. . . .

HANAKO: How pretty . . . the light seems to be dancing on the waves. Your coal mine is out there, in the bottom of the sea.

TOKUGAWA: It just might be out there, in the bottom of the sea. Would you hold my hand?

HANAKO: Your hand, Daddy?

TOKUGAWA: If you don't, I feel like I'll be pulled out into the sea.

HANAKO: Hello! Hello there!

TOKUGAWA: I'm right here.

HANAKO: I know. This time I'm calling out to the bottom of the sea.

TOKUGAWA: The bottom of the sea?

HANAKO: Yes. You see, Daddy, you've completely lost those important memories of the two of us, there in the bottom of the sea. . . . Hey! *(The sea suddenly darkens.)*

Scene 11

(The training room.)

TOKUGAWA: Hello! Hello there!

(KATŌ, NISHI, and KITADA enter with badminton racquets for the next class.)

NISHI: Who are you calling, Toku?

TOKUGAWA: *(Laughing.)* Me, just myself.

(KATŌ and NISHI begin to play badminton.)

KITADA: Is something wrong, Toku?

TOKUGAWA: No, I was just thinking about my daughter.

KATŌ: *(Continuing to play badminton.)* She doesn't look at all like you, does she, Toku?

TOKUGAWA: *(Becoming serious.)* You're wrong. When she smiles, doesn't she look like me? Yes, she does.

KITADA: Smile and let's see.

TOKUGAWA: I can't smile on a cloudy day.

(URAGAMI and IKENO enter with their badminton racquets.)

URAGAMI: No matter what, on cloudy days, my form is off.

IKENO: On rainy days, my form is even worse.

(YAMADA enters from the courtyard with a guitar.)

KATŌ: Hey, look! Look what that guy mistook for his racquet.

IKENO: To hit the birdie, you need something like this.

(Swings his racquet to show YAMADA, who makes the same motion with his guitar. Everybody laughs.)

URAGAMI: This guy shows absolutely no sign of progress.

IKENO: It looks like he's gradually getting worse.

KATŌ: Do you know what that is? It's not a shovel.

YAMADA: It's a guitar. Dr. Kuramochi's. I feel like I can sing again.

URAGAMI: Surely, this guy's memory hasn't returned . . . has it?

IKENO: Look, are we going to destroy our unity?

KATŌ: I'm opposed.

KITADA: Opposed.

NISHI: Any objections? Then, it's passed.

KITADA: I guess you really were the vice-chairman, Nishi.

(KATŌ takes the guitar from YAMADA.)

TOKUGAWA: What a funny feeling. . . .

KITADA: What's funny?

TOKUGAWA: . . . a very, very funny feeling.

KITADA: Is it about your daughter? Maybe you're just worried about what Katō said.

KATŌ: I only meant . . . she surely must look like her mother.

TOKUGAWA: . . . When I was on the hill, I really had a strange feeling.

(All vaguely prick up their ears.)

TOKUGAWA: Suddenly, I wanted to embrace that young woman and kiss her.

(All stop moving and look dumbfounded.)

KATŌ: The hot weather made you feel that way.

URAGAMI: Such a . . . that's strange. She's your daughter, isn't she Toku?

TOKUGAWA: *(Brief silence.)* Just like that, a young woman appeared, even called out, "Daddy, Daddy!"

IKENO: But, there's no doubt you're her father, is there?

URAGAMI: *(Anxiously.)* Now, that's right, you know.

TOKUGAWA: . . . Did you see her hands? First time I ever saw a woman with such gentle hands.

(Brief silence.)

TOKUGAWA: Why are you looking at me like that? They tell me my wife has died. When you see your wives, what's it really like? I wonder if you actually feel those women are your wives.

KATŌ: Sure, I do. She hugged me and cried. No mistaking she's my wife. My father and uncle and others even said so.

IKENO: *(Nervously.)* Stop that kind of talk.

KITADA: I don't want to stop.

IKENO: My wife forgot to hug me.

NISHI: *(Laughing.)* Don't think so much about stupid things. When it gets humid, your head feels strange no matter what you do.

URAGAMI: But, look, think about it. For three years, they've come regularly to see us. No one else would do this, you know. They've brought lunches, clean shirts, things like that. We're being bad to them.

TOKUGAWA: At least that proves they're our families . . . and yet. . . .

KITADA: Why didn't my wife come?

IKENO: It's just one time, isn't it? Hey, there's a guy here who no one ever comes to visit.

NISHI: He's a murderer, you keep your distance.

KATŌ: Nobody knows for sure that he's a murderer.

URAGAMI: But it's strange. Why doesn't his family come forward?

IKENO: His family's lying. They're pretending they don't know him. That's for sure.

(YAMADA abruptly bursts out laughing.)

YAMADA: That's for sure? Pretending they don't know him? But your families lie, too.

KATŌ: What do you mean?

YAMADA: *(Enjoying himself.)* I know perfectly well, about all of you.

NISHI: *(Pointing to himself.)* About all of us?

TOKUGAWA: *(Anxiously.)* You include me in that "all of you"?

YAMADA: *(Pointing to URAGAMI and IKENO.)* Your wives are telling lies.

(URAGAMI and IKENO nervously put their shoulders together.)

YAMADA: Shall I let you in on it? You two were not close friends. You hated one another like enemies.

(The group is dumbfounded.)

YAMADA: You hated each other enough to kill. . . .

(URAGAMI and IKENO nervously move apart.)

YAMADA: You two are no different than me. Try looking back and see. If you do, suddenly it'll be pitch black. *(Laughs.)*

URAGAMI: It's a lie!

IKENO: Help!

(The two pounce on YAMADA. The rest of the group stands frozen in place and looks on blankly. From the courtyard, SAKINO enters, supporting KANAYAMA on her shoulder.)

KANAYAMA: Stop this child's play, that's enough.

SAKINO: If you've got the energy to fight, you can chase after girls. . . .

(YAMAGISHI and KANEKO enter. KANEKO is wearing glasses.)

YAMAGISHI: Stop it!

(YAMAGISHI separates YAMADA and the others.)

KANEKO: You were picking on Mr. Yamada again, weren't you.

TOKUGAWA: He was picking on Ura.

KANEKO: *(To YAMADA.)* Surely you were not. . . .

YAMAGISHI: In any event, let's have the reason.

(The group shuts up. A long silence.)

NISHI: Someone said these two were in fact enemies.

YAMAGISHI: Who said that?

SAKINO: I did. I said it because those women ticked me off.

(TAKEMOTO enters.)

TAKEMOTO: What's going on with all this noise just now?

YAMAGISHI: *(To* SAKINO.*)* How did you know that?

SAKINO: Because my aunt is in the coal mining residence.

YAMAGISHI: But it's just gossip, right?

TAKEMOTO: If it's about men and women, it's usually true.

YAMAGISHI: You please be quiet.

IKENO: It's a lie. He said we were enemies and that we hated each other enough to kill. . . .

YAMADA: You'd better be quiet.

SAKINO: Just ask your wives straight out and see. Anyway, whatever I say is just gossip.

KATŌ: Don't be so sarcastic.

KANAYAMA: You're the only one I believe.

SAKINO: Aaah! I refuse to be dragged in any further than this. . . . I mean, you've been digging up everything you could on me, too.

KITADA: We haven't said that much about you.

TOKUGAWA: Because you're a dull girl.

*(*SAKINO *exits with an air of defiance. Chimes sound.)*

URAGAMI: Call my wife, please!

IKENO: Let me see my wife, please!

YAMAGISHI: What a mess. If we don't call them and talk to them, say tomorrow, these two likely won't be satisfied.

TAKEMOTO: Have them confront each other. If you don't, we'll never get this cleared up. In the future they won't open up at all.

KANEKO: It's useless.

YAMAGISHI: I think so, too. Ms. Takemoto, you amuse yourself too much with people.

TAKEMOTO: What do you mean by that, I wonder? I'd understand if you mean I amuse myself with myself.

KANEKO: *(With passion.)* Mr. Uragami, Mr. Ikeno, please believe your wives. Somebody may try to sneak in the back door, but slam the door shut. Call out to each other, depend on each other, like lovers who've only just met this summer, on a white sand beach glittering in the sun. . . . You should love one another.

TAKEMOTO: Too romantic, makes me want to swoon. I don't want to stick my nose into someone's past, but there are times when the past seems to become important, you see, in order to know a person's true colors.

KANEKO: I'm not interested.

TAKEMOTO: I am. For example, about you. You were in Hakata in the past, weren't you?

KANEKO: I've been there, to that town. . . .

TAKEMOTO: If the associate director types were to know about this, they would be startled.

YAMAGISHI: Ms. Takemoto.

TAKEMOTO: Deceiving us with glasses, that's to be expected.

KANEKO: Is something wrong with my glasses?

IKENO: She's asking if something is wrong with her glasses.

URAGAMI: What about us?

(TAKEMOTO *hysterically grabs* KANEKO*'s glasses.*)

KANEKO: Stop it! You too are all quite happy to dig up someone else's past. What's so much fun about it?

TAKEMOTO: You'll soon be enjoying it well enough.

YAMAGISHI: Ms. Takemoto, that's enough!

TAKEMOTO: Dr. Yamagishi, I came in here to get you. Professor Sasaki from the university wants you to call him. It's urgent.

YAMAGISHI: That's strange. I wonder what Professor Sasaki wants? After all, I'm not much of an academic. Excuse me.

(YAMAGISHI *exits.*)

TAKEMOTO: (*To* KANEKO.) I'm sorry. I'm a woman who's easily misunderstood. Sometime I want you to sit down and tell me about a woman's happiness.

(TAKEMOTO *exits.* KURAMOCHI *enters, moving his body this way and that.*)

KURAMOCHI: Well, everybody . . . let's begin. First, lightly running around the exercise area.

(KURAMOCHI *himself begins with light steps.*)

KURAMOCHI: Don't forget your racquets. (*Sees the guitar in* YAMADA*'s hands.*) What a nuisance, bringing that out without asking. Do me a favor and put it back in my room.

(KURAMOCHI, KATŌ, TOKUGAWA, *and* KITADA *exit.* NISHI *goes over to* KANAYAMA.)

NISHI: (*Gently.*) Hang on to me.

KANAYAMA: It's all right?

NISHI: It's all right. Aren't we in the same room?

(*The two exit like* URAGAMI *and* IKENO *earlier.* URAGAMI *and* IKENO *watch them go and, flurried, exit separately. The* HANDYMAN *enters and begins to clean up.* YAMADA *loiters about, cradling the guitar.*)

HANDYMAN: Morning, noon, and night—three times, three times they eat, and afterward not one thing is cleaned up.

(*Associate Director* NAGAOKA *and* SARUSHIMA *enter.*)

NAGAOKA: Oh, excellent. Here's Mr. Yamada.

SARUSHIMA: News, news.

NAGAOKA: Hey, hey, calm down.

SARUSHIMA: We just now had a communication from the dispatch room of a newspaper in Ehime Prefecture.

NAGAOKA: Mr. Yamada, we've found the person who may be your wife.

(YAMADA *is speechless.*)

KANEKO: What? Really?

SARUSHIMA: Of course, we don't know yet. Anyhow, she's set to arrive here tomorrow.

NAGAOKA: It's been a while, but the Mental Rehabilitation Center may be getting lots of news coverage for the first time in a long time.

SARUSHIMA: In any case, let's contact the company too. They've had their headaches with the problem of workers' compensation. *(Has a coughing fit.)*

NAGAOKA: I'll contact the head of personnel directly.

SARUSHIMA: You're the best one to do that. *(Obsequiously.)* When you have a spare moment, could you take a look at me? I'm wondering if it isn't bronchitis. . . .

NAGAOKA: I'll make the diagnosis. I never expected you to have respiratory trouble. . . .

(NAGAOKA and SARUSHIMA exit. From the direction of the courtyard comes KURAMOCHI's voice, issuing commands for running around the exercise area: "One, two, three. . . .")

YAMADA: Finally, she has appeared. I'm really tired of waiting, it's been such a long time.

KANEKO: Don't be silly, you know she's. . . .

YAMADA: You know there's something so familiar about the way you talk to me.

KANEKO: Oh, I feel like I'm having some crazy hallucination.

YAMADA: Tomorrow, we'll understand everything.

KANEKO: —tomorrow we'll understand everything.

YAMADA: He said Ehime, didn't he. Where is Ehime?

KANEKO: It's in the western part of Shikoku.

YAMADA: There should be a river there.

KANEKO: I don't know. It's an area I don't know.

YAMADA: Near the river . . . there was a long grassy embankment . . . river beds with water tumbling over large, white rocks . . . the daytime stars were dazzling. . . .

KANEKO: What if, what if your wife is a terrible woman who betrayed you? . . .

YAMADA: My wife is not that kind of woman. Why are you speaking ill of my wife?

KANEKO: I'm sorry. Something's come over me. I. . . .

YAMADA: Forget it. You look nice without your glasses.

(YAMADA exits toward the courtyard. KANEKO remains standing for a few moments. Finally, she approaches the empty swing and pushes it. It swings back and forth.)

HANDYMAN: *(Opens a very thick book.)* In the development of productive capacity, one stage will become apparent. Under the various relations at present, the means of transportation as well as the productive capacity to be brought into being at that stage bring only disasters. Before long it is not productive capacity but destructive capacity. And in connection with that, one particular class will be produced. This class receives none of society's benefits but must bear all manner of society's heavy burdens. It is squeezed out of mainstream society and forced into a clear confrontation with other social classes.

(IKKI *enters from the corridor entrance.*)

IKKI: Finally, I've found you. It's time for you to make restitution.

KANEKO: What do you mean?

IKKI: You've committed a crime. There are witnesses. It's your doing, isn't it?

KANEKO: Yes, I'm the one.

IKKI: How cruel to do that to my castle, to the castle I went to all that trouble to make for the gas patients.

KANEKO: *(Hysterically.)* That's enough! Please stop exposing other people's pasts!

IKKI: *(With a blank look.)* Exposing their pasts? You seem afraid for their pasts to come back!

(KANEKO *gives a start and looks around.*)

ACT THREE

Scene 12

(In a spotlight, the conversation exchanged as act 2 ended is being recited.)

IKKI: Finally, I've found you. Well, it's time for you to make restitution.

KANEKO: That's enough! Please stop exposing other people's pasts!

IKKI: Exposing their pasts? You seem afraid for their pasts to come back. *(An explosive burst is heard. A woman's [*KANEKO's*] piercing shriek. Everything sinks into darkness.* IKKI's *voice: "Dammit!" Before long the lights come on abruptly. It's the pit face. The* HANDYMAN *has turned on the light switch.* IKKI *comes out from a hole in the rear and shows an exploded electric heater.)*

HANDYMAN: *(Takes it in hand.)* Guess you won't be using that anymore.

(KURAMOCHI *enters.*)

KURAMOCHI: Are you all right? It sounded like something blew up. . . .

HANDYMAN: Blew up? It's this. *(Shows heater.)*

(KATŌ, KITADA, TOKUGAWA, NISHI, *and* KANAYAMA *enter without a word.*)

HANDYMAN: *(Surprised.)* What's wrong?

(The group is silent.)

IKKI: *(Almost shrieking.)* My god, surely you don't mean you want to destroy this. . . . It's anarchy; violence is the last resort.

(Suddenly, the lights blend with the empty space at the back of the pit face, and

YAMADA *appears.* [*The characters who enter the lighted empty space all say their lines as if in recitation.*])

YAMADA: You people are no different than me. Just take a look back there. You'll suddenly be facing total darkness.

(YAMADA *vanishes.*)

IKKI: Please understand! I'm trying to keep all your interests in mind and to deepen our solidarity. . . . Please put yourselves in my place! I want you to regain your memories as soon as possible.

(KITADA *and the others stare curiously here and there around the pit face.*)

KITADA: It's unexpectedly cool.

KATŌ: The ventilation facilities aren't too bad. . . .

TOKUGAWA: It's rather quiet and relaxing.

KURAMOCHI: Why in hell's name're you here?

KANAYAMA: Why? I'm not sure.

NISHI: There was a big noise, wasn't there?

KATŌ: Right. That's why we came.

IKKI: (*Laughs loudly.*) This is great. They mistook it for a blasting sound just like you, Kuramochi.

KURAMOCHI: Hmmm. But being in such an accident, wouldn't they feel bad?

IKKI: More than that, your body remembers the work it used to do. Something sets off a blast. Boom, your body throbs with pain, you gather coal. Something sets off a blast. Boom, your body in flames. You gather coal.

KURAMOCHI: You mean, like a conditioned response?

IKKI: All right, starting next time, we'll create the sound effects of a blast. The blast'll be the signal for all the gas patients in the rehab center to gather together with their minds on home.

TOKUGAWA: That doesn't sound too bright. You'll mess us up again.

KANAYAMA: Hey! Listen to that. . . .

NISHI: The bones in ol' Kana's feet are knocking.

KANAYAMA: Strange, isn't it, how we've gotten to be such good friends.

NISHI: Probably because it's so somber here.

KURAMOCHI: Well, I don't like such a gloomy place. Midsummer sun, clean air, girls brimming with vigor and vitality. . . .

KATŌ: A feminine fragrance.

KITADA: But an unpleasant one. (*The two sniff* KURAMOCHI.)

KURAMOCHI: (*Flustered.*) That's not so, I don't smell at all, not at all.

TOKUGAWA: What about your pipe, your water-pumping pipe?

IKKI: I wonder if you can remember back to that time.

KITADA: That time?

IKKI: Right after the accident. Shall I lend you a cap lamp? (*Hands one over to* KITADA.)

KITADA: *(Parroting* IKKI.*)* Shall I lend you a cap lamp? *(Hands it over to* NISHI.*)*

NISHI: I'm fine. *(Hands it over to* KATŌ.*)*

KATŌ: You afraid of it? *(Tries to pass it along to the next person.)*

KITADA: Even if I am, we've got to stick it out. . . .

(The spotlights converge on YAMADA, *who is reciting.)*

YAMADA: Everyone was sleeping on the floor. Only the cap lamps were on; they shone on the ceiling, hundreds of them mixed together like searchlights, a sea of mud, an ugly sound, a sound like snakes slithering. . . .

IKKI: No, no. Not to be upset. One step backward, two forward. Have a steady grasp of the mass mind. Go slowly, slowly. . . .

KANAYAMA: Toku, what are you nervous about?

TOKUGAWA: You don't feel uneasy? Isn't everyone worried?

KITADA: Shall we go?

IKKI: It's taken quite some doing to get here. You're all right for a while more, aren't you?

(SAKINO appears in the light in the empty part of the stage.)

SAKINO: I can't believe those good friends Mr. Uragami and Mr. Ikeno used to hate each other enough to kill. . . .

(SAKINO disappears.)

NISHI: I think that nurse is telling lies.

KANAYAMA: I think Ura's wife is lying.

KATŌ: Surely our families and relatives wouldn't lie, would they?

(URAGAMI and IKENO appear in the light in the empty part of the stage. It is as if confrontation and hatred were returning to them just as prior to the accident. It gradually turns into a game of killing each other. URAGAMI suddenly groans.)

URAGAMI: Ike, I can't kill you.

IKENO: *(Shakes his head.)* We hate each other.

URAGAMI: Let's do this the other way. You kill me.

IKENO: You lost at scissors, paper, stone. Going back on that is going back on the truth.

URAGAMI: Being killed is much easier.

IKENO: Right, being killed is much easier.

URAGAMI: Let's get someone else to actually do the killing.

IKENO: Then we'll die good friends.

URAGAMI: Neither of us will be a murderer.

IKENO: The murderer is somewhere, but we have to settle our own matter ourselves. . . .

URAGAMI: I just can't bring myself to hate you, Ike.

IKENO: That's a lie.

URAGAMI: It is, isn't it.

IKENO: What that nurse said is the truth.

URAGAMI: I can't believe it.

IKENO: What you can't believe is the truth.

URAGAMI: What you can believe is a lie.

IKENO: There's only one way out.

URAGAMI: There's only one way out.

IKENO: Come on, kill me.

URAGAMI: I beg you, kill me.

(*The two disappear.*)

NISHI: Doctor. Doctor Kuramochi, please play your guitar.

KURAMOCHI: What a sudden request.

NISHI: Old songs, even I . . . I feel like I can sing songs from when I was a boy.

KURAMOCHI: You don't need a guitar, do you? Go ahead and try.

NISHI: (*Strikes a pose . . . can't recall the words.*) Without a guitar, see. . . . (*Cries.*) If only you'd play the guitar.

KANAYAMA: Nishi, if you cry, you'll make me cry too.

(YAMADA *appears in the lights.*)

YAMADA: (*Sings the song "Those Days."*)

(YAMADA *becomes distant and disappears.*)

KITADA: Listen, Toku, why do you suppose my wife didn't come to see me? She's always been here on visiting day. . . .

(KATŌ'S WIFE *and* UNCLE *appear in the middle of the spotlights and dance with bodies intertwined.*)

KATŌ: That man, my uncle, I wonder if he's really my. . . . Oh! Not with my wife. . . .

(KANEKO *appears in the middle of the spotlights.*)

KANEKO: Please believe your wives. Call out to each other, depend on each other, like lovers who've only just met this summer on a white sand beach glittering in the sun. . . . You should love one another.

(KANEKO *disappears.*)

TOKUGAWA: Hello!

(HANAKO *appears in the middle of the spotlights.*)

HANAKO: Hello! The light seems to be dancing on the waves. You see, Daddy, you have completely lost those important memories of the two of us, there in the bottom of that sea. . . . Hello there!

(*The characters who have appeared in the middle of the spotlight all gather onstage and, bodies intertwined, dance as a group. Before anyone is aware of it,* TOKUGAWA *gets into the truck and thrusts his head out.*)

TOKUGAWA: Hello!

IKKI: (*Seeing this, abruptly becomes agitated.*) That's it! Like that, stay just like that! (*The dancers come to a standstill and finally disappear.*) I got into the cart that way to eat my lunch. It was lunch hour. For some reason I could only eat my lunch in a small place. Then a dull roar sounded in the distance. It was surely from pit face number eight. They were raising a clamor. Someone cried out, "It's exploded!" "Lie down!" "Don't stand up!" "Soak the towels!" "Hurry!" "Douse the lights!" "Cut the motors!" Someone turned the switch off. But it was the wrong switch. The carts suddenly began to move. Eighteen carts, with only me aboard. They picked up speed. I was not letting you die before my very eyes. Someone turned the wrong switch.

KITADA: We have to see it with our own eyes. Someone is telling a lie.

(The HANDYMAN *appears in the middle of the spotlights.)*

HANDYMAN: *(Reading aloud from a magazine.)* We will not permit lies. The mask of an inhuman society must be stripped off.

TOKUGAWA: Well, shall we go?

(The group stands up and slowly moves toward the exit.)

HANDYMAN: As the large coal dust explosion at the Misawa Coal Mine and the lingering symptoms of the ensuing disaster clearly suggest, the patients, who were transformed into hulls of their former selves and their development arrested at childhood, are a declaration of a state of emergency in our world, and we should regard them accordingly as extraordinarily symbolic of that emergency.

(The group exits.)

IKKI: Wait a minute! Aren't you going to listen to what I have to say?

(The group exits.)

HANDYMAN: *(Looking toward the spectators, abruptly begins speaking in a youthful voice.)* In this day we can't avoid the struggle to humanize society. We want to be human. Those of you who've gotten old at twenty, you should recover your youth. You must marshal today the combative strength of youth that was yours yesterday, even though it's like sticking flowers in the air.

Scene 13

(The training room. RYŌKO *enters.)*

RYŌKO: It's a lie. It's nonsense.

*(*URAGAMI *enters.)*

RYŌKO: *(Laughs nervously.)* They say you liked Mr. Ikeno's wife. I'll say it right out, you always used to say behind her back that you hated a gloomy woman like her.

URAGAMI: *(A blank expression.)* I . . . such a thing. . . .

RYŌKO: *(To* URAGAMI.*)* You mustn't believe anyone but me. There's something wrong with all the others. They believe whatever that nurse says.

*(*YAMAGISHI *enters.)*

YAMAGISHI: Ms. Sakino may have made the story up. The patients tend to make up stories, and sometimes it's catching—the doctors and nurses start doing it too. Anyway, this morning I tried to get the story straight from Ms. Sakino. According to her, the rumor is that Mr. Ikeno's wife was involved in a triangular relationship with Mr. Uragami and Mr. Ikeno. . . .

RYŌKO: Well, it looks like I'm the only one not involved.

(TAKEMOTO *enters.*)

TAKEMOTO: I wonder if you aren't very much involved. Mrs. Ikeno did take your husband.

RYŌKO: That's more than enough. Please stop with your insults.

URAGAMI: That's right. To insult is an insult!

IKENO: Please hurry up and call my wife too!

YAMAGISHI: This kind of role doesn't sit well with me. . . . Still, relieving the patients' anxiety is a doctor's job.

RYŌKO: That's what you say, but you just want to amuse yourself at our expense.

YAMAGISHI: That's ridiculous. It is, rather, a trying job for me.

TAKEMOTO: Anyway, we're missing one actor, aren't we?

(TOKUGAWA, KITADA, KATŌ, *and* KANAYAMA, *who is leaning on* NISHI*'s shoulder, enter.*)

YAMAGISHI: Ms. Takemoto, you need to be careful of what you say too.

(*The patients all say "Shh!"*)

YAMAGISHI: You all are annoying.

(KATŌ *abruptly begins drawing a line on the floor with chalk.*)

RYŌKO: What's going on with these people?

KATŌ: No one is to cross this line.

KITADA: (*Stretching out a jump rope like an entrenchment.*) No one is to step over this.

(IKENO *starts to go toward the patients, all of whom shake their heads "No" and murmur in unison: "Ike."*)

TOKUGAWA: Please, don't come over here.

(KANEKO *enters.*)

KANEKO: May I show in Mr. Ikeno's wife?

YAMAGISHI: I'd like you in here as well. By myself I don't think I can handle it.

KANEKO: Nurse Takemoto is here.

TAKEMOTO: That's exactly why he wants you here, because I'll be here. Isn't that right, Dr. Yamagishi?

(YŪKO *enters.*)

KANEKO: Please excuse me.

(KANEKO *exits.*)

YŪKO: I'm sorry I'm late.

RYŌKO: Why did you tell me to go on ahead of you? It's a little suspicious, isn't it, only today coming separately?

(YAMADA *enters quietly and takes shelter behind the others.*)

YŪKO: I, uh, I didn't intend to come today.

YAMAGISHI: Well! A rumor is, after all, a rumor. . . .

YŪKO: I was very afraid.

TAKEMOTO: Oh! You mean it's all right to run away because you're scared?

YŪKO: The rumor is true. I was in love with Mr. Uragami.

IKENO: I was fond of Ura too, you know. (*But is unsure.*)

(*The patients unanimously reproach* IKENO.)

RYŌKO: What're you talking about? . . .

YŪKO: Mr. Uragami also was in love with me.

RYŌKO: How dare you tell such a lie. . . .

URAGAMI: I don't like gloomy women like her. (*But is unsure.*)

(*The patients unanimously reproach* URAGAMI.)

YŪKO: Mr. Uragami and I loved each other. Beyond this I think nothing else need be said. . . .

(*The patients unanimously utter a groan.*)

YŪKO: I . . . if you would let me go home now.

YAMAGISHI: Just a minute, please, Mrs. . . .

YŪKO: For the rest, you can get it all from Mrs. Uragami.

YAMAGISHI: She says it's a lie.

RYŌKO: Lies! Provided they are elegantly touched up, even lies can seem like the truth.

YŪKO: I've got a train to catch.

IKENO: Where are you going?

URAGAMI: To the island! (*But is unsure.*)

YŪKO: I'm sorry. . . . I want to go back to my hometown and think things out.

IKENO: Surely you're not going to leave me, are you?

YŪKO: (*To* URAGAMI.) I loved you. But I don't know anymore what's best to do. I've waited patiently for three years. I can't take anymore. . . . No matter how much we say we loved each other, no one will accept it. Even you don't accept it. I'm leaving both Ikeno and you. (*To* IKENO.) You'll understand my feelings, too, won't you?

IKENO: . . . I'm losing my wife.

YŪKO: Goodbye.

(*Holding back her tears,* YŪKO *exits*).

RYŌKO: Wait, please stop her.

IKENO: I don't know what to say.

URAGAMI: I don't either.

(NISHI *makes as though to run after* YŪKO.)

KANAYAMA: *(Indicating the jump rope.)* Don't cross this line. We should not. . . .

TOKUGAWA: It's a line we can no longer cross.

*(*TAKEMOTO *rushes for the entrance.)*

YAMAGISHI: *(Stops her.)* Miss Takemoto, it's no use.

TAKEMOTO: I'm not convinced of that.

YAMAGISHI: It's not your problem.

TAKEMOTO: You think not? Do you understand it?

YAMAGISHI: Miss Takemoto. . . .

TAKEMOTO: Doctor, what's wrong with living for that cruel spark at just the moment when a man and a woman split?

YAMAGISHI: You are being too unhealthy.

(While jumping rope, the patients, including of course IKENO *and* URAGAMI, *start to move away as a group.)*

RYŌKO: Please wait. Listen to what I have to say too.

(The group stops jumping.)

YAMAGISHI: But, Mrs. Uragami, this is not exactly a trial, so no need to be on edge. . . .

RYŌKO: That was a wonderful performance—a speech even I might inadvertently believe. But what she said is all lies.

YAMAGISHI: Let's grant you your desire to call it a lie . . . but if on the one hand it's a lie, on the other, as fate would have it, it may be true.

TAKEMOTO: He means that, as far as you're concerned, the accident was, rather, a piece of good fortune. Because you've gotten your husband back.

RYŌKO: My husband has always been mine. You don't understand that she planned the whole thing. I was a fool. I'm just now coming to see it.

YAMAGISHI: What is it you want to say?

RYŌKO: She only wanted to leave her husband and made very good use of a totally baseless rumor.

NISHI: My head hurts.

KANAYAMA: Me too . . . give me some medicine.

KITADA: No more shots for me.

RYŌKO: I'm sure she wanted to run away from her present life. She couldn't bear to wait forever for a husband whose recovery was uncertain. That's why she used us.

YAMAGISHI: Then simply in order to separate from Mr. Ikeno. . . .

RYŌKO: The truth is I sometimes felt strangely confused, too. And it wasn't just me. The wives of the other patients all felt that way.

KATŌ: My wife's headache is that uncle of mine.

KITADA: Why hasn't my wife come?

RYŌKO: That's why I can really understand what was going on in her mind. *(Tears well up.)* Surely that's it. Would you believe her rather than me? I'm not much with words. But lies I don't tell.

NISHI: Things have gotten all mixed up.

KANAYAMA: What's really the truth? I'm losing patience.

TOKUGAWA: *(Shakes his head.)* Which one shall we decide on?

(SAKINO and a WOMAN [about twenty-eight years old] enter.)

SAKINO: Oh, you're here together. You look like wedding guests who only came because they had to.

YAMAGISHI: They're that way on account of you. You're an unexpectedly bad bridesmaid.

(RYŌKO suddenly approaches SAKINO and slaps her face.)

SAKINO: What are you doing?

YAMAGISHI: Stop it! That's disgraceful.

(YAMAGISHI and TAKEMOTO move between the two and stop them. RYŌKO exits.)

URAGAMI: That Yamada's a lucky guy.

(URAGAMI hesitates but nervously runs out after her.)

WOMAN: I'm sorry to interrupt when you seem to be having some trouble, but I. . . .

(The group is suddenly aware of the unfamiliar WOMAN.)

WOMAN: I was invited here. . . .

SAKINO: She apparently missed the associate director who went to welcome her. Well, here she is. . . . Mr. Yamada's.

(The group buzzes.)

YAMAGISHI: You're Mr. Yamada's?

WOMAN: No, my name is not Yamada.

YAMAGISHI: Pardon me. We're using the name Yamada temporarily. Mr. Yamada.

(YAMADA stands behind the swing as though intimidated.)

YAMAGISHI: Mr. Yamada.

(YAMADA timidly takes a step or two toward stage center. He stops. The WOMAN stares at him. The NEWSPAPER REPORTER enters. He fusses over setting up his camera; the flash is not properly synchronized.)

REPORTER: Stay in that position, don't move. I'm sorry, one more, please.

(The flash burns out.)

KATŌ: A power outage!

NISHI: Give me some water!

KANAYAMA: Help!

TOKUGAWA: Be quiet!

(A moment of silence.)

WOMAN: That's not him. He's not my husband after all.

(The patients utter a groan. KANEKO *enters.)*

REPORTER: Then you're not this person's wife?

YAMAGISHI: *(To* TAKEMOTO.*)* The symptoms of Parkinson's Disease appear to have gotten worse. Say, has Dr. Nagaoka arrived yet?

REPORTER: He doesn't resemble in any way your missing husband?

WOMAN: Not in any way. It's a case of mistaken identity.

SAKINO: In the past, Mr. Yamada cut his hair short, didn't he? I was just thinking that the shape of one's hair could change one's impression a lot.

TAKEMOTO: What you really want to say is that with women it's easier to fool people just with hairstyles.

REPORTER: At any rate, could you please reconfirm this? *(Clicks his tongue.)* Damn, my watch would have to stop just now. . . .

WOMAN: He's someone I don't know. . . . I've told people in the newsroom there that they are probably mistaken. My husband wasn't built for work in a coal mine, you see. But you said you'd pay my travel expenses, and so I came.

REPORTER: Mr. Yamada . . . you of course, for your part, don't remember her?

YAMADA: Uh . . . I remember a river. By a grassy embankment.

WOMAN: The breeze always used to blow against it. . . .

YAMADA: The thistle flowers in the breeze . . . they made a noise like from a far-off festival.

WOMAN: The marigolds and chrysanthemums were like a sea of flowers from spring to summer. . . .

YAMADA: There is, for sure, a river . . . there's a river in your town.

WOMAN: *(Laughs.)* A town without a river is like the face of a woman who's forgotten how to cry. A stream at a distance from the town. . . . I'm from Ehime, but just a little island in the Inland Sea.

IKENO: An island? You're from that island.

WOMAN: But it grows old from fall to winter, from an island of flowers to an island of stone. . . .

IKENO: Don't talk so sad.

TOKUGAWA: Ike, she's surely referring to an island much farther away.

REPORTER: What time is it now?

SAKINO: *(Twining her body around him and showing him her watch.)* Here.

YAMADA: *(To the* WOMAN.*)* I'd like to see your face where there's more light. . . .

(Associate Director NAGAOKA *and* SARUSHIMA *enter.)*

NAGAOKA: Please forgive me for being so late for this deeply moving encounter.

REPORTER: *(Putting away his camera, addresses the associate director.)* Sir, this story won't make the news.

YAMAGISHI: *(Shakes his head.)* It seems she's not the one, after all.

WOMAN: I am very sorry for you. That he can't remember anything of the past. Isn't there any prospect of recovery?

NAGAOKA: We are making every effort. Mr. Sarushima, what training is scheduled for now?

SARUSHIMA: Let's see, it's time for discussion. Since you've gone to the trouble of coming here, would you like to take a look at the training setup?

WOMAN: I'm exhausted from the night train. *(To YAMADA.)* I'm sorry, I've disappointed you. But even if your wife doesn't appear, you mustn't despair. You shouldn't be so attached to one woman. No woman is that valuable. I wonder if there is anything in this world that is? *(Laughs.)*

(WOMAN exits. SAKINO runs off after her.)

REPORTER: That's right, Mr. Yamada. There are all kinds of women. I'll find ten or twenty women, and you can meet them.

SARUSHIMA: Dr. Nagaoka, how about if we show him our model here of the pit face?

NAGAOKA: *(To the REPORTER.)* It's still in the experimental stage. When we get results, we'll call a press conference immediately. . . .

REPORTER: Some other time. In my business I'm always up against deadlines.

(The REPORTER exits.)

SARUSHIMA: That was a waste of effort, wasn't it? *(To the associate director.)* Sir, a phone call, to the head office?

NAGAOKA: You make it!

(NAGAOKA and SARUSHIMA hurry off after the REPORTER. KANEKO is on the swing.)

TAKEMOTO: Shall I push you?

(TAKEMOTO begins to push.)

KANEKO: Thank you.

TOKUGAWA: That's it! I've got it! That woman just now was lying.

KITADA: Toku!

YAMAGISHI: Then you're saying she's Yamada's wife, are you? Didn't she clearly say she wasn't?

KANAYAMA: But Doctor, how can we say she is telling the truth? She shouldn't be expected to, she can't. . . .

YAMAGISHI: *(Unable to answer at once.)* But she took such trouble to come. There's no need for her to lie.

NISHI: She was saying she didn't want to come.

KATŌ: Maybe she intended to get away by acting like she didn't know.

KITADA: Now you're talking about Ike's wife.

TOKUGAWA: It's the same with that woman just now. We're the people who are a little crazy in the head.

KANAYAMA: After so long a time, even if someone presents herself as your wife, it won't do her any good.

YAMAGISHI: What's happened here? You've suddenly gotten distrustful. . . . It's so stuffy my head seems to be coming off.

KATŌ: It's gotten to where we have no notion at all of what's the truth.

TOKUGAWA: I think that's the way it was even before the accident. What in hell is the truth?

IKENO: If it's lies, then lies are fine. If everyone will just keep telling us lies. . . .

TOKUGAWA: We'll never understand anything anyway until we get over our craziness. And we're not the only ones. . . .

(URAGAMI *enters.*)

URAGAMI: Where is my wife?

(*The group crowds around* YAMAGISHI.)

IKENO: Please give me back my wife!

KITADA: Please call my wife!

KATŌ: Mine, too!

TOKUGAWA: Please give me back my dead wife!

(KURAMOCHI, SAKINO, NAGAOKA, *and* SARUSHIMA *enter.*)

KURAMOCHI: It's all right, it's all right, the doctor has arrived, you can all calm down.

NAGAOKA: Mr. Yamagishi, this would seem to indicate symptoms of increasing volition.

URAGAMI: Liars! All you ever do is tell us to believe. . . .

KATŌ: Tell us the truth.

IKENO: Give back my wife.

NISHI: Give back the truth.

KITADA: Give back everything!

KATŌ: Time! Give that back!

TOKUGAWA: Give back our companions who died.

(*The patients crowd in on the administrators.* NAGAOKA, KURAMOCHI, *and* YAMAGISHI *try to push them back. Suddenly,* KANAYAMA *throws away his crutches and starts to go berserk.*)

KANAYAMA: They're the enemy! These characters are our enemies!

(KANAYAMA *throws the administrators aside one after another.* KURAMOCHI *seems to faint.* SAKINO *runs over to hold him up.*)

YAMAGISHI: Mr. Kanayama . . . what about your foot?

(*Everyone stops moving and focuses on* KANAYAMA, *who stands in blank amazement, then abruptly falls flat.*)

NISHI: Kana. . . . *(Runs to him.)*

SAKINO: He's faking it! A clear case of faking it! He's a fake, a parasite!
(SAKINO exits, holding up KURAMOCHI.)

KANAYAMA: *(Leaning on crutches.)* It is too broken. That much is for certain.

NAGAOKA: *(To SARUSHIMA.)* It's your approach to training by and large
that. . . .

SARUSHIMA: Of course, we are doing exactly as the physicians prescribe.

NAGAOKA: If so, then what about the reports that tests always show a
decrease in their volition?

SARUSHIMA: If you let me explain, what I mean is . . . for the medical
branch to have a more clear-cut policy is. . . .

NAGAOKA: An immediate reexamination, you've got to do a reexamination.
*(NAGAOKA and SARUSHIMA exit. The rest of the group stands about, looking
vacant. KANEKO comes forward.)*

KANEKO: Say, everybody, let's all go over to the hill and have some fun.
There are lots of swallows there now—they're really lovely.

YAMAGISHI: I am thoroughly exhausted. Why don't I go along for the
walk too.

TAKEMOTO: Have a good time. But don't forget that now it's discussion
time.

YAMAGISHI: Right. I can't go for a walk. No reexamination of the training
without me.
(YAMAGISHI exits. YAMADA walks forward unsteadily.)

KANEKO: Mr. Yamada. . . .

YAMADA: I'm not Yamada! That woman, she said there's a river. . . .

KANEKO: There are lots of towns with rivers.

YAMADA: I remember it clearly. I always used to take walks there. Thistle flowers bloomed all over, the water was lukewarm . . . there was
a bridge. A small bridge. Beyond it you could see a red roof. . . .

NISHI: I know that too.

KATŌ: How come?

NISHI: That's the picture on the calendar hanging in your room.

YAMADA: That's a lie. I remember. I always used to take walks there
with someone, maybe my wife. I wore holes in my shoes, pebbles got
in. . . .

IKENO: What a terrible woman! She abandoned you just like my wife
did me.

URAGAMI: Ike. . . .

IKENO: We were deserted!

YAMADA: . . . abandoned, just now, by my wife. . . .

KANEKO: No, you weren't. That's not true.

YAMADA: I was too! You don't understand a thing, so just be quiet. My wife left me.

(YAMADA *goes reeling off toward the garden.*)

KANEKO: (*Turning in his direction.*) No, she didn't. That woman isn't your wife.

(*The patients buzz among themselves saying,"Doctor, how can she?" "How does she," and so forth.*)

KANEKO: I am your wife.

(YAMADA *turns around with a dubious look. The patients, as a group, utter a groan.*)

TAKEMOTO: (*Profoundly surprised.*) Finally, you've come out with it. . . .

KANEKO: She's right. Finally, I've come out with it. I'm your wife.

(*Brief silence. The patients exit singly or in pairs, until only* KANEKO, TAKE-MOTO, *and* YAMADA *remain.*)

Scene 14

(*The pit face.* NISHI, KATŌ, TOKUGAWA, IKENO, KITADA, *and* KANAYAMA *enter. All are silent.*)

IKKI: You're all still young, aren't you? Don't you want to go back to work?

TOKUGAWA: (*Abruptly blurts out.*) Let's dig coal.

KITADA: Right! Let's dig coal.

KATŌ: The safety equipment is no good.

KANAYAMA: The machinery has deteriorated. . . .

NISHI: Leave the hospital negotiations to me.

IKKI: That's right. The coal we dig up here is not phantom coal. Please remember, please remember what we do, especially this next time. If we act with solidarity, there's nothing in this world we can't do . . . let's sing a song or something to brighten things up.

(IKKI *begins to sing. Soon the patients join in the chorus with him.*)

Scene 15

(*The training room.* KANEKO, TAKEMOTO, *and* YAMADA.)

YAMADA: If you're saying this out of pity, that's not a good idea. With time the lie will come out.

(KANEKO *calmly shakes her head.*)

YAMADA: I don't understand. Why keep it a secret till now?

KANEKO: I kept dreaming. That we could have a new love, like a man and woman meeting for the first time.

TAKEMOTO: I wonder why we have dreams when we fall in love but only facts when we part?

KANEKO: *(Drawn to her own words, as if she's halfway making up a story.)* We got married when we were still very young. We led an ordinary modest life, in an apartment with one six-mat room where only the window was large. I lost the courage for a life with you, just the two of us, and I ran away. I learned to do everything necessary for a woman alone to survive. And the more I struggled the more I realized that I loved you even more deeply. Maybe it was a youthful fling, or maybe it was a woman's adventure. But many times along the way I tried to go back to you. . . . I had no confidence. I had no confidence you would forgive me—a selfish woman who would run away and then come back just like that.

TAKEMOTO: When I break up I'll be the one to announce it to him. That's the way to do it. Nobody's going to run out on me.

KANEKO: I was shocked when I read in the paper that your identity was unknown. When the shock passed, I made a decision. I decided that I would appear before you as someone unfamiliar. I thought I would try to have our life start again.

YAMADA: Assuming that's true . . . you're a strong person.

KANEKO: No. Never. I may be a terribly weak one. I can't bear to go on living with my past. The reason I came here to this hospital was simply to see you, simply to have you like me.

TAKEMOTO: For me, the one thing that makes life worth living is that cruel spark when you break up. . . . My body consumed in the sparks shows me I'm a woman. . . .

KANEKO: Living here . . . every time you turned around, I felt you were going to punch me. There was a lingering pain in my love for you that I couldn't get rid of. It's like Mr. Ikki said, I seemed to be terrified of the past coming to life. He was right. I was afraid . . . very afraid.

(Silence. HANAKO*'s voice is heard from a distance: "Hello there!")*

KANEKO: I never intended to tell you. But in the end I did. . . .

TAKEMOTO: *(Looking at her watch.)* Two seconds, three seconds, four seconds . . . I think all this worrying and brooding is a waste of time. I've got to get back to my medical charts.

*(*TAKEMOTO *exits.* TOKUGAWA*'s daughter* HANAKO *enters from the courtyard carrying an animal doll.)*

HANAKO: Say, do you know where my father is?

KANEKO: I wonder if he isn't in the courtyard?

HANAKO: *(Calls out.)* Daddy!

(As HANAKO *tries to leave, a white ribbon falls from the animal doll.)*

KANEKO: Oh!

*(*KANEKO *picks up the ribbon and gives it to* HANAKO.*)*

HANAKO: Thank you. Today is my father's birthday, you know.

KANEKO: What a nice present.

HANAKO: *(Giggles. Indicates doll.)* This face, it's just like when I was small, isn't it.

KANEKO: Well. . . .

HANAKO: I'll ask him to lay it by his bed, to remember when he called me Hanabo.

KANEKO: I see.

HANAKO: My father needs dolls. But I'm growing up, I'm practically an adult.

(HANAKO flutters about like a butterfly and disappears. YAMADA suddenly notices the WOMAN on the swing.)

WOMAN: *(Sings the counting song that the patients were singing before.)*

(YAMADA walks toward the WOMAN.)

KANEKO: *(To YAMADA.)* Dear. . . .

(YAMADA goes to the WOMAN's side without looking back.)

KANEKO: Why are you going back?

YAMADA: *(To WOMAN.)* I want to see your face in better light.

(The WOMAN, leaving behind only her laughing voice, vanishes, together with the swing, into thin air. YAMADA remains standing, dumbstruck.)

KANEKO: I'm sorry. It's all right now. It's all over with.

(YAMADA looks back.)

YAMADA: *(Thinking about what has happened.)* So many things have happened here. I'm completely in the dark about them. I haven't the faintest inkling of who or what you are. To me, you are all people I've only just met here a very brief time ago.

KANEKO: . . . people you've only just met a very brief time ago.

YAMADA: Yes . . . a very brief time ago. . . .

(Tilting his head, YAMADA exits. KANEKO remains standing at stage center.)

KANEKO: Maybe . . . maybe . . . we could begin from this point.

(KANEKO returns to the spectators' seats and again becomes one of the spectators.)

Scene 16

(The pit face. The patients are hard at work. They act as though they are working at the real pit face.)

URAGAMI: Ike, maybe we could begin from this point.

IKENO: Right, I'm not the least bit tired.

(The men laugh together.)

URAGAMI: As long as we're here, our families are complete strangers.

IKENO: You're right, Ura. I've got no memory at all of my wife.

URAGAMI: Let's go over there together sometime, to the island.

IKENO: Yes, let's go together, to the island.

(There is suddenly a deafening roar. The patients are blown over. A strange sort of rustling sound follows. The men exchange shouts.)
The gas! It's exploded!
Lie down! Don't stand up!
Soak the towels! Hurry!
Run! Feel your way along the tracks!
(The pit face collapses into rubble. Finally, a moment of silence. A single individual crawls tentatively out. It is IKKI. He looks around dumbstruck.)
IKKI: *(A soliloquy.)* I've got no luck at all. The only one out alive again. Do I really exist in this world? Somehow, it's gotten so that I can hardly believe myself anymore.
   Curtain.

Notes

1. The real name of the mine is Mitsui Miike. By "Misawa Miyama" Shimizu intends a slightly altered, fictional name that the audience will recognize as referring to Mitsui Miike.

2. The poem "Those Days" is taken from *Songs of Summer Flowers* (Natsubana no uta) (1937) by Tachihara Michizō (1914–1939).

3. Refers to the Great Strikes against the Mitsui Miike Coal Mine in 1953 and 1959–1960.

4. *Tankō bushi,* a song with accompanying dance that mimics coal mining activities, such as shoveling. It is still popular throughout Japan.

The Dressing Room: That Which Flows Away Ultimately Becomes Nostalgia

Shimizu Kunio

TRANSLATION ADAPTED BY CHIORI MIYAGAWA
FROM AN ORIGINAL TRANSLATION BY
JOHN K. GILLESPIE

CAST OF CHARACTERS

ACTRESS A
ACTRESS B
ACTRESS C
ACTRESS D

(Darkness. Several mirrors begin to reflect glittering lights as nostalgic music is heard. The mirrors whisper, "Although the tedium of everyday life deceives you at times, do not embrace sadness and rage. For if you tolerate patiently the sad days, you will without fail be visited by happiness again. . . . Your heart always lives in the future. Present entities aimlessly recollect lonely thoughts. Life in this world flows away in an instant. And that which flows away ultimately becomes nostalgia. . . ."

From the silent darkness, ACTRESSES A and B emerge almost imperceptibly and face the mirrors to begin applying makeup. They are intensely involved in the process. ACTRESS A's eyes are for some reason terribly burnt, and her vision appears to be blurred. ACTRESS B's neck is wrapped in a white bandage with fresh blood soaking through. The two actresses, completely absorbed in the makeup process, are quite serious but at the same time somewhat comical and even slightly sorrowful.

Suddenly, ACTRESS C stands up in front of the full-length mirror. She is dressed as Nina in The Sea Gull. *She holds a lighted cigarette.)*

ACTRESS C: I am a sea gull. . . . No, that's not right. I'm an actress. Ah, well. . . .

(Light slowly grows brighter. It is an ordinary dressing room. She is rehearsing her lines just prior to going on stage. ACTRESSES A and B are indifferent to ACTRESS C and remain involved in their makeup process.)

ACTRESS C: . . . So, he is here, too. . . . Well, it doesn't matter. He didn't believe in the theater; he always laughed at my dreams, and gradually I too ceased believing and lost heart. And then there was the anxiety of love, the jealousy, the constant fears for my baby. I grew petty, trivial, my acting was insipid. I didn't know what to do with my hands, I didn't know how to stand on the stage. I couldn't control my voice. You can't imagine what it's like to feel that you are acting abominably. I am a sea gull.

No, that's not right. Do you remember you shot a sea gull? A man came along by chance, saw it, and having nothing better to do, destroyed it. . . . A subject for a short story. . . . No, that's not it. What was I saying? I was talking about the stage.

I'm not like that now. Now I'm a real actress, I act with delight, with rapture, I'm intoxicated when I'm on the stage, and I feel I act beautifully. And since I have been here, I've been walking, continually walking and thinking . . . and I think and feel that my soul is growing stronger with each day. I know now, I understand, that in our work—whether it's acting or writing—what's important is not fame, not glory, not the things I used to dream of, but the ability to endure. To be able to bear one's cross and have faith. I have faith, and it's not so painful now, and when I think of my vocation, I'm not afraid of life.

(Listening.) Sh-sh! I'm going. Good-bye. When I become a great actress, come and see me. Promise? *(Grasps an imaginary hand.)* It's late. I can hardly stand on my feet. I'm exhausted and hungry. *(Takes a cookie from the dressing table.)* No, no . . . don't come with me. I'll go alone. When you see Trigorin, don't say anything to him. . . . I love him. I love him even more than before. How good life used to be, Kostya! How clear, how pure, warm, and joyous—our feelings were like tender, delicate flowers. . . . Do you remember? Men, lions, eagles, and partridges, horned deer, geese, spiders, silent fish that dwell in the deep, starfish, and creatures invisible to the eye—these and all living things, all, all living things, having completed their sad cycle, are no more. For thousands of years the earth has borne no living creature. And now in vain this poor moon lights her lamp. Cranes no longer wake and cry in meadows. . . . Oops! It's already my cue.

(ACTRESS C suddenly does vocal exercises and runs out of the dressing room. ACTRESSES A and B react for the first time.)

ACTRESS A: I am a sea gull. . . .

ACTRESS B: No, that's not right. I'm an actress. Ah, well. . . .

ACTRESS A: Can you believe she's forty?

ACTRESS B: Look, that idiot forgot her hat.

ACTRESS A: So she did.

(ACTRESS B *stands up, goes over to the hat, picks it up, and puts it on her chair. She then sits on the hat. The hat, of course, is brutally crushed.* ACTRESS C *reenters in a hurry.*)

ACTRESS C: *(Searching)* My hat . . . my hat . . . my hat . . . *(Finds it.)* Ah!

(*She approaches the hat and tries to pick it up.* ACTRESS B *plants herself firmly on the hat.*)

ACTRESS C: What's going on here?

(ACTRESS C *pulls at the hat with greater force. Right at that moment,* ACTRESS B *lifts herself up, sending* ACTRESS C *reeling off balance.*)

ACTRESS C: That's it! I will demand a different dressing room tomorrow.

ACTRESS B: I don't care.

ACTRESS C: *(Glaring at the area occupied by the two actresses.)* Rotten, foul air always hovers around here.

(ACTRESS C *exits in disgust.*)

ACTRESS A: Did you hear that?

ACTRESS B: I heard.

ACTRESS A: She called us "rotten and foul air. . . ."

ACTRESS B: . . . that "hovers."

ACTRESS A: Yeah, "hovers around here."

ACTRESS B: We can't be hovering. That sounds disgusting.

ACTRESS A: What do you mean?

ACTRESS B: Well, if something hovers, it's not solid, is it?

ACTRESS A: Either way, it's a useless image.

ACTRESS B: It sounds poisonous more than useless. We "hover. . . ."

ACTRESS A: You are obsessed with "hovering." My pride is beginning to get hurt. That's enough.

(Short pause.)

ACTRESS B: Anyway, the hats in style these days are abominable.

ACTRESS A: Well, you certainly didn't make it any better by crushing it.

ACTRESS B: When we were performing, we wore far more elegant hats.

ACTRESS A: When we were performing?

ACTRESS B: That's right.

ACTRESS A: Huh. . . .

ACTRESS B: What do you mean "huh"?

ACTRESS A: You talk like you played Nina in *The Sea Gull.*

ACTRESS B: *(Hurt.)* I told you before, I had one opportunity.

ACTRESS A: Only one?

ACTRESS B: What about you? You didn't even have a chance to play a gray starling, never mind a sea gull. You used to feel sorry for yourself all the time. "Ah, I was an eternal prompter. . . ."

ACTRESS A: I can say the exact same about you. Don't condescend to me. I don't run my mouth on lies like you do, but I also had an opportunity . . . Lady Macbeth.

ACTRESS B: Oh my, Shakespeare. . . .

ACTRESS A: That's right. I was on a tour . . . some town on the Inland Sea . . . Lady Macbeth ate too much smelt, the local fish dish, that morning and had a sudden attack of diarrhea. It was serious . . . she was in a coma by noon.

ACTRESS B: I see. There was your big chance.

ACTRESS A: I had been carrying a lucky charm from Kasama Shrine for my protection. I prayed to that charm . . . hurry up and die! Drop dead now!

ACTRESS B: Despite your prayer, your enemy miraculously recovered in the afternoon.

ACTRESS A: Not really.

ACTRESS B: She didn't recover?

ACTRESS A: No . . . by afternoon, I was suffering, too.

ACTRESS B: *(Amazed.)* You ate the smelt, too?

ACTRESS A: *(Nods.)* It was destiny. Everyone eats that fish dish in the Inland Sea.

ACTRESS B: I would have done the same. I have never been able to avoid destiny.

ACTRESS A: Definitely! That dish is delicious.

(Short pause.)

ACTRESS B: Lady Macbeth . . . I envy you. You had your chance, if only once. I didn't, even though I attended Macbeth performances over forty, maybe fifty times as a prompter.

ACTRESS A: So you know all the lines?

ACTRESS B: Of course I do. I recited them more than fifty times. *(Recites.)* "Hoarse is the raven that croaks Duncan's final approach within my walls. Come, you spirits that guide human thoughts, unsex me here. And fill me, head to foot, full of warrior cruelty! Thicken my blood; block up all access and passage to remorse, that no sudden strings of conscience shake my dark purpose nor soften its dread effect. . . ."

ACTRESS A: Hold on a minute.

ACTRESS B: I was just getting into it.

ACTRESS A: Um . . . is it the postwar version?

ACTRESS B: Postwar?!

ACTRESS A: Well, it's different from the version I remember.

ACTRESS B: How?

ACTRESS A: It's different from the beginning.

ACTRESS B: You mean the whole thing?

ACTRESS A: Yeah. . . . *(Striking a somewhat old-fashioned posture.)*
"The raven himself is hoarse
That croaks the fatal entrance of Duncan
Under my battlements."

ACTRESS B: . . . "the fatal entrance"?

ACTRESS A: "Come, you spirits
That tend on mortal thoughts, unsex me here,
And fill me, from the crown to the toe, top-full
Of direst cruelty! Make thick my blood;
Stop up the access and passage to remorse,
That no compunctious visitings of nature. . . ."

ACTRESS B: . . . "no compunctious"?

ACTRESS A: "Shake my fell purpose nor keep peace between
The effect and it. Come to my woman's breasts
And take my milk for gall, you murd'ring ministers,
Wherever in your sightless substances
You wait on nature's mischief!"

ACTRESS B: "Nature's mischief"?

(ACTRESS A stops reciting.)

ACTRESS B: Go on, please.

ACTRESS A: Excuse me if I'm old fashioned. I'm much older than you. I'm from an era when one felt "compunctions."

ACTRESS B: *(Comfortingly.)* I can understand what you mean, in an indirect sort of a way.

ACTRESS A: An indirect sort of way?

ACTRESS B: Well, it slightly lacks sensitivity.

ACTRESS A: Now I'm insensitive. I see. That's why I ended my career being a prompter.

ACTRESS B: There you go getting sulky again.

ACTRESS A: You think us "prewar" people are hardheaded and difficult, don't you?

ACTRESS B: Listen, you claim to be an eternal prompter, but weren't you on stage sometimes? I don't mean as Lady Macbeth or Nina. . . .

ACTRESS A: Yes, yes, of course . . . as Nobleman A or Messenger 2 or Gatekeeper 3. . . .

ACTRESS B: But those are all male roles.

ACTRESS A: I know. For some reason I got only male roles. Maybe because there weren't enough male actors around because of the war. I remember . . . I was even cast in *Macbeth* several times as a boy.

ACTRESS B: A boy? What were his lines?

(ACTRESS A hesitates.)

ACTRESS B: What's wrong?

ACTRESS A: It's just . . . my version is old fashioned.

ACTRESS B: I don't care.

ACTRESS A: I remember . . . I also had a part as a gambler.

ACTRESS B: You mean a punk?

ACTRESS A: Right. In Miyoshi Jūrō's play *Slashed Senta.* Of course, I wasn't Senta.

ACTRESS B: That's a Japanese classic. You don't have to worry about your version being outdated. *(She insists.)*

ACTRESS A: But. . . . *(Suddenly brandishing a backscratcher as a sword.)* "Count me out. In this mortal land, such a manner of gambler should not ever be forgiven. I know that. Yet I insisted on provoking trouble; I want you to know I have no place to escape to or hide in. But please have mercy this night. I wish to be set free. Big bosses, I can make endless excuses because I don't like to kill. I'm not capable of killing. . . ."

ACTRESS B: That's great. Is that your line?

ACTRESS A: No, it's Senta's. . . . "Are you hearing me, bosses. I am, as you can see, a wanderer with neither a name nor identity. I'm just another insignificant pawn. However, if you worry about your reputation being ruined when the word gets out that the one who conquered this gambling joint was a wanderer, make me into a thief. I'm a thief. Right, a thief. But I am not about to use this money for my own pleasure . . . dozens of people's lives will be spared by this money."

ACTRESS B: Look, when do *you* make your entrance?

ACTRESS A: Hush. It won't be long. . . . "I beg you bosses, look the other way just for one night. I will complete my task, and turn myself over to you. I am humbling myself. I understand your rage thinking that I'm another bum, but you are wrong. Think of me as a peasant farmer's son crying his heart out. Do not think that you gave me this one night's take, but think you gave it to peasant farmers, and let me go. Big bosses, I, Senta of Makabe Village, won't forget what I owe you. Wait. . . . *(Looks around and senses danger.)* I don't want to kill. I don't want to destroy life. Can't you understand that?" At that moment, Takijirō of Shimozuma leaps out on stage. . . .

ACTRESS B: Say. . . .

ACTRESS A: "Shut up! Sentarō, what are you babbling about? You don't want to kill? Then I will. I'll rip him apart."

ACTRESS B: Is *that* your role?

ACTRESS A: No.

ACTRESS B: Are we still waiting?

ACTRESS A: I'm already on stage.

ACTRESS B: What? Where?

ACTRESS A: Right around here.

ACTRESS B: Around here?

ACTRESS A: Yes, here. I came leaping out with Takijirō. In the stage
direction it said, "Takijirō leaps out. Seven punks rush out with him.
All have their teeth clenched and remain silent."

ACTRESS B: Remain silent!?

ACTRESS A: Right. Everyone was clenching their teeth . . . but I had to
prompt Senta and Takijirō on top of that, so I couldn't really be
faithful to the stage directions.

ACTRESS B: I can see what you mean. *(Clenching her teeth.)* It's kind of
hard to prompt doing this.

ACTRESS A: *(As if dreaming.)* But I loved that play. I liked the beautiful
women's roles like Otsuta or Omyō . . . but I was moved by Senta,
who gets slashed. . . .

ACTRESS B: *(Staring.)* You don't mean! . . .

ACTRESS A: Mean what?

ACTRESS B: That's why your makeup is. . . .

ACTRESS A: What about my makeup?

ACTRESS B: I've been wondering.

ACTRESS A: Wondering what?

ACTRESS B: About your eternal role.

ACTRESS A: And?

ACTRESS B: Is it Slashed Senta?

ACTRESS A: Give me a break! I *am* an actress. I would like a female role.
What about you? What's your role?

ACTRESS B: It's a secret.

ACTRESS A: Well, *I* know already.

ACTRESS B: No, you don't.

ACTRESS A: It's Nina. *The Sea Gull.* Right on the mark!

ACTRESS B: Wrong.

ACTRESS A: I sensed it when you destroyed that hat. You were as nasty as
a mother-in-law.

ACTRESS B: I said you were wrong.

ACTRESS A: "Nina! My darling. . . . I'm Trigorin."

ACTRESS B: Trigorin!?

ACTRESS A: ". . . these wonderful eyes, this inexpressibly beautiful,
tender smile . . . this sweet face with an expression of angelic
purity. . . ."

ACTRESS B: Stop it! That's creepy. Senta is a far better male role, if you
must.

ACTRESS A: No, I won't stop. Forgive me for my old-fashioned interpre-
tation. "Nina, things have taken an unexpected turn, and it appears
we are leaving today. It's not very likely that we shall meet again. I

am sorry. I don't often meet young girls . . . youthful and interesting. I've forgotten how it feels to be eighteen or nineteen."

ACTRESS B: That monologue suits you well.

ACTRESS A: Be serious. You were also an eternal prompter, weren't you, Nina?

ACTRESS B: "Oh, beautiful lake, romantic forest, splendid big sky. . . ."

ACTRESS A: There you go! But I don't recognize the lines. . . .

ACTRESS B: Never mind. I'm going to say what I like. "A beautiful lake, romantic forest, splendid big sky. When I stand at the edge of the lake, I am surrounded by majestic and generous nature. But, if I could become an actress, I would gladly sacrifice this grand nature and all else."

ACTRESS A: "All else"?

ACTRESS B: "Yes. For the happiness of being an actress, I would endure poverty, disillusionment, the hatred of my family; I would live in a garret and eat black bread, suffer dissatisfaction with myself and the recognition of my own imperfections, but in return I shall demand fame."

ACTRESS A: "Fame. . . ."

ACTRESS B: "Real, resounding fame. . . ."

ACTRESS A: ". . . real resounding fame. . . ."

ACTRESS B: "My head is swimming."

ACTRESS A: "Nina, I am being called . . . to pack, I suppose. But I don't feel like leaving."

ACTRESS B: *(Abruptly raises her head.)* "Do you see the house with the garden on the other side of the lake?"

ACTRESS A: "Where? Oh, yes of course."

ACTRESS B: Can you really see it?

ACTRESS A: *(Trying to focus with her damaged eyes.)* I should be able to!

ACTRESS B: "It belonged to my mother when she was alive. I was born there. I've spent my whole life by this lake, I know every little island in it."

ACTRESS A: "It's lovely here." *(A wig falls at her feet.)* "And what is this?"

ACTRESS B: "A sea gull. Konstantin Gavrilovich shot it."

ACTRESS A: "A beautiful bird." *(Mimes writing something.)*

ACTRESS B: "What are you writing?"

ACTRESS A: "An idea occurred to me . . . a subject for a short story. A young girl like you lives all her life beside a lake; she loves the lake like a sea gull, and, like a sea gull, is happy and free. A man comes along by chance, sees it, and, having nothing better to do, destroys it."

ACTRESS B: My. . . .

ACTRESS A: A good story, don't you think? Actually, it's quite common. It can easily happen to a young actress like you. *(She gives a mean glance to the white bandage on* ACTRESS B*'s throat.)* Oh, my dear Nina, what has happened to you? That bandage . . . my goodness, the blood has soaked through it. Has someone shot you, too, like a sea gull?

ACTRESS B: Stop it!

ACTRESS A: *(Ignoring this, she grabs* ACTRESS B*'s bandage and rips it open.)* Look at this! Numerous little cuts on your neck . . . they look like . . . you did this to yourself. How horrible! I don't understand. Why would you do such a foolish thing? For a play? For a man? Or for both?

*(*ACTRESS B *pushes* A *away.)*

ACTRESS A: *(Continues with a cold smile.)* But Nina, let me give you one piece of advice. Committing suicide for a man is the lowest thing an actress can do. It's fine for countless men to commit suicide for an actress; it's like receiving awards. But the reverse is the most detestable act an actress can commit. Don't you agree?

ACTRESS B: When are you going to quit lecturing me? All right, I'll admit that I'm not qualified to call myself an actress. You know, you were lucky. Your wounds were made glorious by the war. Weapons factories, women's volunteer corps, air raids . . . the whole society looks on the scars of the war with sweet sentimentality.

ACTRESS A: Just exactly what are you trying to say?!

ACTRESS B: Wow, you are scary.

ACTRESS A: If you have something to say, why don't you just come out and say it!

ACTRESS B: Oh, I have nothing special to say. I just thought we should really think about which scar is better—the one caused by the bombing, or the one caused by the kitchen knife.

ACTRESS A: I see. Beating around the bush is the way of postwar realism.

ACTRESS B: Huh, the sly approach is the way of prewar realism, right?

ACTRESS A: Shut up, you sewer rat!

ACTRESS B: Stuff it, you spiny rat!

(They throw objects from the dressing table at each other, then immediately return to their makeup. A long silence.

Frustrated with the results of the makeup, they throw temper tantrums. Long silence.)

ACTRESS A: Um. . . .

(Pause.)

ACTRESS A: I'm sure I'm making a big deal out of nothing, as usual, but what the hell is a spiny rat?

ACTRESS B: A spiny rat is just that, a spiny rat.

ACTRESS A: Do they really exist?

ACTRESS B: Exist? Why do you always ask me things in a stinging way? They exist. They are real. They live on Amami Ōshima Island.

ACTRESS A: What is their habitat?

ACTRESS B: Potato patch.

ACTRESS A: Potato patch? Not bad. Their environment is no worse than sewer rats'. In fact, their standard of living is higher than sewer rats' (ACTRESS B *is mortified.*

ACTRESS D enters quietly. She is younger than the others. She clutches a large pillow to her chest. She stops, looks around the room, and sits in a chair in a corner. She freezes.

[*As you must know by now,* ACTRESSES A *and* B *are not visible to* ACTRESS D *because they are dead.*] *They study* ACTRESS D *intently.*)

ACTRESS A: Who is that?

ACTRESS B: I don't know. She looks familiar, though.

ACTRESS A: One of our acquaintances, maybe?

ACTRESS B: What acquaintances?

ACTRESS A: What is she holding? It looks like a pillow.

(ACTRESS B *stands up.*)

ACTRESS A: Leave her alone.

(*Ignoring this,* ACTRESS B *goes up close to* D *and peers at her.*)

ACTRESS A: So what is it?

ACTRESS B: It's really a pillow.

ACTRESS A: Hm.

(ACTRESS D *is staring motionlessly at a fixed spot on the floor.* ACTRESS B *squats down directly in front of her.*)

ACTRESS B: She is agonizing over something.

ACTRESS A: Agonizing?

ACTRESS B: Either that or she has a fever. I wonder if she is using the pillow to exorcise something.

ACTRESS A: Exorcise what?

ACTRESS B: Maybe her fever comes down when she clings to the pillow.

ACTRESS A: I've never heard of such a thing.

(ACTRESS B *studies* D *persistently.*)

ACTRESS A: Come on, leave her alone.

(ACTRESS B *turns to leave* D.)

ACTRESS D: Mamma.

(*Startled,* ACTRESS B *stops abruptly.*)

ACTRESS D: (*Without taking her eyes off the floor.*) Mamma, did you read my letter?

ACTRESS B: Letter!?

(ACTRESSES A *and* B *look at each other.*)

ACTRESS D: . . . I mentioned it in the letter, didn't I? Finally, I've recovered. In our world, talent is of course important, but health is essential. And the best thing for health is sleep. Yes, I consumed sleep. Moorish people have a saying—"A good pillow for a sound sleep." I have taken that philosophy to heart. Mamma, I'm all right now. Really. I'm the perfect picture of health. So don't worry, Mamma.

(ACTRESSES A and B are dumbfounded. They hastily resume their making up.)

ACTRESS B: Um

ACTRESS A: Yeah?

ACTRESS B: If you were her mother, would you stop worrying?

ACTRESS A: Probably not.

(Music is heard from upstage [where the actual stage is assumed to be]. It is the ending of The Sea Gull. ACTRESS D *raises her head with a start. She moves to the center of the room as if she were acting. The dressing room seems to transform into a stage. A spotlight on* ACTRESS D.)

ACTRESS D: ". . . I'm going. Good-bye. When I become a great actress, come and see me. Promise? It's late. I can hardly stand on my feet. I'm exhausted and hungry. No, no . . . don't come with me. I'll go alone. When you see Trigorin, don't say anything to him. . . . I love him. I love him even more than before. How good life used to be, Kostya! How clear, how pure, warm, and joyous—our feelings were like tender, delicate flowers. . . . Do you remember? Men, lions, eagles, and partridges, horned deer, geese, spiders, silent fish that dwell in the deep, starfish, and creatures invisible to the eye—these and all living things, all, all living things, having completed their sad cycle, are no more. For thousands of years the earth has borne no living creature. And now in vain this poor moon lights her lamp. Cranes no longer wake and cry in meadows. May beetles are heard no more in linden groves. . . ." *(Impulsively embraces a robe hanging nearby and leaves in that pose.)*

(The light fades to black. Pause. From a distance, sound of thundering applause. As it dies, the light in the room returns to normal. ACTRESS C *returns from the stage.)*

ACTRESS C: Oh, it itches, itches!

(As she enters, she takes off her wig and scratches her head violently.)

ACTRESS C: *(Continues.)* That idiot! I couldn't hear the prompter at all. "Do you remember? Men, lions, eagles, and partridges, horned deer, geese, spiders, silent fish that dwell in the deep, seahorses. . . ." Why do I always stumble on this word? Not "seahorses" but "starfish". . . . Well, it's good enough for today. At least both starfish and seahorses live in the ocean.

(She notices ACTRESS D *sitting motionless in the corner, the pillow clutched to her chest.)*

ACTRESS C: Kiiko. . . .

(ACTRESS D *nods.*)

ACTRESS C: I didn't even notice you. Why didn't you say something? When did you get here? Are you feeling better?

ACTRESS D: Yes, thank you.

ACTRESS C: Good. . . . (*She notices the pillow.*) What's with that thing?

ACTRESS D: Yes, uh, this is really nothing, but I would like you to have it.

ACTRESS C: A gift?

ACTRESS D: That's right.

(ACTRESS C *is taken aback by the filthy, stained pillow that* D *presents to her.*)

ACTRESS C: I appreciate your thought, but, I . . . I have plenty of pillows.

ACTRESS D: Please accept it.

ACTRESS C: No, really. (*She pushes the pillow back.*) But I'm glad you are back. That new girl has been prompting for me since you fell ill, but her timing is just terrible. Listen, can you start tomorrow?

ACTRESS D: What?

ACTRESS C: Prompt. For me.

(*Pause.*)

ACTRESS C: What's wrong? You aren't coming back?

ACTRESS D: Look, I . . . I am completely healthy now.

ACTRESS C: Yes, I know. That's why I'm asking you.

ACTRESS D: I'm sorry to have troubled you for such a long time.

ACTRESS C: Never mind. It was nothing. So, you will prompt for me?

ACTRESS D: Prompt?

ACTRESS C: (*Annoyed.*) Yes, prompt.

ACTRESS D: (*Annoyed.*) Haven't you been listening to me? Why don't you understand?

ACTRESS C: Understand what?

ACTRESS D: I am completely healthy now, therefore. . . .

ACTRESS C: Therefore, what?!

ACTRESS D: I want it back.

ACTRESS C: (*Unsure.*) What do you want back?

ACTRESS D: Well. . . . (*Slight laugh as if to say "you know."*)

ACTRESS C: (*Increasingly uneasy.*) I'm taking care of something for you?

ACTRESS D: I wouldn't say "taking care of."

ACTRESS C: Speak up. What do you want back from me?

ACTRESS D: The role of Nina.

ACTRESS C: What?

ACTRESS D: What I'm saying is, I want the role of Nina back.

(ACTRESSES A *and* B *are shocked. They drop their compacts on the floor.* ACTRESS C *also is speechless for a moment.*)

ACTRESS C: Um . . . Kiiko, do you know what you are saying?

ACTRESS D: Yes, of course. Why won't you acknowledge my health? Don't I look much better?

ACTRESS C: Even if you have recovered completely. . . .

ACTRESS D: I've already apologized for causing you trouble for a long period of time.

(As ACTRESS C *searches for words,* ACTRESS D *stares at her.)*

ACTRESS C: You should go back to the hospital. You haven't recovered completely. This is absurd.

ACTRESS D: What's so absurd?

ACTRESS C: Kiiko . . . the role of Nina was mine from the beginning. And you were my prompter from the beginning. I don't really want to say this, but you are not ready for Nina.

(Pause.)

ACTRESS C: OK? Do you understand now?

(Pause.)

ACTRESS C: Go home. I'm going out to dinner with some people.

*(*ACTRESS C *starts to change her clothes.* ACTRESS D, *clutching the pillow, shows no sign of leaving. Mesmerized by the scene,* ACTRESSES A *and* B *have done strange things with their makeup. Suddenly aware how horrible they look, they start fixing their faces.* ACTRESS C *hangs up Nina's costume. She is uneasy with* ACTRESS D *'s glare.)*

ACTRESS D: It's all my fault. I got sick at the height of my career. I wrote many letters to him from the hospital bed. Letters of apology. I feel terrible for the author.

ACTRESS C: You feel terrible for the author?

ACTRESS D: Yes. He wrote such a brilliant role for me.

ACTRESS C: You know who the author is, don't you?

ACTRESS D: Of course I do.

ACTRESS C: He has been dead for seventy years.

ACTRESS D: That's a mere rumor.

ACTRESS C: *(Amazed.)* A rumor!?

ACTRESS D: I talked to him on the phone the day before yesterday.

ACTRESS C: Talked to who?

(Pause.)

ACTRESS C: *(Looking at* ACTRESS D *suspiciously.)* I'm beginning to see it. Go ahead, Kiiko, you can tell me.

ACTRESS D: Yes. . . .

ACTRESS C: Should I guess it? Maybe the author?

ACTRESS D: You are right.

ACTRESS C: How wonderful that you spoke to the author. I have done Chekhov numerous times, but never once had an opportunity to talk to him. I doubt I ever will. So what did you two talk about?

ACTRESS D: Many things.

ACTRESS C: I see. Many things.

ACTRESS D: Before we hung up, he asked me to get well soon and return to the stage. He said that he is looking forward to seeing me all healthy and on the stage once again.

ACTRESS C: Un-huh.

ACTRESS D: That's why I want to play Nina starting tomorrow.

ACTRESS C: I don't think so.

ACTRESS D: But I'm healthy.

ACTRESS C: It won't work.

(ACTRESS D *holds the pillow out to* C.)

ACTRESS C: What are you doing that for?

(ACTRESS D *continues to shove the pillow into* C.)

ACTRESS C: I told you, I don't want it.

ACTRESS D: It's my favorite. I slept so well. Now, it's your turn. . . .

ACTRESS C: My turn? My turn to do what?

(*Pause.*)

ACTRESS C: You are demanding I exchange the role of Nina for this pillow!

(*Pause.*)

ACTRESS C: Where do you get such a mad idea?

ACTRESS D: You must be tired.

ACTRESS C: I'm not.

ACTRESS D: Yes, you are. Very tired. You need rest and sleep for your exhaustion.

ACTRESS C: Stop it! Stop. . . .

(ACTRESS C *grabs the pillow and throws it across the room. It flies in the direction of* ACTRESSES A *and* B.)

ACTRESS C: I have been an actress for a long time, but this is the first time someone insisted I give up a part for a pillow. I've had enough already. I can't waste my time with you. Go home.

(ACTRESS C *sits at the dressing table and starts removing her makeup.* ACTRESSES A *and* B *are curiously looking at the pillow on the floor.*)

ACTRESS B: (*Smells the pillow.*) It's sweaty.

ACTRESS A: I sense her strong determination from it.

(ACTRESS D *approaches the pillow.* ACTRESSES A *and* B *draw back quickly.* ACTRESS D *picks it up and hugs it affectionately.*)

ACTRESS D: (*Mumbles.*) And I went to the trouble of reserving you a room at the hospital.

ACTRESS C: What did you say?

ACTRESS D: I said I already reserved a room at the hospital.

ACTRESS C: A room at the hospital?

ACTRESS D: Yes.

ACTRESS C: For whom? *(Suddenly realizing.)* You mean for me?

(ACTRESS D nods. ACTRESS C is speechless.)

ACTRESS D: I really wanted to get a private room for you, but unfortunately they were all taken. But now I think a large room is better. There is a television set, and you will have a lot of people to talk to. Older people often prefer a large room to a private room. You once said that you were terribly lonely living alone because you had no one to talk to. I thought about that, and came to a real understanding. Loneliness is the worst thing that can happen to anyone.

(ACTRESS C listens in astonishment, her face still half made up.)

ACTRESS D: *(Continues.)* If you really think about it, we actresses get so little reward. We sacrifice everything. Day after day we abuse our degenerating bodies, and what we desperately seek always turns out to be an illusion of love. That's why I'm against a prolonged commitment to this harsh profession. We can endure such cruel work only while we are young. . . .

ACTRESS C: And *you* are going to rescue me.

ACTRESS D: I don't mean to be righteous, but it's not just me, you know. Women my age all feel the same way. They don't say anything, but they all want to liberate you soon from this brutal profession. The role of Nina must be particularly hard for you, moving around like a butterfly. I feel awful that I forced you to take over the role because of my illness. I apologize.

ACTRESS C: Kiiko.

ACTRESS D: Yes.

ACTRESS C: *(Restrained.)* How can I make you understand? You are right about the work being hard. Indeed, we sacrifice so much. And the cruelest factor is aging. Year after year your own body goes on betraying you. . . .

ACTRESS D: I know. . . .

ACTRESS C: Just a moment, that's not what I really mean. There is more to it than your physical being. Youth alone will not bring Nina alive. How can I say this? . . . What's important is accumulation, all kinds of accumulation. You know, loneliness is also a type of accumulation.

ACTRESS D: I can't imagine. . . .

ACTRESS C: I don't mean loneliness is an accomplishment. I mean . . . um . . . I'm confused now. Anyway, I am well aware how heartless this profession is. But I made the choice. Nothing else will do. I don't care how brutal it can get. I will enjoy the savagery all the way. Nothing you can say will make me give up Nina. I will perform it two, three hundred more times! I will perform it when I'm an old hag; I'm hungry for brutality! Oh, I sound ridiculous. I'm not making any sense. What am I saying?

ACTRESS D: See. You are tired.

ACTRESS C: What?

ACTRESS D: I reserved a room for you, you know, at the hospital.

ACTRESS C: Get out!

(ACTRESS D *stares at* ACTRESS C.)

ACTRESS C: (*Continues.*) Don't make me angrier than I already am. I'm afraid of talking to someone like you . . . please . . . I don't want to be ranting and raving and end up feeling miserable.
(*Pause.*)

ACTRESS C: (*Pleading.*) I beg you, please, go home. I'm really tired now. I want to be alone.

(ACTRESS D *presents the pillow.*)

ACTRESS C: Stop it!

(*In a rage,* ACTRESS C *picks up a beer bottle and smashes it on* D's *head. The bottle shatters, and* ACTRESS D *falls.*)

ACTRESS C: (*Realizing what she has done.*) Kiiko. . . .

(ACTRESS C *runs over and takes* D *in her arms.* ACTRESSES A *and* B *cannot hide their curiosity.* ACTRESS D *pushes* C *away and stands up.*)

ACTRESS C: I didn't mean to. . . . How do you feel?

(ACTRESS D *sways.* ACTRESS C *quickly catches her.*)

ACTRESS C: Are you all right?

ACTRESS D: I . . . I'm healthy.

ACTRESS C: I know.

ACTRESS D: Can I have my pillow?

(ACTRESS C *picks up the pillow and hands it to* D. ACTRESS D *unsteadily starts to leave.*)

ACTRESS C: Where are you going?

ACTRESS D: Nothing is better for fatigue than sleep.

ACTRESS C: Kiiko.

(ACTRESS D *exits clutching the pillow.* ACTRESS C *sinks down in a chair.* ACTRESSES A *and* B *are looking at* C *nastily. Pause. Suddenly,* ACTRESS C *grabs a tissue paper box off the dressing table and throws it across the room. It flies in the direction of* ACTRESSES A *and* B; *they dodge it just in time.* ACTRESS C *keeps throwing anything she can get her hands on.* ACTRESSES A *and* B *run around the room dodging them.*)

ACTRESS C: Don't make me laugh! Jesus! I won't be made fun of by that meager actress! Ha, ha. . . . Exchange my role for a pillow? I'm going to laugh so hard I'll burst! Really, the nerve! "Women my age all feel the same way. We all want to liberate you from this brutal profession." I don't need to be *liberated* just because it's the "in" thing to do these days. God dammit!

(ACTRESS C *throws more objects. One of them hits* ACTRESS B.)

ACTRESS B: Shit.

ACTRESS A: Are you all right?

ACTRESS B: Why is everything flying this way?

ACTRESS A: Like she is aiming at us.

(ACTRESS C *pours a brandy and gulps it down.*)

ACTRESS C: Ha. She thinks she can play Nina? A woman with fish-eye lenses for eyes! She is nothing but shine and gloss. . . . If we call *that* passion and youth, then I say this world is full of nothing but grotesque ghosts. . . . And she is huge. It's one thing to be healthy, but it's another to be an overgrown worthless tree trunk. She does not have the body of an actress. On top of that, she moves slower than a hippopotamus in the zoo. Even it moves faster when entering the water. . . . Nina? Sea gull? Ha, ha. . . . (*She takes a drink.*) Look at the time. I've wasted so much time. Stupid.

(*She sits at the dressing table and starts applying makeup for going out to dinner. She suddenly stops and stares at herself in the mirror.*)

ACTRESS C: . . . Kiiko, I'm the wrong person to take on. Your pillow doesn't do anything to me. I'm thick skinned. Think about it. I've been acting for twenty years. There is some accumulation in that. You haven't experienced the feeling. That feeling . . . like blood slowly oozing out from the root of every hair. I've lived through it over and over. I don't expect you to understand . . . that sensation of blood leaking out from every pore of your body. It's like you have to choose either stabbing your adversary or choosing your own death. Have you heard a human howl? Not scream or curse, I mean howl. Locked in the bathroom of your own apartment . . . alone . . . five or six hours . . . all through the night . . . it's the cry of a beast . . . when your dried up throat breaks your voice, you drink water out of the toilet . . . then keep howling. . . . That's how you get a stronger voice. . . . That's accumulation . . . of a nauseating kind. . . .

(*Long pause.* ACTRESS C *lights a cigarette and puts on a record. Music. She stands up and takes off her robe. She is in her slip. She looks at herself in the mirror, taking various poses.*)

ACTRESS C: True, I have sacrificed certain things, but I can justify them. I always know what I'm sacrificing . . . the battle is eternal, my soldier in the mirror . . . (*She hoists a glass.*) . . . as I sit in twilight late alone by the flickering oak-flame . . . musing on long-pass'd war-scenes—of the countless buried unknown soldiers . . . of the vacant names, as unindented air's and sea's—the unreturn'd . . . the brief truce after battle, with grim burial-squads, and the deep-fill'd trenches . . . even here in my room-shadows and half-lights in the noiseless flickering flames . . . again I see the stalwart ranks on-filing, rising—I hear the rhythmic tramp of the armies. . . . (*She laughs.*)

(ACTRESS D *appears clutching the pillow and stands silently in the doorway. Her face is pale.*)

ACTRESS A: Look.

ACTRESS B: That pillow woman is here again.

(ACTRESS C *turns off the record player.*)

ACTRESS C: Let's see. . . .

(ACTRESS C *crosses in front of* D *to get her clothes.* ACTRESS D *wants to say something to her, but* C *does not notice. As* ACTRESS C *gets dressed near* D, *she murmurs Nina's monologue, during which* D *tries several times to talk, but restrains herself.*)

ACTRESS C: ". . . I was afraid you might hate me, Konstantin Gavri-lovich. Every night I dream that you are looking at me and don't rec-ognize me. If you only knew! Ever since I arrived I've been walking here . . . by the lake. I came near the house many times, but couldn't bring myself to come in. Let's sit down. *(Sits at the dressing table and fixes her makeup and clothes.)* Let's sit and talk. . . . It's nice here, warm and cozy. . . . Listen, the wind! There's a passage in Turgenev: 'Happy the man who on such a night has a roof over his head, who has a warm corner of his own.' I am a sea gull. . . . No, that's not right. *(Rubs her forehead and stands.)* What was I saying? Yes, Turgenev. . . . *(Takes her purse and looks back on the dressing room from the doorway.)* 'And may the Lord help all homeless wanderers. . . .' "

(ACTRESS C *exits.* ACTRESS D *wants to follow her but remains and watches* C *leave. Long pause.* ACTRESS D *slowly looks around the dressing room.* ACTRESSES A *and* B *are watching* D. ACTRESS D *stops her eyes on* A *and* B. *They stare at each other for a moment. Then* ACTRESSES A *and* B *quickly look away and resume their makeup.* ACTRESS D *slowly approaches* A *and* B.)

ACTRESS D: Good evening.

(*Shocked,* ACTRESSES A *and* B *fall off their chairs.*)

ACTRESS B: Y . . . y . . . you can see us?!

ACTRESS D: Yes.

ACTRESS A: Then, you too are. . . .

ACTRESS B: *(To* ACTRESS A.) That blow before; it got her good. Poor thing.

ACTRESS D: Excuse me.

ACTRESS A: Yes?

ACTRESS D: May I ask a question?

ACTRESS B: Go ahead.

ACTRESS A: Please.

ACTRESS D: *(Looking at their makeup.)* Were you here doing this every night?

ACTRESS B: Well . . . yes. Didn't mean to invade your space.

ACTRESS D: Oh, no. I don't mind.

(Pause.)

ACTRESS D: . . . I used to feel something.

ACTRESS A: What?

ACTRESS D: I am not surprised at all to meet you. . . . It was never clear, but I always felt your existence.

ACTRESS A: You mean the stagnant air around here?

ACTRESS B: The "hovering" air?

ACTRESS D: No, nothing like that, but I always heard voices . . . silent voices when I came in the dressing room every night.

ACTRESS A: Silent voices?

ACTRESS D: Yes, very low whispers.

ACTRESS B: How pathetic. No matter how hard we try, we can't get away from the curse of being a prompter.

(Pause.)

ACTRESS D: Excuse me . . . may I ask another question?

ACTRESS B: Go ahead.

ACTRESS A: Don't make it too difficult, though.

ACTRESS D: Have you been doing this for a long time?

ACTRESS B: Doing what?

ACTRESS D: You know, hanging out in the dressing room. . . .

ACTRESS B: I'm new. She is an old hand. Very old. Look at those scars. They are from the air raids.

ACTRESS D: Oh, my . . . air raids. You mean in World War II?

ACTRESS A: *(Offended.)* Stop staring at me. You make me feel like a museum exhibit.

ACTRESS D: So have you been coming here ever since then?

ACTRESS A: It's not like I'm obsessed or anything, but there is no other place to go, so. . . .

ACTRESS D: You must be tired.

ACTRESS A: What?

ACTRESS D: I can see it now. You are far more tired than she is. *(Indicating* ACTRESS B.*)*

ACTRESS B: I knew it.

ACTRESS A: *(To* ACTRESS B.*)* Shut up.

ACTRESS D: Sleep is best for exhaustion. . . . This is worn out, but. . . . *(She holds the pillow out to* ACTRESS A.*)*

ACTRESS A: *(Jumping back.)* Keep it. I can't deal with that.

ACTRESS D: You can't deal with a pillow?

ACTRESS A: Right. I have no idea why. . . .

(Pause.)

ACTRESS D: Um . . . isn't it about time?

ACTRESS B: Time for?

ACTRESS D: Time to go on stage. . . .

*(*ACTRESSES A *and* B *look at each other.)*

ACTRESS D: Which play are you doing?
   (Silence.)
ACTRESS D: Which play? . . .
   (Silence.)
ACTRESS D: . . . Well?
ACTRESS B: How noisy you are! Chatter, chatter, chatter, chatter, . . .
   Can't you ever be quiet? Damn, my false eyelashes came off.
ACTRESS D: I'm sorry
   (Pause.)
ACTRESS D: . . . It's Chekhov, isn't it?
ACTRESS B: Chekhov?
ACTRESS A: Oh, yes. You talked to Chekhov on the phone the other day,
   didn't you?
ACTRESS D: Oh, you were listening? . . .
ACTRESS B: OK, let's assume we are doing Chekhov. Can you guess
   which play?
ACTRESS D: Maybe . . . *The Three Sisters?*
ACTRESS A: How can we do *The Three Sisters* with just two of us?
ACTRESS D: Are there only two of you?
ACTRESS B: As you can see, at least here in this dressing room.
   (Long pause.)
ACTRESS D: . . . I understand now.
ACTRESS A: Okay, what do you understand?
ACTRESS D: You don't have a play, do you?
   (ACTRESSES A and B do not answer.)
ACTRESS D: You just sit here doing your makeup night after night for
   nothing. You wait here for your turn forever . . . for the opportunity
   that will never come. Am I right?
   (ACTRESSES A and B remain silent.)
ACTRESS D: Aren't you embarrassed? I wouldn't stand this misery. I
   would rather be in a hospital bed.
ACTRESS A: Huh, then go back to the hospital! And take your precious
   little pillow with you. But your bed isn't there any more. There is no
   such thing as sound sleep for you any more.
ACTRESS D: *(Shocked.)* Do you think I really lost my bed?
ACTRESS A: If you don't believe me, go find out for yourself.
   (Pause.)
ACTRESS B: . . . You will soon get used to waiting, too.
ACTRESS A: Yeah, you will be just like us before long.
ACTRESS B: You know, we are not just wasting our time waiting. We
   keep trying, really. We recollect our past accumulations.
ACTRESS A: Just a little while ago, we nearly lost our voices recollecting.
ACTRESS D: What came out of that?

ACTRESS B: All sorts of things . . . you know, we have a lot of accumulations.

(Pause.)

ACTRESS D: . . . The long night will begin for me, also.

(ACTRESSES A and B look at each other.)

ACTRESS A: You will get used to it soon. You can learn from us how to pass time in many ways. . . .

ACTRESS B: It may look sluggish to you, but we have a certain routine . . . right?

(ACTRESS D suddenly stands up.)

ACTRESS D: But I still think we should do something.

ACTRESS B: We *are* doing something.

ACTRESS D: That's not what I mean. I mean . . . we should decide on an agenda . . . you know, to prepare perhaps for *the* day that will come.

ACTRESS B: What day is coming?

ACTRESS D: We may still get opportunities to go on stage. You never know.

ACTRESS A: Yeah, she *(indicating* ACTRESS B*)* had a similar dream at the beginning. But I tell you, it's never going to happen.

ACTRESS D: . . . You really are tired.

ACTRESS A: Stop it!

ACTRESS D: You are definitely exhausted. *(Edges in with the pillow.)*

ACTRESS A: God dammit! You want my role, don't you. I won't let you take it away! What kind of person are you? You don't discriminate in your attacks, huh? You can chase me all you want with that pillow. I won't give up my role. Get out!

ACTRESS B: Um . . . excuse me.

ACTRESS A: What!

ACTRESS B: What are you talking about? Your role hasn't been decided, has it?

(ACTRESS A is furious. Long silence.)

ACTRESS D: I'm easily misunderstood. Someone encouraged me that to be misunderstood is an asset for an actress. It was a mistake. . . . I don't have the team spirit or the ability to adapt. The fact that I'm misunderstood means that I'm not loved. No one loves me. I'm always alone . . . I have always been alone and I always will be. . . .

ACTRESS B: Wait a minute. Why are you summarizing your life now all of a sudden? Sure, it's hard being misunderstood, but the opposite is just as bad. Everyone always told me how nice I was; for a while even I believed that I was just a nice person. Then it occurred to me that I'm like the air. Air isn't bad, I know. But no one would say "I love you madly" or "I have faith in your talent" to mere air. . . . Do you understand?

ACTRESS D: *(Stubbornly.)* It's okay. I've made my decision already.

ACTRESS B: What decision?

ACTRESS D: From now on, I won't bother you. I will go on by myself. I will wait for the opportunity that may come someday. . . . It must be destiny . . . to spend the long night alone. *(Suddenly breaks into Irina's lines from* The Three Sisters.*)* "Oh, I'm miserable . . . I can't work; I won't work. Enough, enough! I've been a telegraph clerk, and now I have a job in the office of the Town Council, and I loathe and despise every single thing they give me to do. . . ."

ACTRESS B: Where do telegraph clerk and Town Council come from?

ACTRESS A: It's Irina's line from *The Three Sisters.*

ACTRESS B: Oh, she's started already.

ACTRESS D: ". . . I'm nearly twenty-four already; I've been working a long time, and my brain is drying up. I've grown thin and old and angry, and there is nothing, nothing, no satisfaction of any kind. And time is passing, and I feel that I'm moving away from the real, beautiful life, moving farther and farther into some abyss. . . ."

ACTRESS A: Hold it.

ACTRESS D: What?

ACTRESS A: I can't deal with this incredible noise. Who gave you permission to take the role of Irina, anyway?

ACTRESS D: Permission?

(Pause.)

ACTRESS B: The night is forever long.

ACTRESS A: Right. . . . There is no hope for us of ever seeing days filled with sunshine again.

ACTRESS B: Then it's not a bad idea to change our ways a little.

ACTRESS A: I guess so, since there are three of us now.

*(*ACTRESSES A *and* B *look at each other and smile.)*

ACTRESS A: You'll be Masha?

ACTRESS B: Then you'll be Olga.

ACTRESS A: It's been a while since I had a female role.

ACTRESS D: Um. . . .

ACTRESS B: Throw out that pillow. You are Irina, just as you wanted.

ACTRESS A: Let's not rush this. We have plenty of time.

*(*ACTRESS A *gets up and returns with* C *'s brandy. Everyone gets a glass. Brandy is poured.* ACTRESS B *runs to the record player, chooses a record, and puts it on. Music.)*

ACTRESS A: Toast. To our night—a long night.

ACTRESS B: To our eternal rehearsal.

ACTRESS D: And to our forever lost sleep.

(The tone of the music changes. The three actresses stand close together.)

ACTRESS B: *(Reciting Masha's lines.)* ". . . Oh, listen to that music! They are leaving us . . . we are left alone to begin our life over again. We must live. . . . We must live. . . ."

(During this speech, the light dims slowly, and the three figures begin to look like corpses with pale faces.)

ACTRESS D: *(Reciting Irina's lines.)* "A time will come when everyone will know what all this is for, why there is all this suffering, and there will be no mysteries; but meanwhile, we must live . . . we must work, only work! . . . Soon winter will come and cover everything with snow, and I shall go on working, working. . . ."

(ACTRESS A embraces B and D.)

ACTRESS A: *(Reciting Olga's lines.)* "The music plays so gaily, so valiantly, one wants to live! Oh, my God! Time will pass, and we shall be gone forever; we'll be forgotten, our faces will be forgotten, our voices, and how many there were of us. . . . *(The three figures start to fade.)* Oh, my dear sisters, our life is not over yet. We shall live! The music is so gay, so joyous, it seems as if just a little more and we shall know why we live, why we suffer. . . . If only we knew, if only we knew. . . ."

(The dressing room is dark. Then faint moonlight reveals a field of grass. There are countless mirrors resembling tombstones in the field. The mirrors whisper.

      Glorious Town. . . .

      Indigent Metropolis. . . .

      Imprisoned Souls. . . .

      Transcendent Figures. . . .

      Transcendent Figures. . . .)

The Dressing Room is about four actresses, two living and two dead. Shimizu's plays abound in choice female roles. *From right:* Ōshiro Miro, Minamitani Asako, Kuroki Satomi. Mokutōsha, 1988. (Courtesy Shimizu Kunio.)

Matsumoto Noriko in *The Dressing Room*. Her *shingeki* background—the Haiyūza actors school and Mingei (People's Art)—gives her a solid grounding in realism. Mokutōsha, 1988. (Courtesy Shimizu Kunio.)

Terayama Shūji and Kishida Rio

Terayama Shūji (1935–1983) was an avant-garde playwright of international repute. Born and raised in Aomori Prefecture in northern Japan, Terayama attended Waseda University in Tokyo. He first gained attention in his teens as an award-winning *tanka* poet. After spending much of the late 1950s hospitalized with a liver condition, in the early 1960s Terayama established himself as a scenarist for radio, television, and film (he wrote for director Shinoda Masahiro), at the same time pursuing and writing on such passions as horse racing and jazz. Although he had written for the stage as early as 1955 and had his first full-length play produced in 1960, Terayama's most significant theatrical activity began with the establishment of the experimental theater troupe Tenjō Sajiki (The Gallery) and their first production, Terayama's *The Hunchback of Aomori,* in April 1967. Centered on Terayama as playwright, sometime director, and cult figure for many of the disaffected youths of Japan, Tenjō Sajiki maintained a steady pace of activity for sixteen years. By 1969 Terayama and his troupe had begun the frequent appearances in Europe, America, and even the Middle East that garnered international fame. *Jashūmon* (lit., the heretical faith, i.e., Christianity) (1971) won the *grand prix* at an international theater festival in Belgrade. At home, Tenjō Sajiki won critical admiration but was regarded with apprehension by Japanese society at large for its occasional "scandals," such as the thirty-hour street theater piece *Knock* in 1975. The troupe disbanded soon after Terayama's death. Terayama was also an important figure in Japanese cinema, writing and directing such films as *Get Rid of the Books and Hit the Town* (Sho o suteyo machi e deyō) (1971), *A Pastoral Death* (Den'en ni shisu) (1974), and (with Kishida Rio) *Farewell Ark* (Saraba hako-bune) (1982).

Kishida Rio joined Tenjō Sajiki in 1973, a graduate of Chūo University in Tokyo. Although many people had a hand in writing Tenjō Sajiki scripts, Kishida became Terayama's only frequent collaborator. Kishida had begun to stage her own plays as early as 1979, but after Terayama's death she emerged completely from his shadow and established herself as an active playwright with her own troupe, Kishida Jimusho + Rakuten-dan (Kishida Office plus Optimist Company). Conscious of Terayama as her mentor, she regards her current activities and those of other Tenjō Sajiki members as a legacy of Terayama and the troupe he headed. Key figures such as stage and music director J. A. Caesar (also Seazer; born Terahara Takaaki) and actor Salvador Tali (born Kawasuji Tetsurō) are active with Ban'yū Inryoku (Universal Gravitation), a theater company formed soon after the breakup of Tenjō Sajiki. Producer Kujō Kyōko (Terayama's wife from 1963 to 1970) is prominent in Jinriki Hikōkisha (Man-Powered Airplane Hangar), a production company handling Terayama's films.

TERAYAMA SHŪJI:
An Introduction

Robert T. Rolf

THE NEW DRAMA that emerged in the 1960s embraced a rather wide spectrum of dramaturgical approaches. As we have seen, Betsuyaku and Shimizu may, in a sense, be viewed as literary playwrights. Although Betsuyaku uses absurdist techniques and Shimizu delves into complex psychological dilemmas, their plays have a relatively clear structure, one based on language. Terayama Shūji, Kara Jūrō, and Satoh Makoto, on the other hand, directors all, structure their plays with language as merely one element of performance. The impact of their plays emerges from the total performance rather than from the words the characters speak. The reader of their plays, therefore, must imagine the stage action. Otherwise, reading becomes merely an arduous task.

The legacy of this generation of the 1960s is indeed its innovative style. What seemed startlingly new then had become the norm by the 1980s. This underscores the seminal nature of the theater represented in this volume. These playwrights are the respected mentors of the many talented Japanese theater people who have appeared in the past twenty years. The small, rebellious, and dedicated theater companies that such figures as Terayama, Kara, and Satoh headed remain models emulated today. Although it seems fruitless to insist on one of these groups as the most influential, surely none is more wrapped in the glories and mystique of the gone-but-never-forgotten avant-garde of the 1960s than Terayama Shūji's Tenjō Sajiki. A brief discussion of some of his highly personal early works reveals much about Terayama's aesthetic sensibility, the principal force shaping the theater world of Tenjō Sajiki.

Predominant Themes: The Enigmatic Mother and the Lost Father

Although Terayama was a theater innovator, an influential figure in the international avant-garde of the late 1960s and 1970s, his most successful plays derive their power not only from their manner of performance but also from the universality of their themes and imagery. Two recurring themes, especially prominent in his earlier works, involve an ambivalent attitude toward the mother and the search for the father. Pinpointing origins of such preoccupations may be impossible, or even unnecessary, but the events of Terayama's life here seem quite relevant.

Terayama Shūji was born on 10 December 1935, in Aomori Prefecture, where his father was a member of the prewar national Special Police entrusted with the investigation of "thought crimes." His duties allowed Terayama's father to return home only every other day, but the young Shūji insisted on going out to wait for him every evening. As the war in China wore on, Terayama's father was pressed into the military and sent away for three months' training, during which time Shūji refused to eat. Finally, in 1941, Terayama's mother rushed with her child to Aomori Station, having heard a rumor that her husband's unit was to be sent overseas. At the station the anxious crowd was roped off from the soldiers to prevent contact with their loved ones; Terayama and his mother frantically scanned the formations of soldiers until Terayama spotted his father, sneaked into the ranks, and managed a brief good-bye, the last words he would speak to his father, who remained away until his death from illness in the Celebes in 1945.

Deprived of her husband's salary after the defeat of Japan and the subsequent collapse of the government in 1945, Terayama's mother soon went to work at a U.S. military base far away in Kyushu, where she remained for years while Terayama lived with relatives in Aomori. Terayama professed to understand the reasonableness of her motives for the separation, but an ambivalent attitude developed, compounded of his gratitude for the sacrifice she made to support him and his pain at being abandoned.[1]

In *The Hunchback of Aomori,* the obviously Oedipal nature of the hunchback's story takes on additional interest within such a biographical context, but Terayama's genius is to associate this personal ambivalence with the dark, scarcely charted regions of the folk beliefs and tribal mentality of the northern Japanese village. The mother of Terayama's works leads him on an inward journey back into himself, back to his childhood, the dark interior of the snowed-in northern house, the fears and insecurities of life in a society governed by rumor, the world of dreams, and the deepest, most fundamental areas of the individual psyche.

The Hunchback of Aomori is a one-act play of six scenes with titles that reveal its thematic concerns and suggest its macabre atmosphere: scene 1, "The Disappearance of the Official in Charge of Family Registers"; scene 2, "A Lullaby for Abandoned Children"; scene 3, "Graveyard

Bride"; scene 4, "Heredity Flower Card Game"; scene 5, "A Spell to
Write on Blank Paper to Avoid Calamity"; and scene 6, "He Carries a
Tomb of Flesh on His Back." A servant girl, Matsu, was once raped by
the son of her wealthy employer. In revenge she prayed for and delivered a hunchback child. The child was supposedly killed, perhaps by
Matsu herself. Or perhaps a servant took pity on the child and raised it.
In any event, in time Matsu inherits the family's wealth and spends her
years bestowing kindness on young men who pass her way, presumably
looking for her son but also availing herself of them sexually. When the
forlorn young hunchback, who may or may not be Matsu's son,
appears, he is soon at her mercy sexually. The inconclusive ending finds
Matsu denying that the hunchback could be her son (since she herself
killed him) and the hunchback himself more abandoned and loveless
than ever. All is complicated by the stolen family register, which ominously calls out from nowhere the names and places of origin of the area
people.

The eerie, the grotesque, and the traditional are interwoven in a way
that would remain at the heart of the Tenjō Sajiki theater aesthetic. The
play is subtitled as a work in the *naniwabushi* style. The *samisen*-playing
narratress borrowed from this popular genre of emotive storytelling is
woven in as another character, in love with the hunchback.[2] A dwarf
introduces and closes the play; he is labeled a *kōjō*, which refers to "a
verbal greeting to the audience from the [*kabuki*] stage."[3] There are long
passages of Terayama's complex poetry that involve an enumeration of
bird names cast in the style of the satirical Edo period songs known as
ahodarakyō. Shadows of all descriptions dance in pale blue-white light;
incantatory choruses are heard, whose meaning is secondary to their
sound; conversations and cries come menacingly out of the darkness.
Japanese children's games and songs are used, in particular the possibilities of the psychology underlying the common game "guess who's
behind you."[4] The last words of the play's closing chorus thus place
Terayama's personal concerns within the context of the world of Japanese childhood, the underpinnings of the Japanese psyche: "Mother
and father both / Throw them away / Guess who's / Behind you?"

In contrast to the inward journey associated with the mother in
Terayama's works, the search for the father, prominent in such early
plays as *Dr. Galigari's Crime* (Garigari hakase no hanzai) (1969), is an
outward journey, a hunt for a substitute for what has been lost. The
image of the father connects with a spate of impersonal phenomena: the
nation of Japan; the emperor; his police; World War II; the loss of the
prewar value system and the need for a new system of values; and an
unconscious longing for the emotional security and simplistic stability of
an idealized lost patriarchy. Tenjō Sajiki frequently exploited the theat-

rical possibilities of this search: in the street theater piece *Man-Powered Airplane Solomon* (Jinriki hikōki Soromon) (1970), a young actor accosts an unsuspecting middle-aged man on the street claiming that the passerby is his father.[5] Both mothers and fathers are central to *Dr. Galigari's Crime,* an examination of which sheds light not only on these thematic preoccupations but also on the rapid evolution of Tenjō Sajiki's artistic objectives in the two years after *The Hunchback of Aomori.*

The opening directions of *Dr. Galigari's Crime* call for no division between the stage and the audience areas. This makes it immediately clear that the work is designed as an experiment to probe the very nature of the performance space. According to Terayama, the stage set is to look like both a matchbox for people and a simple set. The play explores familiar Terayama territory: the fragility and fragmentation of family relationships; the mindless pursuit of sensual pleasures. These are overlaid with a jumble of images and characters from the world of Japanese boyhood adventure. Terayama exhibits an eclecticism that anticipates the postmodern sensibility dominating Japanese theater today.

Dr. Galigari's three scenes are to start at seven, eight, and nine o'clock, respectively. There is neither a character named nor any apparent relation of the work to Dr. Galigari, and since the different parts of the play occur simultaneously in different rooms of the set, no one in the audience is able to see the whole. The script notes three different actions to begin at seven o'clock. Most significant for this discussion is the one in which Man Forty-One (the forty-first audience member and the only one not invited to the play) rings the doorbell and tries to convince the Servant who answers that he, the Servant, is Man Forty-One's lost father. Although he vehemently denies parenthood, the Servant finally agrees to act the part of the father a little.

It should be stressed that such reconstructions of the "story" are ultimately misleading; unlike *The Hunchback of Aomori, Galigari* is not meant to tell a story. Fairy tales, role reversals, games on stage, jumps from one context to the next—*Galigari's* purpose is not to reassure, entertain, or enlighten but to undermine and undercut both narrative structures and constructs of reality. This is indeed intended as a surrealist exercise, a contemporary avant-garde theater, but the perhaps inadvertent or unconscious result is also to suggest the philosophical dislocation and ensuing psychological disorientation experienced by contemporary Japanese. The play's conclusion reemphasizes the role reversal, the notion that identities are interchangeable, uncertain; as Terayama puts it, the real play—the second act of *Dr. Galigari's Crime*—will be performed by the audience after the actors have gone.

The controlling image and principal icon in many of Terayama's creations is the clock. Time is the one certainty in Terayama's world. The clock measures the progress toward death. The backdrop to *Galigari*'s "card family games" and other expressions of the essential uncertainty of such a basic human relationship as that of parent and child is a human clock, an image of man's imprisonment in time. An old-fashioned wall clock is a fixture in many of Terayama's cinematic and theater works. In addition to suggesting time, aging, and death, these clocks evoke the atmosphere of prewar Japan, nostalgic associations of a lost world. It seems an almost fitting conclusion, then, that, after the air raid that destroyed Aomori City in the last days of the war, the nine-year-old Terayama and his mother were able to identify the site of their house by their wall clock found in the smoldering ruins.[6]

Autobiographical overtones continued to dominate Terayama's, and thus Tenjō Sajiki's, early works. In *Jashūmon*, the familiar ideas are expressed with shocking clarity as "mother killing" and "looking for father." Terayama's conviction that the mother shackles and inhibits one's growth is loudly punctuated with a chorus of "Please die, Mother! Please die, Mother!" The mother is told, "Everyone has to change sometime," and a voluptuous vamp states, "Every man wants my body, but only those who kill their mothers can have me." Terayama's consistent imagery informs the scene: prostitutes in red kimonos, the mother in a nostalgically simple one and carrying the ubiquitous, old-fashioned wall clock. In addition, the immense preoccupation of Terayama's generation with the war and its images, the familiar commingling of nostalgic longing and a sense of betrayal, manifests itself through the presence of a wounded veteran in white as a background character, a saluting Imperial Army soldier identified as a lost father, and a kamikaze pilot apologizing to his mother, "I love you, Mother, though I don't know why I should."

This rejection of parental ties added to both the cult status of Terayama and the appeal of Tenjō Sajiki in the social cauldron that was the 1960s. But, although Terayama's personal concerns played a great role in shaping the aesthetic of Tenjō Sajiki, there are other sources for the aesthetic approaches that account for the company's importance.

Parallels and Sources

In Terayama's world there are both an inward attraction to the familiar but unsettling and an outward journey to a lost unknown. The claustrophobic nature of the former is often expressed by the image of the labyrinth: walls, obstacles, and enclosures are common in his works. In *Opium Wars* (Ahen sensō) (1972), the elimination of performer/audience distinctions had the audience moving through a labyrinth as participant-spectators. In one section of *Knock*—"Human Boxing" (Hyūman bokushingu)—"volunteers" from among the spectators were crated and carted about Tokyo to disorient them and alter their perspective.

Terayama responded enthusiastically to the works of Jorge Luis Borges and frequently referred to him in his writings. This seems not merely a case of a 1960s artist being drawn naturally to an international cult figure. Rather, the two artists arrive at a similar paradigm—the labyrinth—by following different paths, Terayama's idiosyncratic and Borges' formal and intellectual. Borges' *Labyrinths* was a wellspring of ideas and images for Terayama in his endeavor to reduce the primacy of the word in theater. He was attracted to the questioning of language and the critique of logocentrism implicit in the story of Funes in Borges' "Funes the Memorious." Obsessed with naming, Funes has preternatural powers of memory and thus an infinite capacity for the classification of experience and phenomena; he realizes, however, that his remarkable ability and incessant ordering of reality represent an interminable and useless exercise.

Terayama's art also shows similarities to the theories of Artaud, another cult figure of that day. Many of Terayama's artistic aims were obviously Artaudian in conception, and Terayama perceived a kindred sensibility in Artaud's dark images of pestilence and magnificent, defiant posturing. Terayama began reading Artaud in 1966, the year he assembled Tenjō Sajiki, and always routinely listed him as a major influence. The name "Dr. Galigari" *(Garigari hakase)* seems a simple alteration of the Japanese title—*Karigari hakase*—of the German expressionist film *The Cabinet of Dr. Caligari* (Das Kabinett des Dr. Caligari) (1919). In the public bath sequence of *Knock,* Dr. Caligari is mentioned accurately, but "Galigari" and "Caligari" also call to mind "the small town of Caligari, Sardinia," in the opening sentence of Artaud's "Theatre and the Plague," a work that was a seminal influence on Terayama.[7]

Not surprisingly for a playwright who was also a successful poet, Terayama was capable of a rich verbal and visual imagery. In both theater and film, Terayama's landscape is peopled by odd characters reminiscent of the sideshow-like *misemono:* dwarfs, giants, naked women, fat women, grotesqueries of all descriptions seen against bizarre surrealistic backgrounds. Terayama also drew freely on such native sources as Japanese legend, folklore, popular Buddhism, and the world of boyhood adventure as seen in juvenile literature, television, and movies. To what end did he refer so copiously to such facets of the Japanese popular imagination? Although much of what is alluded to is not particularly remarkable in itself—split-tongue sparrows, television masked avengers —there is a cumulative effect. On the one hand, Terayama peels away layers of the contemporary Japanese imagination. At the same time, however, he hints at the composition of his own—the simple popular mythology that sustained him as a virtually parentless youth. The many specific references contribute to his imagistic complexity.

Terayama piles allusion on allusion. If they sometimes create a confusing heap, it might be best understood as mirroring the muddle of thoughts that the mind reverts to when relaxed and unfocused. There is, in that sense, a dual effect: to suggest a sort of collective unconscious (a psychological pool of shared Japanese cultural beliefs and thought patterns) and to hint at the role such a collective unconscious has in the formation of a more distinctively individual psychology. Terayama's plays may puzzle one who insists on purely logical connections, but their layered language and situations also resemble the inscrutability and complexity of life and thought. *Knock* is an excellent example of the provocative lengths to which Tenjō Sajiki carried this approach.

Knock: Street Theater

Knock was a large-scale street performance, an artistic assault on many fronts in Tokyo's Suginami Ward on 19–20 April 1975. It capped a long period of experimentation with street theater by Tenjō Sajiki. Strictly speaking, it is not a work by Terayama Shūji. Playwright/director/cult figure Terayama was the heart of Tenjō Sajiki, but the troupe was very active in experimentation with group authorship. Among other things, their experimental plays were designed to call into question the concept of authorship. This followed naturally from their reduction of the primacy of the text over the physicality of the actor.

Its theoretical basis aside, *Knock* provides a good example of how Tenjō Sajiki's experiments with joint authorship worked in practice. Many people had a hand in putting together its thirty-odd sections. The public bath sequence was composed by Kishida Rio, a combination of her own writing and her selection of excerpts from Terayama's. The dialogue in *Knock* is presented in a simple numbered list, as was often the case with Tenjō Sajiki's experimental works. Among some of the longer items, numbers 64, 65, and 67 are Terayama's and numbers 58, 59, 62, and 63 Kishida's. Number 48 is by Terayama with Kishida's changes and additions. Such close distinctions may violate the spirit of group authorship but are worth noting when discussing a playwright and poet with Terayama's power.

The text of the public bath sequence of *Knock* consists of two parts: a description of the planned theater activity (the "Outline" and "Time Schedule") and a list of the "Lines" that the actors may say if and when they choose. The former is a clear, straightforward delineation of the framework of the performance. The latter is the numbered list of sixty-seven items of speech (to be precise, sixty-six, since number 28 is left suggestively blank), many prosaic, some tending toward the poetic. Most are intended as simple, often humorous non sequiturs; others reveal the psychological and philosophical preoccupations of Kishida and Terayama. Several are lists. The whole theater experiment is in the spirit of Dada and involves undermining both language and everyday routine, a protest against unquestioning acceptance of the primacy of either. The artistic significance of the performance in the public bath should be examined within the context of the overall development of the artistic purposes of Terayama Shūji and Tenjō Sajiki.

Artistic Objectives

A consuming goal of Terayama's stage work with Tenjō Sajiki was to redefine the relation between performer and audience. This involved reconceptualizing both the role of the dramatic text in performance and the nature of the performance space. The dramaturgical differences among *The Hunchback of Aomori* (1967), *Dr. Galigari's Crime* (1969), and *Knock: Street Theater* (1975) illustrate that his plays were designed increasingly to this end.

Although *The Hunchback of Aomori* is extremely theatrical, much of its interest lies in the text. The play unfolds in a basically linear manner; it is enriched by imagery that evokes deep and murky areas of the collective unconscious of a wintry, isolated northern Japanese village. When given a skillful performance, *The Hunchback of Aomori* is a spellbinding work of dramatic literature. But Terayama soon tired of theater that derives its power from literary qualities. He lamented that theater had "become the slave of writing, while the actor's speech is dictated by the printed word." To remedy this, he declared that "first and foremost, theatre must be severed from literature. To do so, we must purge theatre of the play."[8]

Dr. Galigari's Crime reveals the scope of the change in Terayama's dramaturgy. In it the audience encounters, not a plot that develops, but a family with puzzling relationships, deliberate confusion of identities, and frequent role reversals. A clearly defined time span imposes a temporal linearity on the play; however, its unconventional characterization and the fact that none of the audience can watch all the stage action combine to preclude other forms of structural linearity that normally clarify a play's meaning.

Terayama and Tenjō Sajiki experimented with many ways of breaking down such distinctions as those between performer and audience, performance space and audience space, and the reality of a theater performance and that of everyday life. Whereas their first play, *The Hunchback of Aomori*, was meant to be performed at a more or less conventional venue, Terayama's directions for *Dr. Galigari's Crime* call for "no separation of stage and seating area." He invited the audience onto the set for *Origin of Blood* (Chi no kigen) (1973);[9] he transported audiences about the theater in enclosed bleachers mounted on hovercraft for *Directions to Servants* (Nuhikun) (1978);[10] he had audiences threatened, physically harassed, and variously discomfited for *Origin of Blood* and *Blind Man's Letter* (Mōjin shokan) (1973), to name two internationally notorious instances;[11] and, of course, he explored the possibilities of street theater indefatigably, both in Japan and abroad. The thirty-hour *Knock: Street Theater* is a spectacular example of the last; the excerpt presented here, the unannounced invasion of a public bath in Tokyo, was reported in the newspapers alongside accounts of other more customary social disturbances. *The Hunchback of Aomori* sought to shock audiences out of their complacency through its grotesque and bizarre elements; the surrealistic *Galigari* attempted to disorient audiences on the principle that, inasmuch as people go through life uncertain of the nature of the world around them, theater should reflect their confusion rather than offering the customary neat, but false, Aristotelian unities. Finally, a work like *Knock*, especially the bathing sequence, represents a merging with the audience, bringing theater into intimate, in this case literally naked, contact with the audience.

In *Knock* the actors are freed from structural linearity imposed by the logic of the text. The sequence of their actions is dictated by the temporality of a "time schedule," but they speak their lines whenever they wish. Another principle that Tenjō Sajiki came to stress was that the physicality of the actor was as important to a performance as the meaning of the dramatic text. The public bath performance—in which dialogue is left to the discretion of the actors—represents an extreme but theoretically coherent way of insisting on the equality of the physical actor and the metaphysical text. For Terayama and Tenjō Sajiki, the dramatic text came to be not an unalterable itinerary but a "map": "Just as a map may be read in many ways and give rise to many chance encounters, so, too, the text is a guiding plan that enables us to move back and forth between 'interior' and 'exterior' geography on an imaginary theatrical trip shared with the audience."[12] The reduced function of the text heightens the importance of the physicality of the actors, increases awareness of the significance of the performance space, and suggests a metaphor—the trip—for the theater event.

After Knock

The early and middle years of Tenjō Sajiki were characterized by dynamic development and bold experimentation. By the time of *Knock*, however, that unique age—the 1960s and early 1970s—with which the new theater had grown was over. Although *Knock* succeeded in making an impact on the rather unsuspecting citizens of Tokyo's Suginami Ward, the success was only partial; in 1975, the hoped for voluntary participation in street theater would no longer materialize. Shimizu Kunio had lamented the passing of the eventful but brief cultural epoch with his *Not Weep? Not Weep for 1973?* (Nakanai no ka? nakanai no ka? 1973-nen no tame-ni?) (1973), his title inspired by a line from one of Allen Ginsberg's poems, and then lapsed into a two-year silence. Similarly, Terayama and Tenjō Sajiki made a significant move back into indoor theater; they entered on a final period of creativity with *Directions to Servants, Bluebeard's Castle* (Aohigekō no shiro) (1979), two versions of *Lemmings* (Remingu) (1979, 1982), and other works.

The performances of Tenjō Sajiki in Europe and America opened eyes there to another Japanese theater besides that of the great traditional forms. Centered on Terayama Shūji, a theatrical poet of his generation, of childhoods lost to World War II, Tenjō Sajiki was a significant troupe in the history of modern Japanese theater.[13]

Notes

1. For more information on Terayama's life and work, see *Terayama Shūji no sekai* (The world of Terayama Shūji) (Tokyo: Shinpyōsha, 1983); Terayama Hatsu, *Haha no hotaru* (Mother's firefly) (Tokyo: Shinshokan, 1985), his mother's sentimental record of their relationship; Kujō Kyōko, *Sugao no Terayama Shūji: fushigi na kuni no Musshū* (Terayama Shūji unmasked: Musshū in Wonderland) (Tokyo: Shufu to seikatsusha, 1985), his erstwhile wife's chatty reminiscences (Musshū was a nickname for Terayama); Miura Masashi, *Terayama Shūji —kagami no naka no kotoba* (Terayama Shūji—words in the mirror) (Tokyo: Shinshokan, 1987), a collection of essays that explore such areas as the links between Terayama's tanka and his plays; and Carol Sorgenfrei, "Shūji Terayama: Avant-Garde Dramatist of Japan" (Ph.D. diss., University of California, Santa Barbara, 1978).

2. *Naniwabushi* is a style of dramatic narration to the accompaniment of a *samisen,* an expressive three-stringed instrument that slightly resembles a guitar.

3. See Samuel L. Leiter, *Kabuki Encyclopedia* (Westport, Conn.: Greenwood, 1979), 199.

4. This game supplied the title of Betsuyaku Minoru's *Guess Who's Behind You* (Ushiro no shōmen dāre) (1982). Hands over eyes, the child who is "it" squats in the center of a circle of children, who link hands, circle, and sing of the bird in the cage, the crane, and the tortoise. When the children stop circling, the child in the middle is entreated to "guess who's behind" him or her. If the guess is correct, the child guessed goes to the center and the game continues, ad infinitum.

5. Kishida Rio, raised motherless and with a father she regarded with "dislike and awe," feels that "all such searching for an absolutist father leads to the

emperor system *(tennōsei)*" (conversation with Kishida Rio, 21 July 1989). For the numbered lines used in the improvisational street theater piece "Looking for Father" *(Chichi-sagashi)* in European performances of *Solomon* in 1971, see *Terayama Shūji gikyokushū 2—jikken engekishū* (Terayama Shūji anthology 2—experimental theater) (Tokyo: Geki shobō, 1981), 232–234.

6. Terayama Hatsu, *Hahu no hahu u*, 33.

7. See Terayama Shūji, "Haiyū wākushoppu" (actor's workshop), in *Terayama Shūji gikyokushū 2*, 270–272; *"Arutō—waga zankoku engeki sengen"* (Artaud—declaration of my theatre of cruelty), in *Terayama Shūji engekironshū* (Terayama Shūji's collected theater essays) (Tokyo: Kokubunsha, 1983), 238–248; and Paul Ryder Ryan, "Shiraz-Persepolis and the Third World," *Drama Review* 17 (December 1973): 48–50. Terayama quotes the entire lengthy third paragraph of Artaud's "Theatre and the Plague" in "Haiyū wākushoppu," 270.

8. Terayama Shūji, "Manifesto," *Drama Review* 19 (December 1975): 86.

9. Ryan, "Shiraz-Persepolis," 48–50.

10. The hovercraft were employed at European performances in 1978. For an account of the New York production (1980), see Maria Meyers, "Terayama's *Directions to Servants,*" *Drama Review* 25 (March 1981): 79–94.

11. See Ryan, "Shiraz-Persepolis," 50; and Patricia Marton, "Terayama's *Blind Man's Letter,*" *Drama Review* 19 (March 1975): 114–115.

12. Terayama, "Manifesto," 87.

13. That Terayama's plays must be left out of this book is regrettable. Translations of two of them were prepared and included in the original plan. However, Terayama Hatsu, the playwright's mother, who has held the rights to his works since his death from a liver ailment in 1983, insists that his preeminent status requires a separate volume for his works alone. Therefore, the discussion of his plays in this essay was expanded to give a better sense of the accomplishments of Terayama and Tenjō Sajiki. Translations of his major works themselves, however, will have to wait for a planned volume devoted solely to Terayama.

A parody of high school class pictures taken at the Imperial Palace, this photo commemorating Tenjō Sajiki's founding in 1967 reveals its social stance. (Courtesy Shinshokan.)

The set of the 1977 film *The Boxer* (Bokusā), co-written by Kishida Rio and Terayama Shūji, directed by Terayama *(left)*. Kara Jūrō is the referee *(center)*. (Courtesy Shinshokan.)

Tenjō Sajiki Theater, Tokyo; Terayama in front. Writing prose with titles like "The Encouragement of Running Away from Home" made Terayama's theater a destination of alienated youths. (Courtesy Shinshokan.)

The Hunchback of Aomori uses the hallucinatory, the grotesque, and borrowings from Japanese popular and folk culture to explore the themes of lost identity, lust, and mother. Tenjō Sajiki, 1967. (Courtesy Jinriki Hikōkisha.)

Dr. Galigari's Crime calls for no separation of stage and seating areas; the set is a "matchbox for people." Different scenes are played simultaneously in different rooms. Tenjō Sajiki, 1969. (Courtesy Jinriki Hikōkisha.)

Knock: Street Theater was performed in thirty-three locations over thirty hours. Although imaginatively conceived, it encountered changed times; spontaneous participation was slight. Tenjō Sajiki, 1975. (Courtesy Jinriki Hikōkisha.)

Knock: Street Theater

Kishida Rio and Terayama Shūji

TRANSLATED BY ROBERT T. ROLF

(Note: This is a portion of the script of the street theater piece Knock *used by the experimental theater group Tenjō Sajiki for their performance in April 1975. The whole was scripted by Kishida Rio and structured and directed by Maboroshi Kazuma, but the following section is one of those in which Terayama had a hand in the scripting or structuring.*

After months of research on the suitability for performance of several sites in the Shibuya, Suginami, and Shinjuku wards of Tokyo, the play was finally put on simultaneously in thirty-three locations in the Kōenji area of Suginami Ward. Trouble occurred with residents trying to prevent the sudden intrusion of this fiction into their uneventful everyday lives. The newspapers treated it as a scandal and made a memorable clamor in the local news pages.)

An Incident on the Men's Side of a Public Bath at 4–37 East XX, XX Ward: The Plan

An attempt to transfigure time, sending actors as alien objects into a public bath on the casual continuum of everyday life.

Gentlemen in the bath, join us in our male gymnastics; feel with your bodies how the bathing experience is also a party to the dramaturgy of encounter. Wash well! Learn well!

Outline

A   The actor, dressed very normally, goes to the public bath at the predetermined time.

B   He pays the prescribed fee.

C   If possible, he will wear a waterproof watch and leave it on while bathing.

D   However, if there is a wall clock in the bathroom, this will be unnecessary.

E   It is more effective to have many actors; but if that is impossible, one will do.

F   If there are many actors, they will pretend not to know one
        another.
G   If it does not interfere with their other roles, it would help to have
        the actors bearded.
H   They should remain expressionless while carrying out their actions.
I   The actors will choose their lines arbitrarily.

Time Schedule

4:45 P.M.   MAN I arrives at public bath.
4:48 P.M.   MAN I pays bathing fee.
4:50 P.M.   MAN I begins to undress.
4:55 P.M.   MAN I enters bathing room.
            MAN 2 arrives at public bath. (MAN 2's subsequent actions all fol-
            low those of MAN I by ten minutes.)
5:00 P.M.   MAN I enters the bathtub with right arm raised.
5:05 P.M.   MAN I leaves the bathtub with right arm raised. He sits in
            front of the water taps. He lowers his arm.
5:10 P.M.   MAN I washes himself with the liveliness of time-lapse projec-
            tion.
5:20 P.M.   MAN I freezes in the pose he is holding at the time.
5:25 P.M.   MAN I silently dashes water on himself, bucketful after buck-
            etful. It is a ceremony.
5:40 P.M.   MAN I enters the tub with left arm raised.
5:45 P.M.   MAN I leaves the tub with left arm raised. He sits in front of
            the water taps. He lowers his left arm.
5:50 P.M.   MAN I begins to shave. He neatly shaves only the right half of
            his face.
5:55 P.M.   MAN I stops shaving. He washes his face.
6:00 P.M.   MAN I suddenly stands and assumes a rigid upright position.
            (If there are many actors, they all stand.)
6:03 P.M.   MAN I enters the tub.
            (If there are many actors, hereafter they all perform the same actions as
            MAN I.)
6:05 P.M.   MAN I leaves the tub. Stretching his entire body, he dries him-
            self.
6:15 P.M.   MAN I leaves the bathing room; he dresses.
6:25 P.M.   MAN I leaves the public bath.

Lines

*(With every action the actors select their lines with no relation to their
order.)*
1   Where I come from the poets all have beards.
2   My father said he wanted to number all the cities.

3   Early afternoon says it wants to drink the shadows.

4   *Pichi-pichi*—I love that word.[1] *Pichi-pichi*. You and me: we *pichi-pichi*. We speak a mutual language. Let's try a little mutual exploration: *pichi-pichi*.

5   Putting on a little weight around the middle, aren't you?

6   I've got gonorrhea.

7   What the hell makes you think we're prepared to launch into a discussion of class struggle or your relation to abstract forces?

8   Cloudy, followed by clear skies.

9   If a triangle as good as conveys the mysteries of the human body, then the triangle itself is a mystery.

10   Did you clear up your skin disease?

11   Men! They're so easy to fool. *(Feminine speech employed.)*

12   Nothing like a good bath. The water's just right.

13   Well, why don't you have any money? I want some money. Oh, what a worthless man I married.

14   I stared at my navel for a long time, then suddenly I had the feeling it was going to fall off. It started to come loose. I took a deep breath and twisted my navel around once. It had loosened a little more. While I spun it around and around and around and around, I realized it had fallen clean off for good. . . . Hey, you ever seen a man without a navel?

15   It does not serve the objectives of the conference. We were in total agreement to meet at a completely neutral site in international territory.

16   I wonder if Emeron Creme Rinse will really work on my hair?

17   It's man's actions that create history, not his feelings.

18   Oh, dear, I'd like to take off another six or seven pounds.

19   The telephone, the telegraph, the phonograph, the wireless, the movie projector, the slide projector, technical dictionaries, timetables, manuals, official reports.

20   I'd really like to get a look at the women's bath!

21   Nothing ever goes right in the morning.

22   Now we're alone at last, just the two of us.

23   And so, you've become a middle-aged man.

24   The death penalty!!

25   Oh dear me, I'd rather die than ever meet any of my family again.

26   Research follows the circular paths of our mental associations. The pursuit of reality must always proceed not from object to object but from relationship to relationship. Open mouths and windowpanes are interchangeable. Light and sound collide on the skin and sink into the heated ocean. *(Enters the tub.)*

27   I'm really sorry, but can I borrow your soap?

28

29 Look at him. Look at that brat of his over there. Look at that child of yours. Look at that kid. He takes after you: doesn't listen to a word I say. Look at him. He's just like you: not worth a shit.

30 I forgot my new undies!

31 The train ran through the field along the road across from my house. It always ran very fast. Whenever my old man and old lady were fighting—they were always fighting about money—I went to the field and walked along the tracks as far as I could. After listening quietly a while, I held my nose and mouth, holding my breath, so that I couldn't hear them fighting; then I'd cut across the road and go out to the grassy field where it began to slope—I might see a dog pissing. I'd slide down the smooth slope, climb the big hill on the other side, and walk on through the tall grass; when I came to the railroad tracks, I just kept walking. The high grass always cut my fingers and made me cry; but I soon stopped because there was no one around to hear. I always stopped crying at once when I was alone. If someone was with me, I cried and cried and threatened to run away someday and die. I cried and cried—just like this.

32 Your feet are filthy. Hurry up and wash them.

33 I wanted to find out. To try it . . . I didn't know. So I wanted to find out . . . what it was like. *(Feminine speech.)*

34 Ass! Hips! Chest! Legs! Arms! Heels! Thumbs! Ears! Eyes! Back! Navel!

35 He's not worth a shit. He left us in a world of tedium and worry that he never once earnestly tried to change.

36 You're well enough to take baths again now?

37 She sleeps with anybody. *(Feminine speech.)*

38 Have you forgotten? Do you remember?

39 We're losing ourselves in the mementos of our childhood. It's too late now. Understand? There's no possible solution.

40 What happened next was just like a scene from a movie.

41 They are meat, roasting themselves very quietly, very slowly, serving the machine that raises the goats, the machine that raises the big goats.

42 I think that a person begins to die a little when he only gets three or four hours sleep a night for a week.

43 Man is the author of his own destruction.

44 I caught a blind fish. With an invisible line so long it could drift off to the ends of the earth.

45 Where'd my towel go?

46 Find my toothbrush.

47   To name is to arm. The day the great bird comes, the history
      that has yet to be remembered will rise up.

48   Genealogy; two outs, bases loaded; Mickey Mouse; The Origin
      of the Spoon; the Grand Inquisitor; a solitary cat named Clas-
      sics; book wars; hair; The Keys of the Kingdom; Crime Incor-
      porated; the night before last I killed the dog; a bathtub repair-
      man; the past progressive tense; Dr. Ménière; butchered meat;
      The Treatise on Analogous Correspondence; Introduction to
      Wrestling for Youth; I punched Momma; A Study of the
      Beard; The Great Performers Hour; what happened to the old
      detective; The History of the Hat; artificial eye engineering;
      the man-powered airplane; a directory of names; the Kilry
      bird; I ran away from my home in Yamagata; contagious
      magic; A Study of Twins; the haircut ceremony; the empress'
      masturbation; twenty godparents; The Encyclopedia of Gam-
      bling; the world's best razor strap; blood types; Dr. Caligari;
      my father hanged himself three years ago; problem counseling;
      opium; the Pythagorean theorem; shellfish stewed in sauce;
      Medieval Palmistry; forensic medicine; boy airmen; ah, I got
      to get a piece; the Three Brave Human Bullets; Mediterranean
      Express; theories of revolution; A Dark Night's Return Pas-
      sage; Marineland; Chūjōtō;[2] the Korea Strait; a dogcatcher;
      civil war; how are you, Mom?; oneiromancy; mirror divina-
      tion; hunting adults; sailing in a bed; guinea fowl; Boy with a
      Pistol.

49   I caught rickets when I was three years old; then a terrible case
      of scabies, which were cauterized with nitric acid. On top of
      that, I got lame, and now I'm a cripple. A miserable man,
      that's me.

50   Towel and soap; razor and toothbrush; seventy-five yen for a
      bath.

51   I slit my wrists three times trying to kill myself. I botched it
      every time; I've given up trying. Now I'm thinking of opening
      a prop shop.

52   I threw the clock off the roof to run away from time. So now
      every single day alarm clocks keep falling on my head.

53   I'm not on display. Stop looking at me like that.

54   Hey, Honey, want to join me?

55   How many things can you do in the bath? We wash our bodies
      that reek of sweat and masturbation. Accumulated excretions!
      The hot water flows over shoulders and stomach. Filth! Filth!
      Filth! The skin is taut over my flesh and bones.

56   I want to go to the john.

57   My old lady's rheumatism; my old man's sciatica; older broth-

er's trachoma; older sister's barrenness; little sister, does your edema still trouble you?; the carbuncle on little brother's face.

58 Polio, keloids, infantile paralysis, gonorrheal ophthalmia, fluke infestation, infection of the middle ear, geriatric tuberculosis, rabies, diarrhea, jaundice, paratyphoid fever, harelip, rupture, gigantism, stomach cancer, lung cancer, heart cancer, hypertrophy of the pancreas, cholecystitis, plague, leprosy, colon bacillus.

59 Leprosy: a chronic disease due to infection by leprosy bacilli. The latent period is extremely long and may even exceed twenty years. Macular leprosy produces reddish-brown spots; neural leprosy causes cutaneous sensory lesions; tuberculoid leprosy brings nodular protuberances. Concurrent combinations of these forms of leprosy may occur. Hansen's disease; the scourge of Heaven; lepers, beggars, cripples, scroungers, scavengers.

60 Don't come near me. I'll get your disease.

61 It's 19 April 1975, exactly 5 P.M.: I think I'll raise my right arm. It's 5:05: I think I'll lower my right arm. It's 5:40: I think I'll raise my left arm. It's 5:45: I think I'll lower my left arm. Guess I'll do some calisthenics: one, two, three; one, two, three, four; one, two, three.

62 All natural phenomena, human or otherwise, become symbols when they acquire noninherent meaning. Even a part of the body can become a symbol. For example, "phallus" is a word that denotes the erect penis, but it is a symbol, too. That is, "phallus" contains meaning beyond the purely biological; when it has acquired functions serving purposes other than sexual love and procreation, it becomes the symbolic phallus.

63 When the male hamadryas, or sacred baboon, senses the danger of attack by a more powerful male of the species, he averts danger by assuming the attitude of a female baboon desiring copulation. He lifts his tail, arches his back, and exposes his buttocks to the stronger baboon, who then stops his threatening, mounts him, and simulates copulation. Such a pattern was first noted by Zukerman in 1932, but it is not restricted to the sacred baboon. It can also be observed in other animal societies with strictly ranked hierarchies.

64 Hell; corpse; ghost; spirit of the dead; funeral; Buddhist altar; dead child; infanticide; funerary tablet; prayer to Amitābha; starving ghost; funerary light; artificial eye; coffin; artificial limb; madness; the Straits of Abandoned Children; Les Misérables.

65 What is war to a seventeen-year-old boy? What is war to his-

tory? What is war to a freight train leaving? What is war to a faucet one merely pushes for hot water? What is war to the soap in the soap dish? What is war to Vitalis Hair Tonic? What is war to the towel; to the wash bucket; to the tile picture of Mt. Fuji on the bathhouse wall; to the mirror; to the razor, tooth brush, and tooth powder? What is war to the public bath?
Too hot; I've had it.

Dad, who was a local police detective. Dad, alone in the shed masturbating. Middle-aged, black uniform, domestic imperialist reigning alone—Dad. Darwinian Theory of Evolution Dad. Dad, who goes to the railroad tracks to get rid of the vomit he came home drunk and threw up in the washbowl. Dad, who pisses with the toilet door open. Dad the detective, sitting in the convicts' train headed for the prison. Skinny-legged, potbellied Dad. Dad's Sundays. Dad's appendectomy. Dad's solitude, hiding a photograph of Katagiri Yūko[3] in the desk drawer. Dad and his Yamanaka Minetarō[4] map of the Greater East Asia Co-Prosperity Sphere. Dad, whose family line is made up of blood relative lice in the walls. Dad the cop, with the authority of the state, born in the year of the color white and the element water. Dad's continuation and end; where does the horizon begin and where does it end, Dad? . . .

Language

Loquacity without content is merely noise, and at times the silence of the body can articulate thought more eloquently than anything:
So much so that the body and language can gauge one another.
The actors must have just enough language at their disposal to answer the other bathers, should they begin to question their behavior.

Notes

1. *Pichi-pichi* is an onomatopoetic word that refers to a young woman's sprightliness and nubility.
2. A traditional herbal medicine used for female disorders.
3. An actress.
4. Novelist (1885–1966), known primarily for prewar juvenile adventure stories that embraced Japanese nationalism and militarism.

Kara Jūrō

KARA JŪRŌ (b. 1940) is a seminal figure in the new theater that emerged in the 1960s. Classified by Japanese critics under such rubrics as "underground" *(angurā)* and Little Theater Movement *(shōgekijō undō)*, the new theater found a new audience: the young. The phenomenon continues; but whereas once Betsuyaku, Shimizu, Terayama, Kara, and Satoh were all lions of the youth culture, today, with the possible exception of Satoh, only Kara remains a great favorite of audiences twenty or thirty years his junior. The youthful imagery of his plays, the irreverent bohemianism of his troupe the Situation Theater, and the emotional, rather than intellectual, appeal of his plays under his own direction ensure this.

Kara began as an actor and has always considered himself first of all an actor. He claims to have begun writing and directing to fulfill needs within his young troupe. Like Terayama, Kara was a leader in the underground movement, experimenting with alternative configurations of stage/audience space. After several years performing in a variety of venues ranging from conventional halls to outdoor sites, in 1967 Kara and the Situation Theater introduced the Red Tent, which has become their trademark. Like Terayama's Tenjō Sajiki, Kara's Situation Theater went abroad, not to Europe and America, but to South Korea (1972), Bangladesh (1973), and Palestinian refugee camps in Lebanon and Syria (1974).

Kara's successes have included a series of "John Silver" plays (the original *John Silver* [Jon Shirubā] was performed in December 1965); a series of "petticoat" *(koshimaki)* plays, beginning with *Petticoat Osen, One Hundred Montes Veneris* (Koshimaki Osen hyakko no chikyū) in April 1966; and the two plays anthologized here, one of which, *The Virgin's Mask* (Shōjo kamen) (1969), earned Kara the Kishida Prize for Playwriting in 1970. *Kappa* (Kappa) (1978), a work that exhibits similarities to *The Virgin's Mask,* won the Izumi Kyōka Literary Prize for that year. Kara has also written fiction, most notably *Letter from Sagawa* (Sagawa-kun kara no tegami), which involves a recent actual incident, the cannibalizing by a Japanese student of a young woman in France, and which brought Kara the Akutagawa Prize for Fiction in 1983.

INTRODUCTION

John K. Gillespie

UNLIKE THE OTHER playwrights included in this anthology, Kara Jūrō has distinguished himself in every aspect of theater work. Playwright, actor, director, producer, set designer, and theoretician of his art, Kara embodies a complete approach to the stage. As exercises in total theater, his plays are especially good vehicles for actors and, not surprisingly, are reminiscent of *kabuki*.

In fact, Kara sees his troupe as the contemporary manifestation of *kawaramono,* the so-called riverbed beggars who were the first *kabuki* actors. His plays might well be considered *kabuki* brought up to date. Kara crystallized his position in this historical lineage in October 1968 when he set up his now famous Red Tent at Shijōkawaramachi in Kyoto, precisely on the spot where the courtesan Okuni is said to have begun *kabuki*.

Just as Okuni's boldly erotic performances ran counter to the accepted standards of her time, so Kara's unbridled brand of total theater startled the staid world of mainstream *shingeki*. While those plays left the various aspects of performance completely independent one from another, Kara sought in his plays to create a unified whole, as in *kabuki,* with all aspects—body movement, voice, music—interdependent. While mainstream *shingeki* would merely intone a play's lines, Kara's Situation Theater would make the play vibrantly alive. Even his stage design, with elaborate modular sets and modified *hanamichi* (the runway used for entrances and exits leading from the rear of every *kabuki* theater to stage right), is reminiscent of the classic form. Indeed, among the innovative figures in Japanese theater since 1960, perhaps only Terayama—who also drew heavily on classic Japanese forms—was as consistently at the cutting edge of the avant-garde.

Kara's approach to theater is in part a natural result of his upbringing in Asakusa, the old entertainment district of Tokyo that even now retains a certain flavor of the Edo period. Kara was born there in 1940 and attended Meiji University in Tokyo, where he was active in the student drama club. After graduating in 1962, he joined the Youth Art Theater (Seinen geijutsuza, or Seigei) for one year. He then worked for a time at a burlesque house in Asakusa. In 1963 he founded his own theater company, the Situation Group (Shichueishon no kai), soon to become the long-lived Situation Theater.[1]

What are Kara's plays like? They are first of all vehicles for his remarkable ability as a storyteller. He often takes the seed of a play from popular Japanese literature, fertilizes it in the culture of his stagecraft, and produces a flower familiar in some way to virtually all Japanese. His humor, replete with word play, provokes belly laughter rather than thoughtful chuckles—an effect reminiscent of Japanese *manga,* or comic strips. Spectators are drawn to the action like children to "Sesame Street," unable to turn away until they see what happens next.

Paradoxically, the plot in Kara's plays is hardly meant to be followed in the traditional linear sense. Kara offers not a humanistic developmental perspective but a fragmented one. He is, in short, opposed to realism. He teases the spectator with images of illusory reality and realistic illusion. Inside the Red Tent, the atmosphere magically becomes hermetic; time freezes, as in a dream. Such transformation allows Kara freedom to delve into the past, to re-create mythic situations not amenable to the ticking of a clock.

In this, Kara effectively reflects one of the prevailing cultural phenomena of his time: the disorientation of contemporary Japanese youths. Kara feels that Japanese youths in the postwar period, but particularly since the nationwide demonstrations against the U.S.-Japan Mutual Security Treaty in 1960, have lost any sense of history and of their position in it. Kara calls contemporary Japanese youths "the children who have been ostracized from Japanese soil—the soil on which our mothers gave us birth—[and left] to roam about."[2]

Kara's theater is calculated to restore a traditional sense of Japanese history or, as he puts it, to seek "a historical way out of the present state of reality."[3] He would divert the disoriented generation from its labyrinthine wanderings in the present to the historical truths of the Japanese past—dressed, to be sure, in kairotic, mythic overtones. Once inside Kara's Red Tent, there is no fear of being buffeted about as in the real, chronological world.

Indeed, Kara structures his Red Tent world so masterfully as to imbue the particular Japanese setting with universal implications. As his characters wend their way through a maze of obstacles, it becomes

clear that Kara's "way out of the present state of reality" is a way to discover, or rediscover, oneself by reconnecting to a historical—read,
mythic—past. Kara resorts to absurdist means to render this search.
Characters speak to one another, but their words are often geared to
their own private conversations, failing to communicate. The characters too are frequently not single individuals but at any point may
become other characters. This sort of transformation creates a certain
aesthetic distance between the stage action and the spectators, thereby
allowing a clearer, more objective perspective on the search for self.

The Virgin's Mask

The two plays presented here provide examples of Kara's style of playwriting. *The Virgin's Mask* was first published in *Shingeki* magazine in
November 1969 and had already been staged in October by Suzuki
Tadashi and the Waseda Little Theater. This was the first play Kara
wrote for a group other than his own. With its classical, well-organized,
even lyrical structure, it is Kara's most mainstream play.

The style of the play is informed by many of Kara's signature techniques: rapid shifts in mood through sudden entrances, stylized poses,
abrupt changes in music and costume, and revolving scenery. The
action occurs in a subterranean coffeehouse called "The Body," which
is owned by Kasugano Yachiyo, a former heartthrob of the Takarazuka
all-female musical review. Kasugano has fallen on hard times, having
dissipated her body and her talent over many years in the theater.
There remains no body for her to possess. She is nothing more than a
"pitiful ghost gradually fading away." Other relationships in the play
parallel that between Kasugano and her body. There are a Ventriloquist
and a Dummy, for example, whose interaction reflects the separation of
actor and body. And the young virgin, Kai, eager for a life on the stage,
is pressed into the role of Catherine opposite Kasugano's Heathcliff in
an imaginary staging of *Wuthering Heights*, two lost souls begging for the
bodies that will allow them to consummate their love.

These events take on another dimension against the lingering physical and psychological impact of World War II; living underground in
"The Body" coffeehouse is a metaphor for the tortured legacy of that
war. The Water-Drinking Man, for example, having suffered the sear-
ing heat and destruction of the firebombs, guzzles water unslakably.
When the Head Waiter, who has not been above ground since the war,
finally ventures outside "The Body," he returns battered and thirsty to
become another water-drinking man.

Toward the end of the play, as Kasugano seeks to relive a deeply held
bygone passion, her imagination moves the action to a Japanese military hospital in Manchuria, scene of Japan's imperialist past. For Kasu-

gano this past has assumed a reality like that of the romantic fantasies rendered on the Takarazuka stage. These two elements are brought together in Kasugano's vain attempt to play the role that is her pride and obsession—Heathcliff in *Wuthering Heights*. Success is elusive, however, for the ineluctable truth is that the relationship between Heathcliff and Catherine, like that between Japan and Manchuria, is predatory and ultimately doomed. This is made clear from the shockingly specific references to Heathcliff digging up Catherine's remains and joyously consuming her decayed flesh. When Kasugano's one true love from the past, Captain Amagasu of the Imperial Army, finally arrives on stage, he tells her ominously that "this [the Manchurian hospital] is your *Wuthering Heights*" and abruptly leaves her.

Kasugano's dilemma in part emerges from being a woman trapped in a man's body (her breasts reveal her female identity). Her female/male identity complex is bound up with her past (and Japan's). It is a past, moreover, that, as it does her young fans (who appear in World War II costume), holds her (and Japan) in thrall. Reflecting this dilemma, Kai, Kasugano's young protégée—the latest Catherine—who desires nothing so much as to follow in Kasugano's footsteps to stardom, begins to use male pronouns and speech, like her mentor, showing that she will become another Heathcliff.

With this kind of action, Kara recalls the very origin of *kabuki* and the riverbed beggars who were dissipating their bodies for the highest bidder but were looking, perhaps in vain, for a stage body—for some appropriate form on the stage—through which to express themselves. In addition, Kara reminds us in this play that the stage is a place of transformation, a magical realm of the imagination where the physical body paradoxically is essential but easily lost in the illusion rendered. This is Kasugano's dilemma and the fate awaiting the youthful Kai. As one character figuratively says of "The Body" cafe: "You can't get out, and you can't come in." The search for self, in Kara's view, is fraught with dead-end twists.

Two Women

Transformations of character also occur in *Two Women* (Futari no onna), first published in 1978 as a radio drama, *Room Number Six* (Rokugō shitsu). Kara rewrote this piece for the stage and published it in the November 1979 issue of *Shingeki*. The play was premiered in the same month by the important troupe Seventh Sick Ward (Dainana Byōtō), which is led by actor Ishibashi Renji and actress Midori Mako. The plot is loosely based on the conflict in *The Tale of Genji* among Genji, his wife, Aoi, and one of his mistresses, Rokujō. Aoi, pregnant and the fiancée of the psychiatrist Kōichi (avatar of Genji), goes with Kōichi to

see the auto races at the Fuji Circuit. Here Kōichi encounters Rokujō
(the roles of Aoi, Rokujō and the Woman are played by the same
actress), who has recently left the psychiatric ward of the hospital where
Kōichi works and is now selling cosmetics. The famous scuffle in *The
Tale of Genji* between the vehicles of Aoi and Rokujō occurs here in the
racetrack parking lot. Rokujō's spirit then enters the nauseous, sleeping
Aoi. But Aoi pursues Kōichi to Rokujō's apartment, where her intense
passion empowers her transformation into Rokujō. She dies by hanging
as she leaps in a frenzy from the rafters. Is Rokujō dead too? Perhaps,
but a shadowy Woman emerges in the final scene to torment Kōichi,
now himself gone mad.

The Woman is central to an important subtext in the play involving
Kara's ant imagery. A patient in the psychiatric hospital as the play
opens, the Woman is obsessed with ants and creates her own enclosed
ant universe, replete with an ant theater troupe and sonic dune buggy.
Transformed within this universe, she flits about from one thought to
the next in the helter-skelter movements of ants creating a maze of path-
ways in sand. The similarity of this universe to the one within Kara's
Red Tent is hardly coincidental; the ants' characteristic movements call
immediately to mind the helter-skelter lives of Kara's 1960s and 1970s
audiences—in Kara's words, Japan's "aborted" youths, "ostracized
. . . to roam about." In this sense, *Two Women* makes a powerful comment on a Japan no longer moored to deep traditions, adrift on an
uncharted postmodern sea. In part by anchoring his play in *The Tale of
Genji,* a masterwork of the classical past, Kara attempts to chart a way
back to deep Japanese traditions.

All Kara's transformations of character occur sylph-like, lulling the
spectator into his magical stage world. Kara's opposition to conventional, fourth-wall stage realism is clear. He has described this approach
in his essay "To a Cultural Scandalmonger": "If there is anything to
the phrase 'dramatic imagination,' it means the dramatic power that
seeks to negate the reality of the spoken word reverberating rhythmi-
cally inside each actor."[4] In both plays, Kara realizes this crucial aspect
of his theater through the primacy of the physical body on stage. Such is
the body's power that Kara goes so far as to call it something "privileged" *(tokkenteki nikutai).* For Kara, the body is the *sine qua non* of theater; ironically only through the physical body of the actor are illusion
and, ultimately, the negation of reality possible.

Notes

1. For more information on Kara's life and work, see *Kara Jūrō no sekai* (The world of Kara Jūrō) (Tokyo: Shinpyōsha, 1979); Yamaguchi Takeshi, *Dōjidaijin toshite no Kara Jūrō* (Kara Jūrō: Contemporary man) (Tokyo: San'ichi shobō, 1980); and the definitive *Kara gumi—jōkyō gekijō zen-kiroku* (The complete Jōkyō Gekijō—illustrated) (Tokyo: Parco, 1982). Kara now calls his troupe Kara and Company (Kara gumi).

2. Kara Jūrō, *Asahi Shimbun*, 11 September 1967.

3. Cited in Ōzasa Yoshio, *Dōjidai engeki to gekisakkatachi* (Contemporary plays and playwrights) (Tokyo: Geki shobō, 1980), 33.

4. Kara Jūrō, "Bunkateki sukandarisuto e" *(To a cultural scandalmonger),* in *Koshimaki Osen* (Petticoat Osen) (Tokyo: Gendai shichōsha, 1983), 33–34.

Kara Jūrō *(left)* and his Situation Theater, shown here in a revival of his prizewinning play *The Virgin's Mask,* forged a link with the outcast forebears of *kabuki.* Situation Theater, 1971. (Courtesy Kara Jūrō.)

The Virgin's Mask

Kara Jūrō

TRANSLATION ADAPTED BY JOHN K. GILLESPIE
FROM AN ORIGINAL TRANSLATION BY PAUL H. KRIEGER

CAST OF CHARACTERS

KAI, *a virgin*
OLD WOMAN
KASUGANO YACHIYO
VENTRILOQUIST
VENTRILOQUIST'S DUMMY
CHIEF WAITER
WAITER 1
WAITER 2

WATER-DRINKING MAN, *looks like a white-collar worker*
CAPTAIN AMAGASU
NURSE
GIRL IN AIR-RAID HOOD 1
GIRL IN AIR-RAID HOOD 2
GIRL IN AIR-RAID HOOD 3

Scene 1: Flower Ghost

(Lights come up on two figures squatting on the hanamichi, *the runway leading from the rear of the theater to stage right. One is the virgin* KAI, *and the other is the* OLD WOMAN, *who is holding the magazine* Virgin's Friend. *The two are slowly and firmly pulling on black socks. They have large red garters around their thighs.)*

KAI: Say, Granny, when Ms. Kasugano played the role of Heathcliff in *Wuthering Heights* and was crossing the Yorkshire moor, she said she was afraid of getting into a love triangle with those two ghosts of love. But I wonder if she wasn't maybe thrilled to death at the thought.

OLD WOMAN: That's a difficult question.

KAI: If she was, though, Granny, do you think it was wrong of her?

OLD WOMAN: To tell the truth, Kai, you have to be on your guard with what an "eternal virgin" is thinking.

KAI: Eternal virgin?

OLD WOMAN: A Takarazuka actress. You know, a so-called *zuka*-girl. What you're saying about Kasugano sounds to me like *Wuthering Heights* revisited.

KAI: Why? Why is Kasugano like *Wuthering Heights?*

OLD WOMAN: Ask the thrown-away underpants.

258

KAI: What do you mean by that?

OLD WOMAN: Sorry, Kai. I shouldn't have said that to you.

KAI: You know, Granny, I can't see Kasugano so worked up just because that man was amorous. Even now, two hundred years later, the two beggars of love, Heathcliff and Catherine, roaming the Yorkshire moor, are still beggars, you see, beggars of love. The author writes at the end of the book that one could imagine only "unquiet slumbers for the sleepers in that quiet earth." Even though those two are together, they are still searching, still begging for something, while they lie sneezing in the Yorkshire moor. I wonder if maybe Kasugano didn't know that.

OLD WOMAN: No, she didn't know anything.

KAI: Why not?

OLD WOMAN: Kasugano was too busy making money.

KAI: Kasugano was not making so much money.

OLD WOMAN: Kasugano is now, well, an executive.

KAI: Even so, she was young once.

OLD WOMAN: She has a checkered past.

KAI: Say, Granny, don't tease me. Tell me something about what Kasugano knew. What are Heathcliff and Catherine begging for, wandering about Wuthering Heights?

OLD WOMAN: It's what ghosts always want.

KAI: Which is? . . .

OLD WOMAN: A body. *(Sings.)*

> As time goes by the virgin becomes an old woman,
> if time still goes by I wonder if the old woman becomes a virgin.
> I had children in the past,
> only one of them, the smooth talker,
> came back alone from the mountain—
> Zarathustra rubbing his big grimy feet on my thighs,
> this is a superman, rub, rub, rub.
> Listen, mother, the body is big reason.
> If so, son, is reason a big body?
> Then his big feet suddenly stopped. . . .
> *(Spoken, aside.)* "Logic cannot make a U-turn so easily,"
> The creep of a superman with that mouth said,
> in an instant putting his chin in his hand
> like a dwarf.
> Alchemy to Saint-Germain.
> The art of forming the eye to Merleau-Ponty.
> To who the art of forming the body?
> As time goes by the virgin becomes an old woman,

if time still goes by
who knows the U-turn secret
of an old woman becoming a virgin?

OLD WOMAN AND KAI: *(Together.)* More than anything, the body!

(Suddenly, the stage becomes dark, and the Mary Hopkins song "Those Were the Days" begins. The stage is set for the basement coffee house named "The Body." There is a large picture outside the back window of an erupting volcano in ancient times: giant dragonflies are in flight. On the chairs and tables are flower patterns. At stage right is the entrance. At stage left is what appears to be a counter. The CHIEF WAITER is standing by it with a large napkin in his hand. The VENTRILOQUIST is sitting at the table on the right. The VENTRILO-QUIST's life-sized DUMMY sits facing him. The music can be changed from "Those Were the Days" to a melancholy chanson. The WAITER is standing up straight; both his index fingers are covered with white bandages.)

VENTRILOQUIST: *(Looking at the picture of the volcano, speaks in a low voice to the DUMMY.)* How many years old do you think that volcano is?

DUMMY: *(In a high voice.)* Isn't that Mt. Vesuvius?

VENTRILOQUIST: No, it's 200,000 years old.

DUMMY: I see. That's my period.

VENTRILOQUIST: Why?

DUMMY: Because no humans were alive.

VENTRILOQUIST: But there was some evidence of life.

DUMMY: That's not worth talking about because it's before the creation of life. The real creation, see, it's my, that is to say, it's the period of stone or minerals.

VENTRILOQUIST: Don't be so proud of yourself.

DUMMY: The world being what it is, let me show off.

VENTRILOQUIST: Anyway, what would you like, coffee or tea?

DUMMY: Coffee.

VENTRILOQUIST: *(Summoning the CHIEF WAITER.)* Hey, waiter.

CHIEF WAITER: *(Approaching slowly.)* Yes, sir, what will it be?

VENTRILOQUIST: Coffee.

CHIEF WAITER: One.

VENTRILOQUIST: *(In the DUMMY's voice.)* No, two.

CHIEF WAITER: How many?

DUMMY: Two.

VENTRILOQUIST: So it'll be two.

CHIEF WAITER: What do you mean by two?

VENTRILOQUIST: One for me, and one for this guy.

CHIEF WAITER: Oh, I see, one for you *(pointing at the VENTRILOQUIST with his hand in a fist—thereby hiding his index finger)* and *(pointing at the DUMMY with his bandaged index finger)* one for this person.

VENTRILOQUIST: Ah, so that's how you do it, is it?

CHIEF WAITER: Yes, sir.

VENTRILOQUIST: Anyway, give us two.

(*A* MAN, *who looks like a white-collar worker, looks through the door.*)

CHIEF WAITER: (*Looking in that direction.*) Welcome!

(MAN *comes nervously into the room, sweating profusely and carrying an insurance company briefcase. He slowly approaches the* CHIEF WAITER, *then passes by him and fastens his mouth on the water faucet beside the counter.*)

CHIEF WAITER: (*Irritated.*) If you'd like some water, I'll help you. (*While saying this, he goes behind the counter.*)

(MAN *writhes about as he noisily drinks the water.*)

(VENTRILOQUIST *stares at the* MAN.)

CHIEF WAITER: (*Bringing the coffees.*) Sorry to have kept you waiting.

(MAN *leaves the water running and exits in feverish haste.*)

CHIEF WAITER: (*Seeing this.*) Say, how about your order? (*He runs to the door, the coffee tray precariously in hand.*) Shit! (*Returns mumbling to the water faucet and turns it off. Approaches the* VENTRILOQUIST.) I'm very sorry to have kept you waiting. (*Sets coffee in front of the* DUMMY *and, as he is about to serve the* VENTRILOQUIST, *deliberately spills it.*)

VENTRILOQUIST: You idiot!

CHIEF WAITER: I'm sorry. You are there, aren't you?

VENTRILOQUIST: Who would order if I weren't?

CHIEF WAITER: I'll get a fresh cup for you. (*Runs to the counter.*)

VENTRILOQUIST: I've never seen a shop like this before! (*Wipes off the table with a handkerchief.*)

CHIEF WAITER: (*Returning with another coffee.*) I'm sorry to have kept you waiting. (*Placing the coffee on the table, he again spills it.*)

VENTRILOQUIST: Oh no, again?

CHIEF WAITER: I'm sorry. You're there, aren't you?

VENTRILOQUIST: Don't play games with me! You, you don't want me to drink coffee, do you?

CHIEF WAITER: I'm sorry. I couldn't see you.

VENTRILOQUIST: Are you blind?

CHIEF WAITER: No, I'm not blind, not at all.

VENTRILOQUIST: Then what are you doing?

CHIEF WAITER: Just when I'm about to set the coffee down, you cease to exist.

VENTRILOQUIST: But didn't you put a cup in front of this dummy?

CHIEF WAITER: Of course, because he exists.

VENTRILOQUIST: How about me?

CHIEF WAITER: Excuse me, I can't hear you too well.

(VENTRILOQUIST *comes close to the* CHIEF WAITER'*s ear and acts as if speaking in a loud voice.*)

CHIEF WAITER: (*As if hearing him well.*) Indeed.

VENTRILOQUIST: I didn't say anything just now.

CHIEF WAITER: But I could understand what you wanted to say. You think you are a poor appendage of this dummy, right? But I can't sympathize with you. With the nonexistence of existence. What is this dummy's name?

VENTRILOQUIST: Mr. Anonymous.

CHIEF WAITER: Huh, such a nice name. What is the appendage's name?

VENTRILOQUIST: You're talking about me?

CHIEF WAITER: Yeah.

VENTRILOQUIST: It's "Ai."

CHIEF WAITER: Is the meaning "a" from *aho,* the word for "fool," and "hi" from the first part of the word for "nothing to compare"? In other words, "Ahi" or "Ai"—meaning "Incomparable Fool"?

VENTRILOQUIST: It's "Ai" meaning love for the one who has no name.

CHIEF WAITER: That must be a real bother for one with no name. *(The* CHIEF WAITER *sits on the table, knocking over the coffee in front of the* DUMMY *with his rear end. He suddenly hits the* DUMMY.*)* Fool, why didn't you drink this right away?

VENTRILOQUIST: Hey, what the hell are you doing to my dummy?

CHIEF WAITER: Ohhhhh, you get mad after all.

VENTRILOQUIST: Of course.

CHIEF WAITER: Why are you angry? Because it hurts? If you think this is your dummy, do you feel pain if it's pinched like this?

VENTRILOQUIST: Don't touch a person's dummy.

CHIEF WAITER: Which one's the person?

VENTRILOQUIST: It's mine!

CHIEF WAITER: You are the appendage to this dummy, aren't you?

VENTRILOQUIST: Get your damn hands off!

CHIEF WAITER: No, I will not let him go. Not until this dummy asks me to.

VENTRILOQUIST: Damn you, stop it!

CHIEF WAITER: This is what you get for letting the coffee I made get cold. *(Grabs the* DUMMY*'s hair.)* Don't you know my blood boils if you let the coffee get cold? *(He hits and kicks the* DUMMY.*)*

VENTRILOQUIST: Oh! This is terrible!

(CHIEF WAITER *looks down at the limp* DUMMY *and disappears behind the counter whistling.*

The battered DUMMY *and the* VENTRILOQUIST *are aghast.)*

VENTRILOQUIST: *(Cradles the* DUMMY *and smooths down its hair.)* It must've hurt, but you're so good—you didn't cry or anything. You must be mad at me because I couldn't help you. But when you were being hit, I suffered as though my body were being sliced up. Which do you think is more painful—actually being hit or looking on with arms folded? Tell me which. Don't look at me that way. I know I am a cow-

ard, so you always become the victim. If you want, we can split up.
But if we do, can you go it alone? I can't. I can't make it without
you. Let's go live somewhere nobody knows, where we don't have to
deal with people. I wouldn't let you be treated like this anymore. I
am also a man. I will not keep on being quiet. When push comes to
shove, I'll stand up. Well, let's forget It. *(Gives a forced laugh.)* As he
said, I might be your appendage because I worry about you so much.
Nothing ever happens to me.

(Two WAITERS *appear from behind the counter, tap dancing. They are like Fred
Astaire in* Daddy Long Legs *and dance skillfully without dropping the coffee
trays they are carrying. One of the* WAITERS *hurts his ankle and trips. The cups
on his tray slide off.)*

CHIEF WAITER: *(Dashes out in front of the* WAITER *who has injured his ankle and
performs a dance step.)* No, don't think about anything. You are shoes.
Lightweight tap-dancing shoes! Music! *(While dancing, sings.)* When
you see him, quietly say, "The virgin's flower was gone, she lined her
kotex with cute patterned paper and was singing all alone." But he'll
never come, he'll never be back; I'm a total eclipse of the sun. *(Stops
singing.)*

WAITER I: Why do we have to do this? I was only supposed to carry the
coffee.

CHIEF WAITER: Don't be insolent. You are just shoes, you S.O.B. Shoes
to carry coffee.

WAITER I: I am myself.

CHIEF WAITER: You're the only one who thinks so.

WAITER I: If I don't think about myself, who will?

CHIEF WAITER: You can get by without thinking on those lines.

WAITER I: I don't like that.

CHIEF WAITER: Not me . . . I rather like it.

WAITER I: Ah, this is confusing.

CHIEF WAITER: You are shoes. As long as you are working in this coffee
shop "The Body," you will be worked hard as shoes. *(Kicks him.)*
Stand up, young man. Music! *(Sings.)* When you see him, quietly
say, "The virgin's flower was gone, she lined her kotex with cute patterned paper. . . ." *(Sees the* VENTRILOQUIST'*s unpaid bill.)* They left
without paying!

(As he is about to run out the door after them, he meets the virgin KAI *and the*
OLD WOMAN.*)*

CHIEF WAITER: Welcome!

KAI: *(Nervously.)* Is this the coffee shop Ms. Kasugano owns?

CHIEF WAITER: Are you a fan?

KAI: I've sent a lot of letters. Oh, that man! *(Points to* WAITER I, *who has
apparently injured his ankle again.)*

CHIEF WAITER: What? *(Looking over his shoulder.)*

WAITER 1: *(Squatting.)* I don't like it. I am not shoes. I'm much more than that.

(WAITER 2 *is still dancing like a machine.*)

WAITER 1: And also, I'm working like a slave here. I'm pushed so hard, I have no time to think. I want to be a human. I have asthma; this job won't last long. Oh, I hate it!

CHIEF WAITER: *(Kicks him from behind.)* You are shoes. You are shoes that have your name.

WAITER 1: *(Standing up.)* No, as long as I'm being beaten on like that, I am myself with the name "Shoes."

CHIEF WAITER: Hey, that's getting into it too much.

WAITER 1: As long as I stay here, I'll never make anything of myself.

CHIEF WAITER: Suffer, suffer, suffer enough to die.

WAITER 1: *(Running behind counter.)* Oh, I need time to think.

(WAITER 2 *is still dancing like a machine.*)

CHIEF WAITER: *(To* WAITER 2.) Hey, we have customers.

(WAITER 2, *without saying anything, starts to work as if asleep. The* CHIEF WAITER *goes behind the counter.* KAI *and the* OLD WOMAN *sit down. Quiet harpsichord music plays.*)

KAI: We don't have to walk anymore. Here is Ms. Kasugano's shop. Takarazuka is nearby.

OLD WOMAN: Anyhow, my memories of Takarazuka come from the Taishō era.[1]

KAI: But can I really become a *zuka*-girl?

OLD WOMAN: Yes, of course, because you are pretty.

KAI: But I don't think I'll be on stage soon.

OLD WOMAN: Pretty as you are, it won't take long. If it does, it's the organization's fault.

KAI: So I'll sing "Oh, Paris, oh my lovely Paris." Right? But if I start working at Takarazuka without first experiencing love, when will I be able to?

OLD WOMAN: During your life you will be in love with yourself in the mirror, always.

KAI: Doesn't one get weary of that?

OLD WOMAN: If you get infatuated with it, you never get bored.

KAI: Is it so interesting to look at oneself?

OLD WOMAN: If you lived in such a world, no one could hurt you but you yourself. So how could there be any pain, then?

KAI: Oh, I'm *so* lucky!

(*There is a noisy sound behind the counter, but it stops abruptly. The* CHIEF WAITER *and* WAITERS 1 *and* 2 *stand affectedly by the counter.* WAITER 1*'s face is scratched, and he is trying to stanch a nosebleed.*)

KAI: Excuse me, may I have some coffee?

(CHIEF WAITER, not answering, follows a fly with his eyes.)

KAI: Excuse me, waiter, coffee please.

(CHIEF WAITER's eyes become red.

WAITERS 1 *and* 2 *look at the* CHIEF WAITER.*)*

KAI: OK, never mind.

CHIEF WAITER: *(Chases after the fly on tiptoe. Extends his arm as if to grasp the fly but misses. His eyes become increasingly bloodshot. Hissing, he smashes the fly under his foot. This job seemingly out of the way, he takes a breath.)* What would you like, young lady?

KAI: Coffee.

CHIEF WAITER: You should have said so before. *(To* WAITER 1.*)* Hey, coffee.

WAITER 1: We don't have any coffee beans.

CHIEF WAITER: What?

WAITER 1: When you got violent, you spilled them. There aren't any.

CHIEF WAITER: Go and buy some.

WAITER 1: Where?

CHIEF WAITER: Where? Where do you think you buy coffee beans, you idiot . . . at a woman's bath? Go to the police box and ask.

WAITER 1: Oh, what a shop!

(WAITER 1 exits, the MAN who looks like a white-collar worker comes in sweating profusely.)

CHIEF WAITER: What do you need?

MAN: Just a water faucet. . . .

CHIEF WAITER: A plumber? Are you a plumber?

MAN: No, I just need a water faucet.

CHIEF WAITER: What will you do with a water faucet?

MAN: I'll drink.

CHIEF WAITER: Drink?

MAN: Yes, water.

CHIEF WAITER: How?

MAN: I'll put my mouth there and sip it. *(The* MAN *abruptly laughs at his own words.)*

(A chilly silence.)

MAN: *(Advancing.)* Let me borrow the water faucet.

CHIEF WAITER: Go to the station or to the park.

MAN: *(Backing off.)* You're not going to let me use it, are you? You absolutely won't. You've already made up your mind, haven't you? And guys like you never give an inch. A man of will, huh? I've had trouble with characters like you before. *(Exits.)*

CHIEF WAITER: *(To* WAITER 2) Hey, you, throw the salt toward the door.

(From the counter WAITER 2 *brings a lot of salt and scatters it toward the door, but it accidentally hits the* CHIEF WAITER's *face.)*[2]

CHIEF WAITER: *(As if wondering about something, he picks up some of the scattered salt with his finger and slowly licks it.)* Hey, what the hell did you throw?

WAITER 2: Huh?

CHIEF WAITER: You must have thrown sugar *(He raises his hand as if to strike WAITER 2.)*

(WAITER 2 grows pale and crawls to a corner, grasping his head in his arms. As he does so, sugar scatters abundantly from the bag he is carrying.)

CHIEF WAITER: Don't waste it! *(Gathers it up and, moving behind the counter, looks over his shoulder.)* Idiot!

(WAITER 2, still holding his head, bends his bulky body over and breaks into tears.

Music abruptly starts again.)

CHIEF WAITER: *(Slicking down his greased-up hair with his comb.)* Lady, do you have some special business with our owner? Is that why you've come?

(When the CHIEF WAITER approaches, WAITER 2 scurries about along the wall uttering a hissing sound.)

CHIEF WAITER: *(To WAITER 2.)* Hey, get back behind the counter.

(WAITER 2 slowly exits.)

CHIEF WAITER: You, young lady, have you come simply as a fan only to see the face of our owner?

KAI: I came to see Ms. Kasugano for a role in a play.

CHIEF WAITER: A role? Then you mean you're a somebody from somewhere?

KAI: No, I'm still a no-name.

CHIEF WAITER: So . . . the wild camomile flower in a night soil hole. Oh, I'm sorry.

KAI: No, I don't mind. Is Ms. Kasugano here?

CHIEF WAITER: The owner is just now preparing for her bath.

KAI: Let me see her for only five minutes, please.

CHIEF WAITER: Do you have connections?

KAI: Connections?

CHIEF WAITER: Yes, you are not the only young one coming here to see her. You're not the only beautiful young woman. In your world with that old woman there, you may well always have the prerogative of being younger and getting a role, but you, uh, you are young. So what's your name?

KAI: Midorigaoka Kai.

CHIEF WAITER: I see . . . Midorigaoka Kai. Look, ten thousand groupies come here to seek out Ms. Kasugano every day. And do you know how many fans she has in Japan? It's countless. We sometimes gather them all together for a picnic excursion, but then change course through Yumenoshima and get rid of some of the girls there. Most of them are young and fat. By fat, I mean lumps of butter. When I'm surrounded by the fat ones, I no longer understand what the hell youth is—it makes me want to opt for old women. Youth, whether it's conscious or unconscious of itself, is, for me, miserable. Because shame follows after actions. And even that shame is of no great value.

KAI: But youth, love, disappointment, and hope are always described as romantic fantasy, aren't they?

CHIEF WAITER: Are you talking about a young girl's soap opera?

KAI: No, Goethe.

CHIEF WAITER: Goethe?!

KAI: Don't get mad.

CHIEF WAITER: How long is Goethe's glory in comparison to how long it takes the light of a star to reach earth?

KAI: Who knows how long?

CHIEF WAITER: Huh?

KAI: How long it takes for starlight to reach earth!

CHIEF WAITER: I do.

KAI: Do you really know such dizzying numbers?

CHIEF WAITER: I know everything . . . so well that I just breathe it in and spit it back out.

(KAI *laughs her head off.*)

CHIEF WAITER: Hey, you're laughing?

KAI: Where did you learn all that? Did you learn it in the planetarium at Kōrakuen Park or between your mother's legs?

CHIEF WAITER: Where do you think I learned it, young lady?

KAI: I don't know.

CHIEF WAITER: The stage.

KAI: Huh?

CHIEF WAITER: If you're on the stage, you can even see the Icarus star.

KAI: Really, do you think so, Granny?

OLD WOMAN: That's a difficult question.

CHIEF WAITER: On the stage, you can even grab the Icarus star. There's transcendence when you're totally immersed in it—Sarah Vida knew.

KAI: Sarah Vida?

CHIEF WAITER: A Brechtian actor who dances the rumba by the sea.

KAI: I'm sorry. I have no knowledge of the stage. I only know about Ms. Kasugano. But surrounded as she is with so many young people and so much theatrical knowledge, I guess she doesn't have time to see me.

CHIEF WAITER: It is time for the owner's bath.

KAI: Will you let me wait for her?

CHIEF WAITER: Has the weather cleared up outside?

KAI: Please, may I wait?

CHIEF WAITER: Has it cleared up outside?

KAI: It's so bright, you need a parasol.

CHIEF WAITER: Oh, I didn't know that. I haven't been out since the war ended. So the sun hasn't yet died out after all?

KAI: Buildings are going up steadily.

CHIEF WAITER: Three-story buildings?

KAI: No, forty stories.

CHIEF WAITER: *(Incredulously.)* That's crazy.

KAI: Have you really never been outside?

CHIEF WAITER: Has construction started?

KAI: What construction?

CHIEF WAITER: Subways. I've heard subways will run in this area.

KAI: Oh, yes. I saw maybe ten bulldozers stopped at the entrance.

CHIEF WAITER: As I thought.

KAI: Waiter, may I wait here for Ms. Kasugano?

CHIEF WAITER: Come back when you marry and have a baby.

OLD WOMAN: *(Suddenly taking* KAI*'s arm.)* Kai!

CHIEF WAITER: Listen, go marry the young owner of some store, have a kid, enjoy the spring breeze, and, if you're still determined to become a *zuka*-girl, you're welcome to come back.

KAI: If I did all that, I'd. . . .

CHIEF WAITER: And why wouldn't you?

KAI: I, um, wouldn't be that young anymore.

CHIEF WAITER: You don't look so young to me even now. How old are you?

KAI: Sixteen.

CHIEF WAITER: You look more like thirty-two.

KAI: It's the first time I've ever been told that!

CHIEF WAITER: Isn't it about time somebody told you?

KAI: Please . . . if I get married, my passion will . . . uh. . . .

CHIEF WAITER: What? You were going to say your passion will disappear?

KAI: Yes.

CHIEF WAITER: To hell with such cheap passion!

KAI: That's why I'm saying I won't marry.

CHIEF WAITER: Marry, divorce, remarry—it doesn't matter. The question is whether, even if you rip a child out of the womb, you are still attracted by the eternal virgin enacted on stage.

KAI: Such passion is sick passion.

CHIEF WAITER: Sick . . . that's okay. There is not talent without sickness.

(The door opens, and the MAN *who looks like a white-collar worker comes in again.)*

MAN: *(Nervous and exhausted.)* Excuse me, the water faucet please.

*(*CHIEF WAITER *this time is silent, perhaps tired of the game.)*

*(*MAN *goes to faucet by roundabout route, fixes his mouth on it, and drinks rapturously. Continues drinking to end of scene 1.)*

CHIEF WAITER: *(To* KAI.*)* All right, go home and come back some other time.

KAI: If I go home now, I will never come back again.

CHIEF WAITER: Kasugano married thirteen times, aborted thirteen children, and went to divorce court thirteen times. Parts of her body were gnawed away by thirteen men, but after all this she still keeps her youth intact. That's why, when Kasugano dances on the stage and sings, she is the crystallization of a concept far apart from motherhood. By that, I do not mean the body. I cannot stand those thousands of fat would-be actresses looking at Kasugano and trembling all over in the name of inspiration.

OLD WOMAN: Let's go home, Kai.

KAI: I . . . I. . . .

OLD WOMAN: Let's go home, Kai.

(At this point, WAITERS 1 *and* 2 *carry in a bathtub from behind the counter and set it down at stage center. It seems as if the volcano in the picture is erupting directly behind the tub.)*

CHIEF WAITER: Well, young lady, it is time for Kasugano's bath. Are you going home?

*(*KAI *does not move.)*

WAITER 1: *(To the* CHIEF WAITER.*)* Shall I make coffee for you right away?

KAI: One coffee.

WAITER 1: Yes, right away.

CHIEF WAITER: *(To* WAITER 1.*)* She says she's going home.

KAI: I want coffee!

WAITER 1: *(To the* CHIEF WAITER.*)* I bought the coffee beans.

OLD WOMAN: I'll take some coffee too.

WAITER 1: But they say they want coffee.

CHIEF WAITER: The shop is closed for today.

(So saying, he pulls the OLD WOMAN*'s chair away, then kicks her shoulder. She falls flat on her face with a groan and at the same time the magazine* Virgin's Friend *that she was holding also tumbles to the floor.)*

KAI: Granny!

OLD WOMAN: Youth, love, disappointment, hope.

CHIEF WAITER: What are you talking about? *(Picks up the magazine, and, as he throws it toward the* OLD WOMAN, *the cover rips.)*

OLD WOMAN: Oh, no! *(Cradles the torn magazine and looks at the* CHIEF WAITER *with bitter hatred.)*

CHIEF WAITER: Go home, you old piece of cheese.

*(*OLD WOMAN *is beside herself.)*

CHIEF WAITER: When you squeeze fat, it turns to cheese.

OLD WOMAN: My magazine cover, my magazine cover. . . .

KAI: *(Clutches at* CHIEF WAITER, *and strikes him in the chest.)* What do you mean doing such a violent thing?

CHIEF WAITER: *(Lets her hit him, and turns his face away.)* Oh, this smell.

(The song "Those Were the Days" begins, and beautiful Kasugano enters from the hanamichi *in male attire.)*

CHIEF WAITER: The bath is just right.

(The OLD WOMAN *and* KAI *take notice of* KASUGANO. KASUGANO, *the eternal virgin, walks so slowly as to make one nauseous to watch her. The heels of her shoes are far too high.* KASUGANO *acknowledges what the* CHIEF WAITER *has said, and regards her audience with affection, as if she were Don José. During this time she never looks at* KAI. *Obviously,* KASUGANO *here is acting the part of Heathcliff.)*

KASUGANO: *(Abruptly stops.)* Turn the music off. This is not a saloon. *(To the* CHIEF WAITER.*)* Stop the music! *(With a strange male voice, suddenly wriggling her body.)* "You teach me now how cruel you've been—cruel and false. Yes . . . cry; and wring out my kisses and tears: they'll blight you—they'll damn you. You loved me—then *(shouting)* what right had you to leave me? What right? *(Pause.)* Because misery and degradation, and death, and nothing that God or Satan could inflict would have parted us, *you,* of your own will, did it. I have not broken your heart—*you* have broken it; and in breaking it, you have broken mine. Do I want to live? What kind of living will it be when you—oh, God! . . .''

CHIEF WAITER: *(Approaching* KASUGANO, *and speaking respectfully.)* I am exceedingly sorry to bother you while you're rehearsing . . . but the bath is quite ready.

KASUGANO: I see.

CHIEF WAITER: If you don't hurry, you will be late for the executive meeting.

KASUGANO: I see.

CHIEF WAITER: Well . . . please. . . .

(The bath has a ladder. KASUGANO, *remaining clothed, goes up the ladder.* KAI *and the* OLD WOMAN *keep their eyes fixed on her.* KASUGANO *arrives at the top of the ladder and, trousers on, puts one leg into the hot water. She casually looks in* KAI*'s direction.)*

KASUGANO: *(Discovering* KAI, *she speaks with emotion.)* Oh, Catherine!
(KAI *opens eyes wide.*
Again, the music of "Those Were the Days." The MAN *who has been drinking
water from the faucet suddenly turns his head in surprise. The stage becomes
dark. The music continues until the next scene, which soon follows.)*

Scene 2: The Awakening

(Applause. Lights come up on the VENTRILOQUIST *and his* DUMMY *on a stage
lined with flowers. The* VENTRILOQUIST *is in formal dress this time.)*

VENTRILOQUIST: *(Angry at the* DUMMY.*)* You fool, why didn't you tell me?

DUMMY: I thought it better not to.

VENTRILOQUIST: Why?

DUMMY: Such a woman, forget her, already. Still have some lingering
affection for her?

VENTRILOQUIST: It's none of your business.

DUMMY: Don't you talk to me that way.

VENTRILOQUIST: You can't order me around like that. Even if you say
she's such a bad woman, she used to be my wife. We would run in
the rain together and up the steps of our apartment when we went
out to buy pickles. Can't you understand that without my telling
you? And when she visited our dressing room, didn't she leave a
message?

DUMMY: She said, "How are you doing?"

VENTRILOQUIST: And?

DUMMY: I said, "Not well."

VENTRILOQUIST: Surely you didn't tell her about my throat cancer?

DUMMY: I told her.

VENTRILOQUIST: And then what?

DUMMY: She said that must be why you haven't sent the consolation
money.

VENTRILOQUIST: Consolation money!

DUMMY: It's mounting up, isn't it?

VENTRILOQUIST: What is she talking about? She still must be crazy.

DUMMY: She said, if it's hard to pay the whole amount, monthly install-
ments would be fine.

VENTRILOQUIST: Huh, she hasn't changed at all.

DUMMY: Eight hundred million yen in three payments . . . if she
doesn't receive them before summer, she can't buy the wistaria-pat-
tern *yukata,*[3] and she broke into tears.

VENTRILOQUIST: Better let her go. A woman like that won't ever come to
her senses.

DUMMY: Is she that nuts?

VENTRILOQUIST: Yes, listen. She used to be a very nice woman. I was the one who named her Marina Marimura since she had a sweet face like Marina Vlady. I was a curtain puller for a strip theater at that time. I used to bounce pushy customers for her.

DUMMY: So you were intimate lovers?

VENTRILOQUIST: Oh, we were like Paul Newman and Joanne Woodward.

DUMMY: Whatever happened?

VENTRILOQUIST: Wait, not so fast. She got pregnant.

DUMMY: A blessed event.

VENTRILOQUIST: . . . But that was not my baby.

DUMMY: What?

VENTRILOQUIST: Not mine!

DUMMY: Well . . . whose?

VENTRILOQUIST: I don't know. As her stomach got bigger and she could no longer go on stage, she was always irritable. So I said to her, "Marimura, do you really want to have it?" She looked up at me and said, "You don't want me to, do you?" "Not so, Marimura," I answered, "it's not that I don't want you to have it. I just worry about you and me. But, Marimura, please calm down and listen. You and I've pledged our futures to each other. Aren't you unhappy that suddenly we can't trust each other because of a thing like this? Marimura, I won't get angry. Tell me, whose baby is it?"

DUMMY: And then?

VENTRILOQUIST: She didn't say anything. She just stared at the morning glories in the garden all day long. Only said that she would never, for my sake, tell me, and nothing more.

DUMMY: That must've been tough.

VENTRILOQUIST: It was tough for me.

DUMMY: No, I meant for the girl.

VENTRILOQUIST: Hey, why sympathize so much with her?

DUMMY: And when did she go crazy?

VENTRILOQUIST: That was during her fifth month. One day she went to a health fair in the neighborhood and came home feeling faint. She took ten thousand yen that she'd put away in the bureau and ran to an obstetrics clinic. I didn't know where she'd gone. I made her favorite dinner and waited, but she didn't come back the next day or the day after that. I couldn't down so much as a grain of rice, and finally, exhausted with the waiting, I dozed off. Suddenly I woke up, and she was standing there in the dark. When I cried out, "Where have you been?" she answered, "I got rid of it."

DUMMY: The baby?

VENTRILOQUIST: Yes, shhhh, not so loud. And after that I didn't speak to her for days on end. In the daytime she would just sit on the balcony, and by night she would count the knotholes in the wooden ceiling.

DUMMY: She must have become crazy?

VENTRILOQUIST: No, she didn't look crazy yet. She still chatted with the neighborhood wives, and she knew more about the increases in train fare than I did. One evening during a downpour she really became crazy. She was just quietly listening to the rain when. . . . *(Suddenly emits a choking sound.)*

DUMMY: What happened? Are you OK?

VENTRILOQUIST: Fine. That monster in the back of my throat just began hurting again. I'm sure I can get past this one scene. I'm okay. Where was I? Uh. . . .

DUMMY: Just keep talking.

VENTRILOQUIST: All right, listen. Marimura, while concentrating on the sound of the rain, says, "The dead baby is calling in the shadow of the trash can." And I told her, "Listen, Marimura, I can't hear a thing. That's the sound of the wind. Every day, like this, it's tough on me too." And she dashed out without an umbrella. Do you know what she did? She stormed into the obstetrics clinic and said, "Give my aborted baby back!" I guess even the doctors didn't know what to do. Marimura grabbed them one after another and shouted, "Give it back, give it back!" There were ten women there for abortions, but, when they saw her going wild, they changed their minds.

DUMMY: She went completely crazy.

VENTRILOQUIST: A little later a police car came and took her to the loony bin. I first learned about that one week later, but when I went to see her she was tearing her clothes into squares and diapering her pillow. It had been such a long time since I had seen such a happy Marimura laughing and peaceful that I cried.

DUMMY: You cried?

VENTRILOQUIST: I cried!

DUMMY: But didn't you leave her, after all?

VENTRILOQUIST: I couldn't help it. *(Starts to choke again.)* I hate the man who knocked her up. *(Chokes.)*

DUMMY: Do you want to meet him sometime?

VENTRILOQUIST: Yes.

DUMMY: When was all that?

VENTRILOQUIST: About the time when Marimura and I started living together. Right, that was the time when I had decided on my line of work and was really getting into it. It was when I discovered you in a doll store in Asakusa and bought you. *(Starts to choke again.)*

DUMMY: *(With a stern look.)* At that rate, you won't last long either. Marimura asked me to give this flower to you.

VENTRILOQUIST: *(Grasping the white rose presented by the* DUMMY.) Oh, that was my favorite flower—a white rose. *(Starts to choke again.)*
(The VENTRILOQUIST *suddenly vomits blood. The blood gets on the white rose. The* VENTRILOQUIST *falls to his knees in pain.)*

DUMMY: You don't look like you can speak anymore.

VENTRILOQUIST: Yes, I can.

DUMMY: Don't speak. I'll speak for you.

VENTRILOQUIST: You?

DUMMY: Yes, your using me to speak won't work. So this time I will speak for you.

VENTRILOQUIST: But you exist because I speak for you.

DUMMY: No, I existed somewhere you never knew.

VENTRILOQUIST: What do you mean by that?

DUMMY: I'm the one who knocked her up.

VENTRILOQUIST: What?

DUMMY: The aborted baby was mine.

VENTRILOQUIST: Son of a bitch! *(Begins to choke.)* That's impossible! *(Keels over.)*

DUMMY: *(Floating gently in the air, sings.)* My body was artificial arms, artificial legs, an artificial brain and heart, artificial teeth, and artificial shit. And neither are my prick and balls real. Even still, I deceive women by this trick or that one and get them pregnant again.
(The DUMMY *lands softly on the floor on both feet. Thunderous applause. But the* VENTRILOQUIST *remains as he is, on the floor. Another ventriloquist appears on stage, receiving applause. He looks exactly like the* DUMMY, *and the dummy he is holding looks exactly like the* VENTRILOQUIST.)*

SECOND VENTRILOQUIST: You fool, why didn't you tell me?

SECOND DUMMY: I thought it better not to.

SECOND VENTRILOQUIST: Why?

SECOND DUMMY: Such a woman, forget her, already. Still have some lingering affection for her?

SECOND VENTRILOQUIST: It's none of your business.

SECOND DUMMY: Don't you talk to me that way.

SECOND VENTRILOQUIST: Don't *you* talk to me that way.

SECOND DUMMY: Don't you talk to me that way.

SECOND VENTRILOQUIST: Don't *you* talk to me that way.

(Again clapping and applause. The last words of both the SECOND VENTRILOQUIST *and the* SECOND DUMMY *are drowned out by the noise. The stage becomes dark. Scene 3 begins immediately.)*

Scene 3: Beggars of Flowers

(In contrast to the previous scene, the music is upbeat, preferably like a nostalgic Takarazuka girls' chorus. The scene is in "The Body" coffee shop. The props are

as in scene 1. Present are KAI, KASUGANO, *the* OLD WOMAN, *and, standing at attention off to the side, the* CHIEF WAITER *and the* WAITERS. *Gaily decked out,* KAI *is standing on top of the covered bathtub in center stage. In front of the stage* KASUGANO *is affectedly smoking a cigarette. Keeping her distance, the* OLD WOMAN *is sitting next to a* WAITER. *The music is the easy-listening variety.*)

KAI: *(Looking back at* KASUGANO.) Heathcliff!

KASUGANO: *(With emotion.)* Say it again, please . . . again.

KAI: *(Looking back.)* Heathcliff!

KASUGANO: Yes, good . . . you are the virgin of virgins. You are such a nice, pretty girl! Where have you been wandering?

KAI: Along the Mekama Railway Line.

KASUGANO: Don't use concrete words. Please, no concrete words. Okay? Watch your language. If you want to talk about a flower, then I allow only the four concrete words "rose" or "lily of the valley" or "lily" or "autumn bellflower." Absolutely never say "daphne" or "peanut." Never even think about them.

KAI: How about "cloud"?

KASUGANO: "Cloud," but not "cirrocumulus cloud," I generally allow.

KAI: How about "love"?

KASUGANO: There is no taboo in love. Because love is the flower of a young girl, I allow everything. But you should mention at the end which kinds of love—bubbly love, unbearable love, crazy love, and the like.

KAI: How about "death"?

KASUGANO: I'm glad you asked. You should think of death as the flower of an idea. From Onatsu Seijūrō's[4] death to Jean-Jacques' and Robespierre's deaths; and my most precious example, the young woman in the midst of flames, whose very name I want to say only once a day—young Joan of Arc. I have pursued the deaths of these kinds of people, and I'm embarrassed to admit I have enacted on the stage fifty-two times already the death of Joan of Arc. I still do not understand. I still do not understand my one and only true death that is certainly waiting for me in reality. But I would like a splendid, austere manner of dying like those people I have acted. I don't want a violent death or to die for nothing, like a dog.

KAI: How about dying while you're making it?

KASUGANO: *(Looking very upset and in a shrill voice.)* What?!

KAI: Dying while you're making it. . . .

KASUGANO: Concrete language. I mean, don't you see I'm saying to be careful about slang, you foolish girl? Where did you learn such talk? Huh? Did you learn it on the Mekama Line?

KAI: Oh, I will never say it again.

KASUGANO: I won't stand for it. So long as I stage human dramas exclusively with virgins, my theater company will be a strict one, "pure, upright, and beautiful." To always be such a woman, Kai, listen well: you will change your own "stream of consciousness." You want to speak of sweet love, to be wounded fighting for justice, and in every particular to reflect on stage the figure embraced in your lover's breast. To do that, Kai, you need another homeland. Forget right here and now the one in this world where you've formed your sensitivities. Take this place as your second homeland, as your nunnery home. If this sort of world had existed in Ophelia's time, Ophelia would not have had to die. And so, Kai, forget about the Mekama Line.

KAI: Please, Ms. Kasugano, if you say I should forget, I guess I will, but if I do, I'll have to forget my grandmother as well—the old woman sitting right over there. I spent my youth living with her along the Mekama Line. If I were to forget our experiences of shoplifting together and things like that, where should the memory go?

OLD WOMAN: Kai, don't be bothered about me.

KASUGANO: Kai, you are a talent who could shine. If you are ready to kick aside your memories, I will give you more precious experiences.

OLD WOMAN: Kai, really, don't be bothered about me.

(A loud noise overhead like hammering on an iron bar.)

KASUGANO: What is that sound?

CHIEF WAITER: Yes, looks like subway construction has begun.

KASUGANO: Mud is falling from the ceiling!

CHIEF WAITER: Yes, this used to be an air-raid shelter, so the ground is soft.

KASUGANO: Please stop the construction, right now!

CHIEF WAITER: No matter what you say, there are dozens of bulldozers outside.

KASUGANO: Who in hell do you think is living here? Make them stop by whatever means are necessary.

CHIEF WAITER: Yes, by whatever means are necessary. *(He ponders, then soon exits.)*

(KASUGANO paces back and forth like a bear in a cage. Suddenly, with a clap of her hands, she strikes a pose for acting.)

KASUGANO: Catherine, look around you. Are we really the only people in this room?

KAI: *(Responding in song.)* Go to sleep without crying, Mr. Midnight. The baby's mother sleeping in the grave can hear her daughter's night tears.

KASUGANO: *(Continues singing, stomping three times.)* Knock, knock, knock.

WAITERS I AND 2: *(While tap dancing they sing together.)* When you see him, quietly say, "The virgin's flower was gone. She lined her kotex with cute patterned paper and was singing all alone." But he'll never come back, he'll never be back; I'm a total eclipse of the sun.

KASUGANO: "Yes . . . cry; and wring out my kisses and tears: they'll blight you—they'll damn you. You loved me—then what *right* had you to leave me?"

KAI: Oh, Heathcliff.

KASUGANO: OK, one more time.

KAI: Heathcliff!

(Suddenly KAI loses her footing on the bathtub top, and one leg falls into the tub of hot water.)

OLD WOMAN: Oh, Kai! *(Tries to run to her.)*

KASUGANO: *(To the OLD WOMAN.)* Don't touch her. This doesn't concern you. Go sell your cuttlefish or something.

KAI: I'm OK, Granny. Just got my dress wet.

KASUGANO: *(To the WAITERS.)* Have the old woman go replenish her supply of cuttlefish.

WAITER 1: Right. (WAITERS 1 *and* 2 *lead the* OLD WOMAN *away.*)

OLD WOMAN: *(To KAI.)* Keep your chin up. I'm going out to shop. *(Exits.)*

KAI: Ms. Kasugano, can I get down from here and sing?

KASUGANO: No. *Zuka*-girls have always sung and danced on top of the bathtub. When the Takarazuka Girls' Theater Troupe was established in 1928 at the suggestion of Kobayashi Ichizō, their first performances began as entertainment for guests bathing in the Takarazuka hot springs. Plays acted out by virgins began on top of the lids at the large bathhouses where mixed bathing was prohibited. Since then, the Asakusa Opera died out after fifty-five years, but Takarazuka remained. Only "our Takarazuka" is still wringing the tears of young girls from ten thousand cities. Kai, consider it an honor. The bath water your leg fell into is fifty-five years of tears collected from frenzied virgins. Taste it and see. Look, it's salty, isn't it?

KAI: *(Licks some from her finger.)* Yes.

KASUGANO: *(Speaking as a woman.)* Listen, my tears are in there too, or *(corrects herself to speak as a man)* rather my tears. . . . *(Again speaking as a woman.)* Every night when I soaked my body in the bath in the excitement of sobbing together with my fans, I was theirs, and they were mine.

KAI: Ms. Kasugano, you smell.

KASUGANO: What?

KAI: Ms. Kasugano, excuse me, but you really smell. It's because you always get into the same bath. . . .

KASUGANO: You think something smells? It's the smell of virgins. To me your body is much more odd smelling. *(Getting on top of the bath.)* Why, you're not even wearing perfume, are you?

KAI: No, I can't afford it.

KASUGANO: *(Speaking as a man.)* I'll buy some for you.

KAI: Really?

KASUGANO: Yes, leave it to me. That dress must be wet and cold on you. Take it off.

KAI: But if I take it off, I won't be Catherine anymore.

KASUGANO: Kai, you are my eternal Catherine.

KAI: Really, Heathcliff?

KASUGANO: Yes, Catherine. Please call me that one more time.

KAI: Heathcliff. Are you satisfied?

KASUGANO: Yes, completely! *(Placing a suit on Catherine's back.)* And now we, the two of us, have become ghosts of love.

KAI: But Heathcliff, if the ghosts of love have been able to come together, how could they still be roaming the stormy heath of Yorkshire?

KASUGANO: Catherine, listen to me, the ghosts of love have been able to come together, but they're not yet ours, neither yours nor mine.

KAI: Then whose are they?

KASUGANO: The two of us are beggars.

KAI: Beggars?

KASUGANO: Exactly.

KAI: What are we begging for?

KASUGANO: Even if you get into the virgins' bath, and even if Takarazuka prospers, the more I prosper, the more I. . . .

KAI: What are you begging for?

KASUGANO: Ah, the wind that rages in Yorkshire's wilderness—a stormy heath for fifty-five years—wrested everything away from me.

KAI: What?!

KASUGANO: My body. Don't you see? We are ghosts of love and at the same time beggars for bodies.

KAI: You've finally said it, haven't you, Heathcliff. I was waiting for you to say it. But what is the body?

KASUGANO: Look at that over there. *(She points beyond the audience.)* *(Suddenly, there is a loud noise above the stage, and at the same time applause for the virgins wells up like a tidal wave.)*

KASUGANO: My body has been completely taken over by all those girls.

KAI: Who are you talking about? Where are they?

KASUGANO: Virgins whose names I don't even know. That's why when you were not there I always acted on stage merely as a single ghost of love. I never possessed my body. I was a miserable ghost, rapidly growing old. But, you know, I'm glad. Having you as a friend, my sadness has decreased a little. But don't forget that you and I, as always, are still beggars for bodies.

KAI: I don't like that . . . eternally being a beggar for a body.

KASUGANO: Then how will you get it back?

KAI: But I thought you knew.

KASUGANO: Kai, please don't talk nonsense. If you just leave me and go back to town, you could probably get your body back right away. But it's too late for me. I can't be helped.

KAI: I won't leave you alone.

KASUGANO: Really? You won't leave me, will you?

KAI: No.

KASUGANO: If I die, you'll dig up my grave and hold me tightly?

KAI: If I die and you dig up my grave, what will you do for me?

KASUGANO: What will I do?

KAI: Oh, you know.

KASUGANO: If you talk like that to an eternal virgin, she can't really understand very well.

KAI: Stupid. Make love.

KASUGANO: How?

KAI: How? You think you can do it talking on the telephone?

KASUGANO: I will do anything for you. But if you died and I held you and you didn't respond at all, I would plunge a dagger time after time into your belly and your neck.

KAI: My body, my muscles, my bones, when maggots swarm with a scratching sound over my dead body, I will seize your knife in my mouth and never let go.

KASUGANO: Thank you.

KAI: And then the two of us will surely die. After that, Kasugano, we can go looking for our bodies that were taken over by unknown virgins.

KASUGANO: Kai, is it really all right with you?

KAI: What?

KASUGANO: Whether we live or die, we are beggars for bodies. Can you put up with that?

KAI: If I'm with you. If I'm alone, I can't.

KASUGANO: Me too. Kai, come closer to me, but not too close. I don't want you peeking into my secret past.

KAI: Don't consider my smell the same as that of those hateful virgins sitting in the audience.

(*Music comes up softly. Suddenly, the* CHIEF WAITER, *wearing burned and tattered clothes, comes bounding on stage out of breath.*)

KASUGANO: (*Jumps down from the bathtub, thrusting* KAI *aside.*) Hey, what's happened to you?

CHIEF WAITER: I just got burned a little. . . .

KASUGANO: How about the subway construction?

CHIEF WAITER: I tried to stop it, but I was up against some tough-looking workers and their machines. They wouldn't listen to me.

KASUGANO: You mean, they talked you out of it?

CHIEF WAITER: No, I got so provoked I started a fire. There was a gas tank right next to the bulldozers, so I set a fire there.

KASUGANO: There is a fire on the ground right now?

CHIEF WAITER: Yes, and the flames will likely spread to the next section of town. Can I just have some water? *(Drinks from the faucet.)* I have never before seen such stubborn characters. Anyway, they said something about city office or some substitute city center, but even if I went to some government office I wouldn't get anywhere. The way I've done it's got to be faster.

KASUGANO: They won't come in on us here, will they? Nobody saw you coming in here?

CHIEF WAITER: Nobody except for one person.

KASUGANO: So you were seen by somebody?

CHIEF WAITER: Please don't worry. He'll do what I say. Hey, come on in.

MAN: *(Opens door and disconsolately enters. It is the same water-drinking white-collar worker as before.)* I won't say a thing. Just let me drink water. *(He jumps to the faucet and slurps.)*

KASUGANO: How come he's so thirsty?

CHIEF WAITER: I don't know.

MAN: *(Raising his head.)* Burned-out ruins, it's the sun, glaring down on us. It's really strange. I can't believe that after twenty-four years everybody has forgotten how valuable water is. Since that time when B29 bombers were flying about and women whose hair was burned by firebombs were wildly running every which way, I can't believe so much time has passed already. I hate it. I no longer have a home or a life. My family was eating dinner together until the day before, and the next day—dead. I alone was left to stumble around in the burned-out ruins and look for water. I'm very grateful. Grateful that you have provided me with a setting for my daily water-drinking ritual. It serves them right, those people who died. They wouldn't believe me. Anyway *(to the CHIEF WAITER)*, do you feel some resentment toward society?

CHIEF WAITER: Even if society resents me, I don't think I would resent society for any reason.

MAN: Resentment is not the sort of thing you decide to feel. Before you know it, you just do.

CHIEF WAITER: I won't be so careless.

MAN: What a remarkable man you are! Anyhow, can I have another drink? *(Puts his mouth to faucet.)*

CHIEF WAITER: Hey, what do you do for a living?

MAN: Huh? What do you mean by that?

CHIEF WAITER: I'm asking you about your job.

MAN: Whatever I had to sell burned up long ago.

CHIEF WAITER: I see . . . well, how do you live?

MAN: Water.

CHIEF WAITER: How about your staple food?

MAN: I'm telling you, it's water. Eating to stay alive is, after all, just trying to stay afloat. So, why not water? *(To* KASUGANO.) One way to put it, eh, brother?

CHIEF WAITER: Hey, watch that "brother" stuff.

MAN: He looked so smug I just had to say something. Right, brother? *(Approaches* KASUGANO.)

CHIEF WAITER: Don't tell me you have gotten drunk on water.

MAN: *(Approaching* KASUGANO.) Say, you there, the unknown brother, turn that pretty face toward me.
*(*KASUGANO *looks indifferent.)*

MAN: You're not going to look at me? You think it will hurt you to look at me? You don't intend to look at me no matter what? You S.O.B. *(He suddenly leaps on* KASUGANO *and grabs the shoulder of her white shirt.)*

KASUGANO: *(Taken by surprise.)* You hooligan!

MAN: *(Still holding on.)* A hooligan! What an anachronism!

CHIEF WAITER: *(Grabs the* MAN *from the rear.)* Hey!

MAN: Keep a straight face will you, you low-life peon! *(Pulls* KASUGANO'*s white shirt and tears it.)*

KASUGANO: Oh, no. *(Covers her chest, part of which is visible.)*

CHIEF WAITER: *(To* KASUGANO.) My apologies, boss. . . . *(Pulls the* MAN *away from her.)*

MAN: *(Turning pale.)* It's a woman, a woman . . . that's a woman!

CHIEF WAITER: You bastard, I'll flatten you!

MAN: It's a woman, it's a woman! Did you all know that? That's a woman there. You've all been deceived. She's been acting like a man!

KASUGANO: I am a man.

MAN: She's behaving like a man.

KASUGANO: I am a. . . .

MAN: What do you mean, "I am a . . ."? Did you all hear that? I just wanted to try doing it with a woman who says she's a man.

CHIEF WAITER: What are you saying? *(Flings the* MAN *away.)*

MAN: *(Rolling on the floor.)* You threw me down, didn't you. You threw me down in revenge for not being able to throw her down. Isn't that right?

CHIEF WAITER: You S.O.B. *(Kicks the* MAN.)

MAN: You kicked me. You really kicked me. Don't get so mad. What the hell is that woman to you?

CHIEF WAITER: *(Dragging the* MAN *behind the counter.)* You, come here.

MAN: I see, I see. I won't ask anymore about your relationship to her.

(The CHIEF WAITER *takes the* MAN *off stage;* KASUGANO *squats holding her knees;* KAI *sits on top of the bathtub and looks down at her. Easy-listening music continues.)*

KASUGANO: . . . Kai, where are you?

KAI: Here.

KASUGANO: Please, the lights, please turn them down.

KAI: *(Steps down from the bath and turns the light switch.)* I wonder if this will be all right? *(Takes suit from her shoulders and places it on* KASUGANO'*s.)* Are you okay?

KASUGANO: Don't look at me.

KAI: What's wrong?

KASUGANO: Please go away.

KAI: It's me.

KASUGANO: Get away from me!

KAI: What's wrong, Kasugano? It's me.

KASUGANO: *(Sings while in her squatting position.)*

When March 3rd comes,[5] virgins all will remember,
all day from morning till night
you can wear the long-sleeved kimono
and from time to time stamp on rice cakes and laugh.
All of a sudden you become quiet and composed
and comb your own hair.
It was March, early spring,
an age when virgins don't know men.
When March 3rd comes, virgins will secretly remember,
on the summit there beyond the forest
something swirling about so hot and somehow ominous.
And just then it swallows you in
you know not for how many months and years.
Even now you stain
the corridor with blood—
Even now you stain the corridor with blood.

KAI: What do you mean by blood in the corridor?

KASUGANO: I spilled blood in the corridor just now. It's like a doll festival out of season. In the last five years there hasn't been any, but since that water-drinking man ripped my shirt it just started flowing like flowers blooming out of season. Oh, how I want a torrid love affair with whichever man is close at hand! *(Staggers to her feet.)* Oh, so much blood in the corridor. Kai, is this the hospital in Manchuria?

KAI: This is your shop.

KASUGANO: Right, this is my shop, isn't it? But I can hear military songs in the distance. Listen, that's the song I heard at the hospital in Manchuria. The band of the man I loved. At that time the captain was connected with the Manchurian railway. He was really kind to me. Our theater company at that time was on a tour of Manchuria, but I got pneumonia, so they left me there. How could I put on *Wuthering Heights* all alone in a hospital with icicles hanging down? We have to wipe up the blood in the corridor before the captain comes, we have to wipe up the blood in the corridor. *(Stands up.)* Kai, a small can, a small can for my kotex napkins

KAI: You are Heathcliff. Why does Heathcliff need such a can?

KASUGANO: I'm not hysterical. Kai, can't you hear what I'm saying?

KAI: *(Grudgingly brings a white garbage can from the toilet and hands it over.)* Don't make me work so hard.

KASUGANO: Yes, yes, I understand. *(With the white can, she elaborately scoops the floor around her feet.)* The time was February 1941. I was nineteen, and everybody was jealous of my talent. I was alone in Manchuria, eating a porridge of rice and vegetables. The captain said to me, "That porridge is not nutritious. Eat this corned beef." I said, "Captain, wasn't this corned beef expensive?" He said, "No, my uncle has a dry goods store, and he got some corned beef from the Yorkshire plain." "Captain, your relative runs a store with just a handyman, doesn't he." "Oh no. Ah, ha, ha, is it good?" "Yes, very. This meat is scrumptious. Oh, don't trip on the white can under the bed, please. It's exceedingly palatable, utterly delicious. This corned beef, it must surely be Catherine's flesh." "What? What do you mean by Catherine? A kind of saccharin?" "No, Captain, Catherine's flesh is the flesh of a dead person. Every night Heathcliff dug up Catherine's grave and voraciously devoured her flesh. It's quite delicious. How about one piece for you? Here. What? You broke your front tooth? Which part of the flesh did you gnaw on? Huh? The pubic bone? How embarrassing. Go on now, go and die bravely. What's that sound? Oh no, you've finally stuck your shoe in the white can under the bed, and you're splashing it. Shameful. Go on and leave now just as you are. Just as you are, shoulder your gun, and go kill your enemies." *(Runs to a corner of the room, takes out an old album, and stares with a smile of satisfaction at one of the pictures.)*

KAI: Kasugano, I don't know what to do when you act like this.

KASUGANO: Kai, this man. *(Showing her the picture. It is* CAPTAIN AMAGASU.*)* Don't get too friendly with him.

KAI: Which one?

KASUGANO: Captain Amagasu.

KAI: I'm not interested in him.

KASUGANO: If you are not interested, then why are you staring at him with such passionate eyes?

KAI: My eyes, they're always like this.

KASUGANO: You'd take any man, whoever it is, right? You'd sleep with anybody.

KAI: That's not true.

KASUGANO: Don't hide it. I can see the whole thing. So, please, don't involve yourself with this man. Amagasu vanquished some rebels and made good his escape to Manchuria. I don't really want him to have a lover. Look, keep your hands to yourself. What part of his body were you going to play with? I'm going to form a group to save Captain Amagasu. *(Runs to a corner of the room, cradling his picture.)*

(KAI observes KASUGANO steadily, not knowing what to do.)

KASUGANO: *(Addresses the picture.)* That woman is no good. She is just young . . . and lacking in talent. When I get out of this hospital, I will definitely make a name for myself. In *Wuthering Heights.* . . . And then, when I act Heathcliff, I'll make myself up to look just like you. Even though you died a soldier, my face will be your face. On stage your face turns toward the unknown virgins in the audience and shouts, "You bitches must think I am an ogre or the devil or something." See, everyone will be thoroughly frightened. They'll be pissing in their pants. You see? Oh, what's wrong, Captain, your face. . . . You're foaming at the mouth, like a horse. What? You mean, just because those comedians the Crazy Boys, what with all this chaos of the war, were reprimanded for being the crazy guys they are, that I can't even put on a review or something? What are you saying, Captain? We are an artistic theater company with the motto "pure, upright, and beautiful." What? Did you say something just now? That we are riverbed beggars? You said just now "riverbed beggar," didn't you? Is that how you saw me? Weren't you in love with my beauty and my talent? You were, weren't you? Are you saying I should go back to Japan and just be an ordinary housewife? What are you still growling about? Anyhow, clean the white garbage can under the bed, you beggar woman? What are you saying to me? I'll clean, I'll clean, so don't shout at me like that. Hey, you've knocked over the bed. What are you doing, you idiot! How do you like this?! *(Brandishes contents of the white garbage can as if to toss them on the person she has been talking to.)*

(Yelling "you bastard," KASUGANO wields the white garbage can and chases the apparition of AMAGASU around the room. KASUGANO is transformed into a homely looking woman and falls flat, exhausted. Music.)

KAI: *(Approaches KASUGANO.)* Are you okay? Pull yourself together.

KASUGANO: I'm sorry, Kai. That must have surprised you. I've had such strong pride that my lovers have always abandoned me.

KAI: The men who have abandoned you are no big deal.

KASUGANO: When you talk like that, it really helps me.

KAI: *(In a man's voice here and until she approaches the water faucet.)* Look at me, Kasugano. I don't like men anymore. I'm tired of them.

KASUGANO: Oh, that gives me courage.

KAI: What really carries me away now is I'm acting the role of a prince in some foreign country and I have a sweet love and become the ally of justice, and it's just this one moment when I get wounded and fall and my lover holds me to her breast—I'll excite the kids in the audience with my performance.

KASUGANO: But, Kai, if life is an empty struggle and flowers bloom only on the stage, where should I die?

KAI: You're going to die?

KASUGANO: But I have to retire soon. I am afraid of that. When I retire, I'll have to go back again to the hospital in Manchuria. It was very cold there.

KAI: You should warm yourself in the heat of your memories of the stage.

KASUGANO: But I was never even once so excited as the girls in the audience. Seeing other people excited, you somehow get separated from yourself. It's not for me. When I retire, where can I find my own lost body?

KAI: Heathcliff was you yourself, isn't that it?

KASUGANO: Yes, but you are not yet Catherine. Just because you are young doesn't mean that you should put up with being told Catherine is you.

KAI: I will follow after you. Yes, like you I'll go to the hospital in Manchuria. And if I catch up with you there, right, just like you, struck down by pneumonia in a hospital in Manchuria, I would die.

KASUGANO: What about your stage career?

KAI: My stage career. . . .

KASUGANO: How about your spectacular stage career?

KAI: *(Taking KASUGANO's arm.)* It will start after you have died and I dig up your grave.

KASUGANO: You'll turn my body inside out and devour it, won't you? But, Kai, my worry is that those immature kids in the audience might dig me up before you. And what I'm even more worried about, Kai, is that you may not come for me.

KAI: I will come!

KASUGANO: If so, don't speak like that, the way you talk . . . you sound like Heathcliff. Heathcliff is me. Heathcliff would never violate Heathcliff's grave!

KAI: Heh, heh, heh, heh. . . .

KASUGANO: What is that laughing? You mean you're putting on an act?

KAI: Heh, heh, heh, heh. . . . *(Steps back.)*

KASUGANO: Everything up to now, you were faking it, weren't you?

KAI: Weren't you directing me? Wow, am I thirsty.

(KAI goes to the water faucet and turns it on. But there is almost no water. KASUGANO, looking betrayed, stares at KAI. The water finally comes out; but it is not water—it is red blood. KAI touches the red water with her fingertips. The OLD WOMAN *dejectedly emerges from behind the counter with her peddler's basket of dried cuttlefish.)*

KAI: Ah, it's you, Granny.

OLD WOMAN: Kai.

KAI: Did you finish buying cuttlefish?

OLD WOMAN: Kai, let's go home. This place has nothing to do with Takarazuka.

KAI: What's happened to you?

OLD WOMAN: Anyway, we can start out afresh. This is a building unsafe for virgins.

KAI: Is something wrong?

OLD WOMAN: I saw a man killed behind the counter. *(Indicates the running water.)* Look, right here, this is his blood.

CHIEF WAITER: *(Appearing unexpectedly.)* Keep quiet!

OLD WOMAN: *(Runs toward KAI.)* He did it.

KASUGANO: *(To the* CHIEF WAITER.*)* What is it you did?

CHIEF WAITER: Yes, that water-drinking character did such awful things to you that I bottled him up behind the counter, but he kept badgering me for water, and I said no. He gave up then, but when I went out for a few minutes to take a leak he cut through the water-pipe with a hacksaw and was sucking out the water for all he was worth. When I saw him doing that, I got to feeling sad for him. Why I had been feeling so sad wasn't clear even to me, but I put an ice pick through his neck and ended his life so water wouldn't go down his throat anymore. After that I noticed that he was not drinking any water at all. He was just sleeping with his mouth on the pipe. He looked just like a child; he was even smiling. I wonder what he was thinking about. I even feel a little sorry for him. *(Turns off water faucet.)*

OLD WOMAN: *(To KAI.)* Let's go home.

CHIEF WAITER: Where are you saying to go home to? Try and see if you can go home. There's a big fire outside. You can't get out, and you can't come in.

OLD WOMAN: Takarazuka wasn't like this. Kai, who have you been rehearsing for till now?

KAI: *(Pointing to KASUGANO.)* For her.

KASUGANO: *(Sharply.)* It wasn't rehearsal! It wasn't rehearsal, Kai! I'm tired of acting. But I seem to be alone again—Heathcliff, left alone. I won't see anybody again.

(Music of "Those Were the Days.")

CHIEF WAITER: I also will go with you.

KASUGANO: You are the director in this shop, but I don't even want to be directed by you anymore. Wait, did you let someone in here?

CHIEF WAITER: No, nobody besides us.

(Applause for the virgins is heard. From the hanamichi *a nurse and a man in military uniform enter. These two are played by* WAITERS 1 and 2.)

KASUGANO: Who are you?

NURSE: *(To* KASUGANO.*)* Kasugano, how are you feeling? There is a snow storm out on the Manchurian plain now. Even if I tried to give you a hot-water bottle, there's not enough hot water to go around. Please put up with things a little longer. Soon it will be spring in Manchuria. But today I brought a very interesting person with me.

AMAGASU: Kasugano, I'm sorry about before. It's Amagasu. *(Takes off his cape.)*

KASUGANO: Amagasu? Captain Amagasu?

AMAGASU: I thought I wouldn't be able to see you anymore. You have quite a group of dummies around you today. *(Indicates* KAI *and the* OLD WOMAN.*)* Kasugano, even with a popular person like yourself, there is some hidden loneliness, isn't there? But I'm such a boor I didn't understand anything about that, and I blurted out unkind things to you that hurt you a lot. Please, if you can, forget my rudeness.

KASUGANO: What is this place?

AMAGASU: This is the Manchurian Railway Hospital. Pull yourself together Kasugano. *(He approaches* KASUGANO *and makes as if to touch her forehead but doesn't quite do it.)* No, this won't do, too much fever. *(To the* NURSE.*)* You! With so much fever, why have you neglected her? Get rid of these people, get rid of these people!

NURSE: Yes, I'm so very sorry. I didn't notice. But there are no people in this room.

AMAGASU: You idiot, clear away these dummies.

NURSE: Yes, sir. *(Signals the* CHIEF WAITER *and is about to take away* KAI *and the* OLD WOMAN.*)*

KASUGANO: Wait, just leave the dummy of that young woman here.

AMAGASU: Oh, you're partial to her? *(Waves the* NURSE *on with his chin.)* *(The* NURSE *takes the* CHIEF WAITER *and the* OLD WOMAN *away.* KAI *hesitantly sits on a chair in the corner.* AMAGASU *and* KASUGANO *face each other. Sound of wind.)*

KASUGANO: What is that sound?

AMAGASU: The snowstorm.

KASUGANO: I've come back to Manchuria again, haven't I?

AMAGASU: This is your *Wuthering Heights*.

KASUGANO: I've become such an old woman. But, Captain, you haven't aged at all.

AMAGASU: Oh no, I just get myself up to look younger.

KASUGANO: But why have I come back here again?

AMAGASU: I told you   this is your *Wuthering Heights*

KASUGANO: It couldn't be only my *Wuthering Heights*. (*Shouting.*) No, I don't want that!

AMAGASU: Please contain yourself. Your fever is making you delirious.

KASUGANO: Will I die alone in this hospital? Neither as Heathcliff nor as Catherine, without getting any role at all?

AMAGASU: No, even if you can't get a role, I will not let you die alone.

KASUGANO: But there's nobody here. I am after all neither a ghost of love nor a beggar for a body. I'll just die as garbage, and hyenas of the Manchurian plain will prowl for my bones.

AMAGASU: I'm telling you that you will not be alone.

KASUGANO: Who else will be here with me?

(*Sound of wind.*)

AMAGASU: A snowstorm is raging on that hill over there like an armed force of the Devil. I saw your fans there—young women who came looking for you from your home country, Japan.

KASUGANO: My fans?

AMAGASU: Yes, Kasugano, your fans.

KASUGANO: To such a cold place as this?

AMAGASU: Japanese fans who have come at great distance across the sea and over burned-out ruins. You have been calling them your groupies, right? The girls who got into a frenzy at your performances, as if they swallowed down your body and spirited you away. Therefore, Kasugano, you are no longer a beggar for your body. Those virgins have come to return your body to you.

KASUGANO: But when you say this to me, I wonder whether I had a body that can be returned?

AMAGASU: But didn't you really beg for it? Once your body is returned, even supposing that you can't get a role, you can go much further than Heathcliff and Catherine. Kasugano, here are those girls.

(*From the* hanamichi *three* GIRLS *appear, wearing air-raid hoods and long skirts and with their backs stooped over. The air-raid hoods completely cover their faces.*)

GIRLS: (*Sing.*)

> Oh, Paris, oh my Paris
> the town of our love
> the sun sets, bells sound
> as though love just flows away

only life is long, only hope is big
in the town of our love
days pass by, months go by
our love of old never returns.

(The three GIRLS IN AIR-RAID HOODS *stand with heads down.)*

GIRLS; Good evening, Ms. Kasugano. We have something we must return to you.

KASUGANO: Thank you for taking the trouble to come to such a distant hospital. Are you people from the home country?

GIRL 1: Yes, we are from Tokyo.

GIRL 2: We heard you were exceedingly troubled.

GIRL 3: Tokyo is now under terrible air raids. We may not be able to go back again.

KASUGANO: You may stay here as long as you like.

AMAGASU: Hurry up now, return it to Ms. Kasugano.

GIRLS: Yes . . . now.

KASUGANO: But don't surprise me. Even if you say you return my body to me all at once, I know my body I have now is complete, too. . . .

GIRL 1: *(Opens a package wrapped in newspaper and brings out a shoe.)* This is the shoe from a performance of *Mon Paris* in 1928, snatched from your right foot.

GIRL 2: This is one of your sleeves from the next year at *A Tale of Two Cities,* torn off when you were coming down from the stage.

GIRL 3: This is the hair left in your bathtub.

GIRLS: We are returning all of these. *(Lay them on the floor in unison.)*

AMAGASU: Is that it?

GIRLS: Yes.

KASUGANO: What about my body?

GIRLS: Your body?

KASUGANO: My body.

GIRLS: Did you give that to us?

GIRL 1: What you gave us was illusions.

GIRL 2: We have never been able to see the body that you are talking about.

GIRL 3: You have to find your own body, or you have to give it to your husband.

KASUGANO: *(Silent, then abruptly gives a start.)* Captain Amagasu, why did you bring these girls here?

*(*CAPTAIN AMAGASU *is not there. Only his cape is hanging in the window.)*

KASUGANO: Amagasu! *(Pulls at his cape.)* Who in hell are these girls?

GIRLS: We are your fans—your nameless and noble fans.

KASUGANO: I don't want any fans. Right now I don't want any fans.

GIRLS: We'll follow you wherever you go. *(They sing.)*

> Oh, Paris, oh my Paris
> the town of our love
> the sun sets, bells sound
> as though love just flows away
> only life is long, only hope is big. . . .

KASUGANO: I don't want anything—love, body, nothing. Leave me alone. I am not a ghost or a beggar anymore!

(KASUGANO shouts the same thing any number of times to drown out the GIRLS' song. KAI suddenly stands up, goes to the three GIRLS, and pulls off their air-raid hoods. All three faces are identical to KASUGANO's.)

KAI: *(Stepping away.)* Kasugano, look at this. You have finally found your own face.

KASUGANO: *(Looking, suddenly.)* I don't want my face anymore. I am a mere nothing!

(The GIRLS simultaneously turn toward KASUGANO. Immediately audible is the song "Those Were the Days." Darkness. Only the music continues.)

Notes

1. 1912–1926.
2. Scattering or placing salt at the entrance is a talismanic act, done here to counter any evil the MAN seeking water might have brought in. The practice is still common in the Japanese "water trade," where businesses are extremely vulnerable, for example, to protection rackets by organized crime.
3. A light-weight summer kimono.
4. Onatsu Seijūrō, sentenced to death in 1662 for allegedly taking money and attempting to elope with the daughter of an inn proprietor in Himeji; memorialized in a story by Ihara Saikaku and in plays by Chikamatsu Monzaemon and Tsubouchi Shōyō.
5. The annual Doll Festival (Hina matsuri), particularly important for young girls, is celebrated on this day.

The Virgin's Mask (Kara, *right*) is set in a subterranean coffee shop—The Body—
that is a refuge, like a bomb shelter, from Tokyo's gray reality. Kara's Red Tent
is a similar refuge. Situation Theater, 1971. (Courtesy Kara Jūrō.)

Ri Reisen—Red Tent's mainstay for two decades—as Kasugano, the Takarazuka star, in *The Virgin's Mask.* Japan's imperialistic past is interwoven with its materialistic present. Situation Theater, 1986. (Courtesy Kara Jūrō.)

In *The Virgin's Mask,* Kai *(left)* sits on a huge tub of tears shed by virgins driven to a frenzy by Takarazuka romances. She is enamored of the glamor of Kasugano *(center),* who is dressed as Don José in a Takarazuka production of *Carmen.* The Old Woman is at right. Situation Theater, 1986. (Courtesy Kara Jūrō.)

Two Women

Kara Jūrō

TRANSLATED BY JOHN K. GILLESPIE

CAST OF CHARACTERS

WOMAN	PATIENT 1
AOI	PATIENT 2
ROKUJŌ	PATIENT 3, *the* MADMAN
KŌICHI	MOTHER
KOREMITSU	JIRŌ, *little brother to* AOI
NURSE	PARKING LOT ATTENDANT
OLD MAN	REAL ESTATE MAN
YOUTH	

(Note: The roles of the WOMAN, AOI, *and* ROKUJŌ *are to be played by the same actress.)*

Prologue

(A sandy beach. Rosy music. Pat Boone's 1950s hit song "Love Letters in the Sand." A man loiters about.)

My beloved Aoi, how are you? I'm here at Izu; the wind has just died down. It's just the right time to write you a secret love letter in the sand. If my thoughts get through to you, please put on Pat Boone's "Love Letters in the Sand," which we once listened to together, and read this my sweet letter to you. It's so full of sweet talk I'd be embarrassed if someone else read it. And, if the wind blows and destroys my love letter in the sand, I'll take it as a sign that the wind is a mailman delivering my love to you far away. Aoi, a gem so fine it wouldn't chafe even mounted in the eye. I've really got the hots for you. If I could, I'd have the mailman carry me on the wind to your arms. And then I'd corner you in the kitchen and really ravish you. So, Aoi, understand how I feel; I am hoping you won't be taking on dumb men. By the time the Fuji Circuit Grand Prix that you like so much begins, I'll be back for sure. Count on it. The hospital at Izu is depressing, so on my lunch break I always head to the beach, try to forget the world of the sick, and think only about you. Don't two-time me. Koremitsu at the hospital, who, as you know, has been my friend since our intern days, was saying that he would like to see you again—now that you are engaged—the next time he is in Tokyo. But he has a weakness for women, so be careful, OK? Aoi, my Aoi, let's definitely go to the Fuji Circuit Grand Prix. I can just see your face, listening to the roar of those huge engines, wearing your straw hat with the red sash. Until then, for a while, we'll be apart. Finally, I should share a perverse confidence with you. Aoi, listen carefully. The fact is that today while on my rounds at the Izu Hospital I met a married woman, someone I didn't know, who called me "Darling," as if she were my wife.

Scene 1: The Hospital Room

(The patients' lounge—a flimsy affair, partitioned by curtains and about as sturdy as a castle made of sand. Beyond a window with iron bars, the sea breeze is blowing. Splendid sunlight. PATIENTS I and 2, a man and a woman (or two men), are playing house. The two bow repeatedly, then one of them sets about making preparations for supper, going through the hand motions of slicing radishes. The other says, "Mother, is it ready yet?" Then, PATIENT 3 (the MADMAN)—probably an ex-student gone wrong—crawls around on the partition wall. There is also an OLD MAN in a chair in the middle of the room, munching on a pear. He drops a bite of the pear onto the floor and looks intently at something. There is a WOMAN, down on all fours, looking at the same thing. It is unclear what they are looking at.)

CRAWLING MADMAN: Ladies and gentlemen who've gathered here. We must possess the resolve always to pay for our mistakes with respect to our own counterrevolutionary natures. For one counterrevolutionary action, we'll cut off a finger; for the second, cut off another; then another and, again, another. For ten such acts, we'll chop off all ten fingers. The reason we have to be worried is having only ten fingers when we notice eleven counterrevolutionary acts. The problem is where to find one more finger!

OLD MAN: *(Pointing to the MADMAN's feet.)* Don't step there.

MADMAN: *(Pointing to the OLD MAN's finger.)* It's not that kind of finger. "My own unseen eleventh finger! That's what I'm looking for." Pull that finger back. In paying for your mistakes, you are definitely not to borrow another person's finger.

OLD MAN: You S.O.B., I thought I told you don't step there!

MADMAN: All you people, what's that you say?

OLD MAN: You're stepping on the performers!

(MADMAN jumps aside.)

OLD MAN: *(Gets down on all fours.)* Are they all right?

WOMAN: Barely. *(Shows him something she shields with her hand.)*

OLD MAN: Good job.

WOMAN: Not bad.

OLD MAN: That much?

WOMAN: Yes.

OLD MAN: You want to try getting in that much?

WOMAN: Don't you think it'll work out?

OLD MAN: Yes, you can do it. Certainly, *you* can.

WOMAN: They won't treat me mean?

OLD MAN: You think anyone would treat you mean? They'll be your fans. You'll have fans. Look, they're all black, right? If you were to become one of them, don't you know you'd become the star overnight?

WOMAN: But, I want to start at the bottom. . . .

OLD MAN: I'm not so sure that's a good idea.

WOMAN: I have to start at the bottom, or I'll never improve.

OLD MAN: That may be so, but it's a group of circus ants. With your body, no matter how much experience you get at the bottom, you'd be like the Alps to those characters, no?

(WOMAN cries.)

OLD MAN: It does no good to cry.

WOMAN: Say, Mister.

OLD MAN: Don't bat your eyes at me.

WOMAN: What about Gulliver?

OLD MAN: Gulliver?

WOMAN: Right. How was it Gulliver became good friends with the Lilliputians?

OLD MAN: They tied him up.

WOMAN: You mean, S and M?

OLD MAN: No, no sexual passion to it.

WOMAN: What about appetite?

OLD MAN: Well, he must have been hungry, also. *(Drops a bite of pear for the ants.)*

WOMAN: I'm hungry too.

OLD MAN: Want a mouthful of this?

WOMAN: No.

OLD MAN: OK.

WOMAN: I. . . .

OLD MAN: There! Go on! *(To the ants.)* Suck the sweet juice, show us the way out. *(Whereupon he squashes one, and the juice spills over.)*

WOMAN: Once, when I was peeping through a microscope, I dozed off. I believe it was in the science laboratory in fourth grade. When we looked at the bees swarming on flower petals, at some point I was drowsy and got lost in the bees' world and found myself in the bee fortress. They were waiting for the queen to be born any minute and getting terribly bloodthirsty; when the newborn queen came, they decided two females was one too many, and they chased me all over the place. When I woke up from the dream, I went home, and even sipping my soup at dinner, I couldn't forget that blood-tingling, flesh-crawling bees' world. It even made my soup taste bad.

OLD MAN: That sort of thing was a good dream?

WOMAN: I don't know whether it was a good or a bad dream unless I dream it some more.

OLD MAN: In that case, you don't have time to be awake.

WOMAN: That's right. I really hoped I could dream it one more time. But it never came back. Not in junior high or high school either. Zilch. So, then, that was it. I thought, from now on, I'd waste my life on men and money. I'd try to become an ordinary woman. But. . . .

(OLD MAN *looks at her inquiringly.*)

(WOMAN *trembles.*)

OLD MAN: Hey. . . .

WOMAN: Yes?

OLD MAN: You all right?

WOMAN: *Ari,* you know, an ant! *Ari, aari!*

OLD MAN: Ali? Mohammed Ali has retired, you know.

WOMAN: Ant. I had become an ant.

OLD MAN: An ant?

WOMAN: Ah, right.

OLD MAN: Weren't you a bee?

WOMAN: That's why I can get in without being tied up, can't I? Can't I start at the bottom in the ant circus, even without acting sexy?

OLD MAN: If the ants say it's OK.

WOMAN: But they all said we were ants and to say good morning when you meet one. In the evening, good evening.

(OLD MAN *pauses.*)

WOMAN: They all called that hole the secret exit. Sitting with knees drawn up for two days and two nights and nibbling on cookies, they swore they would wait, like ants in the ground. I have nothing in the way of a political creed, but I can become an ant. I was enticed by their idea of organizing ourselves like an army of ants, and at some point I got mixed in with them. But what with the bugs crawling on the back of your neck, and their not giving me anything decent to eat, I started to see things differently: I thought being taken on by the waiters in a cabaret boiler room would be a hell of a lot more fun than this. But I didn't so much as breathe a word about it. I'd had enough of this whole strategy. From the beginning I planned to make a run for it, if anything happened.

MADMAN: *(Abruptly.)* Back when the proletarian vanguard stormed the Bastille, what was the Marquis de Sade doing!?

(WOMAN *walks aimlessly toward the window.)*

MADMAN: Nay, what did they do to de Sade! Mindful of the women he sadistically abused with fart-filled bonbons, they went around setting fire to pages of his voluminous manuscripts.

WOMAN: *(Looking at her feet.)* Hey, the ants are crawling over here.

MADMAN: Nevertheless, that's the reason Justine burned with passion they never dreamed about! Furiously burning like a cathouse sucking on eleven penises! Like a monster pussy sucking in a penis that will be cut off in atonement! *(Unzips his trousers and sets fire to his pubic hair.)*

(He falls over in a burst of flame. Silence.)

WOMAN: Say there.

OLD MAN: What is it?

WOMAN: Is there sand on my back?

OLD MAN: None.

WOMAN: It's full of it.

OLD MAN: Full of it?

WOMAN: Look, when I straighten my back, it makes a sifting noise.

(OLD MAN *pauses.)*

WOMAN: Even then, when I was lying buried in sand, everybody trampled on me. When things got tough, I got scared, and I was grabbed by the police unit that rushed in, so I screamed out that I didn't do anything, that they lured me here, that if anything better comes along I'd quit right away—I blurted out such awful stuff. While I was saying I shouldn't have come and how stupid I was, stuffing my mouth with sand and feeling some remorse, just then a lump of earth toppled over on me, and I really was about to become an ant buried in the ground. And so nobody said a word of criticism to me. First one left and then another until no one was there—that's when he came up. Even while being chased by the cops, he came up and asked me to keep a pass with identity papers and an attached key. And then he piled sand on me and said he'd come again for sure, and he left.

OLD MAN: Well, did he come again?

WOMAN: No.

OLD MAN: He was caught, wasn't he?

WOMAN: Perhaps so.

OLD MAN: Well, then, nothing left but to go home, was there?

WOMAN: But I was there another two days.

OLD MAN: How come?

WOMAN: It really felt good.

(OLD MAN *pauses.*)

WOMAN: I'd suddenly sit up in the dark, grab sand, and pour it lightly on my bare nipples. I felt like a really bad woman, and then I'd squeeze it between my thighs. And when I'd squeeze them tightly together, almost as if to bind them, I felt as if I was giving birth to an outrageous sand monster. Forgive me. Does this sort of talk bother you?

OLD MAN: I'm no longer young and. . . .

WOMAN: You no doubt think this is some lunatic confession, don't you?

OLD MAN: "Here now, here now, dance of the rabbit."

WOMAN: "Taratta, ratta, ratta, ratta, ratta, ratta." (*Jumps about, kicks wall, and sits down.*)

(*Such actions occur abruptly, symptomatic of schizophrenia.*

WOMAN *laughs lightly.*)

OLD MAN: (*Approaching her from the rear.*) Boo!

WOMAN: You don't scare me, you don't scare me.

OLD MAN: Oh, I'm worn out.

WOMAN: Say.

OLD MAN: Huh?

WOMAN: You see, I. . . .

OLD MAN: Yes, you. . . .

WOMAN: I, I'm not me.

OLD MAN: Hm.

WOMAN: Really!

OLD MAN: Really?

WOMAN: Since that time, I've had his pass and key, and I figured out where he works from his identity papers and paid a visit. To Ochanomizu. The autumn sky was very, very high. While looking down at that ditch of a river, I thought about a lot of things. That this is momentary. And that because it is, I'd just take care of this, then quickly get back home. But a woman who swears such a thing in her heart is, on the other hand, also one who sticks to a dreadful plan. And, when I was allowed into the office, before I knew it, I somehow. . . .

OLD MAN: Before you knew it, what?

WOMAN: It went beyond a brief relationship.

OLD MAN: You got on well with him?

WOMAN: No, not all that well, but before I knew it I'd become his wife. . . .

OLD MAN: That is to say. . . .

WOMAN: That is to say?

OLD MAN: Just like that, he got you in bed, didn't he.

WOMAN: Not so! He didn't get me in bed. I only looked like his wife.

OLD MAN: But a man who wouldn't do it to you is not a man.

WOMAN: That's right. But, there in his office, nothing at all really happened. Even while I was politely allowed in as his wife, he never showed up. I couldn't meet him the next day either. So when I went again after several days, this time he used the old "not-at-home" excuse. Then, on the lunch break, when I once slipped in to pilfer the pass and key I'd left behind, this time I was called a thief. . . . So then I idled about for two or three days when I noticed I was standing in front of that hole that had caved in along with their Operation Ant. I thought I'd return the items I'd been entrusted with right to the hole, or, rather, I'd bury them there. At that point, I was caught by the police, who were reinspecting the scene of the crime. I was asked what this pass was. Of course, he was also contacted. . . . That's enough.

OLD MAN: Why is that?

WOMAN: I don't want to talk about it.

OLD MAN: Did you want him to say you were his wife?

WOMAN: No.

OLD MAN: But did you want him to say you had some relationship with him?

WOMAN: Yes.

OLD MAN: And?

WOMAN: He said I was troublesome.

OLD MAN: That was his reaction?!

WOMAN: From his office they even put out a report of the theft to the police, and no matter what I said I didn't get across to them anymore.

OLD MAN: I see.

WOMAN: Then after several days of life in the detention house—I couldn't take it, so I swallowed the cigarettes they'd given me.

(OLD MAN pauses.)

WOMAN: When I did, I ran a temperature, and they sent me to a hospital.

OLD MAN: You were brought here, right?

WOMAN: No. I put in to come here myself.

OLD MAN: Why?

WOMAN: You can hear the rolling of the sea. . . .

OLD MAN: But that's the only good thing. . . .

WOMAN: In addition, when I look at a line of ants, like this, I feel as if I can go anywhere, even to my old science room . . . and also when I talk about all sorts of things like this, sand monsters come out in swarms from inside my panties and (Sings) hey, ta ta ta, ta ta ta. . . .

OLD MAN: One more time.

WOMAN: What?

OLD MAN: Sing that last part again.

WOMAN: *(Sings.)* Hey, ta ta ta, ta ta ta.

OLD MAN: Thank you.

WOMAN: Not at all, don't mention it.

OLD MAN: I really thank you. I was wondering what I'd do without that nonsense refrain. Your confession is too consistent. There is nothing I can say about it. The only thing I can do is cheer up crazy kids. *(Stands up and grasps her shoulders.)* I really thank you. The last part got a little strange. But go ahead, put yourself into it. You can do it. You can do it. You can do it here just as much as you like!

(A clanging sound. The door has been opened. The NURSE's voice can be heard from the door.)

NURSE: Soon we'll be leaving, won't we? I heard so from Dr. Koremitsu, that you have a beautiful fiancée waiting for you in Tokyo?

(Everyone looks in the direction of the voice. PATIENTS 1 and 2, who are playing house, and PATIENT 3, the MADMAN who appears to be a student, start to speak all at once.)

PATIENT 1: Say, have you met his fiancée?

PATIENT 2: Well, Daddy, you probably won't like her.

PATIENT 1: Whether I like her or not, I'm his father, you know.

PATIENT 2: But, Daddy, you always say so and. . . .

PATIENT 3: What the hell is medical treatment to a doctor, anyway! What the hell is care to a patient!

NURSE: Please be quiet.

PATIENT 1: Mother, she says to be quiet.

PATIENT 2: Am I not being quiet?

(PATIENT 3 crawls along the wall.

KŌICHI *stands behind the* NURSE *for some time.*

KOREMITSU *also stands behind the* NURSE *for some time.)*

NURSE: *(To* KŌICHI *and* KOREMITSU.*)* This is about normal for the abnormal.

KOREMITSU: I wonder if what you mean isn't that, rather than the abnormality of normality we face everyday, this is somehow more nakedly open?

NURSE: Certainly it's more nakedly open, but is this "openness" a step forward? It's like fevers babies get that protect them in their own way. It's also a step backward.

KOREMITSU: In that case, they're still not ready to go out into the world?

NURSE: In stages, they could.

KOREMITSU: If only we could know the number of stages.

NURSE: I won't try to stop you from doing whatever you choose.

KOREMITSU: *(To* KŌICHI.*)* This nurse here, she's a bit critical of what I'm doing.

KŌICHI: You mean in this ward lounge?

KOREMITSU: Well, for the time being it is a lounge, but I'm thinking about widening this wall more. In other words, when the patients get up in the morning, their enclosure will be bigger. A meter at a time so it's not noticed, till finally it becomes as big as a gym, and then we'll tear that wall down. In other words, with nothing at all to partition them off, the place will be a really spacious beach!

NURSE: Who would be able to control such a large space?

KOREMITSU: Control. . . .

NURSE: Look, even if you can control it, it doesn't mean a thing at all to the patients. You are thinking that space is freedom, but, inside these people, it's too spacious, and they're not free. If you don't take that into consideration—

KOREMITSU: But who can say Adam and Eve weren't crazy?

NURSE: Instead of that sort of thing, I'll worry about how to pay the plasterer who is going to widen the wall a meter at a time.

KOREMITSU: Do that, and you'll douse my ideal, won't you? *(Touches her rear.)*

NURSE: Stop that, not here! *(Sweeps his hand away.)* Shall we go? *(Starts to leave.)*

WOMAN: *(Taking a step forward.)* Oh! . . . Darling. . . .

NURSE: Darling?

WOMAN: *(Pointing at* KŌICHI.*)* Darling. . . .

KŌICHI: Me? *(Pointing to himself.)*

WOMAN: Don't you remember me?

KOREMITSU: Tell her you do.

KŌICHI: Y-yes.

WOMAN: I am. . . .

KŌICHI: Do you need something?

WOMAN: No, it's all right. *(Tries to withdraw.)*

KŌICHI: You are *(looks at the* NURSE*'s clipboard)* Ms. Rokujō, aren't you? *(*WOMAN *says nothing.)*

KŌICHI: Do you need something from me?

WOMAN: If I could have you dispose of the sand that's accumulated on my back *(with her back to him)*, I think you will understand. *(*KŌICHI *is puzzled.)*

WOMAN: Or else when I show it like this *(lifts up her hair)*, I think I look like somebody. . . .
(She is about to turn around, but the NURSE *steps between her and* KŌICHI.*)*

NURSE: Doctor, there's no end to this.
*(*WOMAN *drops her hair strand by strand.)*

OLD MAN: *(To the* WOMAN.*)* Do it, like that, like his wife!

WOMAN: Right.

OLD MAN: One more time.

WOMAN: Darling!

KŌICHI: What do you want with me?

WOMAN: How many times have I called you "Darling"? It's three times. Three times. Please take note, Kōichi. The third of these three times surely clinches the truth.

NURSE: How stupid. Let's go.

KŌICHI: Yes.

WOMAN: Wait. A little longer. Just a tiny bit.

OLD MAN: Be crazy!

WOMAN: *(Sings.)* Ta, ta, ta . . . ta, ta, ta. . . .

*(*PATIENTS *laugh.)*

NURSE: Don't laugh without reason.

WOMAN: *(Approaching* KŌICHI.*)* I'm leaving here tonight!

KŌICHI: How?

WOMAN: The ants.

KŌICHI: The ants?

WOMAN: Yes, I'll join the ant circus, and from their small house I'll come into your world. Look *(takes out a tree leaf),* I've even received a letter to this effect from the circus director. He's asking me to please come soon and be the star of the company.

KŌICHI: This is a leaf off a tree.

WOMAN: No. It's a pass to the company. A pass.

NURSE: Let's go. It's a classic insane declaration.

WOMAN: I'm not insane! You're a devil!

NURSE: Cut that out now!

KŌICHI: Right, no need to get tough.

WOMAN: Right, it's not good to get tough.

NURSE: *(To* KOREMITSU.*)* Why aren't you saying anything at such a moment as this?

KOREMITSU: The money for the plasterer. . . .

KŌICHI: So that's how it is. Well, it would be good if the director comes for you soon.

WOMAN: He won't come for me.

KŌICHI: Oh? He won't?

WOMAN: I have to go. See, the ant circus will ride a boat made of pear peelings. It will go down a stream, and day and night it will splash right along. When the moon shines, it will look like a blue magic lantern to the crabs lurking on the river bottom. That's why, to overtake it, you have to fly along in a sonic dune buggy at two hundred kilometers per hour, racing along, kicking sand, cutting the wind. And

then, tonight, I want you to park my dune buggy right beneath this
window.

(Holds out a key.)

KŌICHI: Isn't this an apartment key?

WOMAN: Do people who live in apartments have sonic dune buggies?!

KŌICHI: Well, I'll take care of it for now.

(Takes key.)

WOMAN: I'm counting on you.

KŌICHI: But unless you can slip away like an ant from a small hole in
this room, you won't see any dune buggy.

WOMAN: But didn't we once live like ants?

(KŌICHI is silent.)

WOMAN: Well.

KOREMITSU: Yeah.

NURSE: It's time.

(Opens door and leaves. Strained silence.)

WOMAN: *(To the* OLD MAN.*)* Say.

OLD MAN: What?

WOMAN: I made them think I'm crazy, didn't I?

Scene 2: The Corridor

(The cloth at the front of the room falls with a rustle. It becomes a cloth corridor.
KŌICHI *and* KOREMITSU *walk in.)*

KOREMITSU: What a blockhead you are.

KŌICHI: I'm a blockhead?

KOREMITSU: You're a blockhead. I wonder how a blockhead like you
could become a doctor. You took the key, but what do you expect to
come of it?

KŌICHI: Now it doesn't mean I've taken her virginity.

KOREMITSU: It amounts to the same sort of thing.

KŌICHI: I took her key. How much value does a promise sworn to me in
a patient's delusion really have? Is it something that she'll forget
completely after several delusions? Or will she remember her promise, even if she forgets the delusions?

KOREMITSU: You won't know unless you penetrate that woman's brain.
If she begins to feel resentment toward you, it may be a sign of recovery, and if tomorrow she completely forgets about it, she's a normal
patient. And besides—

KŌICHI: And besides? . . .

KOREMITSU: Provided deep down she feels resentment toward you while
her face shows she's completely forgotten, well, this means she leaves
the hospital!

KŌICHI: But that deep down feeling you don't understand. How do you propose to penetrate it?

KOREMITSU: While I'm talking about you with her.

KŌICHI: You'd use me as a tool?

KOREMITSU: Right you are. As far as that woman is concerned, you are the black jack. What matters to her is where that one-eyed jack is looking. . . . Anyway, what are you going to do about the dune buggy?

KŌICHI: I don't need that whole thing.

KOREMITSU: But from now on, wherever you go, won't you see the dune buggy that goes with that key?

KŌICHI: If she could just slip out of here like an ant.

(*Darkness.*)

Scene 3: The Racetrack

(*The Pat Boone song.*)

VOICE: Darling.

(KŌICHI *is silent.*)

VOICE: Darling! (*Louder and stronger.*)

(*Suddenly, the sounds of race cars starting up one after another.*)

AOI: What are you thinking about?

KŌICHI: I was just thinking about the letter I sent you.

AOI: Look, there! It's Kurosawa. Kurosawa's about to start. There, the yellow Porsche. He had a one-year suspension; this is his first start in a long time. He looks like a gentleman, but, that man, once he's in his car, there's no telling what he'll do. (*She is in pain from morning sickness.*)

KŌICHI: Of all the dumb things. You are hurting from morning sickness because you look at Death when you're pregnant.

AOI: That's so. But it doesn't hurt. Not at all.

KŌICHI: Looks like it's threatening to rain.

AOI: If it doesn't, it'll surely be a wicked, nasty race.

KŌICHI: Did you get over your nausea?

AOI: Argh.

KŌICHI: What luck. We come all the way out to the track, and your morning sickness is awful.

AOI: I don't like being a woman.

KŌICHI: Why?

AOI: The design of our bodies is a real pain.

KŌICHI: God made it. It can't be helped.

AOI: Listen, put your hand on my back.

KŌICHI: Like this?

AOI: It would be nice to have some grapefruit.

KŌICHI: I'm having Jirō go get some right now. Are you all right? Shall . . . should we go to the toilet?

AOI: I'm fine, fine. If we go to the toilet, someone will take these good seats you went to such trouble for.

KŌICHI: Jirō's slow, isn't he?

AOI: Would you get my handkerchief from my handbag, darling, my handkerchief?

KŌICHI: We should have listened to your mother. But we couldn't wait until the ceremony. She told us to stay conservative, inconspicuous, not to attract attention, to be newlyweds with a clean slate; but if somebody sees you suffering like this, there'll be no hiding what we did before the marriage then. Aoi, are you all right?

AOI: Kōichi, put on that song, that song.

(KŌICHI *switches on the Pat Boone song. Sound of a race car passing by.*)

KŌICHI: Isn't it growing a little cold?

AOI: A bit.

KŌICHI: Shall we go back to the car?

AOI: I'll stay here. But what about the grapefruit?

KŌICHI: I'll go see.

AOI: Please don't go.

KŌICHI: But after it starts to rain, it'll be too late to go and see.

(JIRŌ *arrives.*)

JIRŌ: Hey, Sis.

AOI: You're late, you bum. What about the grapefruit?

JIRŌ: Here you are.

AOI: What took you so long?

JIRŌ: Late or not, the parking lot was packed, junk-heap jalopies getting in the way, and cars coming in one after another clogging things up. I could only barely get through to the car, slipping between other cars. It took some doing. Here's the key.

AOI: This is not our key.

JIRŌ: Oh, this one's your key.

AOI: Look, whose key is it?

JIRŌ: I met up with my buddies over there, and I'm going to their place for just a little while. You two go home together.

AOI: Hold it.

JIRŌ: See you later.

AOI: Jirō. (*Chases after him.*)

(*Sounds of race cars zipping by. An announcer's voice. This noise changes to the sound of waves.* KŌICHI *squats down and scoops up a handful of gravel. As he does so, the words of his love letter suddenly flow from his mouth: "My beloved Aoi, how are you?—."* The WOMAN *approaches him.*)

WOMAN: Doctor. Aren't you the doctor?

KŌICHI: *(Vacantly.)* Eh?

WOMAN: It's me. It's me. Rokujō.

KŌICHI: Rokujō?

WOMAN: Yes. With my hair dyed like this, you might have forgotten me, but, look, here I am, the Rokujō you ran into at the hospital in Izu.

(KŌICHI *is speechless.*)

WOMAN: You needn't be so surprised.

KŌICHI: But. . . .

WOMAN: Yes, I left the hospital one month ago. The one you were just with, is she the one you're going to marry?

KŌICHI: Yes. You said your name was Miss Rokujō?

WOMAN: Your face says you still don't believe me.

KŌICHI: The actual fact is I am surprised. I remember clearly what you spoke to me about. . . .

WOMAN: Oh, you do. When we were at the place by the sea, I spoke of absurd things. It may have been quite annoying to you. But now that I'm back in normal society, please forget all that.

KŌICHI: Have you often been to the racetrack?

WOMAN: No, it's my first time. Right now I'm doing cosmetic sales in this town, and, by chance, I saw a poster on a telephone pole about some star named Kurosawa who, I thought, really looked like a person I'd met somewhere, so I brought my car right here. Then I unexpectedly bump into you, and we talk about old times. I wish it were that simple, but things are a lot more complicated. Actually, there was some trouble over at the parking lot, and I chased someone as far as here. . . . Doctor, do you have the key?

KŌICHI: Key?

WOMAN: The one who was here a little while ago, he's your brother-in-law, right?

KŌICHI: Yes.

WOMAN: Didn't he hand you a key?

KŌICHI: What about it?

WOMAN: It's my key.

KŌICHI: What did you say?

WOMAN: There was a mix-up in the parking lot. When I went to get a parking coupon, your brother-in-law deliberately moved my car, see, squeezed it to the back so he could get his car out easily. That's okay, but he even took my key.

(JIRŌ *comes running in.*)

JIRŌ: Kōichi, my sister over there! . . .

(ROKUJŌ *recognizes* JIRŌ.
Seeing ROKUJŌ, JIRŌ *jumps and tries to flee.*)

KŌICHI: *(Grabs him.)* What's happened to Aoi?

JIRŌ: *(Struggles to get away.)* Go see for yourself.

ROKUJŌ: *(Stands directly in JIRŌ's way, and slaps him on the face.)*

JIRŌ: *(Falls over.)* What the hell are you doing? You slut!

ROKUJŌ: You little bastard, you think you can take me for a fool!

JIRŌ: Who the hell is this character? *(To KŌICHI.)* Don't tell me you know her.

KŌICHI: If you have the key, give it back right now!

PARKING LOT ATTENDANT: Uh, we have to close up now. . . .

WOMAN: I don't have my key. . . .

JIRŌ: You want the key, it's right here. *(Produces it.)*

ROKUJŌ: *(To KŌICHI.)* This is the one.

KŌICHI: *(Tries to take it.)*

JIRŌ: *(Draws back.)* First, decide which you want—my sister or this.
    (KŌICHI says nothing.)

JIRŌ: She's collapsed with morning sickness!

KŌICHI: Anyway, just give it back.

JIRŌ: So that's how it is. *(Throws key.)*
    (ROKUJŌ picks it up.)

JIRŌ: Is that how it's going to be?

KŌICHI: What do you mean?

JIRŌ: You and her!
    (JIRŌ leaves.
    KŌICHI starts to go look for AOI.)

ROKUJŌ: Doctor.

KŌICHI: *(Stops briefly.)* That was inexcusable. I apologize for him.

WOMAN: You don't have to apologize. I don't like you apologizing to me.

KŌICHI: Well, take care.

WOMAN: Doctor, I'm no longer angry. Please convey this to your wife and her brother. That I'm not offended. That's right. *(Opens her bag.)* This is what I'm selling now. Please give it to your wife to show there's no hard feelings.

KŌICHI: Thank you. Well, take care.

WOMAN: Also, I'm planning a business trip to Tokyo soon. I have a favor to ask you. If there is someone you know in real estate, I'd like to have them look into an apartment for me.

KŌICHI: I can at least ask about it. . . .

WOMAN: Yes, that's all I want. Please. I'll be calling you. I'm sorry to lay this on you all at once.

KŌICHI: Well, then. *(Leaves.)*

WOMAN: *(To self.)* Oh, and Doctor, how wonderful it wasn't you that got burned to death just before the pit stop.

(The PARKING LOT ATTENDANT *runs in from the* hanamichi.)

PARKING LOT ATTENDANT: We have to close up now. . . .

ROKUJŌ: Oh. *(Heads toward* hanamichi)

PARKING LOT ATTENDANT: Is that your car?

*(*ROKUJŌ *suddenly falls down.)*

PARKING LOT ATTENDANT: Madam! *(Runs to help her.)*

ROKUJŌ: Say it once more.

PARKING LOT ATTENDANT: Huh?

ROKUJŌ: Madam.

PARKING LOT ATTENDANT: What's happened to you?

ROKUJŌ: Nothing really.

PARKING LOT ATTENDANT: Do you feel bad?

ROKUJŌ: A bit nauseous. . . .

PARKING LOT ATTENDANT: That's not good. *(Leans over.)*

ROKUJŌ: *(Places his hand on her stomach.)* It's like something being stirred up in there. . . .

PARKING LOT ATTENDANT: Oh, that's not good. *(Pulls hand away.)*

ROKUJŌ: What's wrong?

PARKING LOT ATTENDANT: My hands are unworthy of touching a woman's body. They take a tremendous beating in the parking lot. In the olden days, I'd be like a groom for horses. Please, madam, don't take hold of such hands as these.

ROKUJŌ: You. . . .

PARKING LOT ATTENDANT: Yes.

ROKUJŌ: You have a sweetheart?

PARKING LOT ATTENDANT: No. . . .

ROKUJŌ: But you must have at least one?

PARKING LOT ATTENDANT: It's no use.

ROKUJŌ: Why not?

PARKING LOT ATTENDANT: Not someone like me.

ROKUJŌ: Why's that?

PARKING LOT ATTENDANT: I'm lacking something.

ROKUJŌ: You're not lacking anything.

PARKING LOT ATTENDANT: No, I've already given up. It's always a holiday here.

ROKUJŌ: Holiday?

PARKING LOT ATTENDANT: It's a long, long Sunday, madam, so I'm accustomed to seeing everything that way. And you're telling me to be attached to someone?

ROKUJŌ: Are you weeping?

PARKING LOT ATTENDANT: Does it look like I am?

ROKUJŌ: That, or it could be something else.

PARKING LOT ATTENDANT: That's because you're looking at my shadow.

ROKUJŌ: Your shadow?

PARKING LOT ATTENDANT: Look, it's wavering there, isn't it? *(Sways his body.)* But a shadow'll just get blown away by a big storm someday. Then I can tell you who I am, if you want.

Scene 4: The Room

(While the conclusion of the previous scene is taking place on the hanamichi, *the stage is changing into* AOI's *house.* AOI's MOTHER *and* KŌICHI *are in front of the sliding doors. The two are playing cat's cradle. Their shadows fall against the sliding doors.)*

MOTHER: Why didn't you come earlier?

KŌICHI: I just didn't know there was a call for me at the hospital. How is Aoi?

MOTHER: The rain that day must have cast an evil spell on her. The fever won't go down.

KŌICHI: I'm sorry I didn't take better care of her. Even though I was with her, I noticed hardly any change. If only it were a simple cold.

MOTHER: *(Referring to cat's cradle.)* Oh, there, you've got to do it like this.

KŌICHI: But isn't it like this? *(Their game may continue if it takes time for* AOI *to enter.)*

(Sounds of sliding doors opening.)

AOI: Mother, who's there?

MOTHER: It's Kōichi.

AOI: The "cosmetics" you gave me recently was pomade, not cosmetics.

KŌICHI: But I asked for cosmetics, and that's what I bought.

AOI: My face got all chapped from being in bed so long, and when I put some of the stuff on a while ago it got sticky and stuck to the pillow. I was just now cleaning it off with a tissue. That's why I'm so annoyed, see, the things men buy! Where did you pick that stuff up?

*(*KŌICHI *says nothing.*

The phone rings.)

MOTHER: *(Answers.)* Yes, this is Miyamoto. Kōichi? Just a minute, please.

KŌICHI: Thanks. *(Takes phone.)* Hello. . . . Hello. . . .

AOI: Who is it from?

KŌICHI: . . . Hello? *(Hangs up.)*

AOI: What a strange call. Mother, would you throw out the stuff in this wastebasket? It still smells.

MOTHER: I'll go change your ice pack.

AOI: Yes.

(The MOTHER *opens the sliding doors and goes out.)*

AOI: Hey, come here, come a little closer.

KŌICHI: How long have you had a fever?

AOI: Since I left you. Also, my stomach sometimes cramps up.

KŌICHI: Your fever doesn't seem terribly bad, but I'm concerned about your stomach.

AOI: Tell me, where did you go?

KŌICHI: Huh?

AOI: After that, you saw my brother, didn't you?

KŌICHI: Yeah.

AOI: I called your place all night long

KŌICHI: I just met up with an old friend.

AOI: Tell me, do you still smell it?

KŌICHI: What?

AOI: Put your face a little closer. Doesn't that pomade smell?

KŌICHI: No.

AOI: Perhaps you met her?

KŌICHI: What are you trying to say?

AOI: At times like this, my intuition is clear. You went to return the key, didn't you?

(KŌICHI *says nothing.*)

AOI: I heard it from my brother. That you did everything but beat it out of him, and then he finally handed it over to her.

(*The telephone rings.*)

KŌICHI: (*Answering.*) Yes?

WOMAN'S VOICE: Uh, doctor? It's me. Excuse me for calling you in such a place.

KŌICHI: What is this?

AOI: Who's it from? Who's it from?

WOMAN'S VOICE: Finally today I found a room. This is with your help. Thank you. And one more thing. Tomorrow if possible I'd like to celebrate in that room my new life in Tokyo. Do you think you could come by?

KŌICHI: Just now I'm terribly wrapped up with something. . . .

WOMAN'S VOICE: Wait, I also want you to return my key.

KŌICHI: Your key? Haven't I returned it?

WOMAN'S VOICE: I don't have it yet. Look, it's the key I once gave you in Izu. Heh, heh, heh, if I can't have it back, I won't be able to ride in the vehicle of my dreams. I'm sorry. That's a joke. Just a joke.

KŌICHI: Enough's enough, please. (*Hangs up phone.*)

AOI: What is she saying to give back?

KŌICHI: A key.

AOI: Not this key, is it?

KŌICHI: How did you get that?

AOI: When you came back from Izu. I found it stuck in a corner of your suitcase. I didn't think it was the key to your room, but I thought I'd try it once to find out.

KŌICHI: Throw it away, Aoi, throw that thing away.

AOI: This is that woman's room key, isn't it?

KŌICHI: That's stupid.

AOI: Since when, since when have you taken up with that crazy woman?!

KŌICHI: What do you mean? Give it here, I'll throw it away for you!

AOI: No. This is my key! You think you can take it away? Just try. Look, here and here. *(Laughs in a strangely husky voice.)* Ha ha ha ha, the key you love is here. You can tell by the scent of pomade on it. Let's turn out the lights, shall we? While you grope about catching the scent of my pomade, you can crawl slowly over here. Listen, darling, darling, darling, darling—why do you make me call you as many as four times? Please come closer.

KŌICHI: Aoi, pull yourself together, Aoi.

AOI: What are you going to do?

KŌICHI: Aoi.

AOI: No. Because my body's still clean and unsullied, ha ha ha, ha ha *(gradually her voice turns into* ROKUJŌ's), I say no. What're you doing, climbing up on top of me? Isn't your sweetheart waiting for you somewhere? You don't need to be concerned with a woman like me. It's better if you move on quickly. I say no. Don't touch my breasts. I won't have it. I won't. Do you hear me? I'm going to leave here. I'll be leaving this hospital, and, when I do, then I'll let you. What do you think you're doing? You're hurting my stomach. Where's my director.

KŌICHI: Aoi, it's me. Do you understand? Aoi!

(Ambulance siren in the distance slowly takes over the slightly feverish dynamic between these two. AOI's *hollow laughter.)*

AOI: I won't give you the key. Absolutely not! You think I'd go back to that kind of hospital?!

KŌICHI: Aoi.

Scene 5: *On the* Hanamichi

(The PARKING LOT ATTENDANT *and the* OLD MAN *are drunk, stumbling about and hanging on one another.)*

PARKING LOT ATTENDANT: Are we going to get there soon?

OLD MAN: No, not yet, not yet.

PARKING LOT ATTENDANT: Do you really have a house?

OLD MAN: Do I look like I don't have a house?

PARKING LOT ATTENDANT: That's not what I meant. Just that before, when I picked up a person who'd fallen over drunk like this, he started to look for his former house, and when we got near the Edo River, he said to cross it. . . .

OLD MAN: Well, did you?

PARKING LOT ATTENDANT: No way. We couldn't really swim across, so we take an old boat, and when we're about halfway, he thrusts his hands into the water and calls out the name of his dead son.

(OLD MAN *vomits.*)

PARKING LOT ATTENDANT: Are you all right?

OLD MAN: . . . Then, what happened then?

PARKING LOT ATTENDANT: Morning came.

OLD MAN: What are you?

PARKING LOT ATTENDANT: Huh?

OLD MAN: I said what are you?

PARKING LOT ATTENDANT: Let me see.

OLD MAN: What the hell are you!?

PARKING LOT ATTENDANT: I'm me.

OLD MAN: You lie.

PARKING LOT ATTENDANT: You say I lie, but I'm just being myself.

OLD MAN: But not everyone acts like you.

PARKING LOT ATTENDANT: Is that so?

OLD MAN: They run around frantically just looking out for number one. Are you doing this to drunks!? (*Makes a sign with his finger to indicate a pickpocket.*)

(PARKING LOT ATTENDANT *looks at a dim light in a room in front of them.*)

OLD MAN: What are you looking at?

PARKING LOT ATTENDANT: The little. . . .

OLD MAN: You mean the little happiness of home?

PARKING LOT ATTENDANT: No.

OLD MAN: Then, what, what, what?

PARKING LOT ATTENDANT: The little flickering flames of the will-o'-the-wisp.

OLD MAN: Hmm.

PARKING LOT ATTENDANT: Kind of hazy, like they're taking shelter in each one of those apartments over there. Sometimes they're beyond the discotheque and other times in the big appliance stores in Akihabara. I'm sorry, you're not the one who's drunk, it's me.

OLD MAN: Even you can. . . .

PARKING LOT ATTENDANT: Even I can what?

OLD MAN: Even you can be happy someday.

PARKING LOT ATTENDANT: It won't work. Not for me.

OLD MAN: But you're young.

PARKING LOT ATTENDANT: No, I'm dead.

OLD MAN: Dead?

PARKING LOT ATTENDANT: Look. . . . *(Puts the palm of his hand on the* OLD MAN.*)*

OLD MAN: *(Withdrawing.)* You're young. Still so young, aren't you? *(Exits.)*

(Silence.)

PARKING LOT ATTENDANT: *(Lends his shoulder to an imaginary person.)* Well, old fellow, let's go.

Scene 6: The Room

(The echoing sound of an ambulance leaving.)

WOMAN'S VOICE: Doctor, Doctor.

(Sound of ambulance farther away.)

WOMAN: Doctor!!!

KŌICHI: What?

WOMAN: What happened to you?

KŌICHI: Was I having a bad dream?

WOMAN: Yes. You looked really terrible. I didn't intend to wake you up.

KŌICHI: *(Gets up.)* Didn't an ambulance just go by?

WOMAN: There's an emergency hospital right behind here.

KŌICHI: I see.

WOMAN: I wanted to invite your wife too. Will you give her my regards?

KŌICHI: Yes. May I have some more wine?

WOMAN: Sure. Well, how is she now?

KŌICHI: Well, women during pregnancy on occasion will experience some confusion.

WOMAN: Confusion?

KŌICHI: She speaks with your, with your voice.

WOMAN: Don't say such a frightening thing to me!

KŌICHI: I've seen that sort of spirit medium before, but it never occurred to me that she was capable of such a stunt.

WOMAN: Does she really sound exactly like me?

KŌICHI: Not *like* you, it *is* you.

WOMAN: Is it acceptable for a scientist to say such things?

KŌICHI: It was the same thing with that other spirit medium. I couldn't forget the younger female factory worker who had worked together with me when I was eighteen. So I asked the spirit woman to enter the spirit world and call her back. But you know what became of her? She got separated from herself. In other words, at the moment she entered into the spirit world, she began to look for her real self that had possessed that girl, using the voice of that female factory worker.

WOMAN: But I haven't been looking for your wife or anything like that.

KŌICHI: No, but you are always there in the palm of her hand.

(WOMAN *pauses.*)

KŌICHI: Do you remember the key you gave me in Izu?

WOMAN: Let's stop talking about that.

KŌICHI: You did give me the key. And it's the one that's in Aoi's hand right now

WOMAN: Really?

KŌICHI: That's why, you know, when she closes her fingers around it, she can change into you and also speak with your voice.

WOMAN: I have no intention of being an apparition of a living person, and, for that matter, I've got no reason to possess her.

KŌICHI: The cosmetics you gave me, wasn't it some pomade?

WOMAN: I wouldn't call it cosmetics, my goodness, Doctor. Didn't I say pomade?

KŌICHI: You said pomade?

WOMAN: That's right.

(KŌICHI *says nothing.*)

WOMAN: Why are you looking at me like that?

KŌICHI: It's that smell.

WOMAN: Huh?

KŌICHI: You have on the same stuff now too, don't you?

WOMAN: Yes, the same stuff.

KŌICHI: You still have a lot of it?

WOMAN: Huh?

KŌICHI: Don't you have ten or twelve dozen in the closet?

WOMAN: What are you getting at?

KŌICHI: This is half-used already, but I'll return this jar to you. And the key, too, that you left with me at the hospital in Izu. A little while ago, I snatched it from her hand while she was sleeping. I want to return all this to you.

WOMAN: You didn't come to congratulate me, did you?

KŌICHI: Here, I've set everything here.

WOMAN: *(Places her hand on his.)* And then. . . .

KŌICHI: And then?

WOMAN: What about the dune buggy?

(KŌICHI *pauses.*)

WOMAN: Didn't you promise? That if I could sneak out like an ant, you'd have the dune buggy waiting for me?

KŌICHI: You've even got me aboard that invisible vehicle?

(WOMAN *laughs lightly.*)

KŌICHI: Why would you do that?

WOMAN: What do you mean?

KŌICHI: Why did you say such things back then? I've been thinking about it ever since. And why is it you remember only those kinds of things?

WOMAN: Because you were my you.

KŌICHI: Do you think you could speak clearly?

WOMAN: Don't you think everything is clear?

KŌICHI: Is this what you mean by being clear? You weren't crazy. You were faking it. You found your way into the field of mental rehabilitation, and finished your training just for fun. And even now, you would "insert" me into your laughable experience.

WOMAN: *(Grasps his hands.)* That's not so.

KŌICHI: OK, just try and tell me in what way you were crazy!

WOMAN: In all sorts of ways.

KŌICHI: What the hell's that mean?

WOMAN: I . . . I'm. . . .

KŌICHI: What's this climbing all over me!

WOMAN: I can't say it well, but I was thinking only of you. It was a one-way passage. Whether my one-way ticket made me brood like that over you I can't tell, but at some point everything about the time when I met you somehow or other came into focus for me. And I wanted to know more, to taste more. I had no intention of becoming your wife, but from the time I was told I resemble your wife, it was a greater honor than being in your wife's place. These thoughts will surely not amount to real-life happiness. They're just something really very tiny, like peeking through a microscope, like a brass key and sand and ants being hemmed in together. But from long before, ever since I was a child, I wanted to go back there and was hoping someone would take me.

KŌICHI: It's not that I don't understand what you're saying. . . .

WOMAN: Please understand.

KŌICHI: But it doesn't have to be me.

WOMAN: If not, why did you entrust the key to me?

KŌICHI: The key is. . . .

WOMAN: To me, small as an ant?

(Sound of knocking on the door.)

MAN: Excuse me. Miss Rokujō. Miss Rokujō.

WOMAN: She's not here.

MAN: You say not, but she's here, isn't she?

(He opens the door.)

MAN: Is there a Mr. Kōichi here?

(WOMAN does not answer.)

MAN: How about it, he's here, isn't he?

KŌICHI: Who is this?

WOMAN: It's the real estate man.

KŌICHI: What do you mean, coming here so late?

MAN: I'm sorry. She badgered me into directing her here at all costs.

KŌICHI: Who did?

MAN: She said her name was Aoi.

KŌICHI: What are you saying? Aoi's supposed to be in the hospital.

MAN: She was in the hospital? No wonder she was so pale and very much in pain, but she implored me to bring her here.

KŌICHI: Well, where is she?

MAN: She's there.

KŌICHI: There?

MAN: There, there. My god! She's been eavesdropping on the two of you. . . .

KŌICHI: Aoi. . . .

(*Rushes out of the room.*)

WOMAN: Say.

MAN: Yes.

WOMAN: How is it outside?

MAN: It's very. . . .

WOMAN: The wind is whistling?

MAN: Not only the wind.

WOMAN: What else?

MAN: Something.

WOMAN: What something?

MAN: It's really awful.

WOMAN: Then, for a sick person. . . .

MAN: Right, it's rough.

(KŌICHI *returns, slumps to the floor.*)

WOMAN: Did you look in the direction of the pedestrian overpass?

KŌICHI: No.

WOMAN: She must be there. (*Goes out.*)

(KŌICHI *and the* REAL ESTATE MAN *remain.*)

MAN: I'm sorry. Perhaps I shouldn't have accompanied her.

KŌICHI: How did she know?

MAN: Huh?

KŌICHI: How did she know about this place?

MAN: May I have a piece of cake?

KŌICHI: Maybe. . . .

MAN: May I have a piece of cake?

KŌICHI: The wind is. . . .

MAN: Well. . . . (*Nibbles cake.*)

KŌICHI: . . . blowing from this apartment toward the hospital, isn't it?

MAN: Yes.

KŌICHI: Then the fragrance of the pomade may well have wafted that far and. . . .

MAN: No, the fact is she received a phone call.

KŌICHI: A phone call?

MAN: Yes. That said you were here.

KŌICHI: Who from?

MAN: I don't know. She said that's why she ran over dressed like she was, and she showed me her bare foot stuck with glass.

VOICE: Darling.

KŌICHI: What?

(Stage grows dark.)

AOI: Darling, I'm here.

(KŌICHI looks up and sees AOI kneeling on one of the ceiling crossbeams. Startled, he is speechless.)

AOI: I've been here all along.

KŌICHI: What are you doing there?

AOI: So you were at her place.

KŌICHI: Come down.

AOI: Don't come near me. I'm about to bear your child. I don't want anything to do with a father who'd fool around with that sort of woman. I'm saying don't come near me! A while ago, when I woke up in bed, my key was gone. I knew what had happened. But, while I was dozing off again, the phone rang. It was a strange call, someone like me was calling me. Even her face I could vaguely see. And a feeling came over me like I could forgive everything. Because being attracted to a person like me means, after all, that you won't forget me.

KŌICHI: Just a minute.

AOI: Kōichi, you're the one who will be my husband. Both in the past and now I've decided it would be that way, and that's why I've been intimate with you. And so from now on too you are the one who must be my eternal husband. Listen closely, Kōichi. I will remove from your eyes forever that woman Rokujō. Forever! When I do, you and I will be alone, and until that time comes you are not to approach me. Kōichi, she is going to disappear just like that from in front of us.

(She stands up. The lower half of her body is covered with blood.)

KŌICHI: Aoi! Come down from there!

AOI: Darling, listen well to my voice. Do you know who I am? Look, this key, the key she left there, I picked it up. Now, the key is in my hand again—the wind will be blowing from here to there. Then you will surely smell this very pomade. Well, come on, turn out the lights

all over Tokyo, and grope your way over here. *(AOI's voice.)* I am
Rokujō, your wife, ha, ha, ha, ha, ha.
*(She leaps down from the lintel with her full weight and stops with a jerk in
mid-air. She is hanging by her neck; the key slips out of her hand and falls to the
floor. Music.)*

Scene 7: A Sandy Beach.

(The sound of waves from afar. This is the beach by KOREMITSU*'s hospital in
Izu.)*

KOREMITSU: Well, what will you be doing from now on?
*(*KŌICHI *says nothing.)*
KOREMITSU: Any idea? Don't you plan to be at the hospital in Tokyo?
*(*KŌICHI *still says nothing.)*
KOREMITSU: You should take a trip somewhere. Stay for even half a year
    at such a remote hospital and you have to long for the craziness of the
    city again.
KŌICHI: No, I'm not going on a trip.
KOREMITSU: Well, what are you going to do?
KŌICHI: Would you admit me here to room number six?
KOREMITSU: What?
KŌICHI: I want to get to the bottom of what that woman was thinking in
    that room.
KOREMITSU: You're carrying this game too far.
KŌICHI: C'mon. Just get me into that room.
KOREMITSU: What can you learn in a place like that?
KŌICHI: Things about me reflected in that woman's eyes, things about
    Aoi, who has died. . . . When I think about it now, she didn't say
    the pomade was pomade. She simply handed it to me, but there's no
    doubt she even had in mind that Aoi would mistake it for something
    to put on her face.
KOREMITSU: Do you hate Rokujō that much?
KŌICHI: When I think of Aoi, crushed as she was like a ripe tomato, you
    can't imagine how much. . . . *(Utters a groan.)*
KOREMITSU: It simply won't do for me to put you in that room.
KŌICHI: Why, why not?
KOREMITSU: I'm telling you, being in that room with your frame of
    mind, you won't learn a thing about Rokujō!
KŌICHI: You're wrong, you're wrong! What I'd learn is how Rokujō
    recovered her health so quickly!
KOREMITSU: If I could answer that question, I would not be this kind of
    doctor!
KŌICHI: You're the one who stirred her up so she'd be obsessed with me.

KOREMITSU: Hey, hey, do you know what you're saying?

KŌICHI: Before, why didn't you take charge of the key I got from her? You just let me have it! You took me, your friend, as a guinea pig and used me so that that woman would completely recover!

KOREMITSU: You say that, and you're a doctor in the mental ward?

KŌICHI: I am a patient. That's why I'm telling you to just get me in room number six.

KOREMITSU: But, look, there's no place here to put the likes of you, a seriously ill person!

KŌICHI: There's room number six, room number six.

KOREMITSU: Right now it's filled with less seriously ill patients.

(The NURSE *approaches.)*

NURSE: Doctor, there's someone who says he wants to meet someone.

KOREMITSU: Meet with a patient?

NURSE: No, with you. It's about the patient in room number eight.

KOREMITSU: Ah, that one who wants to pay for his mistakes with his ten fingers?

(The man comes out. It is the PARKING LOT ATTENDANT.*)*

KOREMITSU: Yes?

*(*PARKING LOT ATTENDANT *lowers his head, has something wrapped with a large cloth in his hand. Somehow he resembles the patient who had set fire to his pubic hair.)*

KOREMITSU: What's on your mind?

PARKING LOT ATTENDANT: This. *(Holds out the cloth bundle.)*

KOREMITSU: What is that?

PARKING LOT ATTENDANT: It's underwear.

KOREMITSU: You want to deliver it?

PARKING LOT ATTENDANT: Directly, if possible.

KOREMITSU: I wonder if we could manage that.

PARKING LOT ATTENDANT: Doctor.

KOREMITSU: Yes.

PARKING LOT ATTENDANT: Concerning my older brother, I believe I have given you letters for some time. . . .

KOREMITSU: Right. I took a look at them.

PARKING LOT ATTENDANT: If he wants to grovel against the walls, he can do that in my apartment too. If he wants to set fire to his "eleventh finger," I could even buy him a substitute from an adult toy store.

KOREMITSU: Hmmm. . . .

PARKING LOT ATTENDANT: Recently I caught the students playing mah-jongg and made them confess. My older brother was only caught in the dorm toilet by a med student whose part-time job was hunting up patients. Don't you think a job like that is odd, if crying all alone in the restroom means you're crazy?

KOREMITSU: However, he can't in fact take care of himself, can he?

PARKING LOT ATTENDANT: I'm thinking I'll give him a ride on the ferry.

KOREMITSU: On the ferry?

PARKING LOT ATTENDANT: The ferry that crosses the big river. It's a river big as an ocean where once several hundred fingers were washed ashore from a neighboring country. Even with swollen, rotting fingers and the corpses and garbage drifting about in the river, if he just gives himself over to the trip, he'll free himself of the walls where he cringes and buries his voice. I thought he'd understand that. Doctor, my older brother is a fragile man, like a virgin. Did you see his white fingers? Did you hear his cramped, bird-like voice? Those things are stains of the city that fly away when he clings to a rusty deck and gulps down the river wind. Otherwise, how shall the blood-curdling, flesh-tingling juvenile classics make our hearts boil?

(In the distance, the siren sounds, ending lunchtime.)

KOREMITSU: Well, anyway *(to the* NURSE*)*, look after the underwear for him.

NURSE: Yes. *(Tries to take it.)*

PARKING LOT ATTENDANT: No. You people won't deliver it. You'll only wonder if there isn't something in them and even take out the rubber from the briefs—you would cut open even a tube of toothpaste with a knife—and in the end you'd deliver a discarded husk.

NURSE: Don't be rude.

KOREMITSU: Let's go.

PARKING LOT ATTENDANT: Doctor. *(Grabs him.)*

KOREMITSU: What? Why are you putting a hand on me?

PARKING LOT ATTENDANT: Please look closely at my face. My older brother looks like me, doesn't he? I'm the younger brother. When we were kids and I'd force my hand into the milk bottle and look at my hand and cry at how weird it looked, my brother would look at me and laugh. But now that hand has become my brother's face. Why? Doctor, why did my wrist look so weird then? And why does my brother act so strange now? It's because he is on the other side. On the inside of the glass bottle—behind the iron bars! And while we're here wasting time, that other side is gradually moving farther and farther away from us.

KOREMITSU: Hey, take it easy.

*(*KOREMITSU *pushes the* PARKING LOT ATTENDANT *away.)*

PARKING LOT ATTENDANT: If you don't believe me, throw me into the hospital for just as long as my brother has been here. And *(grasps a handful of sand)* I give my word to you on these smoothly crumbling playing cards of sand that, even while acting like my older brother, if you put your ear to my breast, you can hear the gong of the ferry crossing the river!

(Music. KOREMITSU *and the* NURSE *exit. The* PARKING LOT ATTENDANT *stands in silhouette. The sand spills from his hand. Sound of waves. Lights up on* KŌICHI. *He is writing in the sand a love letter he once wrote.)*

KŌICHI: My darling Aoi, how are you? I'm here at Izu; the wind has just died down. It's just the right time to continue my love letter to you that I once wrote in the sand. If my thoughts reach heaven, please put on Pat Boone's "Love Letters in the Sand," which we once listened to together, and read this my sweet letter to you.

(Sound of frothy waves. A woman—it is ROKUJŌ *herself—peeks out from behind the silhouette of the* PARKING LOT ATTENDANT. *It's as though she has emerged from his shadow.)*

WOMAN: Doctor.

KŌICHI: So it's you, isn't it, the one standing there.

WOMAN: I heard from Dr. Koremitsu that you were at the beach. . . . I won't stay long. I'll be going soon.

KŌICHI: And you'll call to me again from behind?

WOMAN: No, I probably won't be calling you again.

KŌICHI: Are you going away somewhere?

WOMAN: Yes. To a place where you'll be out of reach even if I tried to call you.

KŌICHI: Goodbye.

WOMAN: You even went to room number six, didn't you? Dr. Koremitsu told me. And also that you really have it in for me.

KŌICHI: Let's forget it. Haven't I said goodbye? I beg of you, won't you leave me alone? I'm just now writing a letter.

WOMAN: Yes, I know. I read it.

KŌICHI: I wasn't writing it to you. I. . . .

WOMAN: It's for Aoi, isn't it?

KŌICHI: That's right. I have to choose the right moment when the wind calms and write quickly.

WOMAN: But, now, with waves washing up, look, it's completely disappeared, hasn't it?

KŌICHI: Then I'll write it any number of times. Any number of times.

WOMAN: No, it's one time only for love letters written in the sand. High tide will be coming on.

KŌICHI: Now, you've made me forget what I was writing.

WOMAN: Doctor, look, I know I've been a big nuisance to you, but I've come here because it occurred to me that there was at least one thing I had to give back before we part.

KŌICHI: The tide is rising. Look there, the waves are as far as where I was sitting a while ago.

WOMAN: Yes, now the love letter you wrote in the sand, you can no longer see it.

KŌICHI: The wind has gotten stronger, hasn't it?

WOMAN: Doctor, no need to write love letters to heaven anymore. I'm
the one who had your pass and key, who was looking down that day
at that ditch of a river and was mistaken for your wife when I went to
your office. I'm right here.

KŌICHI: You're Rokujō.

WOMAN: Listen to my voice, close your eyes and listen to my voice,
because the thing I must give back to you is this very voice. My voice
that didn't answer when you called to me in that shrine of a sand hole
I was in. If you had heard it then, we might have gotten by without
taking this sort of roundabout route. But I knew that, unless I
worked twice as hard at it, the memory of that ant that you've forgotten and forsaken would never cut its way into your heart.

KŌICHI: All that is. . . .

WOMAN: Don't talk. Just be silent and look over there. My tongue is the
waves in the sea. It has completely licked away the love letter you
gave me. Now then, try closing your eyes slowly. It's like there's a big
lens above our heads, and sunshine is pouring through, like we're in
a big laboratory. That's right. That's the spirit. We'll be getting
smaller and smaller now, we'll enter the world of the microscope.

KŌICHI: *(Intending to kill her.)* You, you're Rokujō, Rokujō from room
number six! *(Grabs her by the neck, and pushes her down.)*

WOMAN: *(Turning the tables and getting on top of him.)* No, there's no room
number six here. No Rokujō here. We have to go slowly back home,
like this.

*(Throws a handful of sand. The two writhe about in the sand, and, as though
dragged into it, they disappear like ants going back into the sand.)*

Two Women (1979) was premiered by Seventh Sick Ward, which is led by actor Ishibashi Renji and actress Midori Mako. Veterans, they appeared in some of Shimizu's early successes. (Courtesy Kara Jūrō.)

Two Women: the beginning of the doctor's fatal entanglement. "Darling. . . . Don't you remember me?" the woman asks. Seventh Sick Ward, 1979. (Courtesy Kara Jūrō.)

The end of *Two Women* finds Kōichi, the woman's psychiatrist, caught in her net and dragged down into the sand. Seventh Sick Ward, 1979. (Courtesy Kara Jūrō.)

The woman in *Two Women* holds a round Japanese pear, whose peelings an ant circus of her fantasies will use for a boat. Ants working underground is a metaphor for the ultimate futility of New Left political activism. Seventh Sick Ward, 1979. (Courtesy Kara Jūrō.)

Satoh Makoto

SATOH MAKOTO (b. 1943) has long been the principal playwright and director of the important troupe Black Tent Theater 68/71 (Kokushoku tento roku-hachi nana-ichi). The BTT 68/71 grew out of earlier groups and underwent several name changes, achieving its present form by 1969 and acquiring its well-known Black Tent in 1970. The huge black tent, like Kara's smaller red one, is trucked about Japan, providing access to a variety of audiences. The most political in purpose and intellectual in approach of the major troupes to appear in the 1960s, BTT 68/71 specializes in leftist critiques of society and history, presented in a lively, often humorous fashion that skillfully exploits the troupe's considerable musical talents.

A native of Tokyo, Satoh attended Waseda University but left before graduating to attend the drama school of the Actors Theater (Haiyūza), which he completed in 1965. His career as a playwright began with the productions of *Ismene* in 1966 (under the direction of Kanze Hideo as the initial performance of the Free Theater, one of the precursors of BTT 68/71) and *My Beatles* (Atashi no Bītoruzu) in 1967 (directed by Suzuki Tadashi for the Waseda Little Theater). Satoh soon became active as a director, too, with his own production of *My Beatles* (1967), adaptations of O'Neill's *The Emperor Jones* (1967) and *The Hairy Ape* (1968), and a production of Megan Terry's *Viet Rock* (1968), all for the Free Theater. The first production in the Black Tent was *The Dance of Angels Who Burn Their Own Wings* (Tsubasa o moyasu tenshitachi no butō) (1970), directed by Satoh and coauthored by Satoh, Yamamoto Kiyokazu, Katō Tadashi, and Saitō Ren. For his revival of *Nezumi Kozō: The Rat* (Nezumi Kozō Jirokichi; lit., rat apprentice Jirokichi) (1969), Satoh was awarded the Kishida Prize for Playwriting in 1971. He had received the Kinokuniya Drama Award in 1970.

With a number of other remarkable plays, like the trilogy *The Comic World of Shōwa* (Kigeki Shōwa no sekai) (1975, 1976, 1979), Satoh the playwright was a key contributor to the new theater of the 1960s and 1970s; but in the 1980s, despite an occasional new play, he has become primarily a director. Satoh and the BTT 68/71 developed an interest in exploring the cultural heritage and social conditions of other Asian countries, leading to such distinctive achievements as their *Journey to the West* (Saiyūki) (1980), an inventive and musical staging of the Chinese classic, adapted and directed by Satoh.

INTRODUCTION

David G. Goodman

SATOH MAKOTO's *Ismene* was the playwright's first produced work and one of the plays in his maiden trilogy: *Hello, Hero! Three Episodes in the Unending Ending* (Harō Hīro! Owaranai owari ni tsuite no sanshō).[1] All three plays in *Hello, Hero!* are based on Sophocles' *Antigone*. *Ismene* retells the Antigone story from the point of view of the heroine's younger sister; *The Subway* (Chikatetsu) centers on Oedipus, Antigone's father; and *The Changing Room* (Hikaeshitsu) was originally conceived as a psychological portrait of Haemon, Antigone's fiancé.[2]

In *The Subway,* Satoh suggests that all men and women are passengers on a subterranean railway hurtling through a narrow tunnel in time. The train is piloted by Oedipus, "the tragic hero," who has been traveling the same route for three thousand years. Everyone assumes that he knows where he is going, but he is blind and in fact does not. The train is out of control, and not even the nuclear holocaust that envelops the world as the play ends can alter its course.

Tragedy is what Satoh means by "unending ending." For him, tragedy a dramatic form where nothing ever ends, where the ultimate purpose is not true resolution but the affirmation of the ineluctability of tragedy itself. Satoh's tragedians are attired in modern dress and drink Coca-Cola because *Hello, Hero!* is a meditation on tragedy in its modern, Hegelian form.

Satoh's purpose in *Hello, Hero!* is to reject modern, Hegelian tragedy and its conception of history. "The Hegelian and post-Hegelian idea of tragedy," Raymond Williams has written, "is inevitably concluded with the achievement of order through disorder, with tragic resolution as much as with tragic suffering, and thence with active and affirmed

meanings."³ But in *Hello, Hero!* Satoh argues that tragedy, which may
have made some sense in Sophocles' time and perhaps even in Hegel's,
is fatally dangerous today, when conflict promises not order out of disorder but extinction through nuclear war. Satoh is saying, in effect, that
we must find some other vehicle for the human adventure, that it is time
to find a driver with a clearer vision of where we are going.

The Changing Room suggests the alternative that Satoh has in mind.
The play is a monodrama about a gladiator preparing to enter the arena
to engage in a duel to the death. Isolated as he is, however, he is not
alone. He is engaged in a dialogue with a transcendent "presence" that
ordains his struggles and gives them meaning. By identifying and
engaging this unnamed "presence," Satoh believes, there may be a way
to disembark from the tragic vehicle of human history; indeed, that is
the major thrust of his subsequent plays.⁴

Ismene

Hello, Hero! commences with *Ismene*, which introduces two elements that
are more or less constant in Satoh's work and that help define it. The
first is the figure of the waiting woman. There is a sex-specific division
of labor in Satoh's plays. Men are committed to tragedy, and their
activity, even their revolutionary activity, ultimately reaffirms the status
quo: women act instinctively and offer the promise of transcendence.
Waiting women appear in most of Satoh's plays. Passive and patient,
they wait for someone to rescue them from the monotony of life. When
no one appears, they rebel, creating the fissure in time through which
authentic change might be introduced.⁵

The prototype of the waiting woman appears in *Ismene*. Ismene's
elder sister, Antigone, has been waiting patiently for something to happen: for Haemon to marry her, for peace to come, for life to take on
meaning. When none of these things happens, she takes matters into
her own hands and defies her uncle Creon's order to leave Polyneices'
body unburied on the field of battle. Her act does not produce the antic-
ipated effect, however. It is not what Ismene calls an "adventure": a
risk-free foray into the adult world. Antigone learns that actions have
consequences, and thus from her point of view the play concerns the difficult transition from the moratorium of childhood to the world of adult
responsibility.

Satoh's real focus of attention is Ismene, however, and from her point
of view the events taking place around her are arbitrary and bewilder-
ing. Ismene is too young to act; the best she can do is react to events set
in motion by her elders. When the play ends, despite the momentous
happenings that have radically reshaped her world, Ismene is left just as

she was at the outset, longing for salvation, "the dawn of a new day." The waiting women in Satoh's later plays are descendants of this adolescent Ismene.

Ismene is Satoh's alter ego. Underlying *Hello, Hero!* (and the rest of Satoh's work, for that matter) is the playwright's experience in the 1960 demonstrations against renewal of the U.S.-Japan Mutual Security Treaty. The treaty was objectionable because, by providing for American troops to be stationed on Japanese soil, it makes Japan complicit in American military and political policy. Satoh was born in 1943, and he participated in the demonstrations, the largest in postwar history, as a high school student. He was thus in much the same position as Ismene, for the course of his life was altered by events he had not initiated and over which he had no control. Like Ismene, Satoh would have liked to be able to say, "I did it!" but he was too young, and his convictions were as yet unformed.

Satoh's Ismene is thus an adolescent thrust into the adult world suddenly, unprepared, naive. It is a world characterized by Coca-Cola, pervaded by American influence, dominated by modernity, tragedy, and realpolitik.[6] Ismene has no taste for any of these things. She dreams only of some day escaping to "the next city," a utopian world free of death and longing.

Aiding and abetting her in this dream are Nobody A and Nobody B. They are the second element characteristic of Satoh's work that is introduced for the first time in *Ismene*. Mysterious characters like these appear in most of Satoh's plays. They promise to help the waiting woman fulfill her fantasy of escape and aid her in her quest for Utopia, but they ultimately betray her, diverting her from her dialogue with the transcendent presence in her life (the sun) and delivering nothing but death and disillusionment.[7]

As becomes apparent in Satoh's later work, these characters are numina, sinister manifestations of the Japanese pantheon. Even in *Ismene* there is the distinct implication that Nobody A and B are more than they seem and that they and their vending machine are somehow responsible for the war between Thebes and Argos. Satoh is not merely implying in orthodox Marxist fashion that war is the result of the exigencies of capitalism; nor is he simply denouncing American culture as a baleful influence on pristine Japanese tradition. On the contrary, as borne out by his later plays, Coca-Cola is just the latest device employed by the gods to ensnare the Japanese and preserve their hegemony over them.[8]

The trilogy *Hello, Hero!* is an excellent introduction to the drama of Satoh Makoto. The plays describe a world endangered by the threat of nuclear war but moving inevitably toward catastrophe because of its commitment to tragedy. As he makes clear in *The Changing Room,* Satoh sees mankind involved in a dialogue with a transcendent presence, and he sees a possible avenue of escape in this dialogue; but the dialogue is continually interrupted and sabotaged by autochthonous spirits, local deities, representatives of the Japanese pantheon like those who deliver death and disappointment to Ismene. What Satoh tries to do in his later work is describe and find some means to elude these deities so that the dialogue with the transcendent "presence" can fulfill its promise, the realization of the millennium.

Notes

1. This translation was originally completed in 1972 at the request of Duryea Smith of Alfred University. Smith was preparing an anthology of Antigone plays from around the world, and he approached me for a work from Japan. Sadly, he passed away before he could bring his plan to fruition. This translation is respectfully dedicated to Duryea Smith's memory in the hope that it will be at least a partial fulfillment of his dream.

2. Conversation with Satoh, 9 November 1980.

3. Raymond Williams, *Modern Tragedy* (Stanford, Calif.: Stanford University Press, 1966), 37.

4. I have analyzed Satoh's work at length in "Satoh Makoto and the Post-Shingeki Movement in Japanese Contemporary Theatre" (Ph.D. diss., Cornell University, 1982). For translations of three of Satoh's plays, see n. 4 of Takahashi's introduction to this volume.

5. Jenny the Prostitute in *Nezumi Kozō: The Rat* is an example of such a character. For a discussion of Jenny and a more complete analysis of the waiting woman, see David G. Goodman, ed., *After Apocalypse: Four Japanese Plays of Hiroshima and Nagasaki* (New York: Columbia University Press, 1986), 258–267.

6. Satoh has told me that he got the idea of using a Coca-Cola vending machine as the centerpiece for his play from a painting by Jasper Johns.

7. Heh-heh, So-so, and Bo-bo in *Nezumi Kozō: The Rat* and the Quartet in *My Beatles* are examples.

8. Thus, in *My Beatles,* the gods appear in the guise of a rock group; and, in *Nezumi Kozō,* the numina Heh-heh, So-so, and Bo-bo appear at the end of the play wearing blond wigs, chewing gum, and claiming that they are Santa Claus.

Satoh Makoto, leader of the Black Tent Theater from its inception until 1991. (Courtesy Black Tent.)

The Black Tent has been in use for more than twenty years. In 1991, the troupe's name was finally changed to, simply, Black Tent. (Courtesy Black Tent.)

Black Tent rehearsals. Satoh Makoto *(second from left)*; actor Saitō
Haruhiko, the new head from 1991 *(third from left)*. (Courtesy Black Tent.)

In *Abe Sada's Dog* (Abe Sada no inu; 1975), part 1 of Satoh Makoto's *Comic
World of Shōwa* trilogy, murderess Abe's idiosyncrasy contrasts with the social
conformity and moral paralysis speeding Japan down its fascist path. (Courtesy
Black Tent.)

Part 2 of Satoh's trilogy *Cinema and the Phantom* (Kinema to Kaijin; 1976) explores the mythology behind Japan's predatory behavior in Manchuria. *From left:* key Black Tent performers Shimizu Kōji, Saitō Haruhiko, and Arai Jun. (Courtesy Black Tent.)

Fantasy scene from the opening of *The Killing of Blanqui, Spring in Shanghai* (Buranki-goroshi, Shanhai no haru; 1979), the final link in Satoh's trilogy, which concerns Japanese militarism and the mindless brutality of revolutionary terrorism. (Courtesy Black Tent.)

Satoh's adaptation of the Chinese classic *Journey to the West* (1980). With the disintegration of New Left activism into factional violence in the 1970s, Black Tent turned to the Asian cultural heritage. (Courtesy Black Tent.)

Satoh Makoto's *Night and the Night's Night* (Yoru to yoru no yoru; 1981), a portrayal of contemporary Japanese youths, showcased Black Tent's musical and parodic skills. (Courtesy Black Tent.)

A 1990 production of *The Threepenny Opera* (Sanmon opera). Black Tent has specialized in Brecht's works. (Aoki Tsukasa, courtesy Black Tent.)

Ismene

Satoh Makoto

TRANSLATED BY DAVID G. GOODMAN

CAST OF CHARACTERS:

ISMENE	SOLDIER
ELDER SISTER	NOBODY A, *a Coca-Cola delivery man*
FATHER	NOBODY B, *a Coca-Cola delivery man*
MOTHER	BROTHER, *Polyneices' corpse*
UNCLE CREON	

(The Setting: A room much like the inside of a wood-frame warehouse: big, crude, empty. A Coca-Cola machine dominates the scene. The empties strewn around the room augment its overbearing presence with cacophonous silence.

There is a very large window beyond which, as if pasted to it, looms a depressing sky, an unchanging, stagnant yellow pall that obscures the hour. The sun cannot be detected.

There are doors, two of them. Door 1 leads outside, and Door 2 leads to the dank interior. There are appropriate pieces of furniture in no particular style. Things are in disarray.

The place: let's call it Thebes.

The curtain rises. ISMENE *is asleep with her head on the table, stage center. She looks as if she might have cried herself to sleep. She wears a white robe reminiscent of ancient times. It is a morning of uncertain promise.*

Beyond Door 2 a man and a woman are laughing. The man is trying to sing something, and the woman appears to be trying to stop him. They start laughing again, then stop abruptly.

ELDER SISTER *steals melodramatically through Door 1. She is wearing a long white robe like* ISMENE*'s, but hers is covered with stains. Even from a distance, it is obvious that the stains are blood. Her expression is fixed, a tragic mask. Keeping a sharp eye on the sleeping* ISMENE*, she glides stealthily to Door 2, cocks her ear, and listens. Silence. A long moment passes.*

All at once ELDER SISTER *relaxes. She saunters from Door 2 to the vending machine, produces a coin, and inserts it. The machine grunts, then vomits up that familiar dark-green bottle. Carelessly,* ELDER SISTER *removes the cap, then waltzes through Door 1, swallowing the contents greedily as she goes.*

   As if this were her cue, ISMENE *sits upright at the table with quick, well-defined movements.)*

ISMENE: *(As if speaking to the audience.)* Good morning! *(She rises and goes to the window. It is her intention "to have a talk with the sun.")* Hi! . . . How do you like that? *(She leans out the window.)* Where are you? *(She looks around.)* It's all right. Never mind. You needn't bother this morning. What's the difference anyway? You're here, and we have our little talk. You're not here, and we don't. So? What do you think? You don't care either way? I see. In the morning, when you've had a bad dream, tell your troubles to the sun. That's what Mom told me when I was little. Everybody does it. It's what you're supposed to do. Right? But for your sake, I decided to tell you only my good dreams. Tsk, what a mess! *(She begins picking up the bottles scattered on the floor.)* And you've been nice to me back. *(Puts a bottle to her eye as if it were a telescope.)* But this morning, when I really need you, you're not here. You're not anywhere. Merci beaucoup! *(She kneels to return the bottle to the floor and begins to sob without getting up.)*
(Door 2 opens. MOTHER *enters and, a few steps behind her,* FATHER. MOTHER *goes directly to the vending machine.* FATHER, *verifying each step with his cane, taps his way to the center of the room, where he seats himself.* FATHER *is blind.*

   In contrast to their daughters, MOTHER *and* FATHER *are attired in simple, modern dress: he wears a sweater and slacks, for instance, she a one-piece shift.*

   MOTHER *takes two bottles from the machine. She hands one to* FATHER *and drinks from the other herself.)*

MOTHER: What's the point? *(She gazes in the direction of Door 1, through which* ELDER SISTER *exited.)*

FATHER: Of what?

MOTHER: Oh, you know. . . .

   *(*FATHER *and* MOTHER *clutch each other in a firm embrace and kiss greedily. Pause.)*

MOTHER: *(Running her hands frantically over* FATHER's *body, to* ISMENE.*)* Will you please quit that bawling already!

ISMENE: *(Her head still buried in her hands.)* Aren't you even going to ask me why?

MOTHER: I couldn't care less. I'm just sick and tired of all these tears.

FATHER: Tears of sadness, you mean. For all we know, she could be weeping for joy. *(To* ISMENE.*)* You wash your face yet?

MOTHER: *(Her face buried in* FATHER's *lap.)* Tears of joy?

FATHER: For instance. *(He drinks cola.)*

MOTHER: *(Again to* ISMENE.*)* Well?

ISMENE: All right, if you say so.

MOTHER: All your crying won't bring back the dead. If tears could do that, don't you think I'd be crying my eyes out? What time is it, anyway?

ISMENE: I don't know. It's so overcast you can't see the sun

FATHER: It'll be nine soon.

MOTHER: Nine? No wonder I'm hungry. Is there anything to eat around here?

ISMENE: Maybe some leftovers from last night, unless somebody's eaten them.

MOTHER: Who, for instance? Your sister was out all night.

ISMENE: Were you awake?

MOTHER: Yes.

FATHER: Have you washed your face yet this morning?

ISMENE: No, Father.

FATHER: Then get to it. Even dogs wash their faces in the morning. They line up at the well with their tails wagging. *(He laughs as he remembers.)* Ever see them?

ISMENE: No, sir.

FATHER: Before I gouged out my eyes. . . .

MOTHER: *(To* ISMENE.*)* Where are the leftovers from last night?

ISMENE: In the pot. Shall I warm them for you?

MOTHER: Don't bother. Where? Oh, I see. Will you look at this mess? It's this damn war. The flower bed behind the fish market was wrecked completely. *(She carries the large pot to where* FATHER *is sitting.)* I wish you could have seen it, dear. It was the dearest little flower bed, filled with these precious yellow flowers. Now it's just so much mud. *(*ISMENE *takes dishes from the cupboard and helps her parents with their late breakfast.* MOTHER *sets the table, then sits opposite* FATHER. ISMENE *does not sit with them but stands alone near the window.)*

MOTHER: *(Dishing the thick soup-like substance onto plates.)* Is this all that's left?

ISMENE: There's still an apple if. . . .

MOTHER: No thanks. You and your half-rotten apples! Really good for nothing, aren't you? "Were you awake?" she wants to know! What kind of parents do you think we are? You'd have to be pretty callous to doze off with your own flesh and blood lying there dead in front of you!

FATHER: I slept all right. Maybe even a little better than usual.

*(*MOTHER *looks at* FATHER *but sips her soup without comment.)*

FATHER: *(To* ISMENE.*)* Is everything ready for the celebration?

ISMENE: *(Looking out the window.)* There are already a lot of people in the plaza, and the altar's ready, too. They'll be herding in the lambs any minute.

FATHER: I'll bet it'll be fun. It's been a long time since we've had anything to celebrate.

ISMENE: The end of a war, that's worth celebrating. Everyone's smiling, decked out in finery.

MOTHER: Let them celebrate. They like to dance, so let them dance. What do they care about Eteocles? Who was he to them?

ISMENE: The war's over, and that's all that matters. Last night, the armies of Argos retreated beyond the mountains. People won't have to spend their nights peeping through cracks in the city walls, watching enemy bonfires anymore. They're happy. That's all that matters to them.

MOTHER: Of course it is. The war is over. The war's gone off somewhere and taken poor Eteocles with it. Who am I to quarrel with the celebration?

FATHER: Hey, there's a chunk of salt in here! Ismene, did you make this?

ISMENE: No, sir.

MOTHER: You try to blame everything on someone else. It's a very unattractive habit. *(Peering into* FATHER*'s plate.)* Where?

FATHER: I ate it.

MOTHER: The whole chunk? It'll be the death of you, you know.

FATHER: That doesn't seem likely.

MOTHER: *(To* ISMENE.*)* From now on, be more careful. Do you understand?

ISMENE: Yes, Mother.

MOTHER: You and your sister are the only ones we have left. You have to learn to do your share.

ISMENE: Yes, ma'am.

FATHER: Let's go see Polyneices.

*(*ISMENE *and* MOTHER *look at* FATHER *in surprise.)*

FATHER: If we climb up the city walls, we should be able to see where they left him.

MOTHER: You must be joking! Have you forgotten the edict Creon issued last night?

FATHER: All Creon said was that no one was to touch Polyneices' corpse. I only want to go out where they left him.

MOTHER: Even so, if Creon finds out, he won't like it. Polyneices was a traitor. He turned his bow against the city of his forefathers and murdered his own brother, King Eteocles.

ISMENE: They were both my brothers, and they're both dead. If Polyneices was guilty of murder, so is Eteocles. Daddy, I'm trying to understand, but Uncle Creon's edict seems so unfair!

FATHER: A new king makes new laws. That's a king's job.

MOTHER: *(To* ISMENE.*)* Eteocles was king of Thebes. That king died by the hand of his brother, who had gone over to the enemy. Anybody can understand that. Polyneices is guilty; Eteocles was an upstanding. . . .

ISMENE: No, Mother, you're not being fair to Polyneices. After all, Eteocles has to share part of the blame for the war. It was Eteocles who failed to honor Daddy's decision to rotate the throne between his sons and refused to give Polyneices his turn. That's why Polyneices joined forces with Argos in the first place.

MOTHER: Enough of that. You're obviously incapable of. . . .

FATHER: They were both sissies.

ISMENE: *(Persistently.)* But only Eteocles is to get a proper burial. Only Eteocles is a martyr to his country's cause. Meanwhile Polyneices has been labeled a traitor and left to rot on the field of battle. Even his own family can't go near him. Before long he'll be food for the vultures. Could there be anything more awful? Daddy, is that what you call justice?

FATHER: The king must have his reasons. All we can do is obey the king's orders. That's just the way things are.

MOTHER: Ismene, try to understand how we feel.

FATHER: Let's go. We've been stuck in this house so long, I feel like I'm going to suffocate. Let's go some place quiet. Like that parapet overlooking the river. I'll bet you can smell the flowers there, just like before. We're worn out. It's about time we had a rest.

MOTHER: Yes, dear.

FATHER: We'll look down on the peaceful field, free from the sound of war and. . . . *(He chuckles.)* What matters is I'm still alive! So are you. We're entitled to a little relaxation.

*(*MOTHER *rises, places her empty bottle on the floor, and goes to the vending machine for another.)*

MOTHER: *(Pointing to the flock of empty bottles on the floor.)* Look how they've accumulated! Ismene, tidy up around here.

ISMENE: Yes, ma'am.

MOTHER: And while you're at it, try to find your sister. *(To* FATHER.*)* Shall we go, dear?

FATHER: Ready when you are.

*(*MOTHER *goes to Door 1 leading* FATHER *by the hand. They are both carrying cola bottles.)*

FATHER: *(Exiting.)* You can hear the music of the celebration!

MOTHER: We won't have a minute's peace all day.

(They both leave. ISMENE *sees her parents to the door.)*

ISMENE: *(Smiling.)* Now I've got all the rotten apples to myself!

*(*ISMENE *slams the door hard. Then, going to the box of apples, she indiscriminately chooses one and begins munching it noisily.)*

ISMENE: It's sweet. Not tart at all. *(To the apple.)* You stupid apple! Ah, who cares? I could eat a horse!

(She goes toward Door 2 as she chomps on the apple. She opens the door a crack and looks in.)

ISMENE: It's dark. You in there, Eteocles? No answer. Must be sleeping. You have a bad dream? Aren't you going to sing? Hey! Aren't you going to sing for me anymore? Get out of bed already! The weather stinks, but it's morning. Get up and say, "Morning everybody! What's for breakfast, the same lousy porridge?" Say it! Don't just lie there! Come on, say something! Anything! All right, if that's the way you want it. Go ahead and sleep. You can sleep forever for all I care. Here, a stupid apple for a stupid brother!

(She flings the apple inside and slams the door. She turns and looks at the bottles strewn on the floor.)

ISMENE: How's anybody supposed to clean up a mess like this?

(She picks up one of the bottles and blows on it. The bottle releases a low, unintelligent sound.)

ISMENE: Raise the gangplank! No one allowed on board! No one allowed! Haemon . . . I'm setting sail alone!

(The green bottles are the sea. In her white robe, ISMENE is the ship. Rolling gently, she sets sail. The horn sounds again.)

ISMENE: I'm off into the unknown. Off to somewhere far away. Off to the next city!

(ISMENE closes her eyes. The ship sails forward smoothly. ISMENE no longer blows on the bottle, but there is occasionally the sound of a ship's horn.

There is the sound of a truck coming to a halt. NOBODY A pokes his head in through Door 1.)

NOBODY A: Good morn. . . . *(Spying ISMENE, he signals to NOBODY B behind him. The two of them tiptoe swiftly toward her.)*

(All three are now on board, playing their well-loved game of "Let's Pretend.")

NOBODY A: Full port rudder!

NOBODY B: Full port rudder!

NOBODY A: Aye-aye, sir!

(ISMENE's ship heels to port.)

NOBODY A: A fine wind. Can't beat a wind like today's.

NOBODY B: Aye! A wind to carry us 'cross desert sands. *(He wets his finger and judges the direction of the wind.)* Seven minutes at this clip. We'll be in the next city before you can say "shiver me timbers"!

NOBODY A: Did you hear that, milady?

ISMENE: *(Eyes closed, affirmatively.)* Mm.

NOBODY B: You're alone, aren't you? Always alone. At this rate you'll never have a real. . . .

NOBODY A: Don't worry. Someday, she'll. . . . This is only a practice run. Thirty degrees to starboard!

NOBODY B: Thirty degrees to starboard!

NOBODY A: Aye-aye, sir!

NOBODY B: Someday she'll what?

ISMENE: Run away!

NOBODY B: Carrying a basket filled with bread and dried fruit. . . . But who will take your hand?

NOBODY A: Why, Haemon, of course!

ISMENE: *(Adamantly.)* No!

NOBODY A: You're not going alone?

NOBODY B: No!

ISMENE: Yes, I will!

NOBODY A: But what about your adventure? You haven't given up on your adventure, have you? That'd be terrible! *(To* NOBODY B.*)* Right?

NOBODY B: Terrible!

ISMENE: Ten degrees to starboard!

NOBODY B: Ten degrees to starboard!

ISMENE: Ahoy! Ahoy!

NOBODY A: We're already aboard ship, sailing across a sea of silver sand, the wind filling our sails! . . . *(Trying to excite her imagination.)* See?

ISMENE: Yes, thanks, but it's all right, really.

NOBODY B: But running away all by yourself? That's sad! Come on, take Haemon with you. We'll help.

NOBODY A: It's not like you.

ISMENE: Maybe. . . .

NOBODY A: Then?

NOBODY B: *(Abruptly.)* Well, here we are. All ashore who's going ashore!
   *(*ISMENE *opens her eyes, slowly, expectantly.)*

ISMENE: Darn!

NOBODY B: Hello!

NOBODY A: Haven't seen you for a while!

ISMENE: No.

NOBODY A: I guess we just weren't in the mood for sailing today. And today of all days!
   *(*ISMENE *cleans off the table.)*

ISMENE: Take a load off your feet. What's so special about today?

NOBODY B: Looks like it's our last.

ISMENE: Last? You quitting?

NOBODY A: In a manner of speaking. We really are going to the next city.

ISMENE: *(Indicating the vending machine.)* Want some?

NOBODY A: You kidding?

ISMENE: *(Offering* NOBODY B *a chair.)* You, too, have a seat.

NOBODY B: Thanks.

ISMENE: *(To* NOBODY A *and* B.*)* Tea as usual?
   (She begins to prepare the tea.)

NOBODY A: They're really whooping it up outside.

ISMENE: They're celebrating the end of the war.

NOBODY A: So I understand.

ISMENE: Why are you leaving?

NOBODY A: For a lot of reasons, I guess. But, you know. . . .

NOBODY B: *(Looking at the flock of empty bottles.)* Certainly have piled up, haven't they?

NOBODY A: Thanks to our devoted clientele. *(Whispering.)* Of course there are some people who shall remain nameless who wouldn't go near it.

ISMENE: I just don't care for it. Don't ask me why.

NOBODY A: I was only kidding. Never touch the stuff myself. Frankly, I don't know what people see in it.

ISMENE: People who do?

NOBODY A: Yes.

(They both laugh.)

ISMENE: It doesn't stop you from taking their money, though, does it?

NOBODY A: Business is business. *(To NOBODY B.)* Right?

NOBODY B: *(Distractedly.)* Right, yes.

NOBODY A: Hey, what's wrong? *(Suspiciously.)* Oh, I get it.

NOBODY B: Huh?

NOBODY A: I thought there was something funny going on! You've got your eye on our friend here, haven't you?

NOBODY B: Don't be ridiculous.

(The tea is ready. ISMENE brings it to the table with the sugar pot. There is a cup for her, too.)

NOBODY A: Thanks. By the way, my partner here thinks you're pretty special.

NOBODY B: Hey, cut it out!

ISMENE: Why, thank you very much.

NOBODY A: *(To NOBODY B.)* On the other hand, you know she's. . . .

ISMENE: Help yourself before it gets cold.

NOBODY B: Thanks. *(To NOBODY A.)* Pssst!

NOBODY A: What?

(NOBODY B signals to NOBODY A with his eyes. NOBODY A remembers something.)

NOBODY A: Oh, yeah, right! I almost forgot. We brought you a present. Somebody asked us to drop it off.

ISMENE: A present? What is it? Is it for me?

NOBODY A: Don't know exactly. We were just asked to bring it by.

ISMENE: Is it something I'd like?

NOBODY A: Couldn't say, actually. All we do is make deliveries. It's in the truck. Maybe we'd better. . . . Be back in a jiffy.

NOBODY B: Right away.

(NOBODY A *and* B *exit.* ISMENE *is left alone with her tea. After a few moments,* NOBODY A *and* B *enter carrying a large object wrapped in a sheet.*)

NOBODY A: Hey, watch where you're going! That's it. Okay.

ISMENE: My goodness, it's big, isn't it?

NOBODY A: Would you mind clearing a space over there, please?

ISMENE: Here?

NOBODY A: Yes.

(ISMENE *hurriedly clears the table.* NOBODY A *and* B *set the object down.*)

ISMENE: What could it be?

NOBODY A: Whatever it is, it's awful heavy. Well, perhaps we'd better get down to business. Bring in some cases, will you?

NOBODY B: Right-o!

(NOBODY B *exits.* NOBODY A *begins gathering the bottles scattered around the floor.*)

ISMENE: Do you think it would be all right to take a peek?

NOBODY A: (*As he works.*) What? Sure, why not?

(ISMENE *begins tentatively to loosen the ropes. Suddenly she is seized with foreboding and stops, but then she continues until all the ropes have fallen away. She hesitates, then removes the sheet.*

POLYNEICES' CORPSE *lies on the table attired in a common, olive-drab uniform.*

ISMENE *might want to scream, but she utters no sound.* NOBODY A *stops what he is doing and watches* ISMENE. NOBODY B *enters, carrying cases for the empties.*)

NOBODY B: Got the cases.

NOBODY A: (*Turning to* NOBODY B.) Let's go. We'll come back later.

NOBODY B: What's wrong?

NOBODY A: Never mind. Come on.

(NOBODY A *and* B *exit.* ISMENE *gazes vaguely at the corpse for a few moments.*)

ISMENE: (*Quietly.*) Why?

(*Realizing what this means, she hurriedly covers the corpse, then goes to Door 1 and peers outside. There's no one in sight, but she can't be too sure, so she goes first to the window and then, pointlessly, to Door 2. No one is there. No one is watching. Gradually, she begins to regain her composure. She approaches the corpse and peels the sheet back from the face. A kiss.*)

ISMENE: You're back. Finally. Do you have to keep your eyes shut so tight? It's dark and gloomy in here. But I guess it's too bright for you. You left while I was sleeping. When I woke up you were gone. Polyneices is home! But this time I'm awake, and you're the one who's sleeping. What a strange game of hide-and-go-seek!

(*She fetches a towel and wipes the blood from the corpse's forehead.*)

ISMENE: All I can do is wipe the blood from your forehead. You really used to love me. But you weren't the only one. You know that. Eteocles used to love me, too, and now he's in the other room, grown stiff just like you. Eteocles used to love me, too. Why should two people who loved the same. . . . How could it happen? Why did you have to become enemies and kill each other? Or . . . or was it all a lie? Every night you'd whisper, "Sweet dreams," and kiss me. Were those kisses only lies? And what about the armloads of daisies? You picked so many you could hardly carry them! Were they lies, too? Who needs a brother, anyway? Who needs brothers who can't answer, who can't cry? I hate you! . . . Here, have an apple.

(She brings an apple and places it gently next to POLYNEICES' *head. After a few moments, she carefully pulls the sheet back over his face.)*

ISMENE: I have to hide you. . . .

(She looks toward Door 2 and tries to drag the table toward it. It won't budge.)

ISMENE: I can't do it alone.

(A SOLDIER *opens Door 1 and enters without making a sound. He is wearing the same threadbare uniform as the corpse. On his head is a wreath of flowers.)*

SOLDIER: Ahem. . . .

*(*ISMENE *is startled and confused.)*

ISMENE: *(Finally managing to speak.)* Can I help you?

SOLDIER: A Coke?

ISMENE: *(Trying to make the corpse as inconspicuous as possible.)* The machine's over there.

SOLDIER: Thank you.

(The SOLDIER *is in no hurry as he moves to the machine.)*

SOLDIER: *(Inserting a coin.)* Aren't you going to the celebration?

ISMENE: No. . . .

SOLDIER: *(Pretending he has just noticed where he is.)* No, of course not. Terrible what happened, terrible! Please accept my condolences.

ISMENE: Thank you.

SOLDIER: His death was glorious, though, glorious! Nearby at the time, I was. Saw the whole thing. Both of them fought magnificently, magnificently! *(He drinks cola.)*

ISMENE: Are you on duty?

SOLDIER: Hm?

ISMENE: Today. . . .

SOLDIER: Oh, yes. Crowd control, that sort of thing, you know.

ISMENE: You must have your hands full.

SOLDIER: No! Listen, I'd choose this detail over battle any day. I know how that must sound, but guys like me, we're just not cut out for being magnificent or glorious. Strolling around, patrolling a festival or two, believe me. . . .

ISMENE: Everyone feels the same way, I'm sure.

SOLDIER: Maybe, maybe not. Must be different for those with reasons.

ISMENE: Reasons?

SOLDIER: For fighting, you know.

ISMENE: Reasons. . . .

SOLDIER: Sure! You've got to fight when you've got a reason. I mean, what choice do you have? That's just the way things are. The problem's with us, called up to serve, not knowing what we're fighting for.

(ISMENE is silent.)

SOLDIER: Well, I'd better be getting back. You mind if I take the bottle with me?

ISMENE: No, go ahead.

(ELDER SISTER enters through Door 1 as the SOLDIER is leaving. ISMENE is startled but relaxes when she recognizes her sister. ELDER SISTER is dressed in the same white garment as before. She carries an empty cola bottle in her hand.)

SOLDIER: Well, thanks for the drink. *(He salutes ELDER SISTER and exits.)*

(ELDER SISTER pauses until the SOLDIER has left.)

ELDER SISTER: *(Nonchalantly.)* It came, huh?

(She gives the corpse a passing glance, then proceeds to the vending machine for a fresh bottle.)

ISMENE: Then you? . . .

ELDER SISTER: The boys delivered it, did they? Who was that just now?

ISMENE: He just wanted a Coke. Said he's policing the celebration.

ELDER SISTER: I see.

ISMENE: *(Indicating the corpse.)* You? . . .

ELDER SISTER: Yes.

ISMENE: Why?

ELDER SISTER: I couldn't very well manage it all alone. I went out while it was still dark and tried, but it was all I could do to drag him to the foot of the city walls. They happened by, so I asked them to bring the body here.

ISMENE: But why?

ELDER SISTER: What do you mean why?

ISMENE: You heard, didn't you?

ELDER SISTER: You mean about Creon's edict?

ISMENE: Yes.

ELDER SISTER: That cretin! This king business has gone to his head.

ISMENE: Even so. . . .

ELDER SISTER: Arrived in one piece, though, eh? I was afraid the legs were going to come off.

(ELDER SISTER goes to the table and unceremoniously yanks the sheet off the corpse. She notices the apple.)

ELDER SISTER: What's this?

(She throws the apple on the floor. ISMENE *picks it up.)*

ISMENE: Are you out of your mind? Do you know the penalty for what you've done?

ELDER SISTER: Death by stoning? *(Laughs.)* I hardly think our spineless uncle's up to that, do you? But if that's what he wants, so be it.

ISMENE: He's the king. Uncle Creon's king now. Maybe he's. . . .

ELDER SISTER: Yes, maybe.

ISMENE: He can do anything he wants.

ELDER SISTER: I suppose he can.

ISMENE: I know how you feel. I think the edict Uncle Creon issued last night is unjust. But still. . . .

ELDER SISTER: That's not the point. I only. . . .

ISMENE: You only what?

ELDER SISTER: I just got this urge, that's all.

ISMENE: Urge? But. . . .

ELDER SISTER: I admit it's strange, crazy even. But what can I tell you? I heard the edict last night, and all of a sudden—I don't know—all of a sudden I had to resist. Before I knew it I'd made up my mind.

ISMENE: How could you!

*(ELDER SISTER *does not answer. She drinks from her bottle.)*

ISMENE: What are you going to do? What are you going to do when Uncle Creon finds out and comes to get you?

*(ELDER SISTER *does not respond but continues to drink her Coke.)*

ISMENE: You're not the only one, you know. Mom and Dad will suffer, too. And what about? . . .

ELDER SISTER: You? That's what you're really worried about, isn't it?

ISMENE: *(Indignantly.)* I am not!

ELDER SISTER: There's nothing to be ashamed of. You have to look out for your own interests. But don't worry. I'll take full responsibility. After all, this is none of your affair.

ISMENE: I'm not thinking of myself! You just don't understand!

ELDER SISTER: I don't understand? What don't I understand?

ISMENE: That's not it at all!

ELDER SISTER: You're right, I don't understand.

ISMENE: What are you going to do?

*(ISMENE *covers the corpse as she speaks.)*

ISMENE: *(Repeating.)* What are you going to do?

ELDER SISTER: About what?

ISMENE: You know.

ELDER SISTER: Haemon?

ISMENE: Yes, Haemon. If anything should happen to you . . . if you're arrested and sentenced to death, he'll go out of his mind, I know it!

ELDER SISTER: Maybe you're right, but what can I do? He's my fiancé, and . . . and, I love him. Yes, now I can say it out loud. I love him. But that's beside the point.

ISMENE: Beside the point?

ELDER SISTER: Yes, beside the point.

ISMENE: You're not making any. . . .

ELDER SISTER: Haemon likes to talk about the life we'll have together: peaceful afternoons when we'll sit quietly and sip tea, enjoying each other's company. Haemon says he wants to start a ranch. Did you know he writes poetry?

ISMENE: Poetry?

ELDER SISTER: Yes, he carries a little blue notebook, and every so often he writes something down in it. He showed it to me once. They're short poems, mostly about the stars. There's a tiny little window in his room. He says he spends a lot of time there at night, gazing at the stars. The day the war started, we spent the whole night together up there in his room. It was the first time. We didn't sleep a wink. Haemon described the constellations to me one by one and told me all kinds of things. He said that when he's got his ranch started, he wants to build us a little house with the same tiny window in the attic. Every night we'll go up there, and he'll talk to me and write poetry. Sounds wonderful, doesn't it?

ISMENE: Yes.

ELDER SISTER: Of course I'd like to wait for Haemon. I'd like to wait until he's built his ranch and come to fetch me. I'd like to wait forever.

ISMENE: So?

ELDER SISTER: So I could wait. That's what bothers me. I want to wait for him, and I hate myself for it. The day Haemon left for the war, he came by in his uniform and asked me to wait for him until he got back. I felt . . . I felt depressed and sad, but I said yes, I'd wait for him, and I tried to sound as enthusiastic as I could. Then he laughed and said good-bye and went off to war. He might have been killed, but he didn't seem to mind and went confidently off with the others. Haemon the poet, Haemon the astronomer, that's the man I . . . that's the Haemon I know. But there's another Haemon, isn't there? Haemon the man, gallant in his uniform, the image of the warrior. There are two Haemons. But there's only one me, the one he knows: the woman who waits. Quiet, persevering, small, and happy. That's why I. . . .

ISMENE: Yes?

ELDER SISTER: Maybe there are other reasons, but that's what I was thinking at the time.

ISMENE: I don't understand.

ELDER SISTER: It doesn't matter. I'm not sure I understand myself.

ISMENE: But. . . . (*Reconsidering.*) I suppose what's done is done.

ELDER SISTER: What about you?

ISMENE: Me? Polyneices' corpse is already here! It's always been this way, ever since we were little. You'd stride off ahead and call me from the most unexpected places. I'd have to run to catch up, and by the time I got there, you'd already be gone.

ELDER SISTER: This time I won't be calling you. I'm on my own now. That's the way I want it.

ISMENE: What now?

ELDER SISTER: I'm going to wash and prepare Polyneices' body for burial.

ISMENE: And then?

ELDER SISTER: I'll place it next to Eteocles and give them both a proper funeral.

ISMENE: And then?

ELDER SISTER: Then I'll bury them together in the family plot.

ISMENE: But what if Uncle Creon finds out? He's sure to hear before you have a chance to bury Polyneices.

ELDER SISTER: Let him. I'll figure out something. I'll tell him I'm only doing what's right, or that I acted out of obedience to the law of the gods, not the law of the king. Something like that. In any case, I'll do what I can before he realizes what's happened.

ISMENE: I see.

ELDER SISTER: Maybe I'm hoping he'll kill me, kill me in the most gruesome way. It would prove what I did had some meaning, wouldn't it? You see what I mean? Then it wouldn't just be something I concocted on impulse, for no particular reason. That's it! Maybe then the crowd cavorting down there in the plaza would understand that the war isn't over, that it will never be over, that there's just a new king who's started a new war. Maybe they'll wake up. How about that? That's not a bad way of looking at it, is it?

(*Door 1 bursts open, and* MOTHER *enters, followed by* FATHER. *They both carry empty Coke bottles.*)

FATHER: You just overlooked him, that's all. You just couldn't see from there.

MOTHER: I'm the one who brought him into this world. I should know my own son!

(MOTHER *sets her empty bottle on the floor and automatically goes to buy another.*)

MOTHER: (*To* ISMENE *and* ELDER SISTER.) He's gone. Polyneices's disappeared.

(ISMENE *and* ELDER SISTER *exchange glances.*)

FATHER: Get me one too.

(FATHER *hands his empty bottle to* MOTHER, *goes to the table, and sits down.* MOTHER *extracts a new bottle from the machine and hands it to her husband.*)

FATHER: *(Half to himself.)* Strange, isn't it? The way this stuff grows on you. *(He takes a drink.)* Before you know it, you can't do without it.

MOTHER: What could have happened to him? I'm sure he was out by that black tree last night.

FATHER: You didn't go out there?

MOTHER: *(Apologetically.)* Oh, it was before Creon issued his edict, you see, and I, well . . . I never imagined anything this awful was going to happen. Polyneices' corpse up and vanishing! And after Creon issued that edict, too!

ELDER SISTER: Don't worry. Polyneices' body hasn't disappeared.

MOTHER: Don't try and tell me, I just saw with my own two eyes. . . .

ELDER SISTER: He's here.

FATHER: Here?

(ELDER SISTER *removes the sheet from the corpse.* FATHER *examines it with his hands.*)

MOTHER: Then it *was* you!

ELDER SISTER: What's that supposed to mean?

MOTHER: *(Taking a swig of her Coke.)* I knew it! But really, I didn't think . . . I was watching you through a crack in the door before, when you waltzed in here covered with blood, and the thought occurred to me, you know, that we'd really be in for it if you'd gone and done something foolish, but. . . .

FATHER: Why'd you do it?

ELDER SISTER: I don't know.

FATHER: You understand what this means, don't you?

(ELDER SISTER *does not answer. Her attitude is openly contemptuous.* ISMENE *is standing a little apart from the others.* MOTHER *approaches the corpse but stops short.*)

MOTHER: This is the last straw! It's the end of everything! We're done for this time! It's all over for us!

ISMENE: Mother. . . .

(ISMENE *goes to support her* MOTHER *but is rebuffed.*)

FATHER: *(Forcefully.)* Why?

ELDER SISTER: I told you, I don't know.

MOTHER: But you . . . you're the one who. . . . It's just not like you. You were always Mommy's good little girl. Now you go and do a thing like this. Heaven knows. . . .

ELDER SISTER: I knew what I was doing. I knew well enough.

MOTHER: But you've got your whole life ahead of you! Your father and I don't really matter, our best years are behind us. But you! Just when you were about to marry Haemon. And now Haemon's going to be the next king of Thebes! What could you have been thinking? You're, why, you're the next queen! You could have been the queen of Thebes, just as I was.

ELDER SISTER: Easy come, easy go.

(FATHER *rises slowly and slaps* ELDER SISTER *without a word.*)

ISMENE: Daddy!

FATHER: *(Grumbling.)* Going to get herself killed, the fool!

ELDER SISTER: Yes, it was a foolish thing to do, a foolish, selfish thing to do. I'm not calculating like you, Father.

MOTHER: Don't speak that way to your father! What's gotten into you today?

ISMENE: *(To* ELDER SISTER.*)* Daddy has his own way of thinking about things, too. You can understand. . . .

ELDER SISTER: That's not the point. Father, you were once king of Thebes. And not any ordinary king, either. You solved the riddle of the Sphinx and saved the city from the plague. You acceded to the throne because the people universally acclaimed you king. But then, albeit unknowingly, you committed the sin of incest by wedding your own mother and were cursed by the prophet. It would have been better if you'd taken your own life right there and then. You should have atoned for your sin with a swift, clean thrust of your sword. But no, you had to live on in shame and blindness. And what's worse, each day you roam the streets of Thebes, this city you once ruled, a wretched beggar, led by Mother, the witness of your sin. You say all you want to do is live. All you want to do is affirm life by continuing to love Mother. Well, it makes me sick!

FATHER: It's my way of doing penance.

ELDER SISTER: No, it's your cowardice!

MOTHER: How dare you!

FATHER: It's all right, leave her alone. Perhaps you haven't noticed, but this isn't the first time she's spoken of me this way. And besides, I'm used to it. People stone me and set their dogs on me. What's a little criticism from my own flesh and blood compared to the way people treat me in the street every waking day?

ISMENE: Daddy. . . .

FATHER: So you've taken it on yourself to defy Creon's edict in my place and brought your brother's corpse here. Your kindness overwhelms me.

ELDER SISTER: I did it because I wanted to, that's all.

FATHER: Very interesting. *(He drinks Coke.)* I thought you were smarter than that.

MOTHER: But listen, dear, don't you think you should reconsider? It's not that I don't understand how you feel, after all you're still very young. When you've made up your mind to do something, you want to see it through, but even so. . . .

ELDER SISTER: If there's any meaning at all in what I've done, it's simple respect for the dead and my desire to protect the honor of this family. I don't see how I can be faulted for that.

MOTHER: You're right, of course, but. . . .

FATHER: Don't talk to me about honor! You acted out of selfishness, you just said so yourself.

ELDER SISTER: I said that honor was the only meaning my act had if it has any meaning at all.

FATHER: And it doesn't.

ELDER SISTER: Even if I die for it?

FATHER: You bet! You think defying death is a big deal, that it takes courage, that you can prove something by dying. But there's another way to prove something, and that's by fearing death, by running from it, by surviving. That's perfectly normal human behavior, too. It's the way I feel. It's better to live than to die. I want to live.

ISMENE: She doesn't want to die; she's just saying if worst comes to worst. . . .

FATHER: Yes, you're probably right, but I sense something. . . .

(ISMENE *looks questioningly at her father.*)

FATHER: Haste. I sense her trying to tie all the loose ends of her emotions to her death, trying to take care of everything she can't understand with one decisive act.

ELDER SISTER: Your own guilty conscience makes you hypersensitive, doesn't it?

FATHER: Yes, and you just love raking the muck of my life, don't you? You're disgusting. (*He laughs sarcastically.*)

ELDER SISTER: Go ahead and laugh. It's a good way to evade the truth.

MOTHER: Dear, won't you reconsider . . . wouldn't you like to take the body back where it came from before anybody notices it's missing?

ELDER SISTER: No.

MOTHER: But listen, dear. Will you listen to me? For my sake, then, won't you? . . .

ELDER SISTER: Please, Mother. You and Father and Ismene go in the other room with Eteocles. I'll stay here, and. . . . If someone comes you'll be implicated. Please go in the other room. I want to be alone.

MOTHER: It's not that easy, darling.

FATHER: (*Drinking.*) Ah, that really hits the spot! Never mind, we'll go.

MOTHER: But dear. . . .

FATHER: (*Mimicking.*) But dear. . . . (*To* ISMENE.) Come on, you too.

ISMENE: I'll stay and help.

FATHER: As you wish. But I'm going.

(FATHER *gets to his feet. He takes two or three steps toward Door 2 but falters.* MOTHER *hurries to his aid. Carrying their bottles of Coca-Cola, the two exit together.*

For a few moments ISMENE *and* ELDER SISTER *stare in silence at the door through which their parents have gone.*)

ISMENE: Maybe you're right.

ELDER SISTER: Do you think so?

ISMENE: Everyone thinks they'll have an adventure sometime, but when the time comes. . . . Maybe that's what I've been doing, maybe I've been waiting, too. I just haven't been able to find the right moment, that's all. The way things are going, the right moment may never come. I've got a feeling.

ELDER SISTER: Do you suppose this is an adventure?

ISMENE: What a strange. . . .

ELDER SISTER: Not so strange. Suppose . . . I mean, does something have to be right to be an adventure?

ISMENE: Of course it has to be right. An adventure has to be right and true.

ELDER SISTER: Oh. . . .

ISMENE: *(Referring to the corpse.)* Let's begin. There isn't much time.

ELDER SISTER: You're right.

ISMENE: First we'll wipe the blood away and then perfume the body.

(As the girls are about to set to work, there is a knock at Door 1. They stand motionless and listen. There is more knocking, this time louder and more persistent than before. ISMENE *rushes to cover the corpse.*)

ISMENE: Come in.

(UNCLE *enters. He is a peasant type: suntanned, sturdily built, rustic. He looks as if he might be slightly older than* FATHER *and is obviously uncomfortable in his three-piece suit. He carries a small bunch of yellow posies.*)

ELDER SISTER: Uncle Creon!

(UNCLE *does not return the salutation but goes to the vending machine and removes a bottle. He drinks and sits down near the table.* ISMENE *and* ELDER SISTER *do not move.*)

UNCLE: *(Having drunk half the bottle's contents.)* Morning! Sleep well last night?

ISMENE: Very well, thank you.

UNCLE: Good, good. Where are your mother and father this morning?

(ISMENE *indicates Door 2.*)

UNCLE: Never mind, you don't have to call them just now. *(He takes another drink.)*

(Pause. Door 1 bursts open without warning, and the SOLDIER *enters. Noticing* UNCLE, *he does not venture in further but stands at the door, fidgeting.*)

ISMENE: Can I do something for you?

SOLDIER: *(Hoarsely.)* Yes . . . I mean no.

UNCLE: *(Handing the flowers to* ELDER SISTER.*)* Oh, I almost forgot. They're from the owner of the fish market on the corner. You can give them to your mother later. *(Casually indicating the object on the table.)* What's this?

UNCLE: *(Repeating, deliberately.)* What is this?

ISMENE: *(In a whisper.)* Eteocles.

UNCLE: What?

ISMENE: It's Eteocles.

UNCLE: Ah, I see. *(He stands and is about to pull back the sheet but stops.)*

SOLDIER: *(Uneasily.)* Ahem. . . .

UNCLE: *(To* ISMENE.*)* Maybe it would be best if your parents were here. *(Indicating Door 2.)* Call them, will you?

*(*ISMENE *walks mechanically to Door 2, but before she arrives, it is opened from within.* FATHER *enters, followed by* MOTHER, *who carries a bottle of cola.)*

UNCLE: Good morning!

FATHER: Ah, your majesty, shining glory of Thebes, protector of our fair city, welcome to our humble abode. *(He bows obsequiously.)*

UNCLE: Come on, cut it out! *(To the* SOLDIER.*)* At ease.

MOTHER: *(Brightly.)* It's so nice of you to come! Please do sit down. Ismene, don't just stand there, bring your uncle a cup of tea!

*(*ISMENE *prepares the tea without a word, but she is still preoccupied with* POLYNEICES' CORPSE.*)*

UNCLE: *(To* MOTHER.*)* Please, don't go to any trouble.

FATHER: Have you met with the elders yet? They've got most things pretty well figured out. You'd be wise to consult them often.

UNCLE: Yes, of course.

FATHER: I'm looking forward to a display of our new king's political acumen.

UNCLE: Do I really have to be king?

FATHER: Now what's wrong? Both of my sons are dead, so my closest male relative succeeds to the throne. That's you.

UNCLE: But I'm satisfied running my vineyard. Of course if some morning I were called to defend my city, I wouldn't hesitate. I'd be ready to give my life at a moment's notice, that goes without saying, but soldiering's one thing, and being king's something else. I'm just not cut out . . . I mean, I don't have the qualifications to be king. You know that better than anybody.

FATHER: Don't worry, everything's going to work out fine.

ELDER SISTER: *(To* MOTHER.*)* Uncle brought you these.

MOTHER: How nice! Thank you. What a lovely scent. Ismene, put them in some water, and set them on the table.

(ISMENE *does as she is told.*)

FATHER: We need a ruler. Somebody has to be king.

UNCLE: It frightens me, that's all. I was happy living with the missis and our Haemon and watching the grapes ripen on the vine.

FATHER: Everyone has their little happiness. The feeling of waking bright and fresh in the morning; the striped cat that crawls into bed with you; the baby that has just learned to say its name. To the fellow at the fish market, it's that little flower patch in his backyard. But who's going to protect him from the people who trample his flowers, who don't respect his picket fence? Happiness may grow in the warmth of people's hands, but it's fragile. They can't defend it or themselves.

UNCLE: Yes, I understand that. (*Simply, awkwardly.*) The king defends the people and their happiness. (*He drinks cola.*)

FATHER: That's right.

UNCLE: You heard my edict?

FATHER: Yes, it was perfect.

UNCLE: I did just as you said.

(ISMENE, ELDER SISTER, *and* MOTHER *all stop in their tracks and stare at* FATHER *and* UNCLE. *They are shocked to learn that* FATHER *is responsible for the edict.*)

UNCLE: (*As if reading from a document.*) "The corpse of Polyneices shall be left on the open plain. No one, be he even of the dead man's flesh, shall lay a hand on it. Anyone defying this order shall be put to death by stoning." To be perfectly frank, I don't understand it.

FATHER: You will.

ISMENE: Then, Daddy, you. . . .

FATHER: No. The edict is Creon's.

ISMENE: But. . . .

UNCLE: (*Hastily.*) Ismene, it's just as your father says. The responsibility for that edict is mine. He just gave me the benefit of his knowledge and experience. I suppose you think I'm cruel, and you're probably right. It's a despicable edict. But that seems to be the business of kings.

SOLDIER: (*To* UNCLE.) Ahem. . . .

UNCLE: I know. I know.

FATHER: What is it?

UNCLE: Nothing, really. It's nothing important, believe me. He just likes to pester me, that's all.

ELDER SISTER: (*Deliberately.*) Uncle, was this just a social call this morning?

UNCLE: Eh? Well, as a matter of fact . . . but it doesn't matter. (*To the* SOLDIER.) Let's go.

SOLDIER: But. . . .

ELDER SISTER: Why did you come?

MOTHER: *(Sensing* ELDER SISTER*'s purpose.)* No!

UNCLE: Nothing, really. This fellow got a crazy idea into his head, that's all.

*(*ISMENE *has silently moved to the table and now whisks away the sheet covering the corpse.)*

ISMENE: Is this the crazy idea?

FATHER AND MOTHER: *(Together.)* Ismene!

*(*UNCLE *closes his eyes for an instant, then with an air of deep regret looks first at the corpse, then at* ISMENE. *He then goes to the* SOLDIER *and counts out several gold pieces from the purse in his breast pocket. Clutching his reward, the* SOLDIER *bolts through the door.)*

ISMENE: This is Polyneices' corpse. You said you'd execute anyone who touched it.

UNCLE: I can see who it is.

ISMENE: *(Fervently.)* Your edict of last night was wrong, Uncle. Polyneices may have been a rebel who betrayed his country, but it is no justice to villainize the defenseless dead and profane their remains. That's why, even if you. . . .

UNCLE: *(Interrupting.)* I know, I know. *(Turning to* FATHER.) What am I going to do?

*(*FATHER *is silent.)*

ISMENE: Even if you threaten me with death, I. . . .

UNCLE: *(Desperately.)* Tell me what to do!

*(*FATHER *still does not respond.)*

ISMENE: Uncle. . . .

UNCLE: That's enough, Ismene. I get the point. *(To* FATHER.) I can't go through with it. I'm just not cut out to be king. You be king again. That's the best way. You could. . . .

FATHER: *(Softly.)* If I could, I would, believe me. I'd give almost anything to regain power in Thebes. But there's not much hope of that. No one would follow me. I've lost my charisma. The people despise me.

UNCLE: *(To* ISMENE.) Personally, I think you did the right thing. The edict was a mistake. . . .

ELDER SISTER: Not so fast. The king's word is law. And those who break the law must be punished.

UNCLE: *(With intensity.)* Why?

ELDER SISTER: Ismene didn't do anything. She's lying. I brought the corpse here. Mother and Father know the truth.

UNCLE: You? *(To* MOTHER.) Is it true?

*(*MOTHER *does not answer.)*

FATHER: *(Answering in* MOTHER*'s place.)* Yes.

ELDER SISTER: *(To* ISMENE.*)* Thank you, Ismene. But now I understand. What I really wanted was to rebel, to rebel against the king.

UNCLE: *(Shocked.)* Rebel? Against me?

ELDER SISTER: Against the edict you gave.

UNCLE: *(Without thinking.)* But it wasn't my   *(He looks at* FATHER.*)*

(Unaware of UNCLE*'s gaze,* FATHER *goes to* MOTHER *and puts his arm around her shoulder.)*

UNCLE: What have I done? Ismene!

*(*ISMENE *is silent. She continues to stare at* UNCLE.*)*

FATHER: You issued the edict. Now you have to pass judgment.

ISMENE: *(At last, in a voice hardly audible.)* I did it. . . .

UNCLE: *(To* ELDER SISTER.*)* What have you done!

*(*ELDER SISTER *is silent.)*

UNCLE: *(To* MOTHER.*)* What do you expect me to do?

*(*MOTHER, *too, is silent. Several moments pass.)*

UNCLE: *(Struggling to control his emotions, to* FATHER.*)* You bastard! . . .

*(*FATHER *does not respond. Long pause.)*

UNCLE: All right, now I see. It's a plot to get me to. . . . You want me to suffer as you have suffered.

FATHER: No.

UNCLE: Oh, shut up! I . . . I didn't know what I was doing! . . . Damn! How could I get myself into this mess?

*(*UNCLE *is shaking with rage. He swallows some Coke to settle his nerves, but it doesn't help.)*

ELDER SISTER: Do whatever you think is best. I'm prepared for the worst.

ISMENE: Uncle, please. . . .

UNCLE: All right!

ISMENE: *(Hopefully.)* Then?

UNCLE: I will judge.

ISMENE: Then please. . . .

UNCLE: I said I will judge. I will pass judgment here and now.

(There is a long silence. UNCLE *collects his thoughts.* FATHER *continues to fondle* MOTHER. ISMENE *and* ELDER SISTER *stand, watching* UNCLE. UNCLE *takes one of the yellow flowers from the bouquet on the table and begins pacing back and forth in the middle of the room, his gaze fixed on the floor, avoiding the others' eyes. Then. . . .)*

UNCLE: All right. *(There is a new, ominous tone in his voice, betraying his effort to control his emotions and think clearly.)* The problem before us is to decide what measures are to be taken. Are you ready to hear our judgment?

ELDER SISTER: *(With studied composure.)* Yes.

UNCLE: First, Polyneices' body shall be returned to the place from which it was taken. He chose his grave when he betrayed his country. As for you. . . .

ISMENE: Uncle. . . .

UNCLE: We hereby banish you and your father from our city.

ELDER SISTER: (*Spontaneously.*) Banishment? With Father?

UNCLE: Yes, banishment. (*He laughs. It is a queer, empty laugh.*) Does that surprise you? I thought you were prepared for anything.

ELDER SISTER: But. . . .

UNCLE: (*Laughing loudly.*) You didn't actually think I'd sentence you to death, did you? No, that would be playing into your hands. My purpose is to punish you, not put the finishing touches on your scheme.

ELDER SISTER: But you're subverting your own edict. You said that anyone who touched Polyneices' corpse would be stoned to death.

UNCLE: I'm the one who issued that edict, not you or your father. I issued it, and I can change it. I don't see anything wrong with that.

ELDER SISTER: But why? Why banish Father too?

UNCLE: (*Laughing.*) No reason, really. Maybe I just feel like rebelling myself. Unlike you, though, I am king. I can explain my actions any way I like. For example: your father has polluted our city; we expelled him to protect our subjects. How about that? (*He laughs.*)

ELDER SISTER: But. . . .

UNCLE: I'm not going to say it again. You take your father and leave the city before anyone catches on.

MOTHER: (*To* FATHER.) The city . . . he says you have to leave the city. The two of you.

UNCLE: That's right. I want them both out of Thebes.

FATHER: (*Moving away from* MOTHER.) Creon. . . .

UNCLE: Yes?

FATHER: Me too? Do I have to go, too?

UNCLE: You too. Especially you.

MOTHER: That's terrible! Creon! Both at once?

UNCLE: I may be your brother, but I'm also king, and it's my job to pass judgment. (*To* ELDER SISTER.) Go, get ready to leave.

MOTHER: But what about us? What about Ismene and me? From now on how will we? . . .

UNCLE: You and Ismene can remain here as before. Well, I'm leaving. I'll send a patrol around in thirty minutes. See that you're gone by then. And be careful not to let anyone see you leave the city. Use the confusion of the celebration to make your escape.

MOTHER: But, Creon, but. . . .

(UNCLE *takes a new bottle from the vending machine and is about to make a hurried exit.*)

ISMENE: Uncle. . . .

UNCLE: *(Stopping.)* What?

ISMENE: What about Haemon?

UNCLE: Haemon?

ELDER SISTER: Where is he?

UNCLE: He was still sleeping when I left this morning.

ELDER SISTER: Sleeping?

UNCLE: *(Laughing.)* Yes, he's sleeping round the clock. Poor boy, the fatigue hit him all at once. *(To FATHER.)* Good-bye. Starting today I'm king of Thebes. Yes, I am king! *(Exits.)*

ISMENE: *(To ELDER SISTER.)* Well?

ELDER SISTER: Haemon's sleeping. He's asleep!

ISMENE: Yes.

ELDER SISTER: I'll bet he's having pleasant dreams. Anyway, there's no sun to tell your nightmares to. *(To ISMENE.)* Like this one. *(Her lips curl in a melancholy smile.)*

MOTHER Aaah-ah!

(MOTHER collapses, sobbing. ISMENE and ELDER SISTER go to comfort her.)

FATHER: Exile. So he's finally done it. He's finally become king. *(He chuckles to himself.)* Wouldn't you just know it, though? Damn! *(To ELDER SISTER.)* Well, I'm ready. You want to pack?

ELDER SISTER: Pack? No.

FATHER: Then let's go.

ELDER SISTER: I'd prefer to go alone.

FATHER: Well, that's a problem. I can't go alone.

ISMENE: *(To ELDER SISTER.)* Please, lead him.

ELDER SISTER: Lead him? . . .

ISMENE: Please?

FATHER: Look, we'll go as far as the next city together. We can decide what to do after we get there.

ELDER SISTER: All right.

ISMENE: To the next city. . . .

MOTHER: Cruel, Creon, too cruel!

(MOTHER weeps hysterically. NOBODY A and B enter.)

NOBODY A: We're back!

(NOBODY A notices that something is amiss and stops at the door. ISMENE looks at the two of them and has an idea.)

ISMENE: *(Softly, to herself.)* My ship . . . that's it, the next city! *(To ELDER SISTER.)* Listen, what if? . . .

ELDER SISTER: *(Preoccupied.)* What if what?

ISMENE: I mean. . . .

(MOTHER continues to sob. ISMENE looks at her, then kneels and embraces her.)

ISMENE: *(To ELDER SISTER.)* Never mind.

ELDER SISTER: No, tell me.

ISMENE: It was nothing, really. The adventure's over, isn't it?

FATHER: *(To* MOTHER.*)* Don't cry, dear. Things don't just happen. They're the consequences of our own actions.

ELDER SISTER: But what did I do? It all seems so anticlimactic.

FATHER: You've done exactly this, nothing less and nothing more.

ELDER SISTER: But it's all wrong! Everything. It wasn't supposed to turn out like this.

FATHER: I wonder.

(As unobtrusively as possible, NOBODY A *and* NOBODY B *are moving the vending machine toward the door.)*

ISMENE: *(Matter of factly.)* You're taking it with you.

NOBODY A: Yes. *(To* NOBODY B.*)* Okay. Ready? Push.

FATHER: You done with this city?

NOBODY B: For the time being.

FATHER: Why?

NOBODY B: Well, the war's over, and. . . .

NOBODY A: *(Interrupting.)* Actually, we don't understand ourselves. The main office makes these decisions. We just follow orders.

FATHER: I see.

NOBODY A: Are you going to the next city? We could give you a lift if you like.

FATHER: That's kind of you. *(To* ELDER SISTER.*)* Shall we?

ELDER SISTER: I don't care.

FATHER: Then if you really don't mind. . . .

NOBODY A: You get ready. We'll have this thing out of here in a jiffy.

FATHER: We're as ready now as we'll ever be.

NOBODY A: Then you can go ahead and get in the truck. We'll load this beast and tidy up and be with you right away.

ISMENE: Do you think? . . .

NOBODY A: Huh?

ISMENE: Do you think you could leave some of the bottles? I'd like to play with them.

NOBODY A: Well. . . . *(To* NOBODY B.*)* It'd be all right, wouldn't it?

NOBODY B: Sure.

NOBODY A: *(To* ISMENE.*)* We'd be glad to.

ISMENE: Thanks.

NOBODY A: Go ahead, sir. *(To* NOBODY B.*)* All right, you ready? Ready, get set, heave!

*(*NOBODY A *and* NOBODY B *move the vending machine out.* FATHER *goes to his weeping wife. He is about to embrace her but thinks better of it and kisses her softly on the hair instead.)*

FATHER: Well. . . .

ELDER SISTER: Take care of yourself, Mother. *(To* ISMENE.*)* Say good-bye
to Haemon for me.

NOBODY A: *(Calling from outside.)* We're ready!

FATHER: *(Calling back.)* Be right there! *(To* ELDER SISTER.*)* Shall we?

(After a moment's hesitation, ELDER SISTER *turns her back on* MOTHER *and*
ISMENE, *who clings to* MOTHER *in silence. She takes* FATHER*'s hand and exits.*
A few moments pass.

The truck's horn is heard. It sounds exactly like a ship's horn. The truck
shifts into gear and departs.

MOTHER *jumps to her feet and rushes to Door 1.)*

MOTHER: *(Calling.)* Wait! Wait!

*(*ISMENE *does not move. She remains seated on the floor, staring at the bottles.*
The truck moves off into the distance. MOTHER *collapses near the door and sobs.*
Long moments pass. Suddenly MOTHER *looks up.)*

MOTHER: Haemon, that's it!

(She gets to her feet and goes to ISMENE.*)*

MOTHER: It's just the two of us now, Ismene. Let's make the best of it,
all right? *(She rests her hand gently on* ISMENE*'s shoulder.)* It's not the end
of the world. There's still hope. You just wait and see. These things
happen. Our luck's bound to change. Things can't go on like this forever. You'll be getting married, and. . . . Someone special will come
along, you'll see. What about him, for example, you know,
Haemon? You could do a lot worse. *(Her tone is hopeful, but her expres-*
sion grows more and more desperate as she speaks.) Right? He wouldn't be
bad at all. I mean, when you consider that he was engaged to your
sister, well. . . . We know he's reliable, and he's just the right age for
you, too. If you two got married, all our. . . . Haemon would make
you happy, I'm sure. You'd make a very nice couple. As soon as
things have quieted down a bit, I'll have a talk with your Uncle
Creon. I wouldn't be surprised if he's already. . . . What do you
think? Then you'd be. . . .

(She lifts her Coke bottle to her lips, but it is empty. She turns to the vending
machine out of habit but realizes it is gone.)

MOTHER: *(Suddenly realistic.)* When it rains, it pours. No more of that stuff,
either. Wait a minute, maybe there's some left in your father's bottle.

*(*MOTHER *exits through Door 2.* ISMENE *remains seated on the floor. She picks*
up an apple, lifts it to her lips, and takes a small bite.)

ISMENE: Sour!

(Tears well up in her eyes. She leaps to her feet and rushes to the window. She
leans out and shouts at the top of her voice.)

ISMENE: Hey! Come out already, will you? Hurry up! I've got to tell you
something! I need someone to talk to. Hey, come out! Please! Hey!

(The curtain falls very fast.)

CONTRIBUTORS

JOHN K. GILLESPIE was raised in Osaka and graduated from the Canadian Academy in Kobe, Japan. He received his B.A. from Houston Baptist University and his Ph.D. in comparative literature from Indiana University. He has conducted research in Germany, France, and Japan on the mutual impact of Japanese and Western theater and has written several articles on the nature and processes of that impact. As director of the Japan Film Center and the Performing Arts Program at the Japan Society in New York from 1986 to 1989, he was instrumental in introducing two outstanding contemporary Japanese playwrights, Inoue Hisashi with *Makeup* (Keshō) and Ōta Shōgo with *Water Station* (Mizu no eki), to North American audiences. His original translation of Shimizu Kunio's acclaimed play *The Dressing Room* (Gakuya) was adapted by Chiori Miyagawa and staged off Broadway in fall 1991 by the Pan Asian Repertory Theater. He is currently an intercultural specialist and consultant on Japan with the Clarke Consulting Group and resides in New York City.

DAVID G. GOODMAN has produced numerous studies and translations of the works of modern Japanese playwrights, in particular those of Satoh Makoto and other figures associated with the Theater Center 68/69, but also Kubo Sakae, Hotta Kiyomi, Tanaka Chikao, Betsuyaku Minoru, Fukuda Yoshiyuki, Akimoto Matsuyo, Kara Jūrō, and Kishida Kunio. From 1969 to 1973 he edited *Concerned Theatre Japan*, an English-language theater journal associated with Theater Center 68/69. He has recently published *Long, Long Autumn Nights*, translations of the poems of Oguma Hideo, and is currently at work on a history of modern Japanese drama. He is a graduate of Yale University, received his doctorate in Japanese literature from Cornell University, and is a professor of Japanese and comparative literature at the University of Illinois.

PAUL H. KRIEGER is a specialist on the works of Abe Kōbō. He received his doctorate in Japanese literature from the University of Minnesota and is an assistant professor of Japanese language and literature at the University of the Pacific.

ROBERT N. LAWSON did his undergraduate study and received his doctorate in English literature from the University of Kansas. A Shakespearean scholar, he is a professor of English and theater at Washburn University in Topeka. Since the 1970s he has also pursued a deep interest in modern Japanese drama, in particular the works of Betsuyaku Minoru. He has translated several of Betsuyaku's plays.

CHIORI MIYAGAWA is literary manager of Arena Stage in Washington, D.C. She was formerly assistant literary manager at Actors Theatre of Louisville, where she served as dramaturg for several productions in the Humana Festival of New American Plays. She has also worked in New York at the Brooklyn Academy of Music and as an auditor for the New York State Council on the Arts. She is treasurer of Literary Managers and Dramaturgs of the Americas.

ROBERT T. ROLF has lived mostly in Japan, following the development of Japanese theater, since the mid-1970s. A graduate of Indiana University, he received his doctorate in Japanese literature from the University of Hawaii. He is the author of several articles on nontraditional Japanese theater, and has been a visiting professor at Washington University in St. Louis, where he lectured on contemporary Japanese drama. He has also taught Japanese literature and language at Duke University and the University of Florida. He resides in Tokyo and lectures at Yokohama National University.

TAKAHASHI YASUNARI is both a noted specialist of English drama and a well-known critic of contemporary Japanese theater in Japan. He has produced many Japanese translations of and commentaries on English drama and prose, in particular the plays of Samuel Beckett and the writings of Lewis Carroll. He has been an active participant in academic conferences in Japan, the United States, and Great Britain. He is a professor of English and comparative literature at the University of Tokyo, where he also completed both his undergraduate and graduate study.